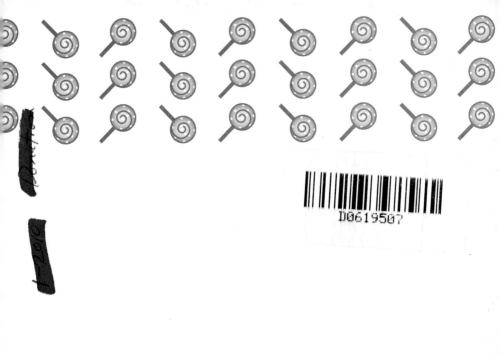

1

Gong GooGoo
Sugarholic

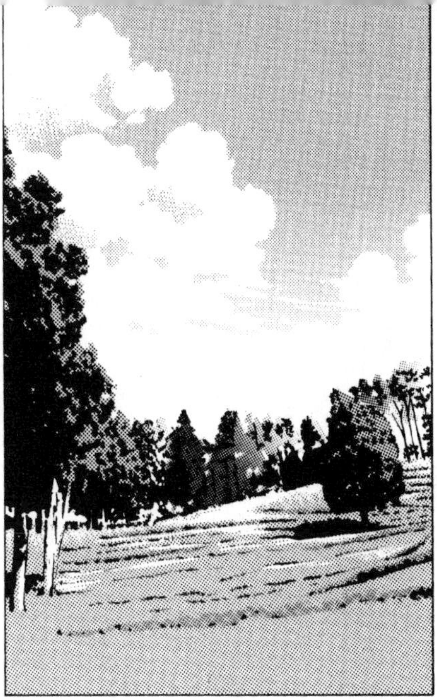

EVERYONE HAS AT
LEAST ONE MEMORY THEY'D
RATHER FORGET.

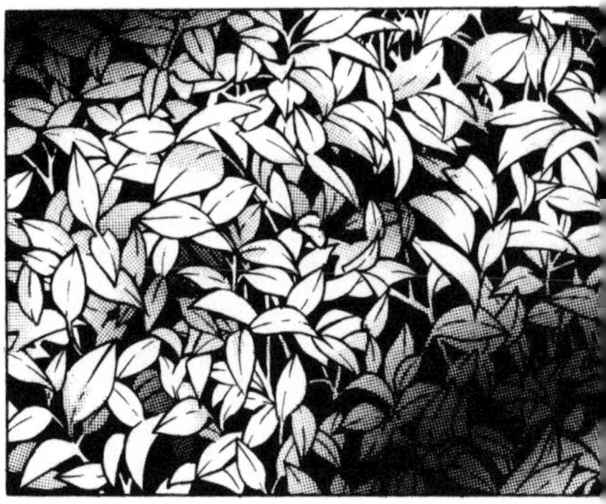

HERE, YOU
CAN HAVE THESE
GLASS BEADS.

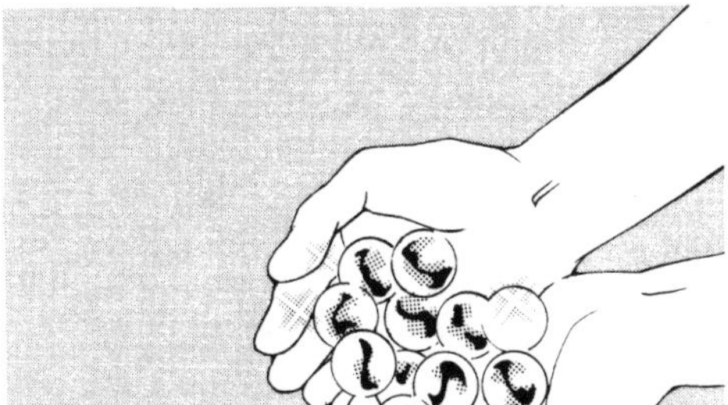

JUST TELL
ME IF YOU
WANT MORE.

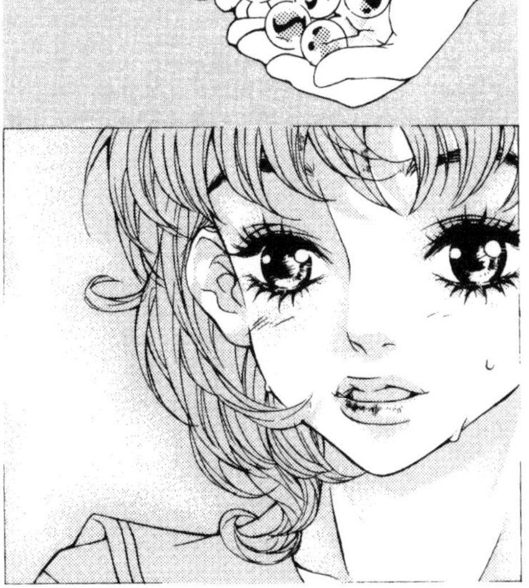

I'VE GOT TONS OF
THEM AT HOME.

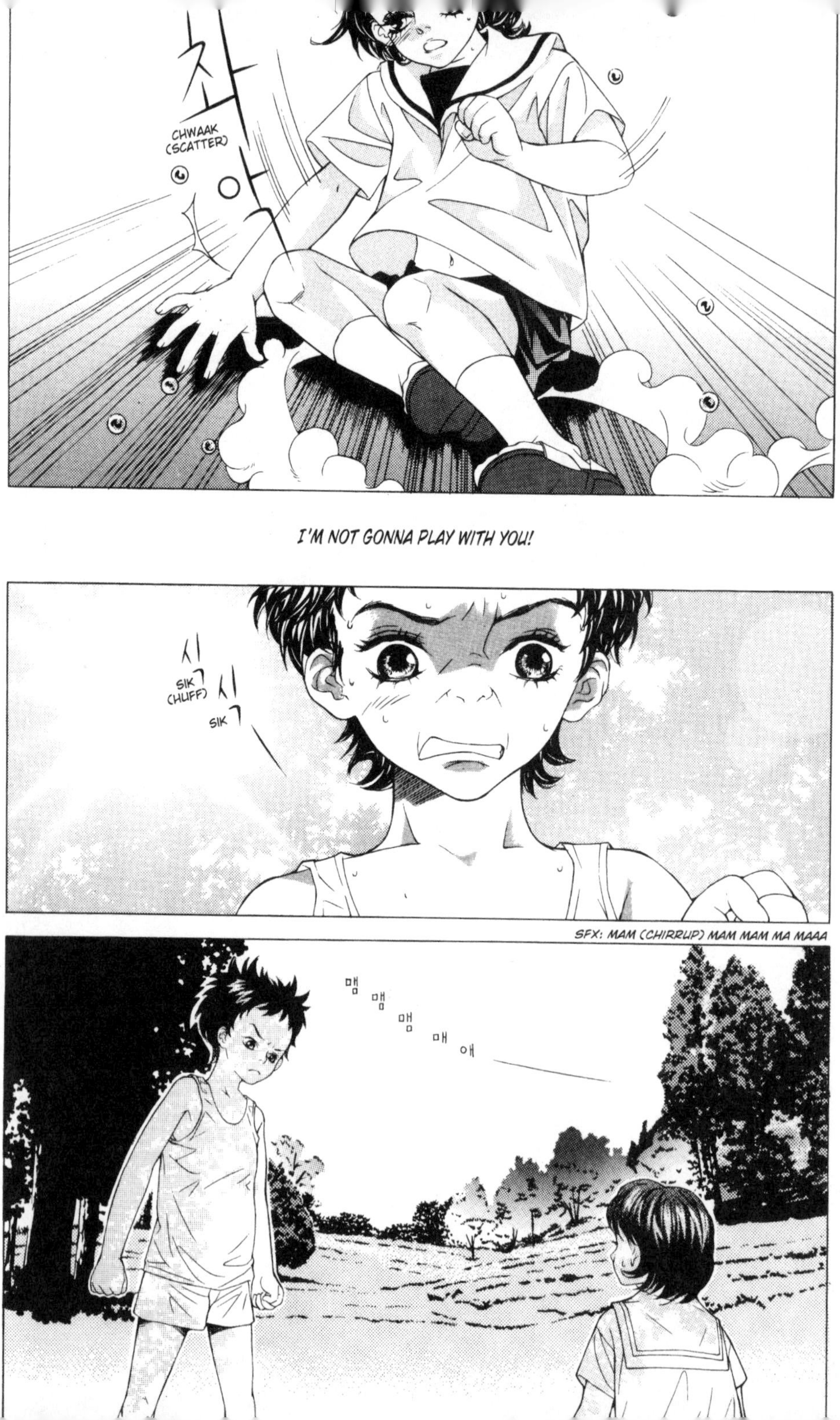
촤악
CHWAAK (SCATTER)
I'M NOT GONNA PLAY WITH YOU!
식 식
SIK (HUFF)
SIK
SFX: MAM (CHIRRUP) MAM MAM MA MAAA
맴 맴 맴 매 애

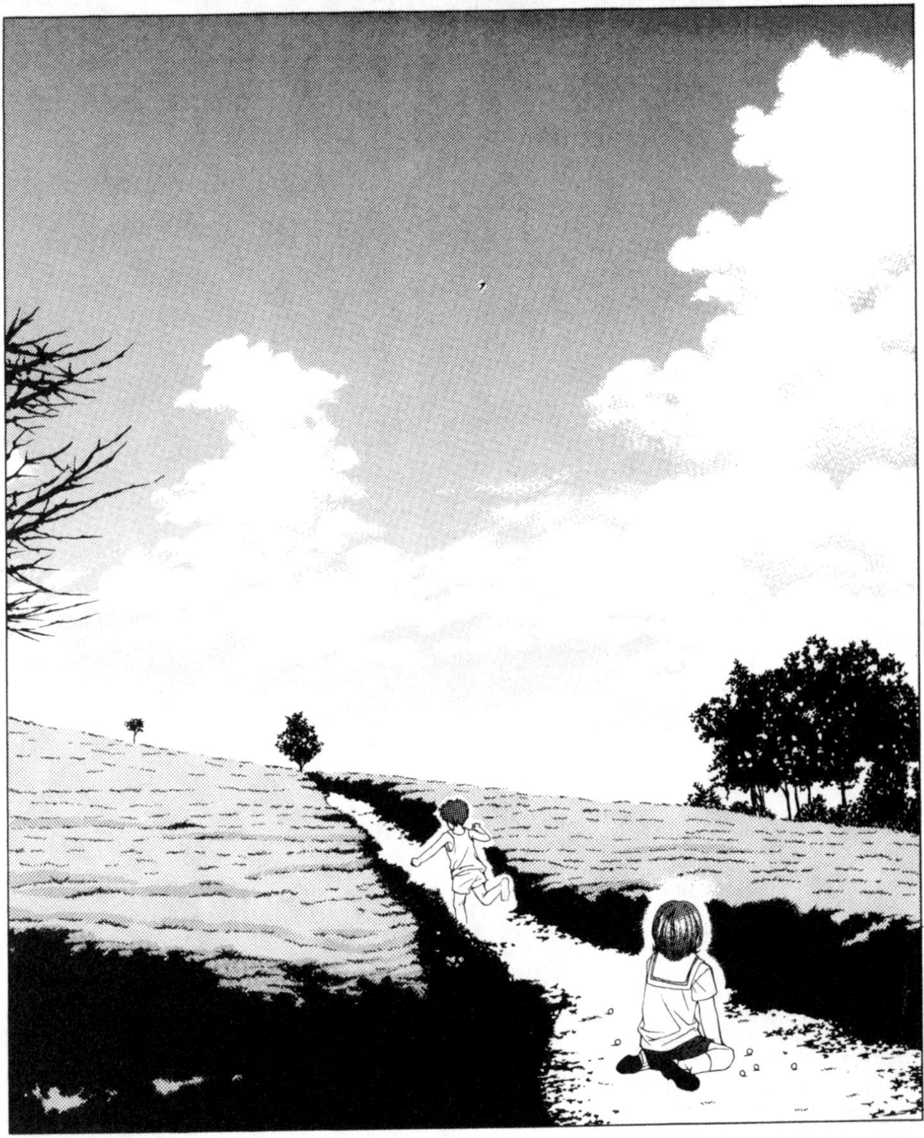

IT HAPPENED ONE
SUNNY SUMMER IN A
FIELD OF GREEN TEA.

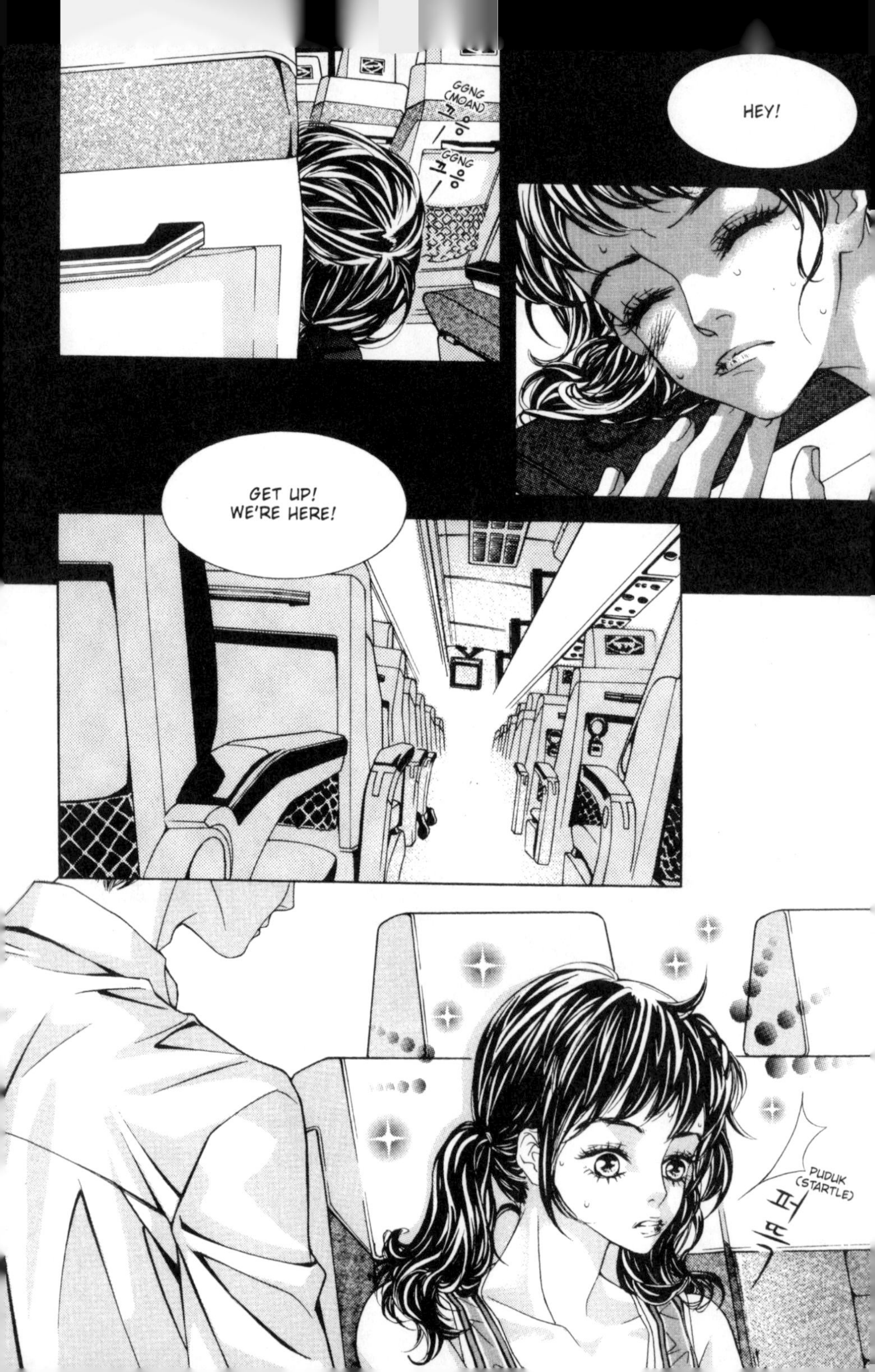
GGNG (MOAN)
GGNG
HEY!
GET UP! WE'RE HERE!
PUDUK (STARTLE)

CAN'T YOU SEE EVERYONE ELSE IS ALREADY GONE? WIPE YOUR MOUTH.

SUP (WIPE)
습

I DREAMED OF THAT BOY... THE ONE I NEVER WANT TO THINK ABOUT.

BUS: SEOUL   SIGNS: TO JEON-NAM / TO SOK-CHO

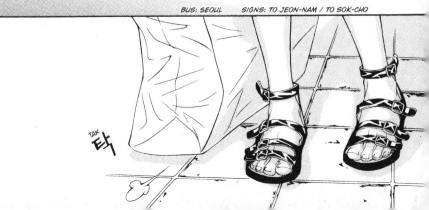

TAK
탁

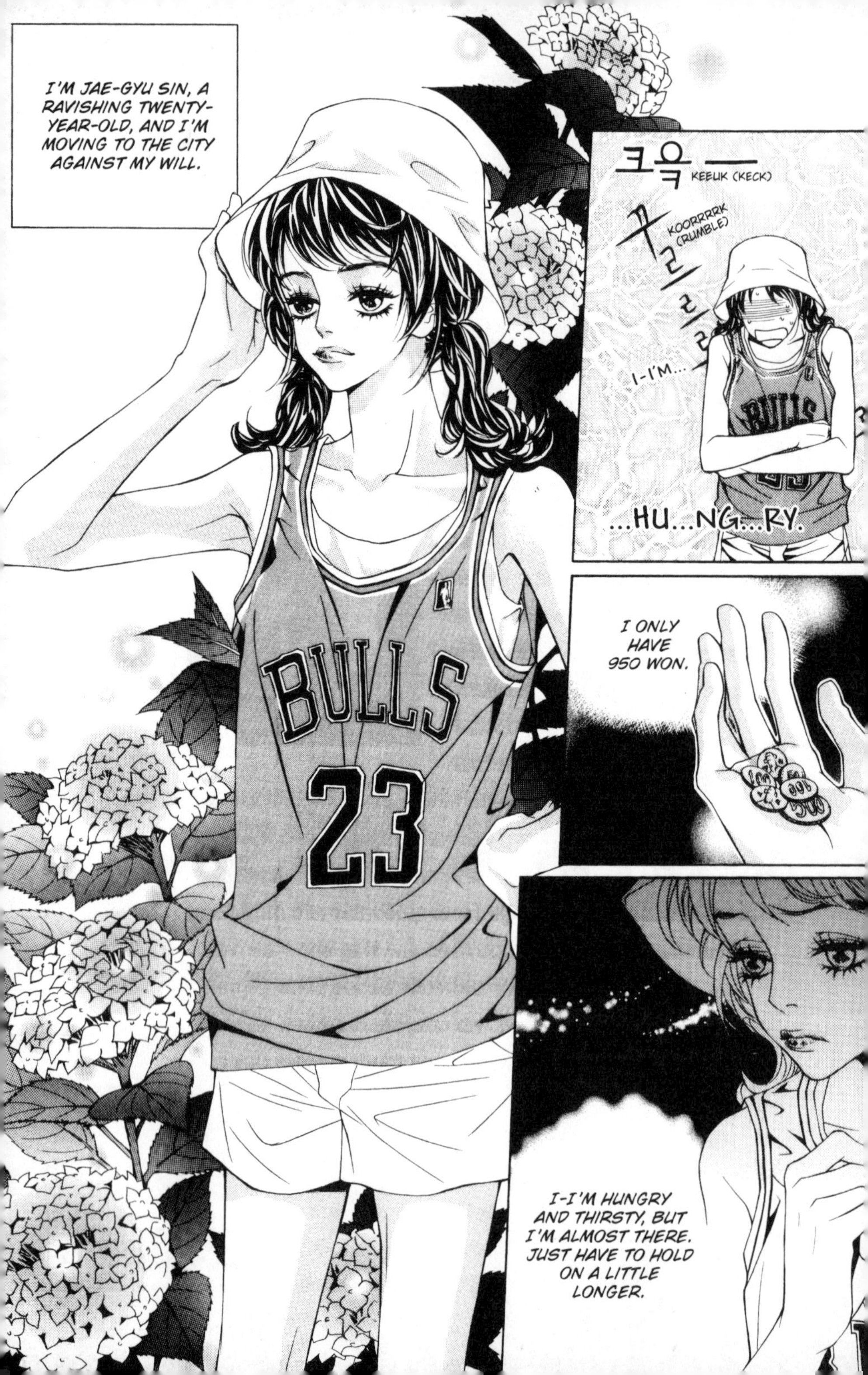
I'M JAE-GYU SIN, A RAVISHING TWENTY-YEAR-OLD, AND I'M MOVING TO THE CITY AGAINST MY WILL.
크윽 —
KEEUK (KECK)
KOORRRRK (RUMBLE)
I-I'M...
...HU...NG...RY.
I ONLY HAVE 950 WON.
I-I'M HUNGRY AND THIRSTY, BUT I'M ALMOST THERE. JUST HAVE TO HOLD ON A LITTLE LONGER.

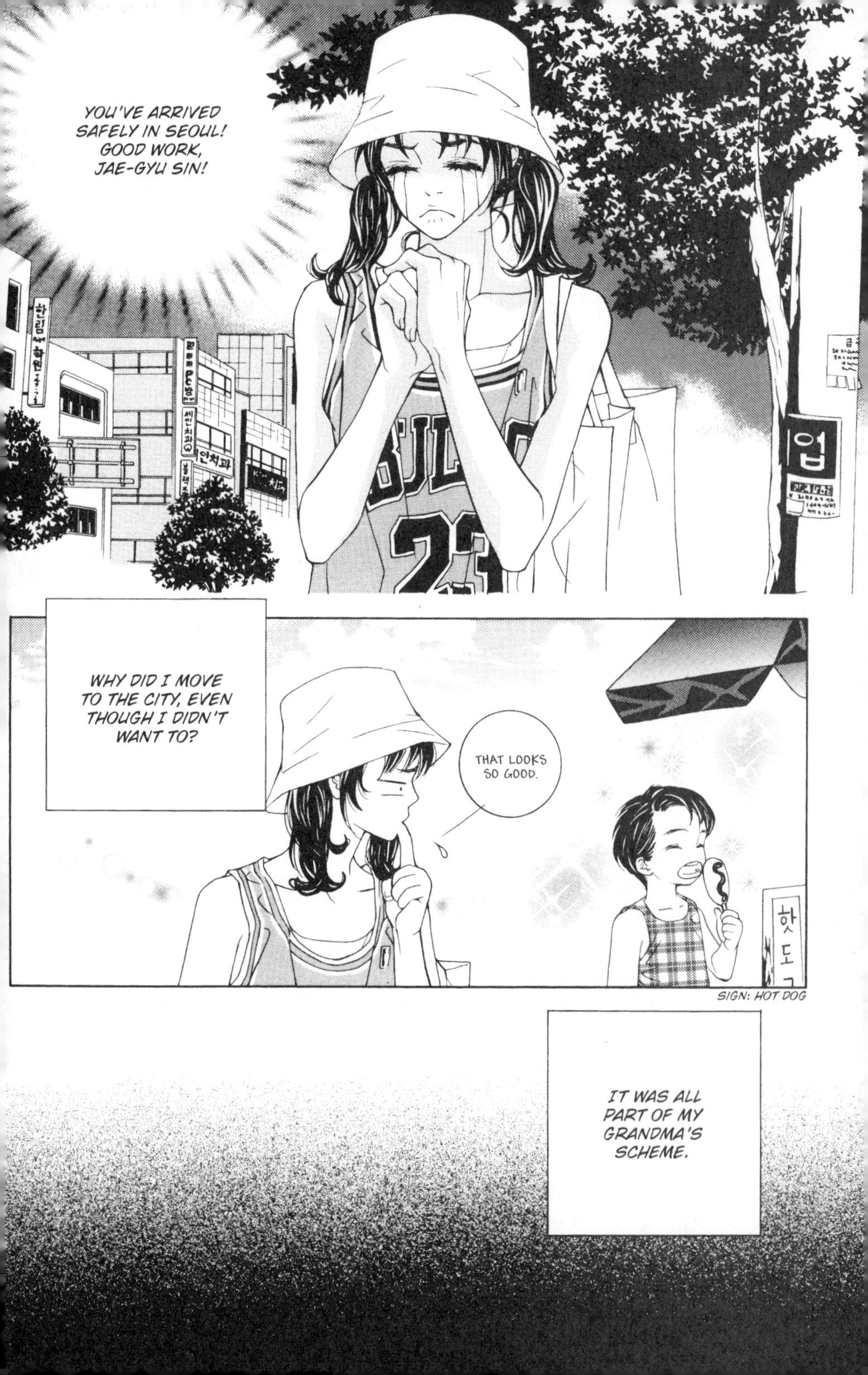
YOU'VE ARRIVED SAFELY IN SEOUL! GOOD WORK, JAE-GYU SIN!
WHY DID I MOVE TO THE CITY, EVEN THOUGH I DIDN'T WANT TO?
THAT LOOKS SO GOOD.
SIGN: HOT DOG
IT WAS ALL PART OF MY GRANDMA'S SCHEME.

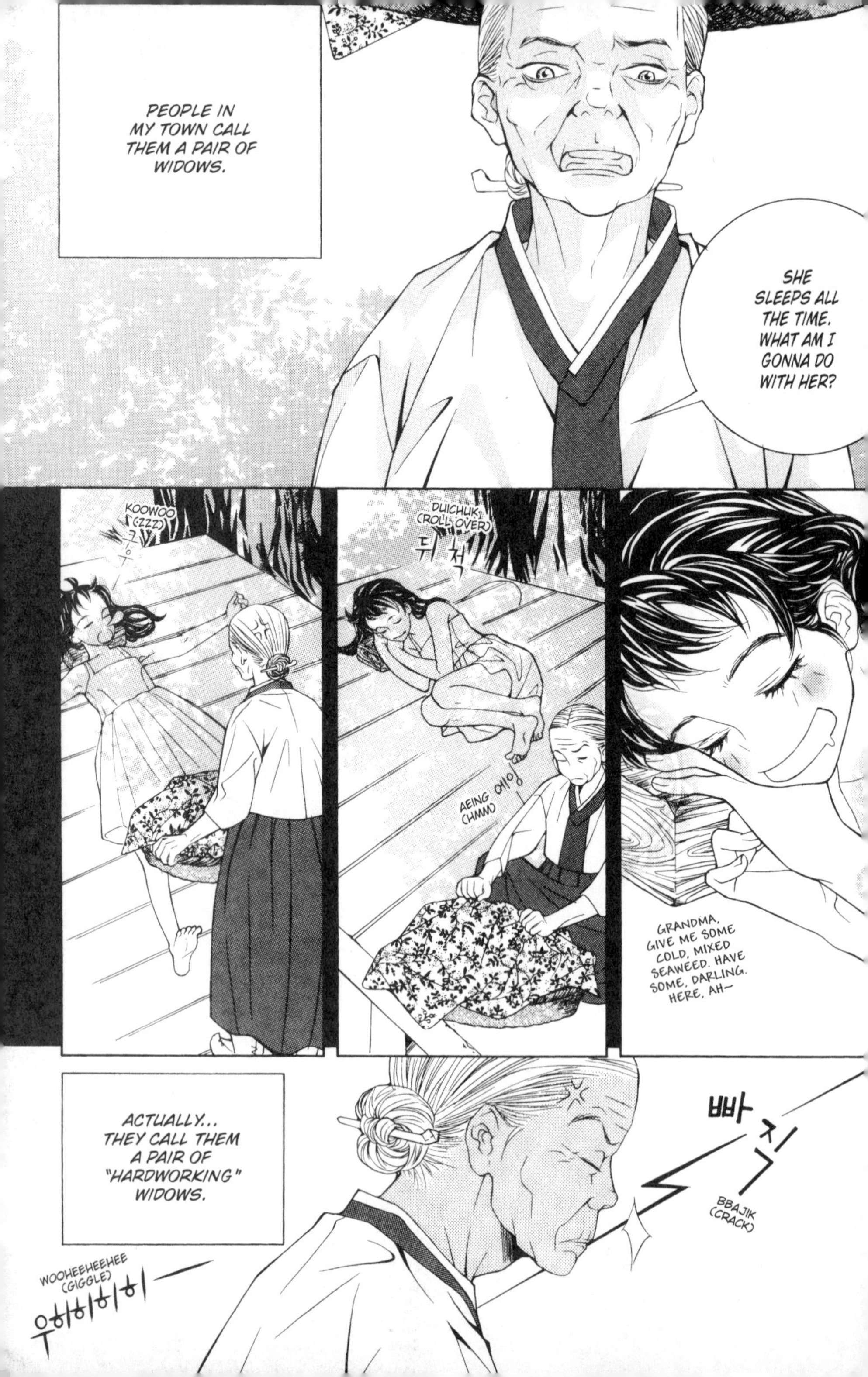
PEOPLE IN MY TOWN CALL THEM A PAIR OF WIDOWS.
SHE SLEEPS ALL THE TIME. WHAT AM I GONNA DO WITH HER?
KOOWOO (ZZZ)
DUICHUK (ROLL OVER)
뒤척
AEING (HMM)
에잉
GRANDMA, GIVE ME SOME COLD, MIXED SEAWEED. HAVE SOME, DARLING. HERE, AH~
ACTUALLY... THEY CALL THEM A PAIR OF "HARDWORKING" WIDOWS.
빠직
BBAJIK (CRACK)
WOOHEEHEEHEE (GIGGLE)

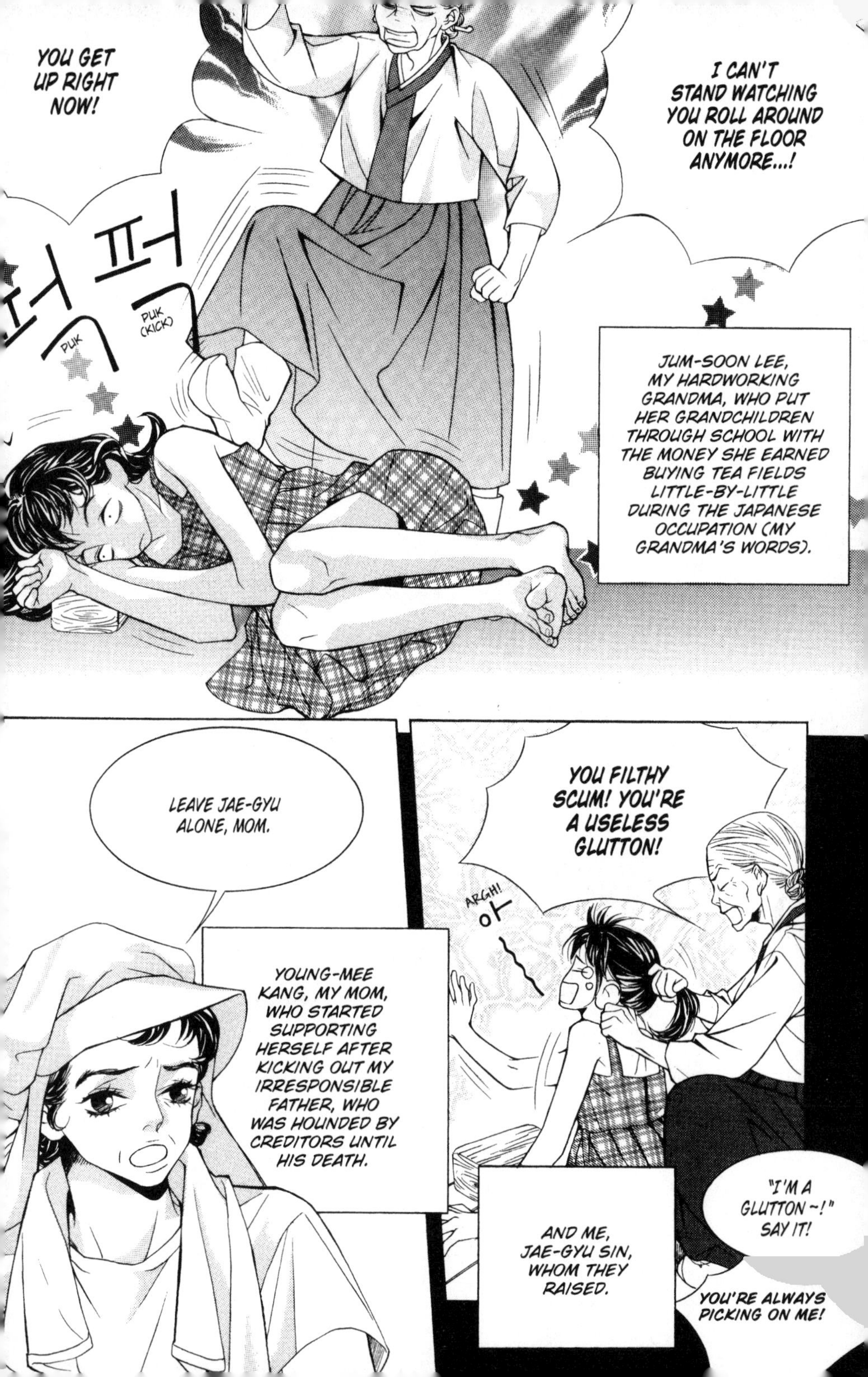
YOU GET UP RIGHT NOW!
I CAN'T STAND WATCHING YOU ROLL AROUND ON THE FLOOR ANYMORE...!
퍽
PUK
퍽
PUK (KICK)
JUM-SOON LEE, MY HARDWORKING GRANDMA, WHO PUT HER GRANDCHILDREN THROUGH SCHOOL WITH THE MONEY SHE EARNED BUYING TEA FIELDS LITTLE-BY-LITTLE DURING THE JAPANESE OCCUPATION (MY GRANDMA'S WORDS).
LEAVE JAE-GYU ALONE, MOM.
YOUNG-MEE KANG, MY MOM, WHO STARTED SUPPORTING HERSELF AFTER KICKING OUT MY IRRESPONSIBLE FATHER, WHO WAS HOUNDED BY CREDITORS UNTIL HIS DEATH.
YOU FILTHY SCUM! YOU'RE A USELESS GLUTTON!
아~
ARGH!
AND ME, JAE-GYU SIN, WHOM THEY RAISED.
"I'M A GLUTTON~!" SAY IT!
YOU'RE ALWAYS PICKING ON ME!

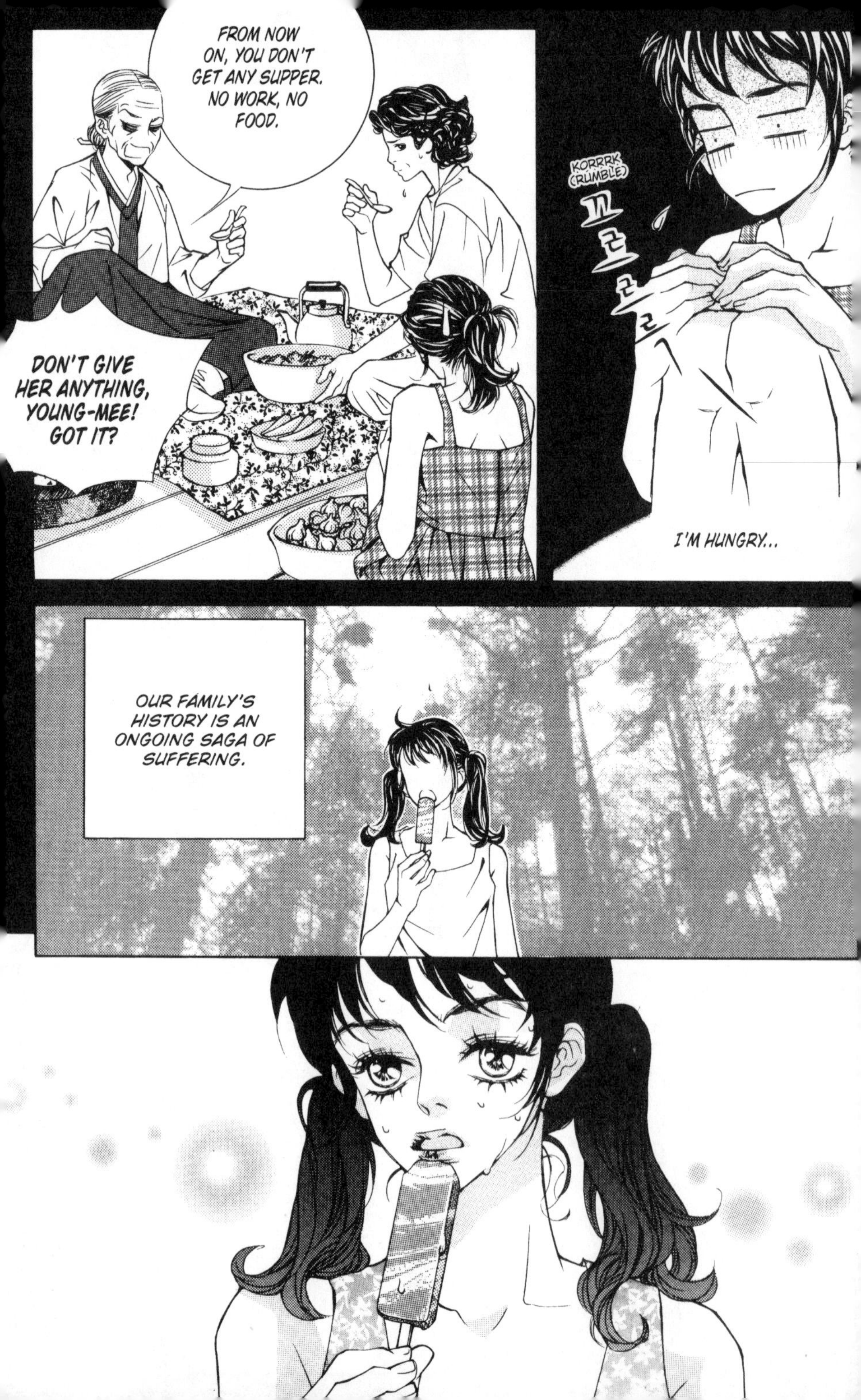
FROM NOW ON, YOU DON'T GET ANY SUPPER. NO WORK, NO FOOD.
DON'T GIVE HER ANYTHING, YOUNG-MEE! GOT IT?
KORRRK (RUMBLE)
꼬르르르
I'M HUNGRY...
OUR FAMILY'S HISTORY IS AN ONGOING SAGA OF SUFFERING.

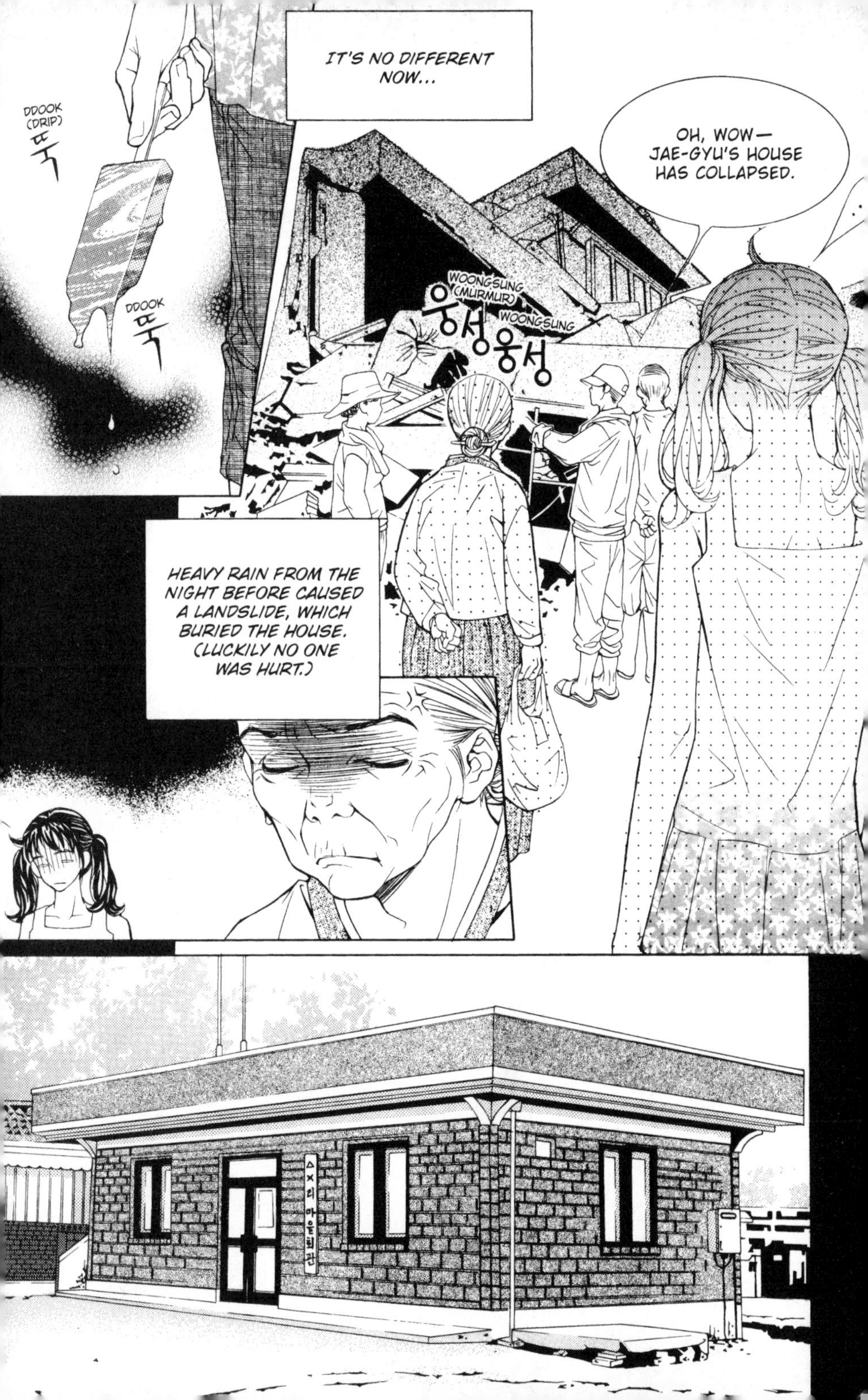
DDOOK (DRIP)
뚝
DDOOK
뚝
IT'S NO DIFFERENT NOW...
OH, WOW— JAE-GYU'S HOUSE HAS COLLAPSED.
WOONGSUNG (MURMUR)
WOONGSUNG
웅성웅성
HEAVY RAIN FROM THE NIGHT BEFORE CAUSED A LANDSLIDE, WHICH BURIED THE HOUSE. (LUCKILY NO ONE WAS HURT.)

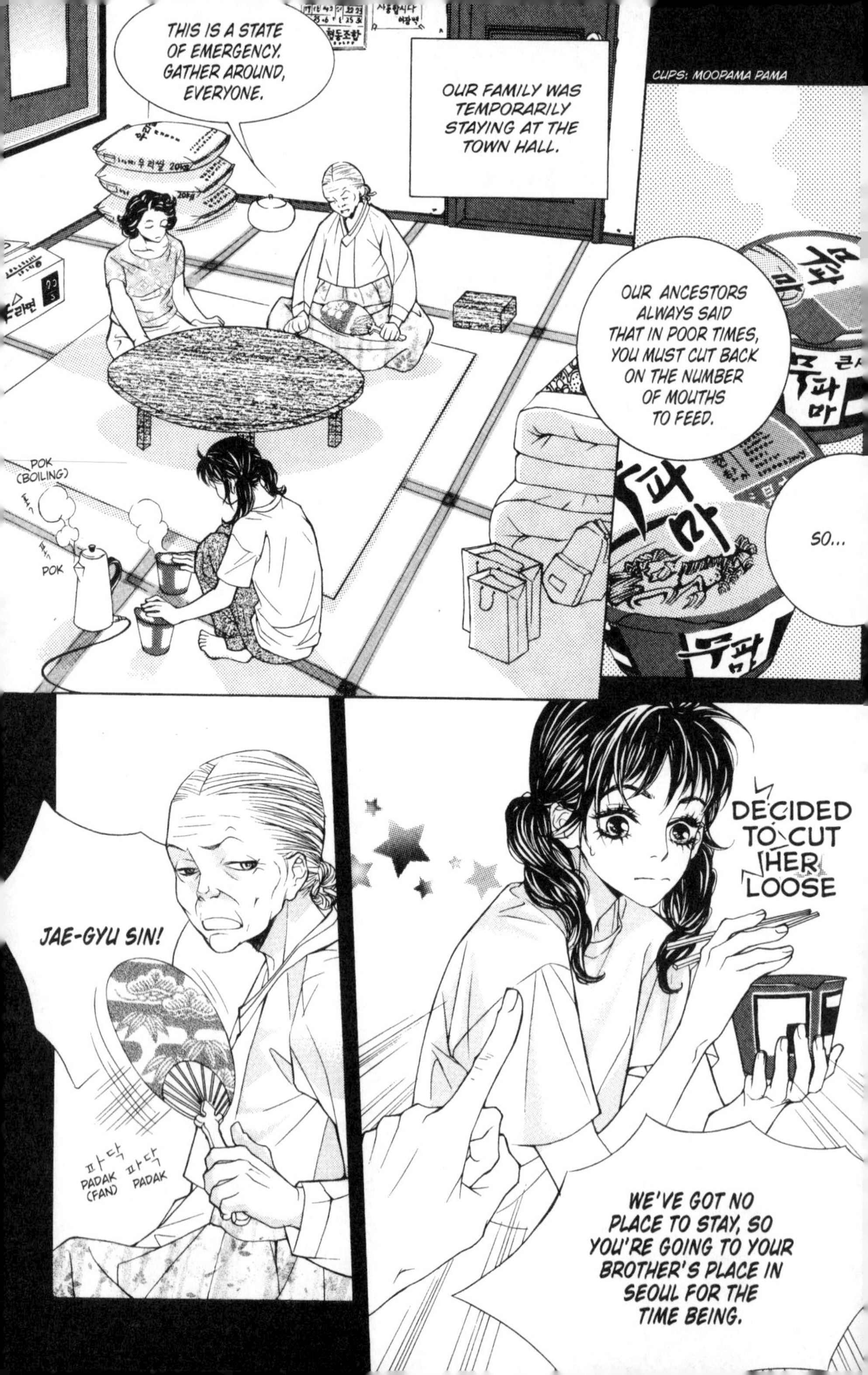
THIS IS A STATE OF EMERGENCY. GATHER AROUND, EVERYONE.
OUR FAMILY WAS TEMPORARILY STAYING AT THE TOWN HALL.
POK (BOILING)
POK
CUPS: MOOPAMA PAMA
OUR ANCESTORS ALWAYS SAID THAT IN POOR TIMES, YOU MUST CUT BACK ON THE NUMBER OF MOUTHS TO FEED.
SO...
JAE-GYU SIN!
파닥 파닥
PADAK (FAN) PADAK
DECIDED TO CUT HER LOOSE
WE'VE GOT NO PLACE TO STAY, SO YOU'RE GOING TO YOUR BROTHER'S PLACE IN SEOUL FOR THE TIME BEING.

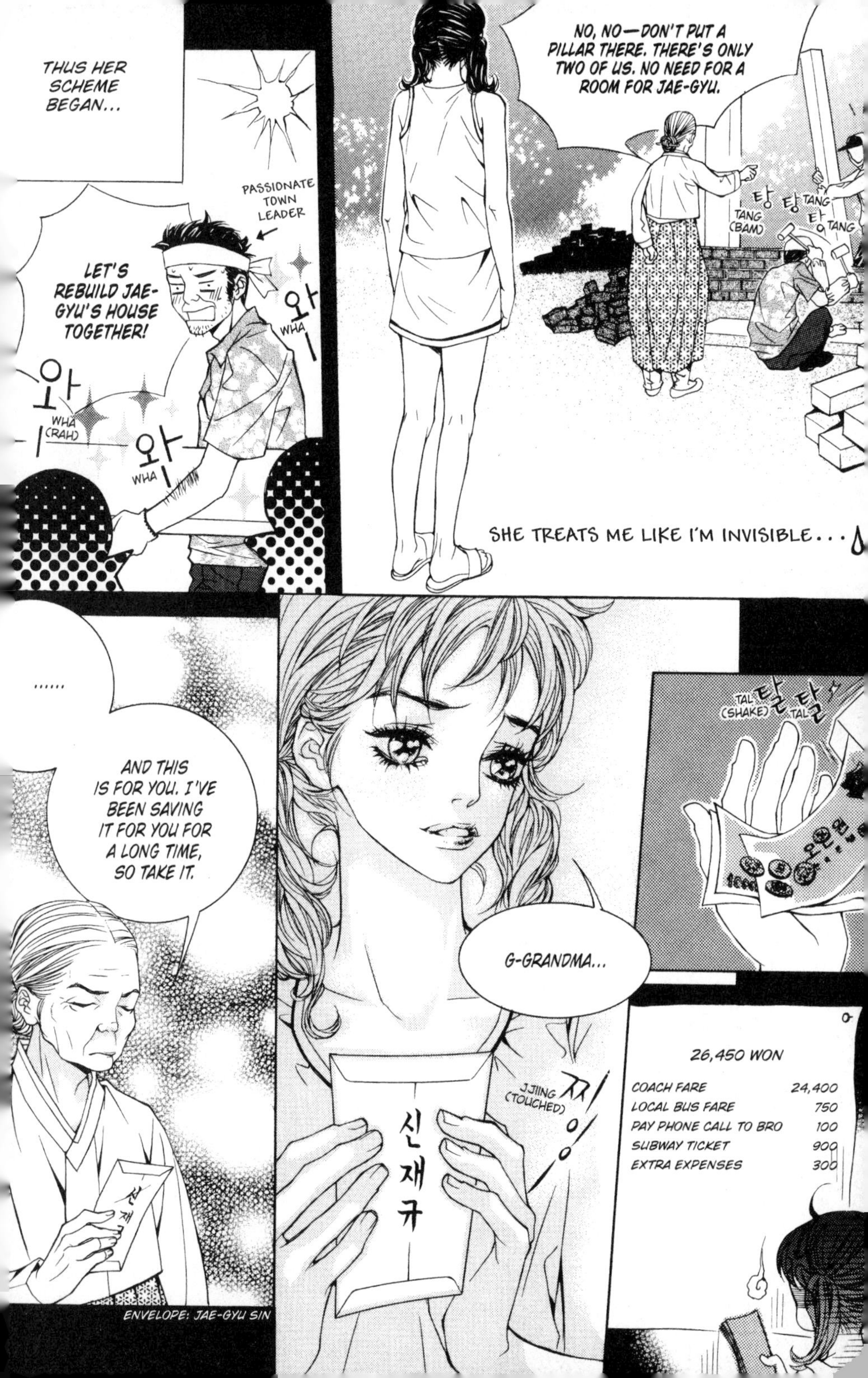
THUS HER SCHEME BEGAN...
PASSIONATE TOWN LEADER
LET'S REBUILD JAE-GYU'S HOUSE TOGETHER!
와 WHA
와 WHA (RAH)
와 WHA
NO, NO—DON'T PUT A PILLAR THERE. THERE'S ONLY TWO OF US. NO NEED FOR A ROOM FOR JAE-GYU.
탕 TANG (BAM)
탕 TANG
탕 TANG
SHE TREATS ME LIKE I'M INVISIBLE...
......
AND THIS IS FOR YOU. I'VE BEEN SAVING IT FOR YOU FOR A LONG TIME, SO TAKE IT.
ENVELOPE: JAE-GYU SIN
G-GRANDMA...
신재규
찌잉 JJIING (TOUCHED)
탈 TAL (SHAKE)
탈 TAL
오원
26,450 WON
COACH FARE 24,400
LOCAL BUS FARE 750
PAY PHONE CALL TO BRO 100
SUBWAY TICKET 900
EXTRA EXPENSES 300

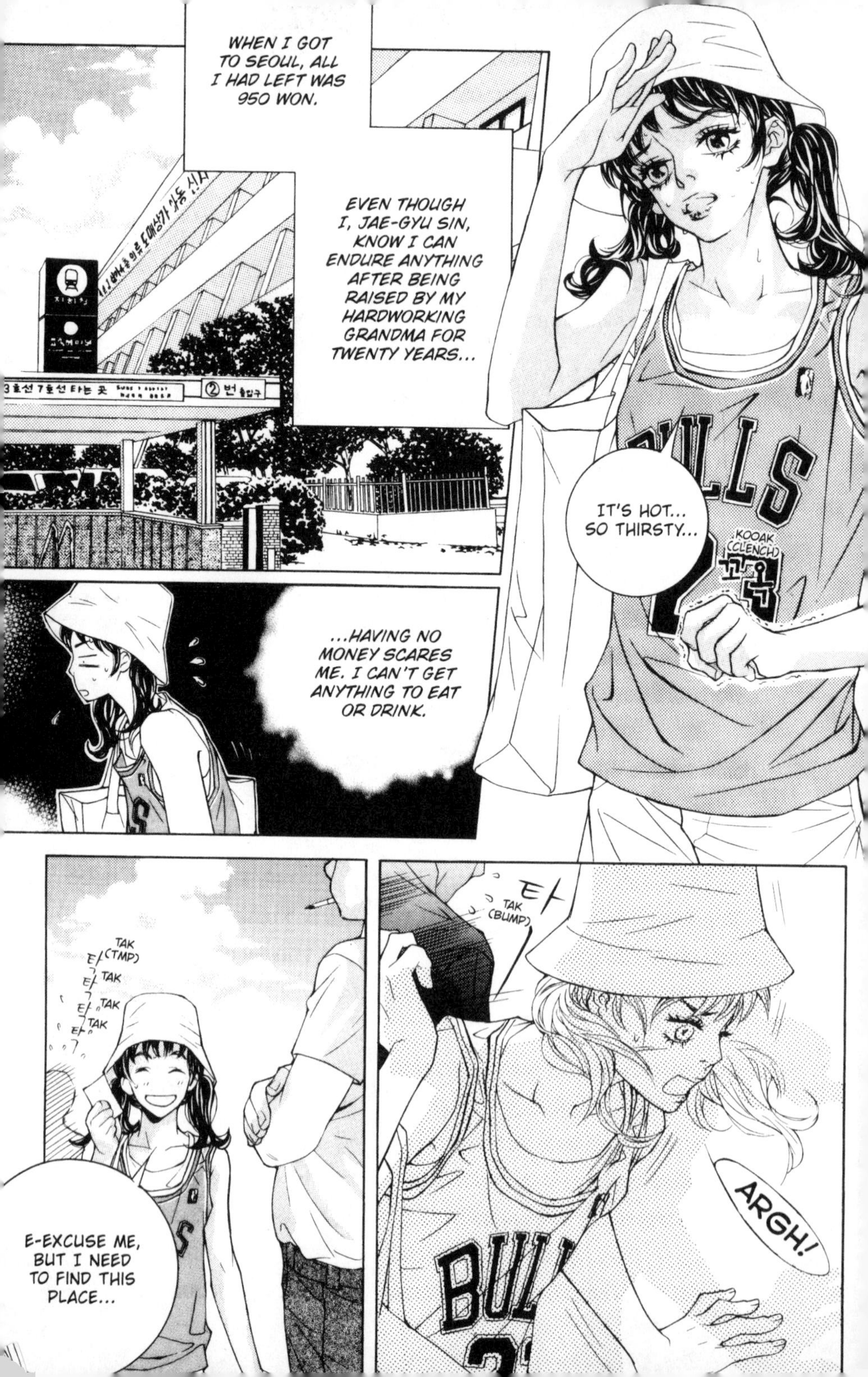
WHEN I GOT TO SEOUL, ALL I HAD LEFT WAS 950 WON.
EVEN THOUGH I, JAE-GYU SIN, KNOW I CAN ENDURE ANYTHING AFTER BEING RAISED BY MY HARDWORKING GRANDMA FOR TWENTY YEARS...
...HAVING NO MONEY SCARES ME. I CAN'T GET ANYTHING TO EAT OR DRINK.
IT'S HOT... SO THIRSTY...
KOOAK (CLENCH)
꽉
TAK (TMP)
TAK
TAK
TAK
E-EXCUSE ME, BUT I NEED TO FIND THIS PLACE...
탁
TAK (BUMP)
ARGH!

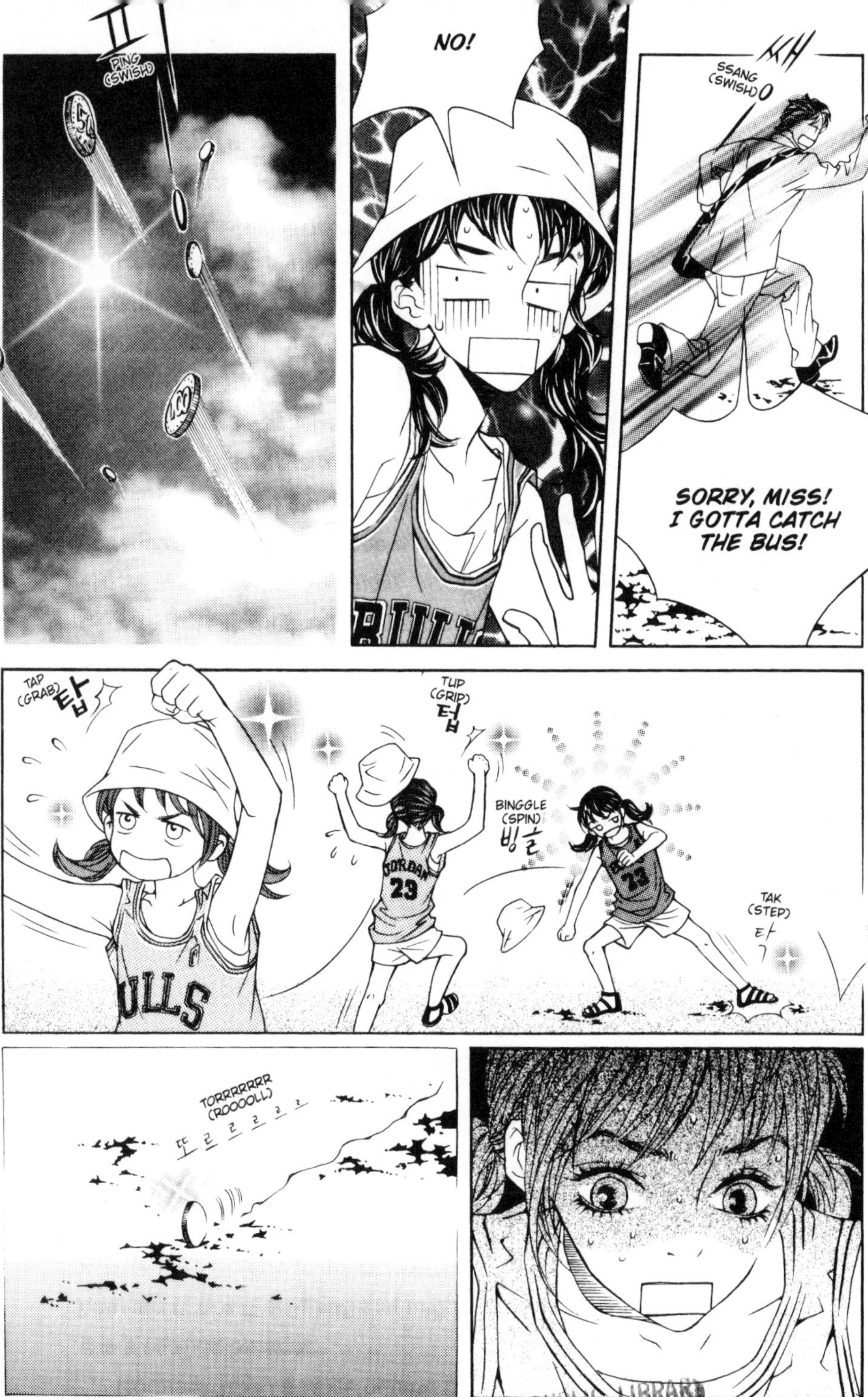
PING (SWISH)
NO!
SSANG (SWISH)
SORRY, MISS! I GOTTA CATCH THE BUS!
TAP (GRAB)
탑
TUP (GRIP)
텁
BINGGLE (SPIN)
빙글
TAK (STEP)
TORRRRRRR (ROOOOLL)

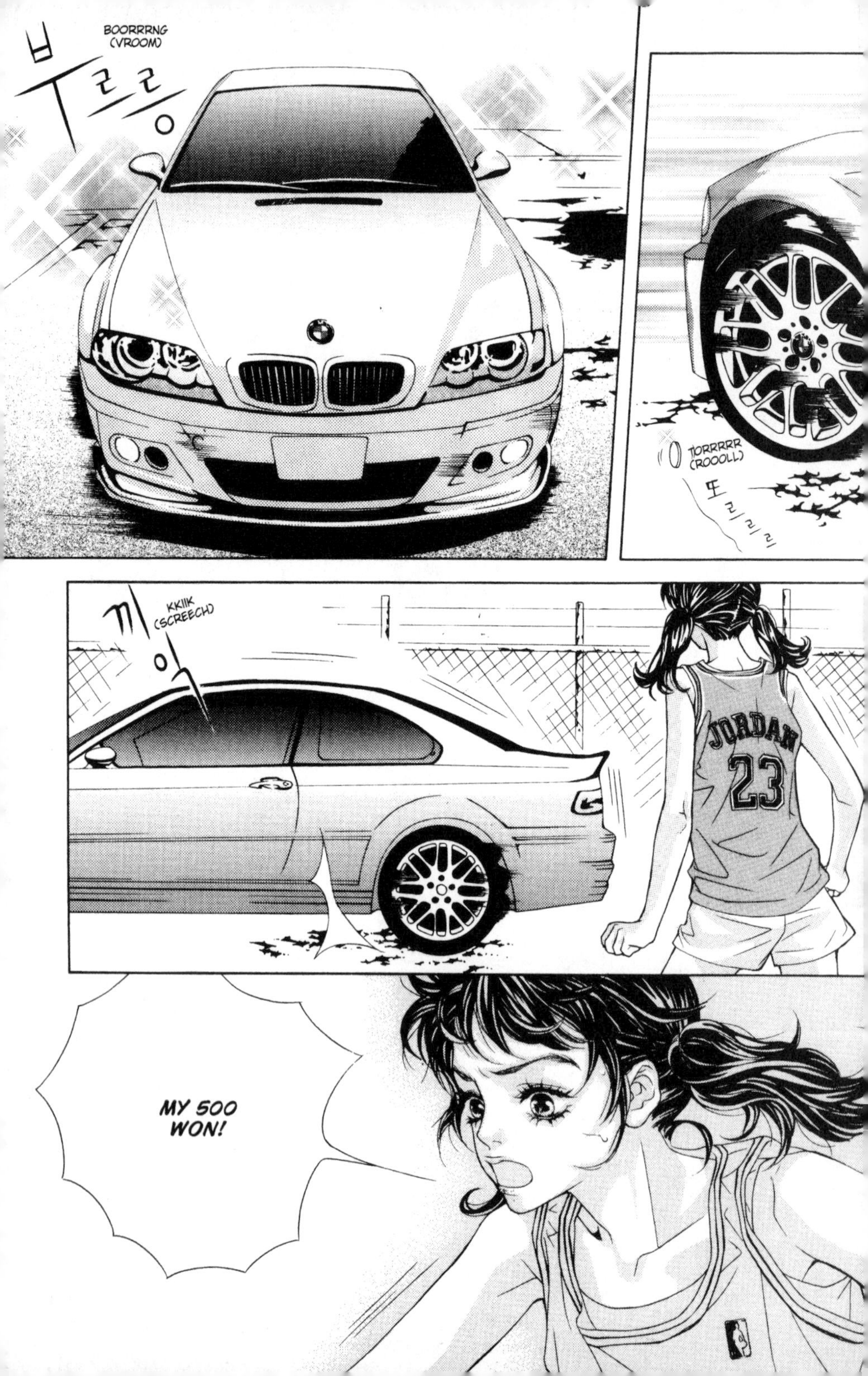

BOORRRNG
(VROOM)
TTORRRRR
(ROOOLL)
KKIIK
(SCREECH)
MY 500 WON!

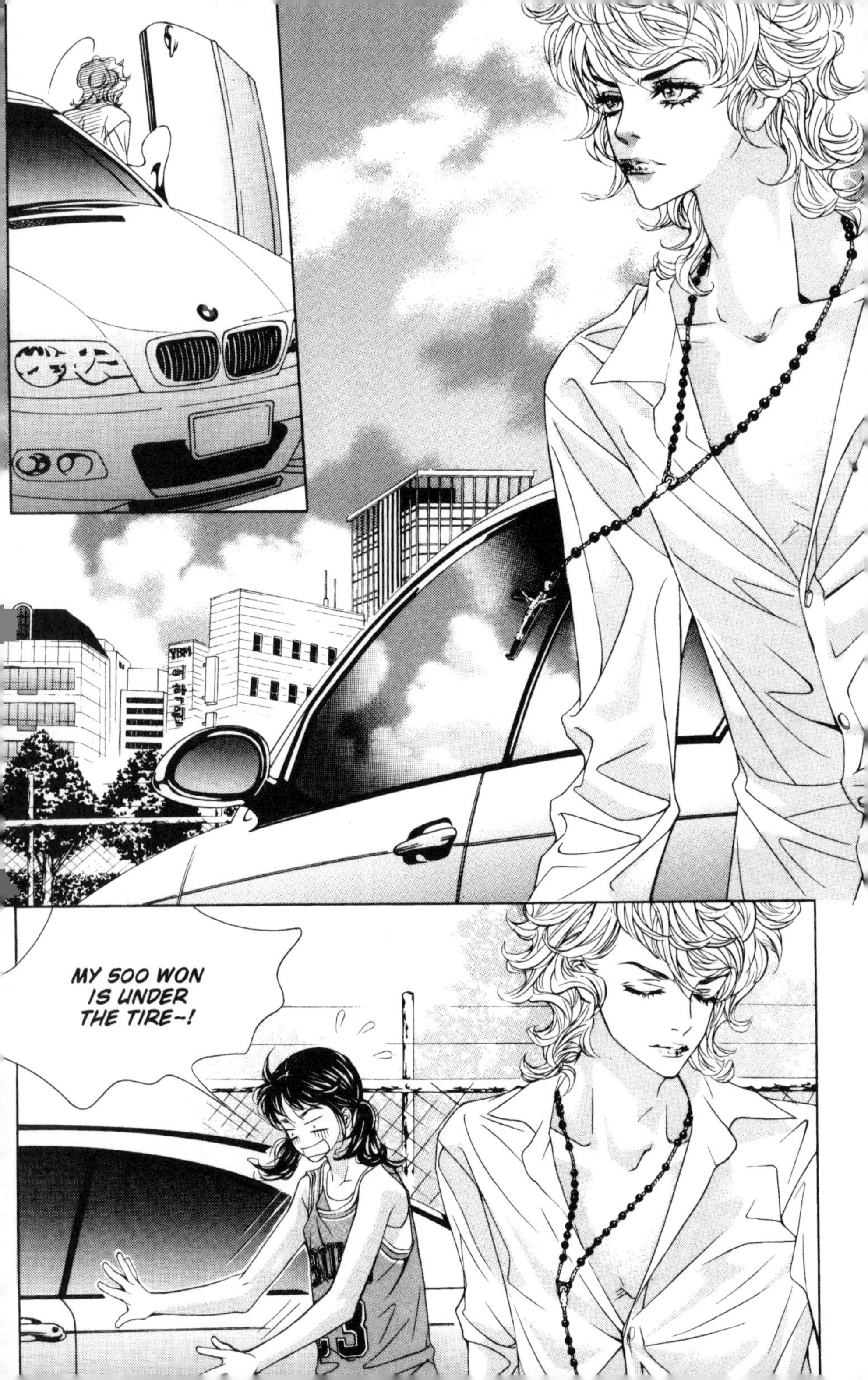
MY 500 WON
IS UNDER
THE TIRE~!

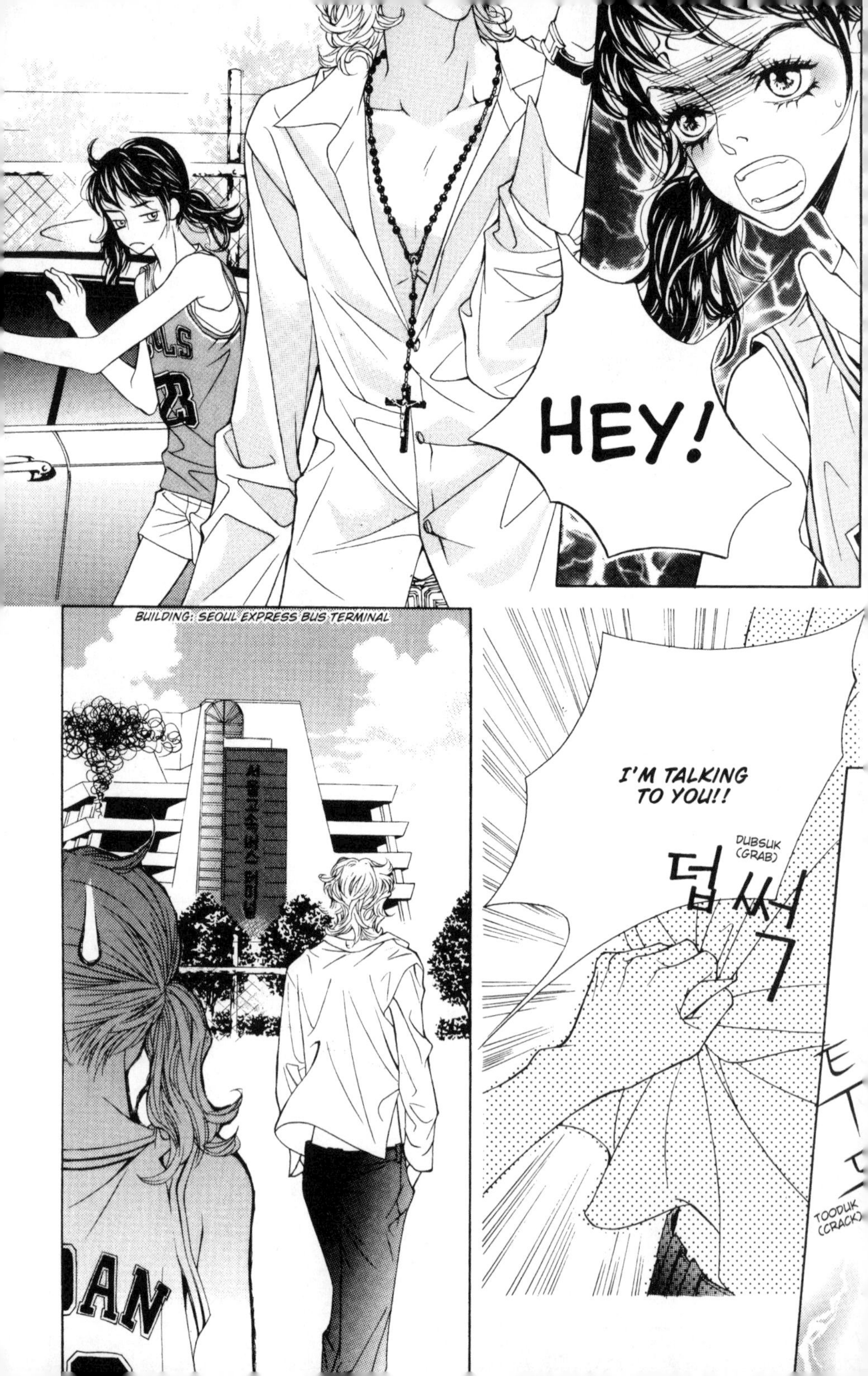
HEY!
BUILDING: SEOUL EXPRESS BUS TERMINAL
I'M TALKING TO YOU!!
DUBSUK (GRAB)
덥썩
TOODLIK (CRACK)

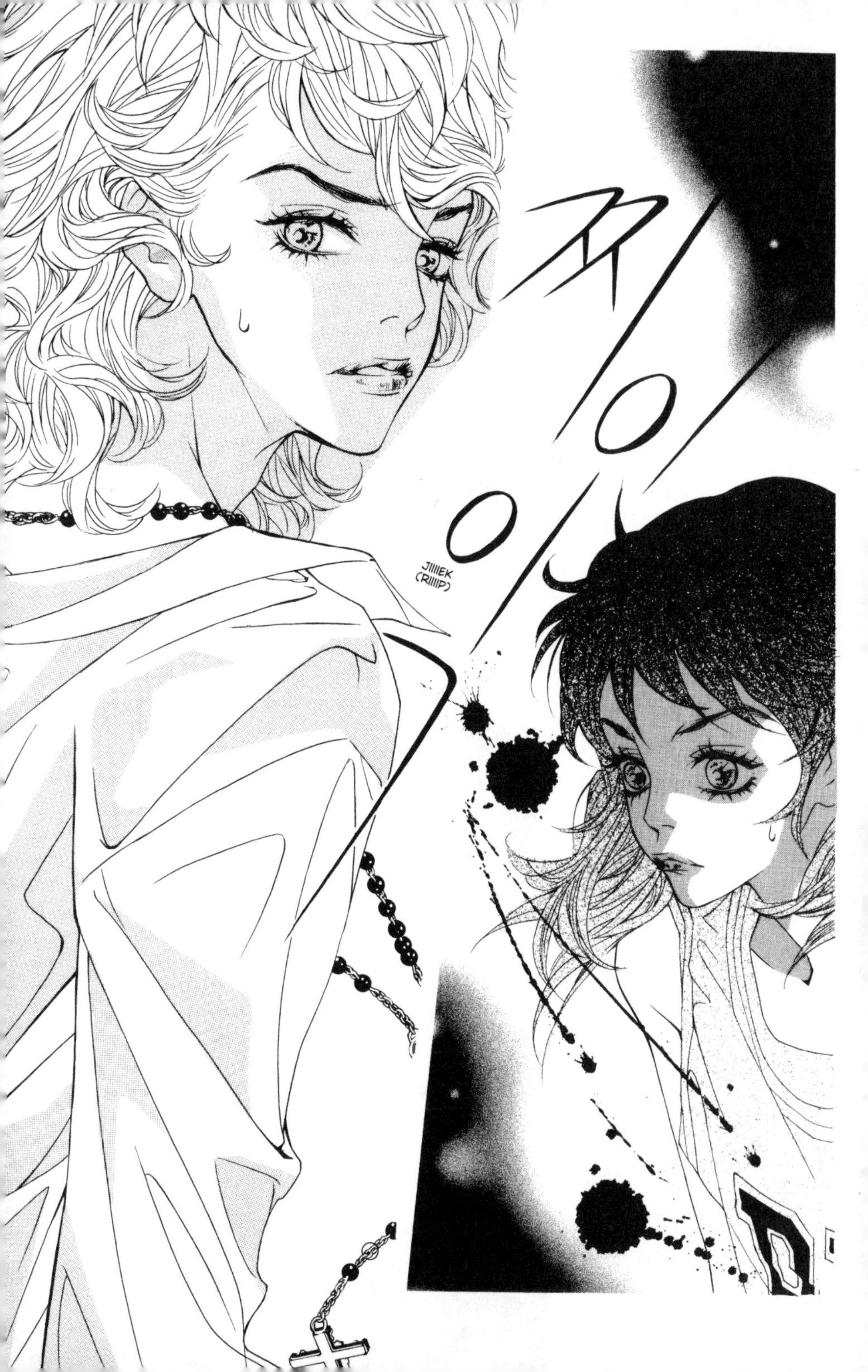
찌이익
JIIIIEK
(RIIIIP)

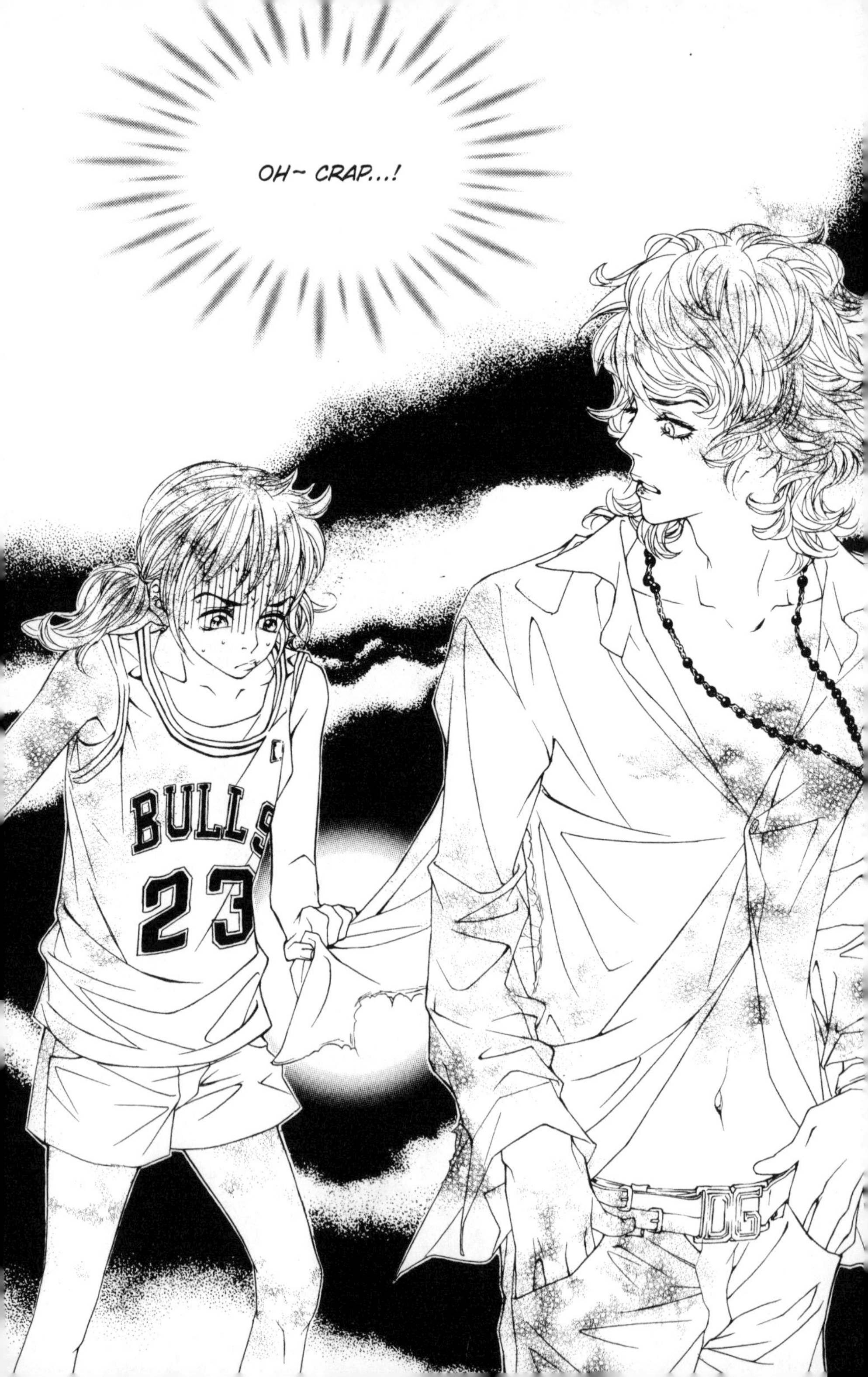
OH~ CRAP...!
BULLS
23
DG

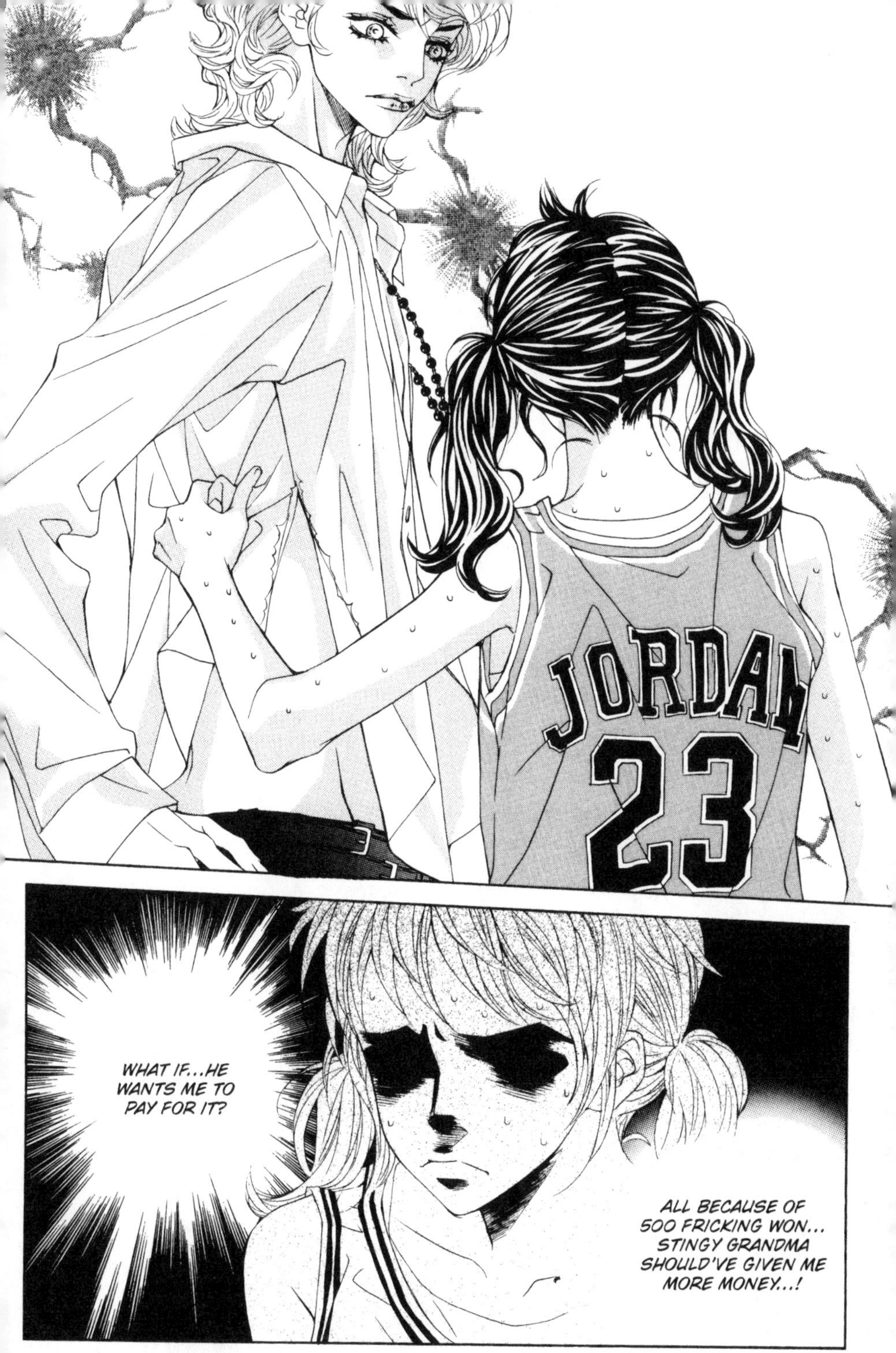
JORDAN
23
WHAT IF...HE WANTS ME TO PAY FOR IT?
ALL BECAUSE OF 500 FRICKING WON... STINGY GRANDMA SHOULD'VE GIVEN ME MORE MONEY...!

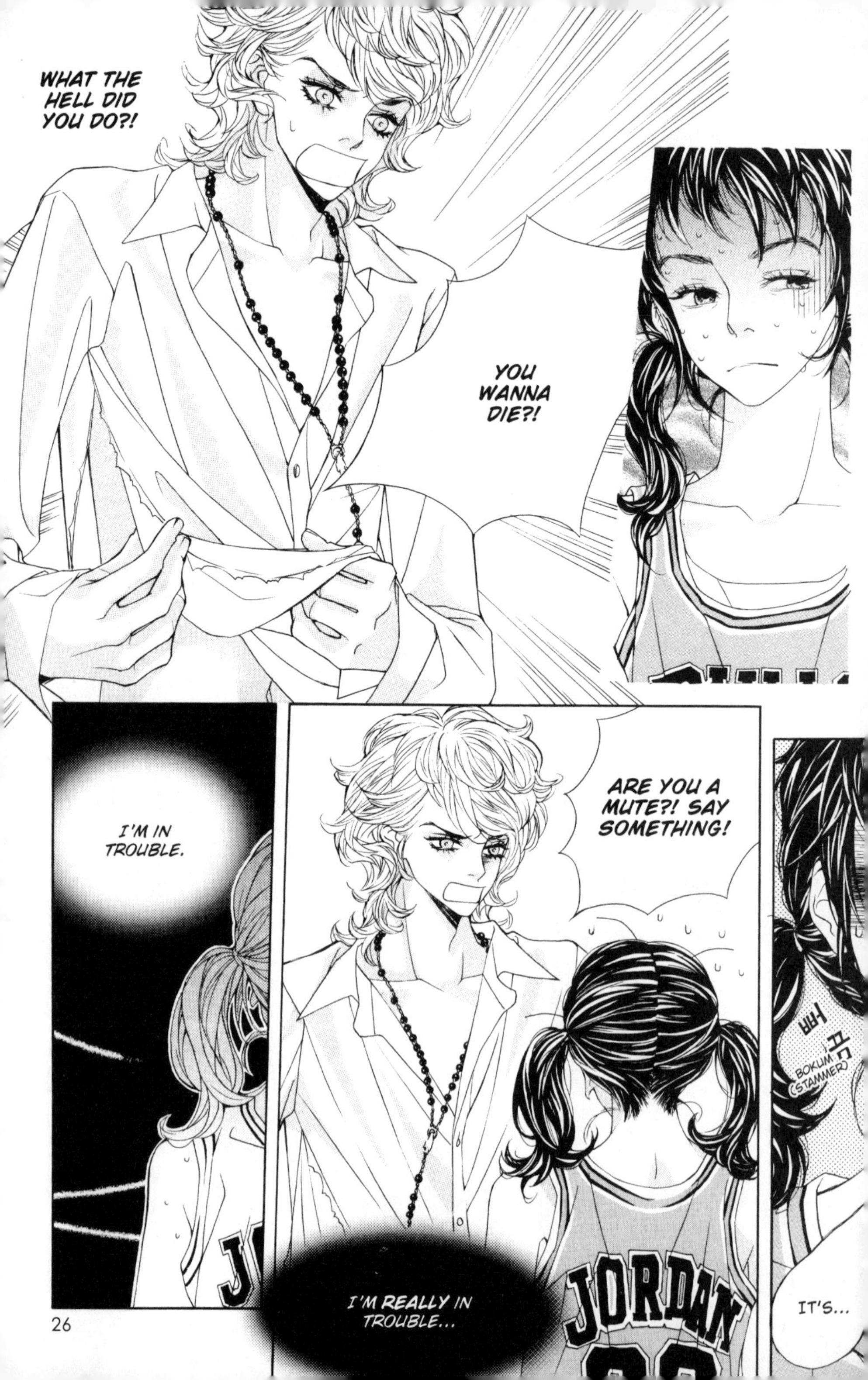
WHAT THE HELL DID YOU DO?!
YOU WANNA DIE?!
I'M IN TROUBLE.
ARE YOU A MUTE?! SAY SOMETHING!
I'M REALLY IN TROUBLE...
BOKUM (STAMMER)
IT'S...

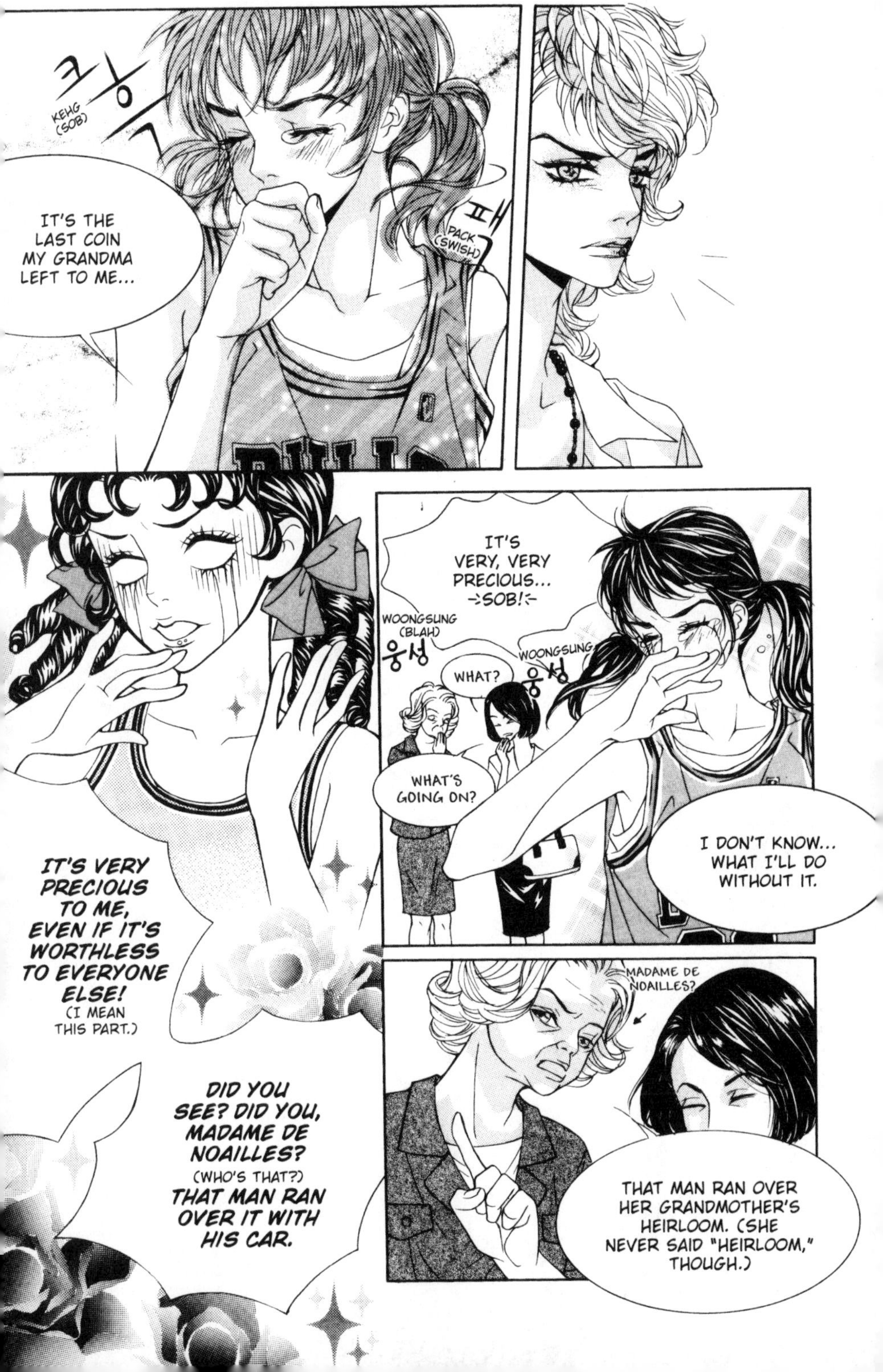

크흥
KEHG (SOB)
IT'S THE LAST COIN MY GRANDMA LEFT TO ME...
패
PACK (SWISH)
IT'S VERY PRECIOUS TO ME, EVEN IF IT'S WORTHLESS TO EVERYONE ELSE!
(I MEAN THIS PART.)
IT'S VERY, VERY PRECIOUS... -SOB!-
WOONGSUNG (BLAH)
웅성
WOONGSUNG
웅성
WHAT?
WHAT'S GOING ON?
I DON'T KNOW... WHAT I'LL DO WITHOUT IT.
DID YOU SEE? DID YOU, MADAME DE NOAILLES?
(WHO'S THAT?)
THAT MAN RAN OVER IT WITH HIS CAR.
MADAME DE NOAILLES?
THAT MAN RAN OVER HER GRANDMOTHER'S HEIRLOOM. (SHE NEVER SAID "HEIRLOOM," THOUGH.)

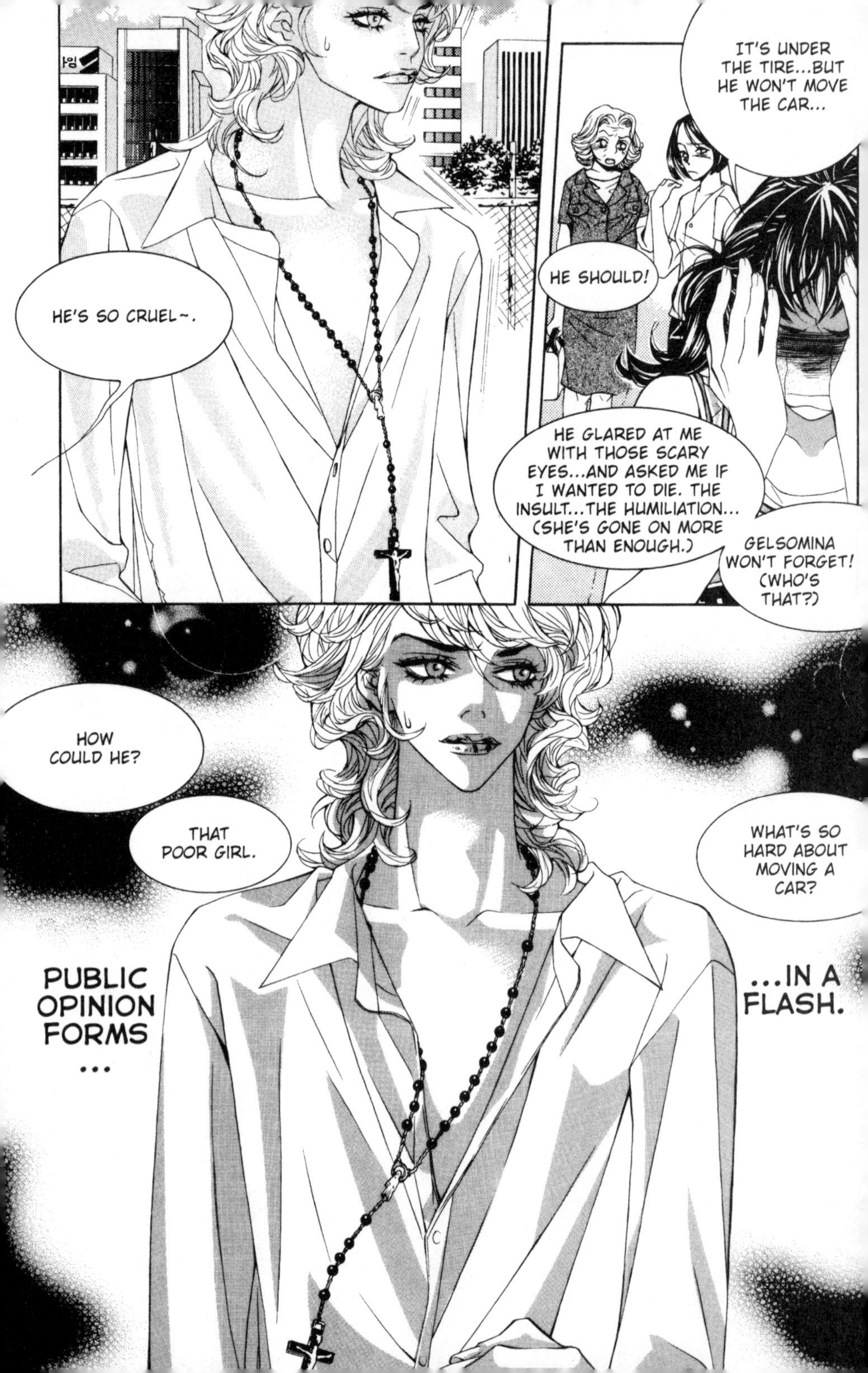
HE'S SO CRUEL~.
IT'S UNDER THE TIRE...BUT HE WON'T MOVE THE CAR...
HE SHOULD!
HE GLARED AT ME WITH THOSE SCARY EYES...AND ASKED ME IF I WANTED TO DIE. THE INSULT...THE HUMILIATION... (SHE'S GONE ON MORE THAN ENOUGH.)
GELSOMINA WON'T FORGET! (WHO'S THAT?)
HOW COULD HE?
THAT POOR GIRL.
WHAT'S SO HARD ABOUT MOVING A CAR?
PUBLIC OPINION FORMS ...
...IN A FLASH.

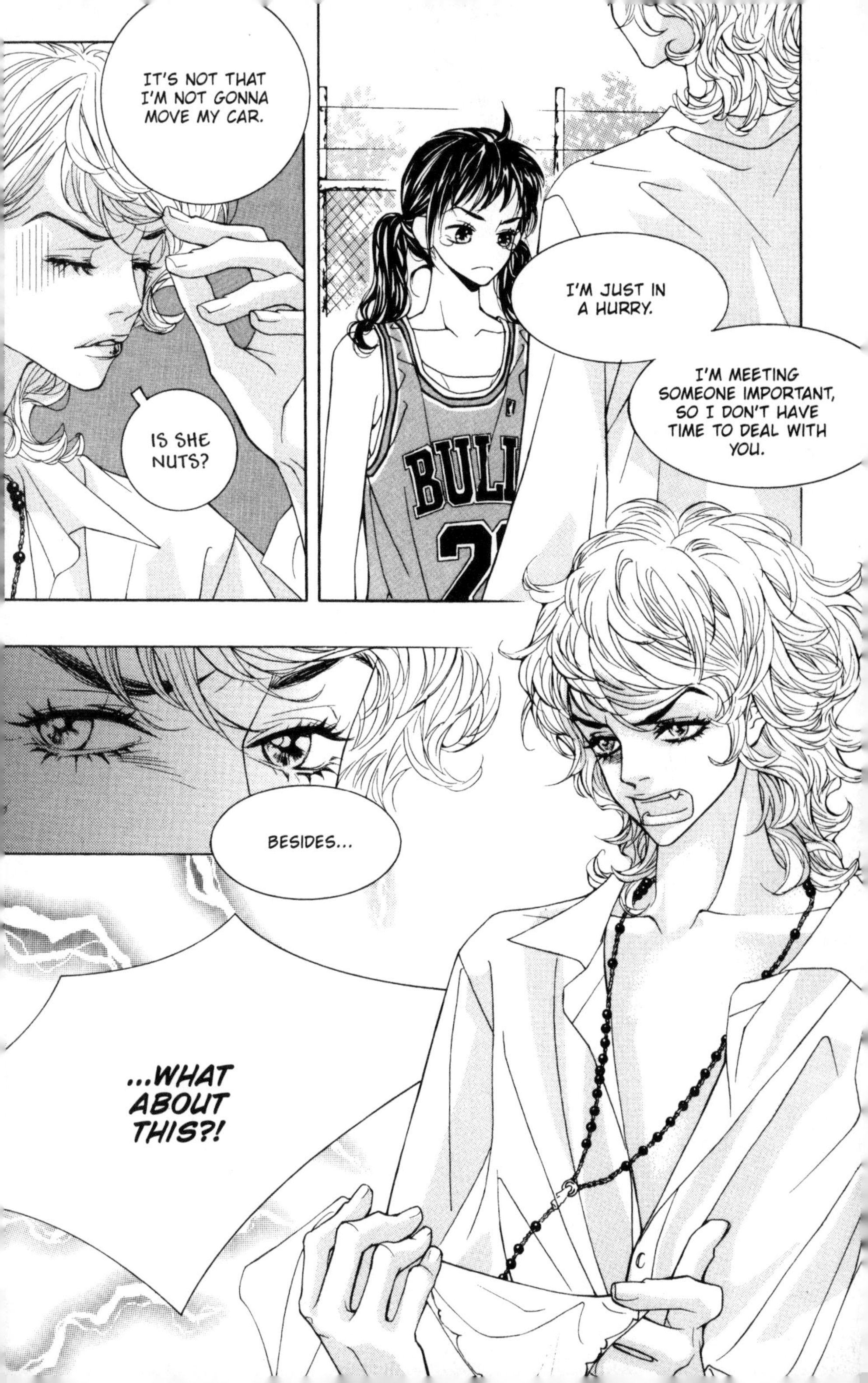
IT'S NOT THAT I'M NOT GONNA MOVE MY CAR.
IS SHE NUTS?
I'M JUST IN A HURRY.
I'M MEETING SOMEONE IMPORTANT, SO I DON'T HAVE TIME TO DEAL WITH YOU.
BULL
BESIDES...
...WHAT ABOUT THIS?!

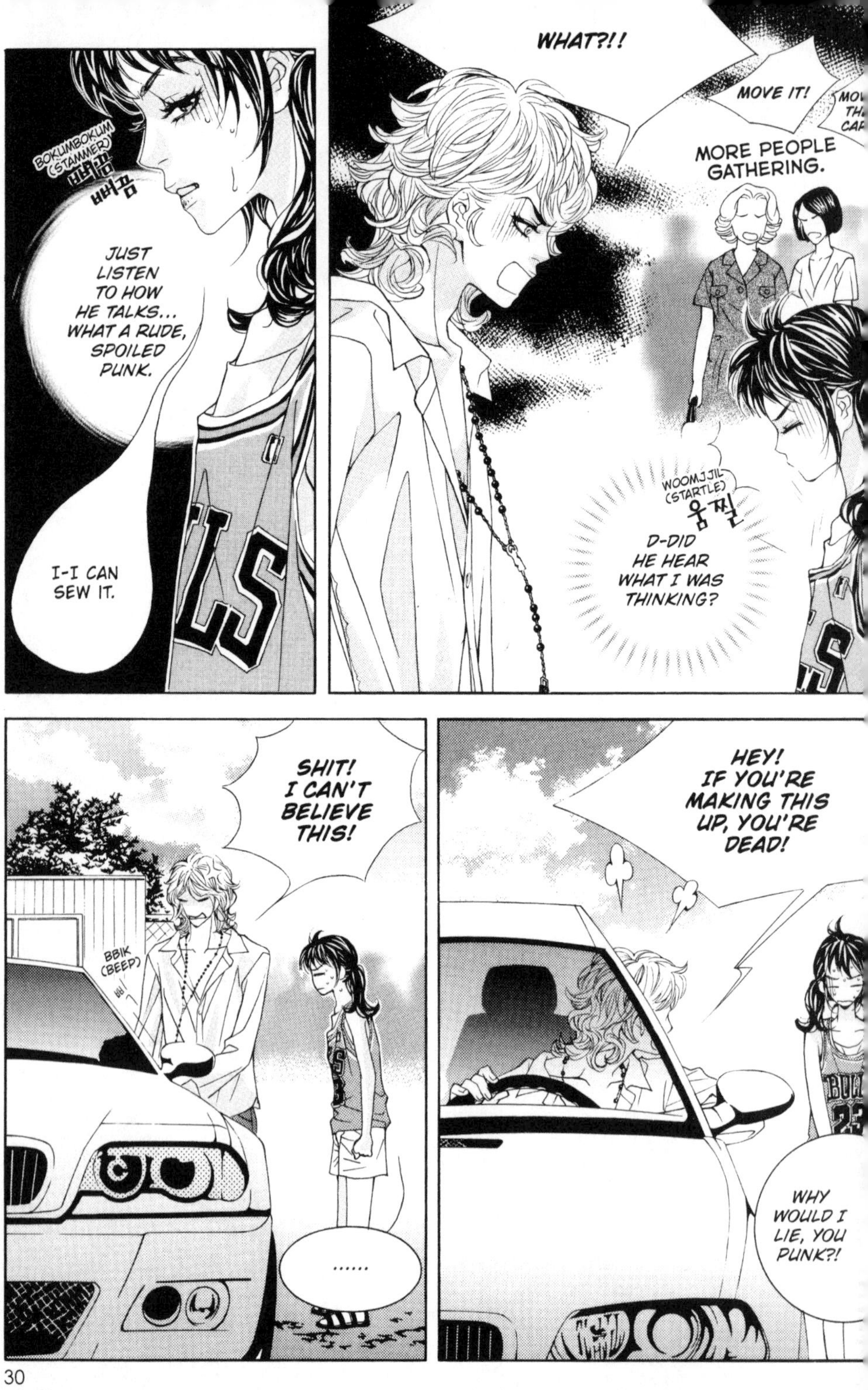

BOKUMBOKUM (STAMMER)
JUST LISTEN TO HOW HE TALKS... WHAT A RUDE, SPOILED PUNK.
I-I CAN SEW IT.
WHAT?!!
MOVE IT!
MORE PEOPLE GATHERING.
WOOMJJIL (STARTLE)
움찔
D-DID HE HEAR WHAT I WAS THINKING?
SHIT! I CAN'T BELIEVE THIS!
BBIK (BEEP)
......
HEY! IF YOU'RE MAKING THIS UP, YOU'RE DEAD!
WHY WOULD I LIE, YOU PUNK?!

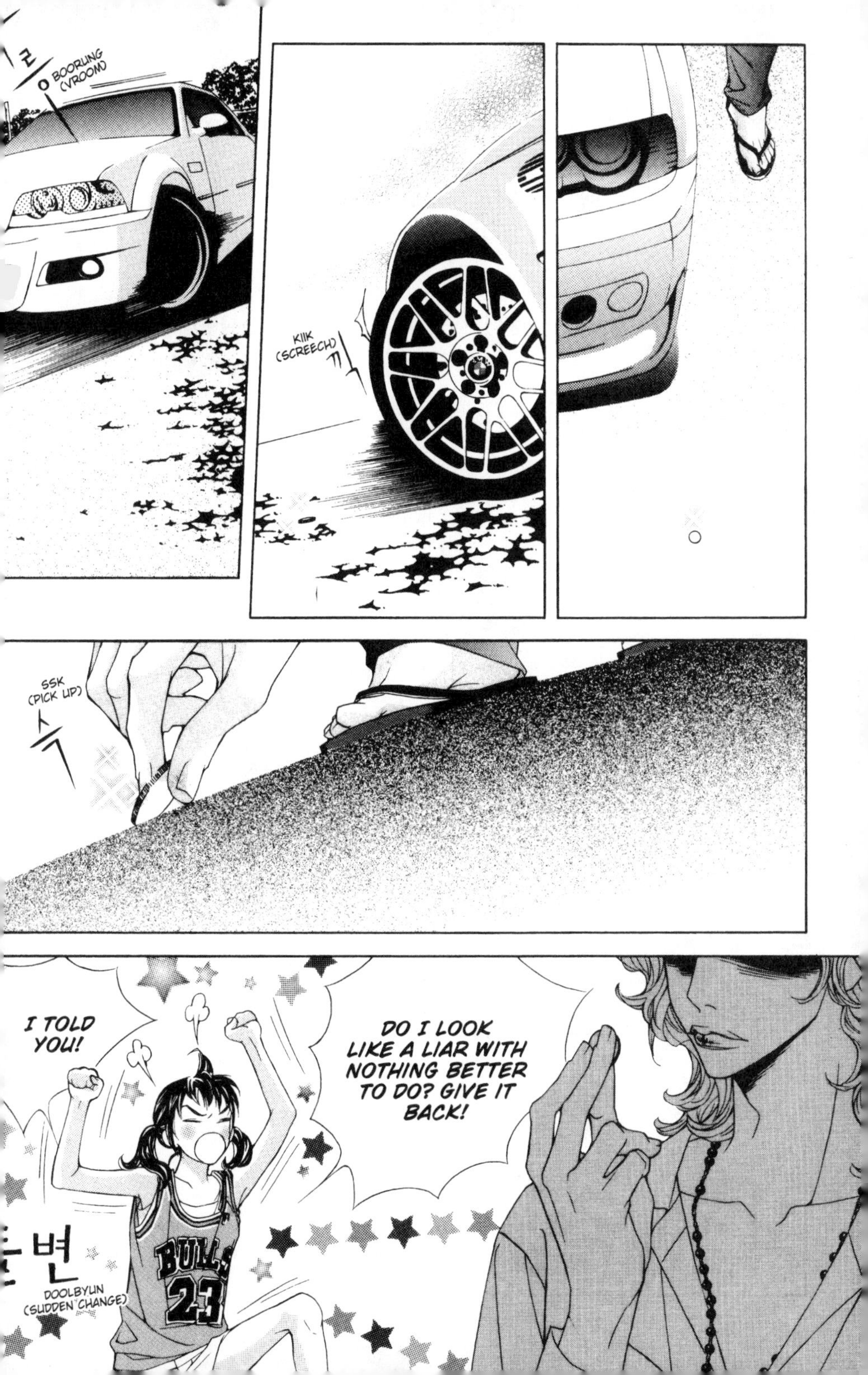
BOORUNG (VROOM)
KIIK (SCREECH)
SSK (PICK UP)
I TOLD YOU!
DO I LOOK LIKE A LIAR WITH NOTHING BETTER TO DO? GIVE IT BACK!
DOOLBYUN (SUDDEN CHANGE)

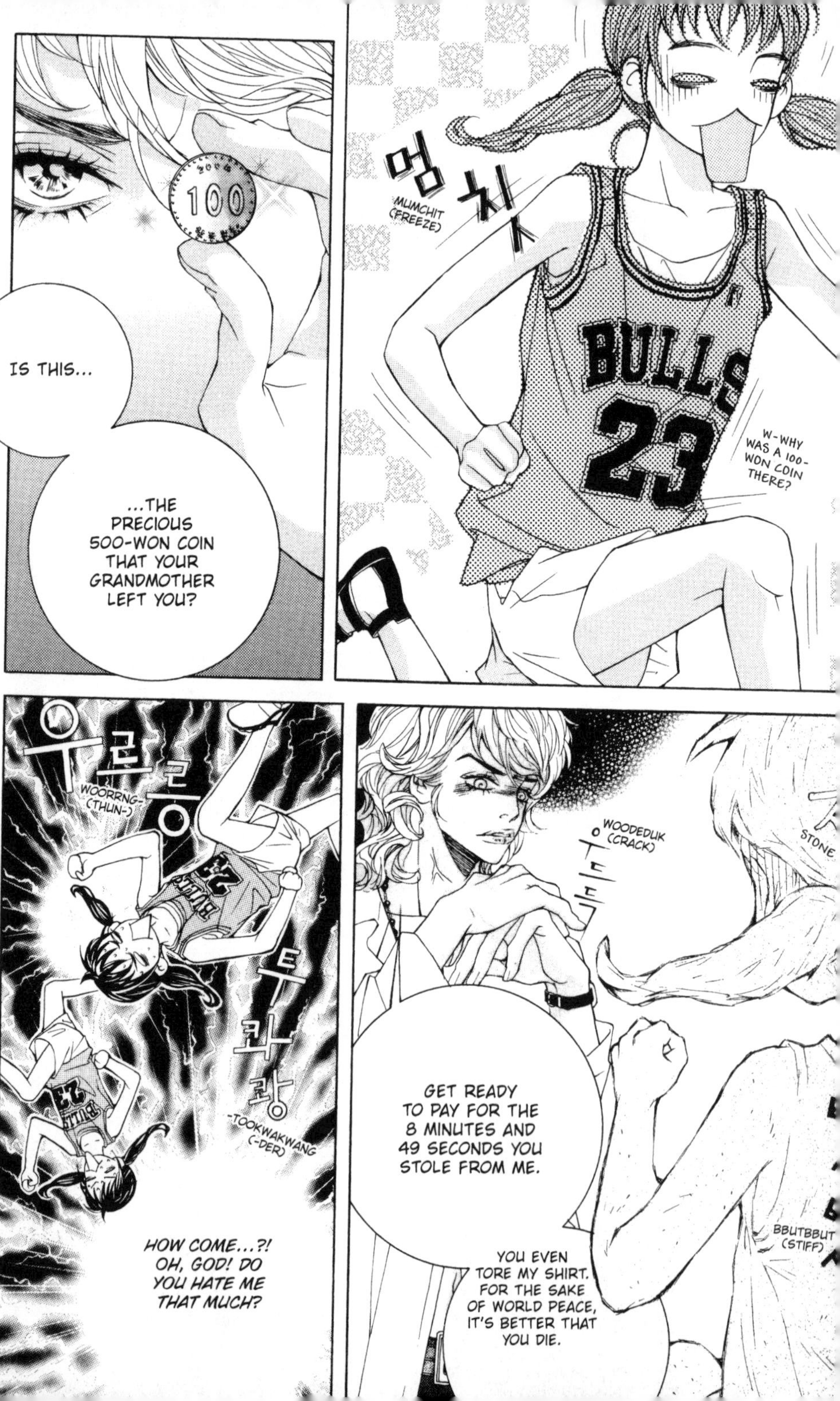
IS THIS...
...THE PRECIOUS 500-WON COIN THAT YOUR GRANDMOTHER LEFT YOU?
멈칫
MUMCHIT (FREEZE)
W-WHY WAS A 100-WON COIN THERE?
BULLS 23
우르릉
WOORRNG- (THUN-)
투콰쾅
-TOOKWAKWANG (-DER)
HOW COME...?! OH, GOD! DO YOU HATE ME THAT MUCH?
WOODEDUK (CRACK)
STONE
GET READY TO PAY FOR THE 8 MINUTES AND 49 SECONDS YOU STOLE FROM ME.
YOU EVEN TORE MY SHIRT. FOR THE SAKE OF WORLD PEACE, IT'S BETTER THAT YOU DIE.
BBUTBBUT (STIFF)

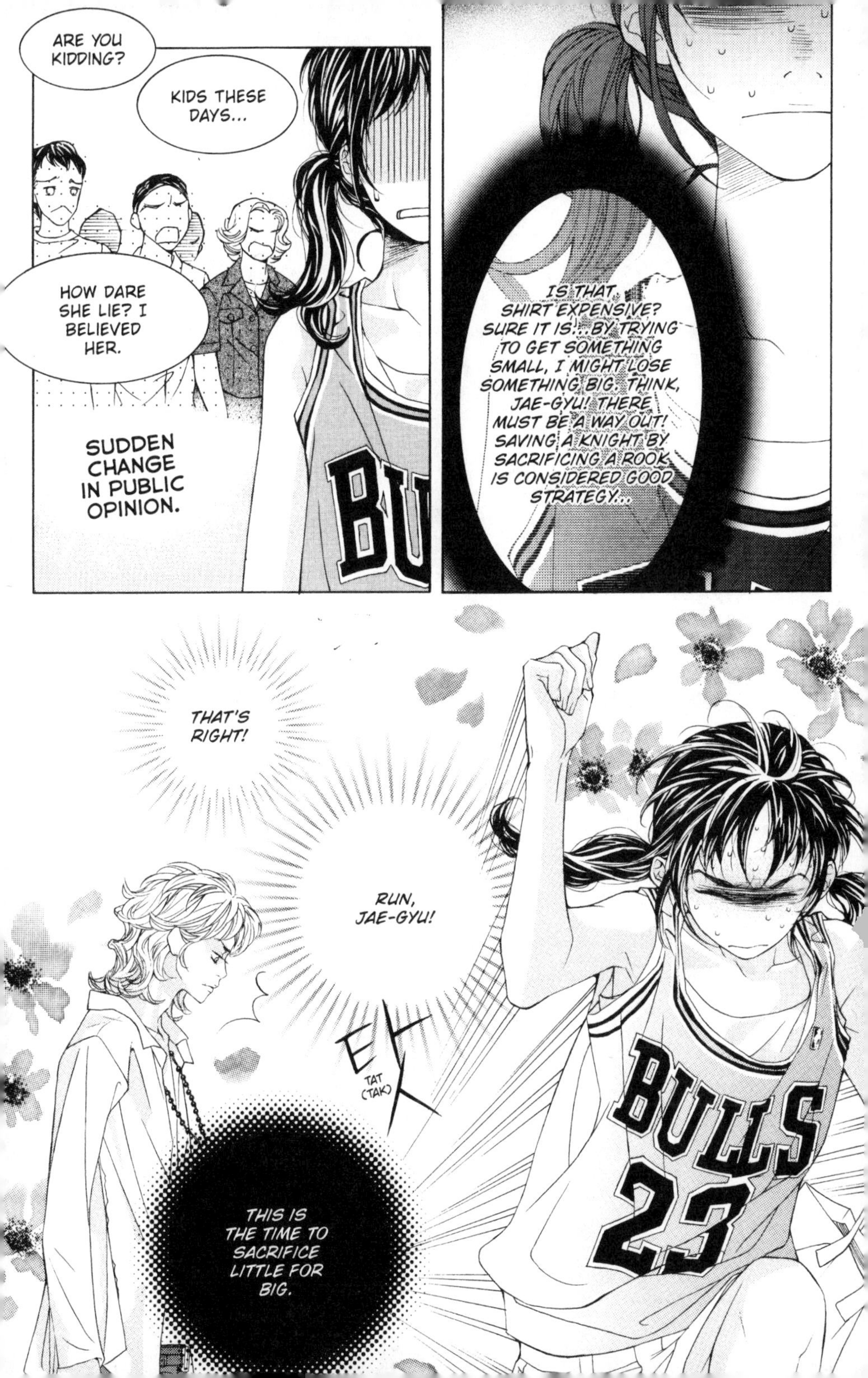
ARE YOU KIDDING?
KIDS THESE DAYS...
HOW DARE SHE LIE? I BELIEVED HER.
SUDDEN CHANGE IN PUBLIC OPINION.
IS THAT SHIRT EXPENSIVE? SURE IT IS...BY TRYING TO GET SOMETHING SMALL, I MIGHT LOSE SOMETHING BIG. THINK, JAE-GYU! THERE MUST BE A WAY OUT! SAVING A KNIGHT BY SACRIFICING A ROOK IS CONSIDERED GOOD STRATEGY...
THAT'S RIGHT!
RUN, JAE-GYU!
TAT (TAK)
THIS IS THE TIME TO SACRIFICE LITTLE FOR BIG.

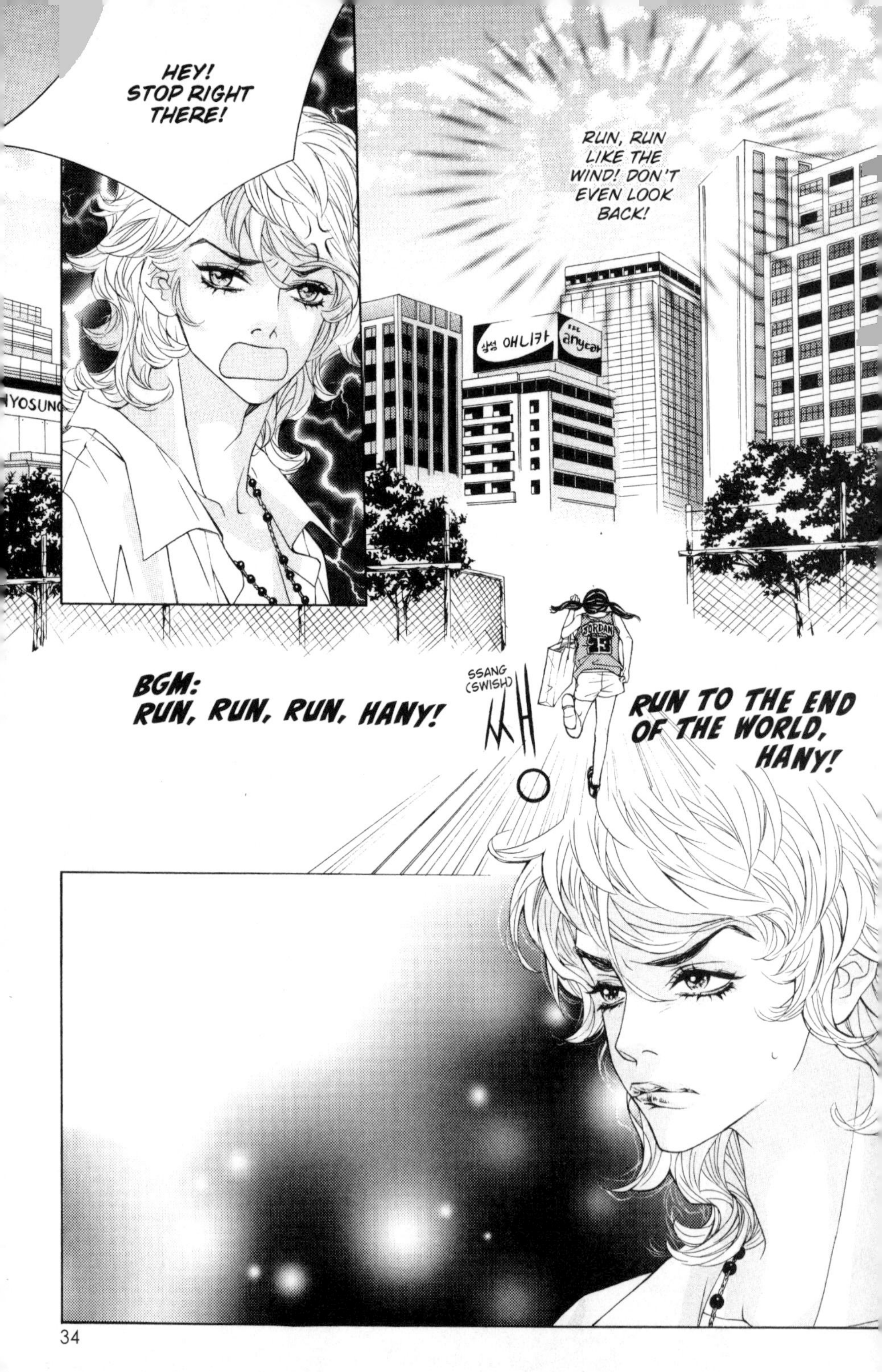
HEY! STOP RIGHT THERE!
RUN, RUN LIKE THE WIND! DON'T EVEN LOOK BACK!
삼성 애니카
anycar
BGM: RUN, RUN, RUN, HANY!
SSANG (SWISH)
RUN TO THE END OF THE WORLD, HANY!

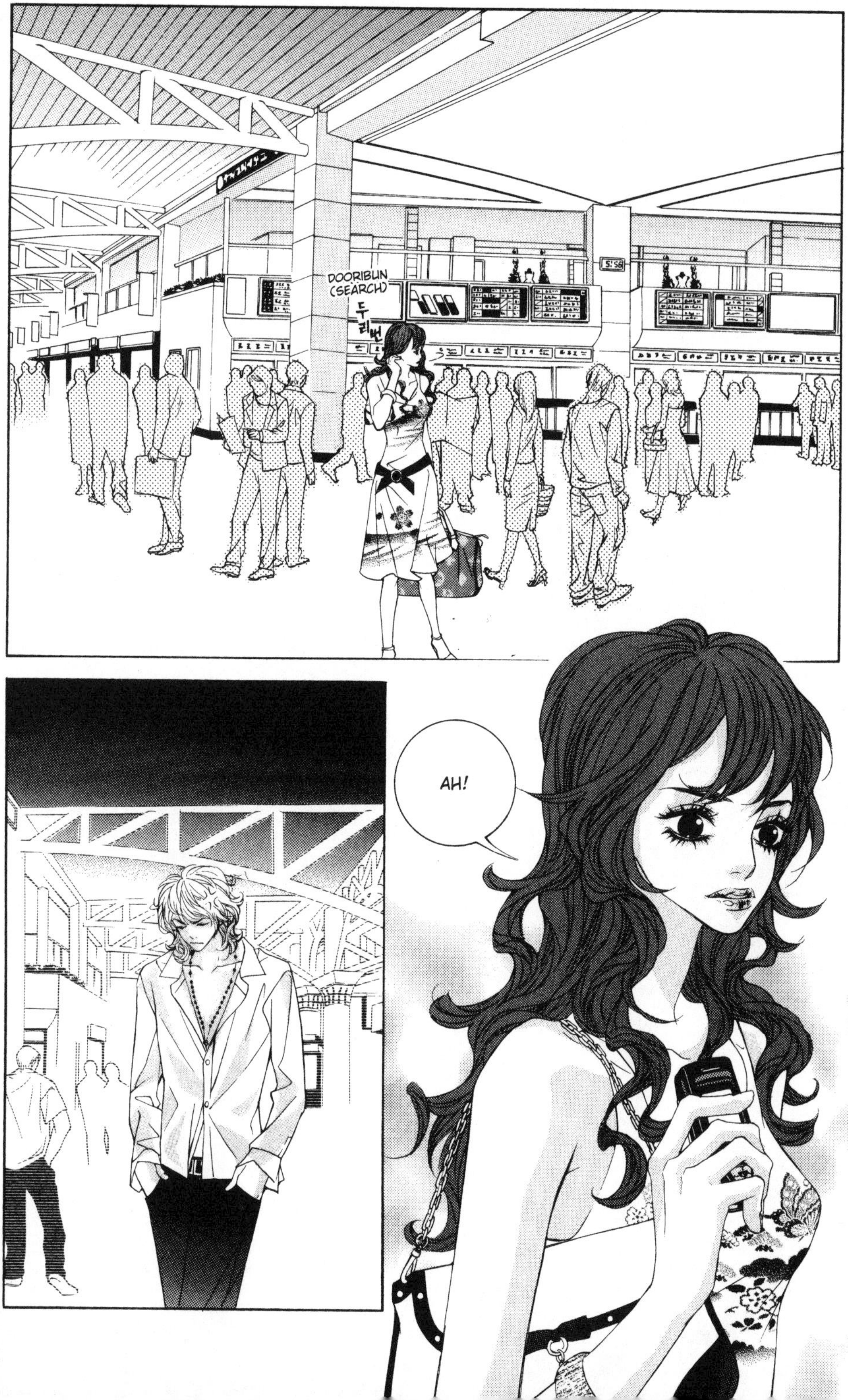
DOORIBUN (SEARCH)
두리번
AH!

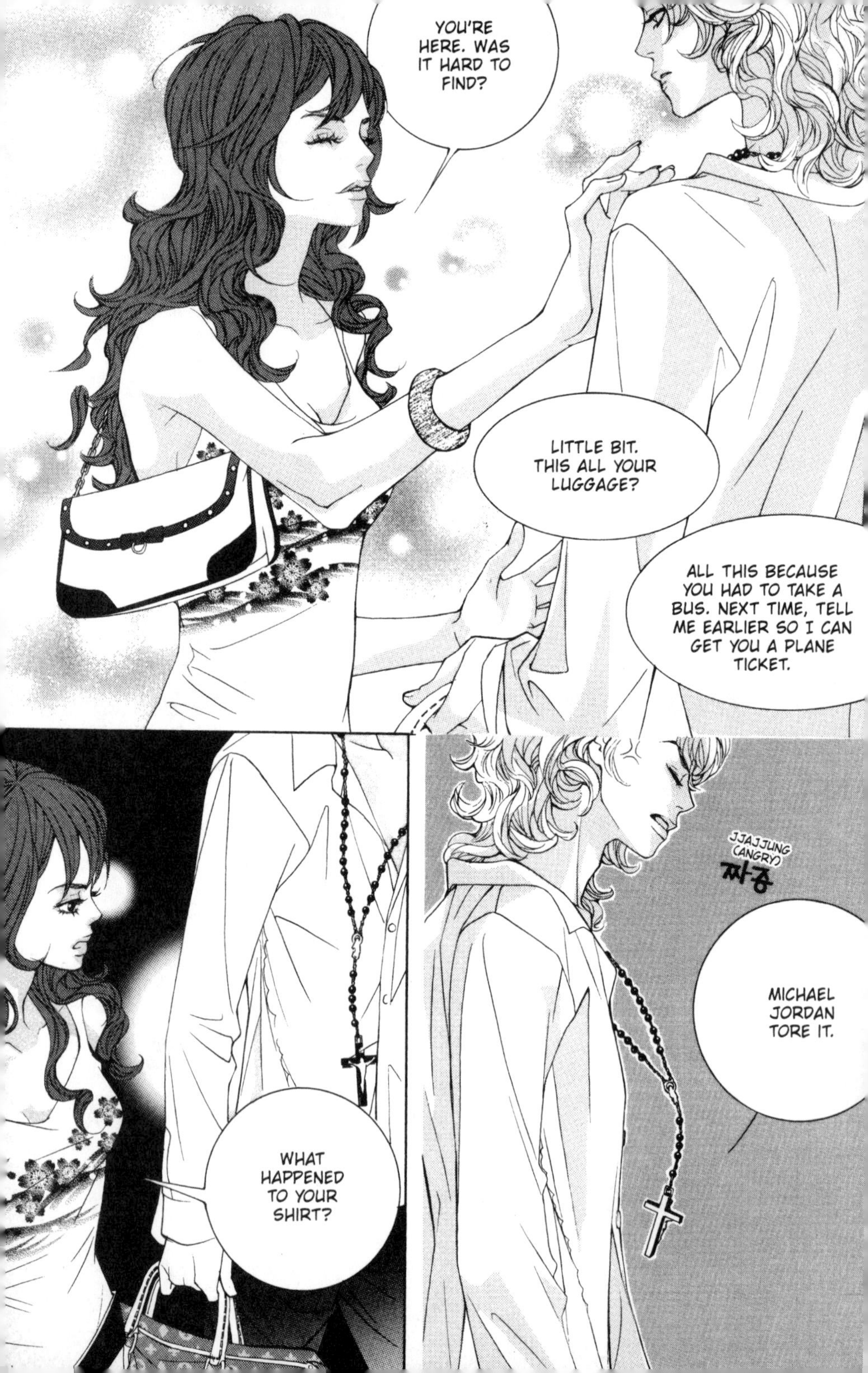
YOU'RE HERE. WAS IT HARD TO FIND?
LITTLE BIT. THIS ALL YOUR LUGGAGE?
ALL THIS BECAUSE YOU HAD TO TAKE A BUS. NEXT TIME, TELL ME EARLIER SO I CAN GET YOU A PLANE TICKET.
WHAT HAPPENED TO YOUR SHIRT?
JJAJJUNG (ANGRY)
짜증
MICHAEL JORDAN TORE IT.

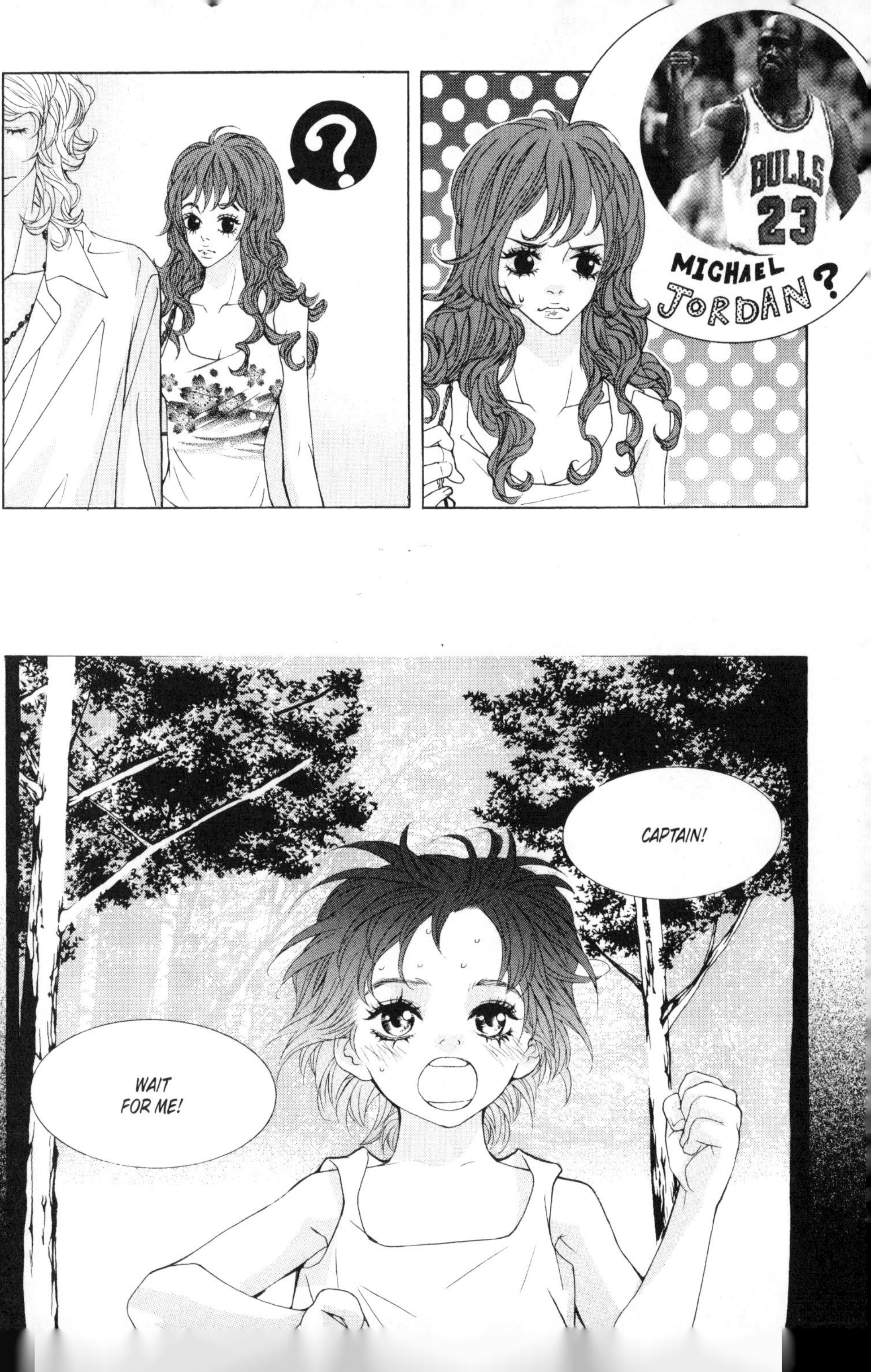
?
MICHAEL JORDAN?
CAPTAIN!
WAIT FOR ME!

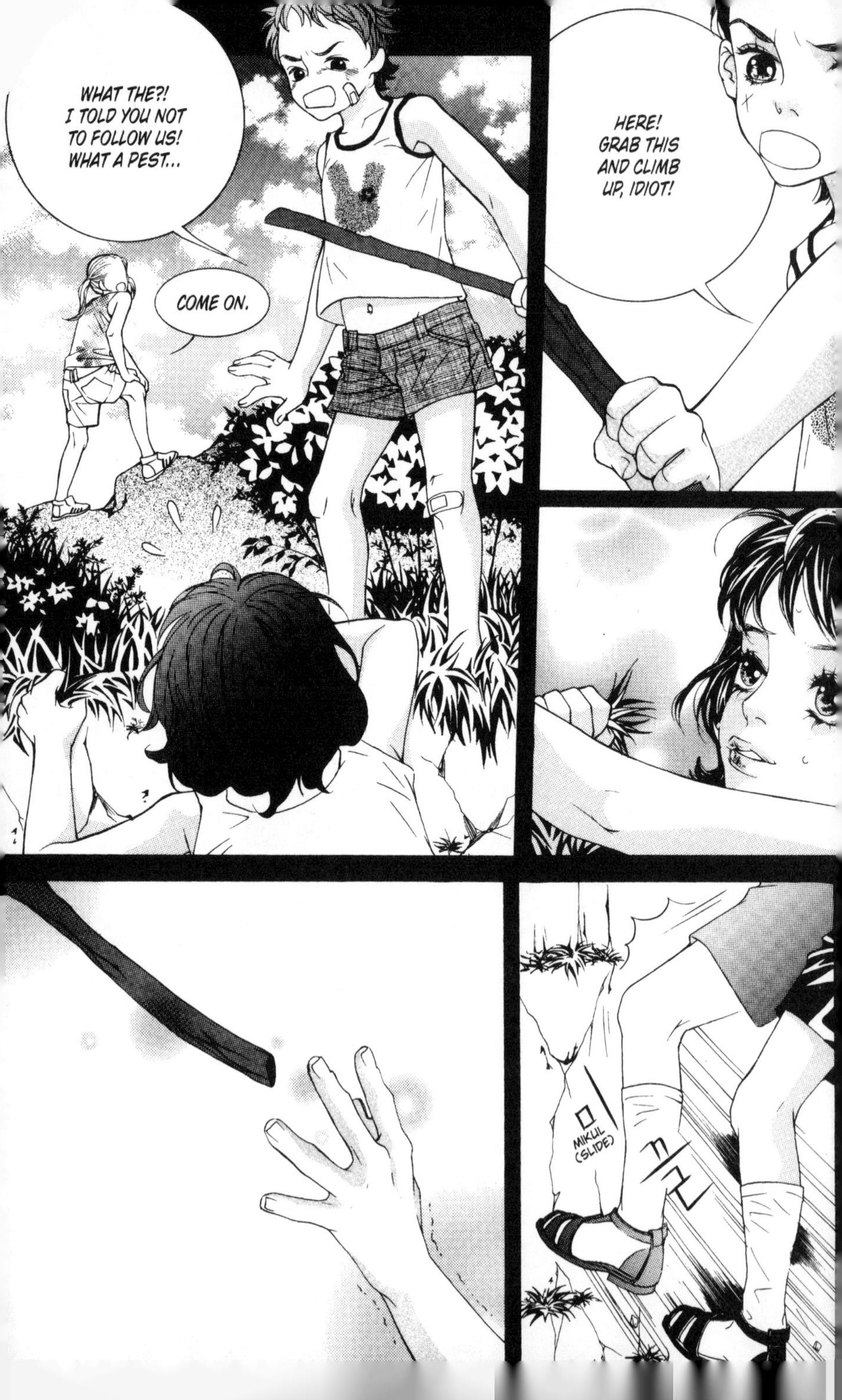
WHAT THE?! I TOLD YOU NOT TO FOLLOW US! WHAT A PEST...
COME ON.
HERE! GRAB THIS AND CLIMB UP, IDIOT!
MIKUL (SLIDE)

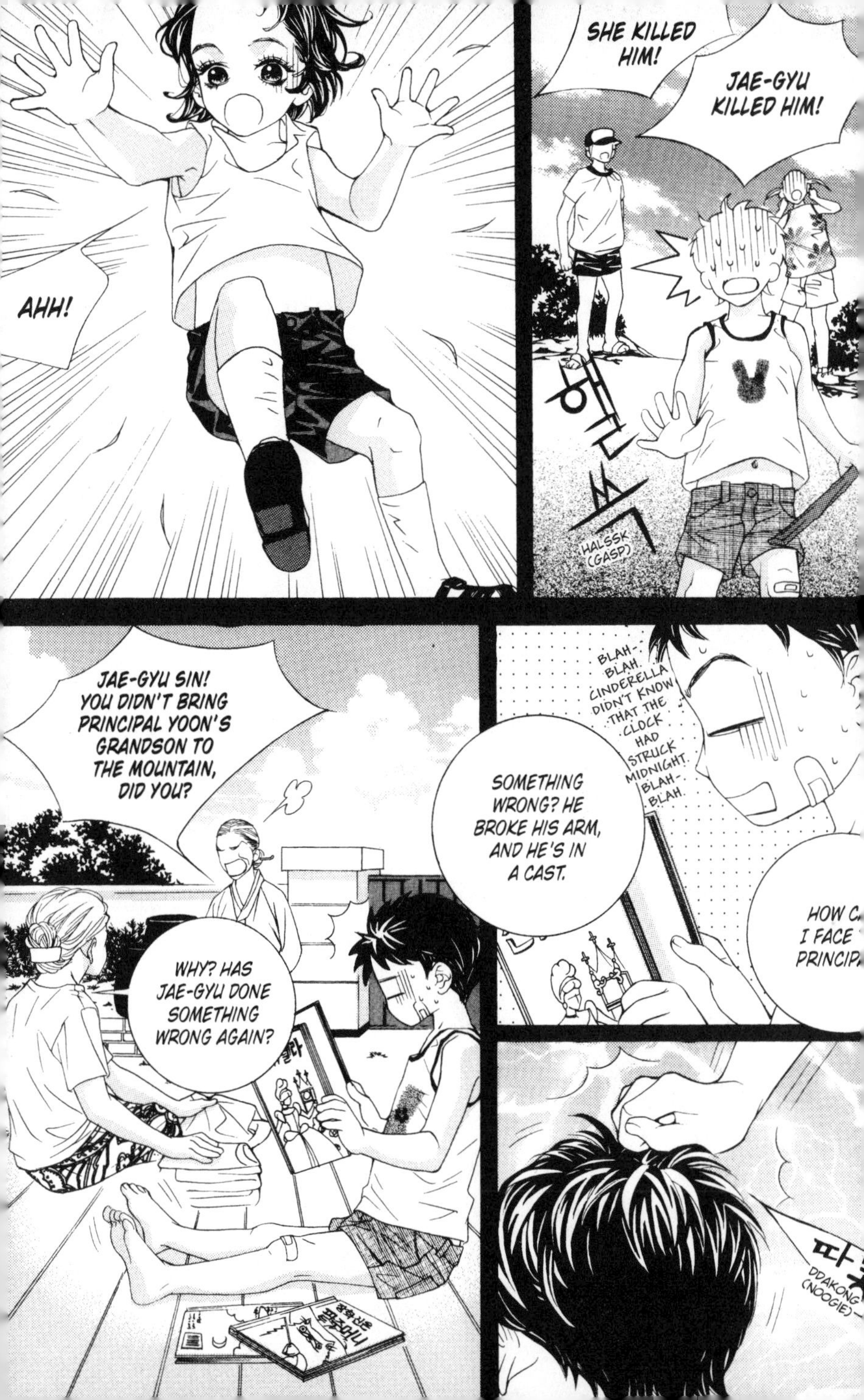
AHH!
SHE KILLED HIM!
JAE-GYU KILLED HIM!
HALSSK (GASP)
JAE-GYU SIN! YOU DIDN'T BRING PRINCIPAL YOON'S GRANDSON TO THE MOUNTAIN, DID YOU?
WHY? HAS JAE-GYU DONE SOMETHING WRONG AGAIN?
SOMETHING WRONG? HE BROKE HIS ARM, AND HE'S IN A CAST.
BLAH-BLAH. CINDERELLA DIDN'T KNOW THAT THE CLOCK HAD STRUCK MIDNIGHT. BLAH-BLAH.
HOW C I FACE PRINCIP
DDAKONG (NOOGIE)

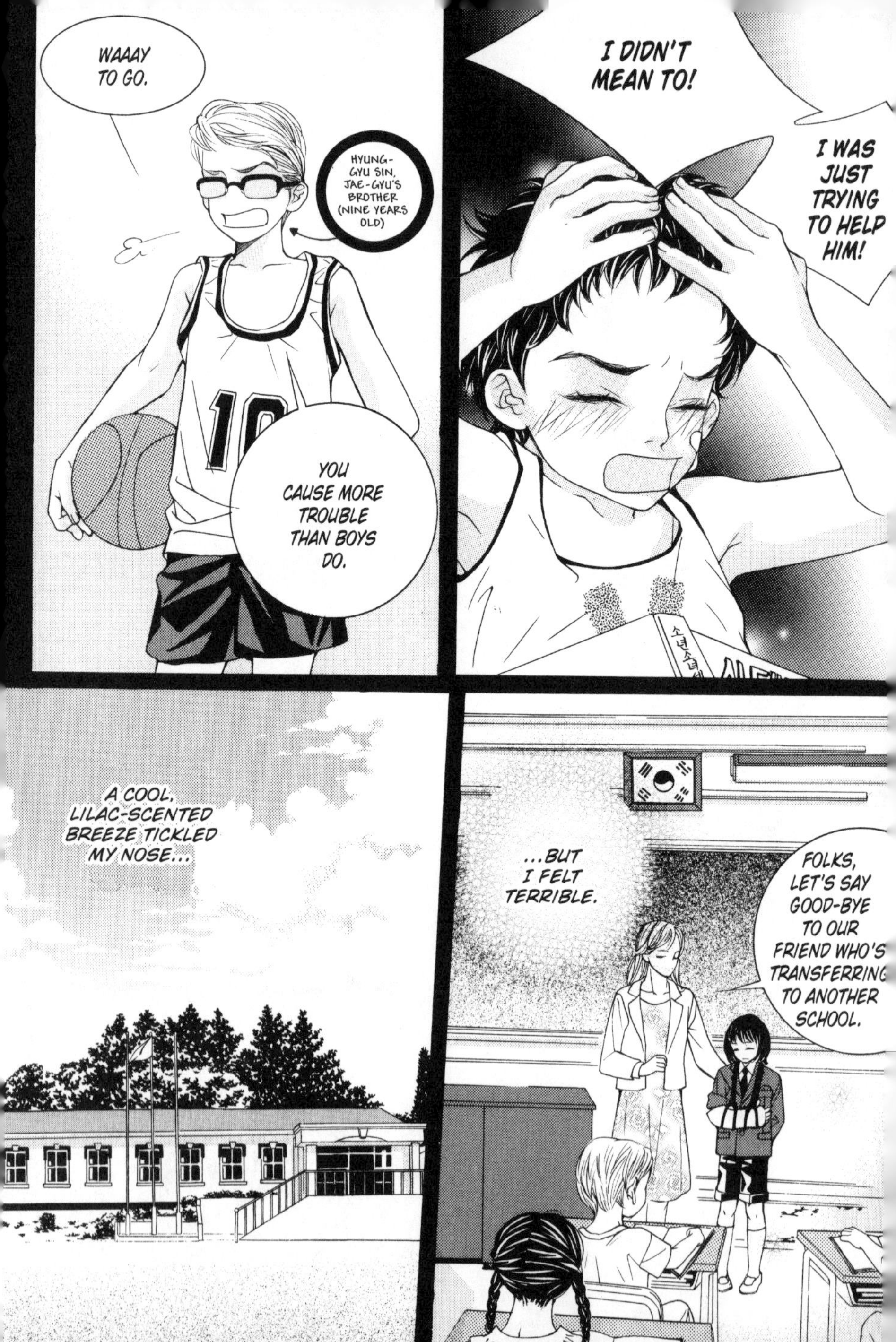
WAAAY TO GO.
HYUNG-GYU SIN, JAE-GYU'S BROTHER (NINE YEARS OLD)
YOU CAUSE MORE TROUBLE THAN BOYS DO.
I DIDN'T MEAN TO!
I WAS JUST TRYING TO HELP HIM!
A COOL, LILAC-SCENTED BREEZE TICKLED MY NOSE...
...BUT I FELT TERRIBLE.
FOLKS, LET'S SAY GOOD-BYE TO OUR FRIEND WHO'S TRANSFERRING TO ANOTHER SCHOOL.

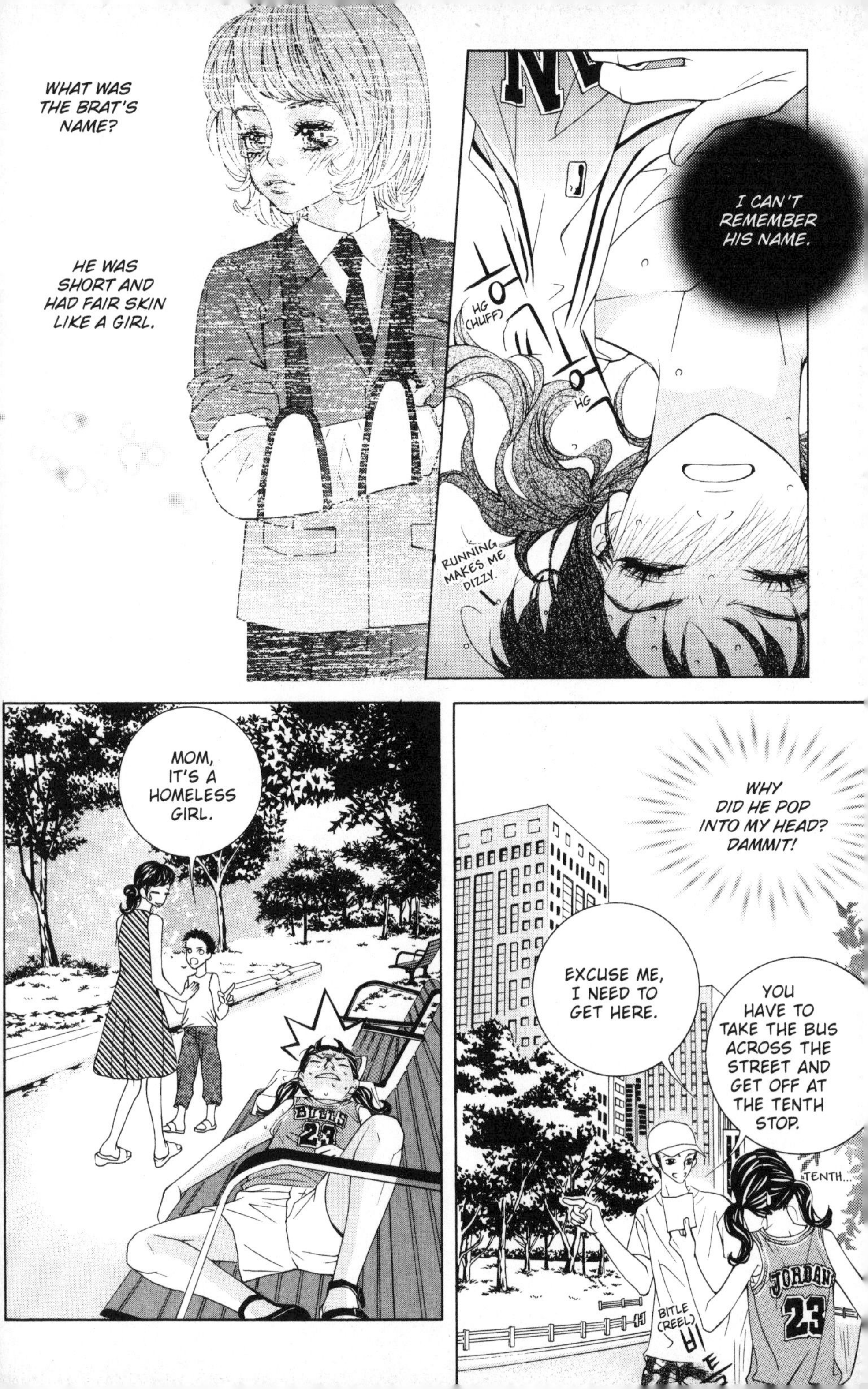
WHAT WAS THE BRAT'S NAME?
HE WAS SHORT AND HAD FAIR SKIN LIKE A GIRL.
I CAN'T REMEMBER HIS NAME.
HG (HUFF)
HG
RUNNING MAKES ME DIZZY.
MOM, IT'S A HOMELESS GIRL.
WHY DID HE POP INTO MY HEAD? DAMMIT!
EXCUSE ME, I NEED TO GET HERE.
YOU HAVE TO TAKE THE BUS ACROSS THE STREET AND GET OFF AT THE TENTH STOP.
TENTH...
BITLE (REEL)

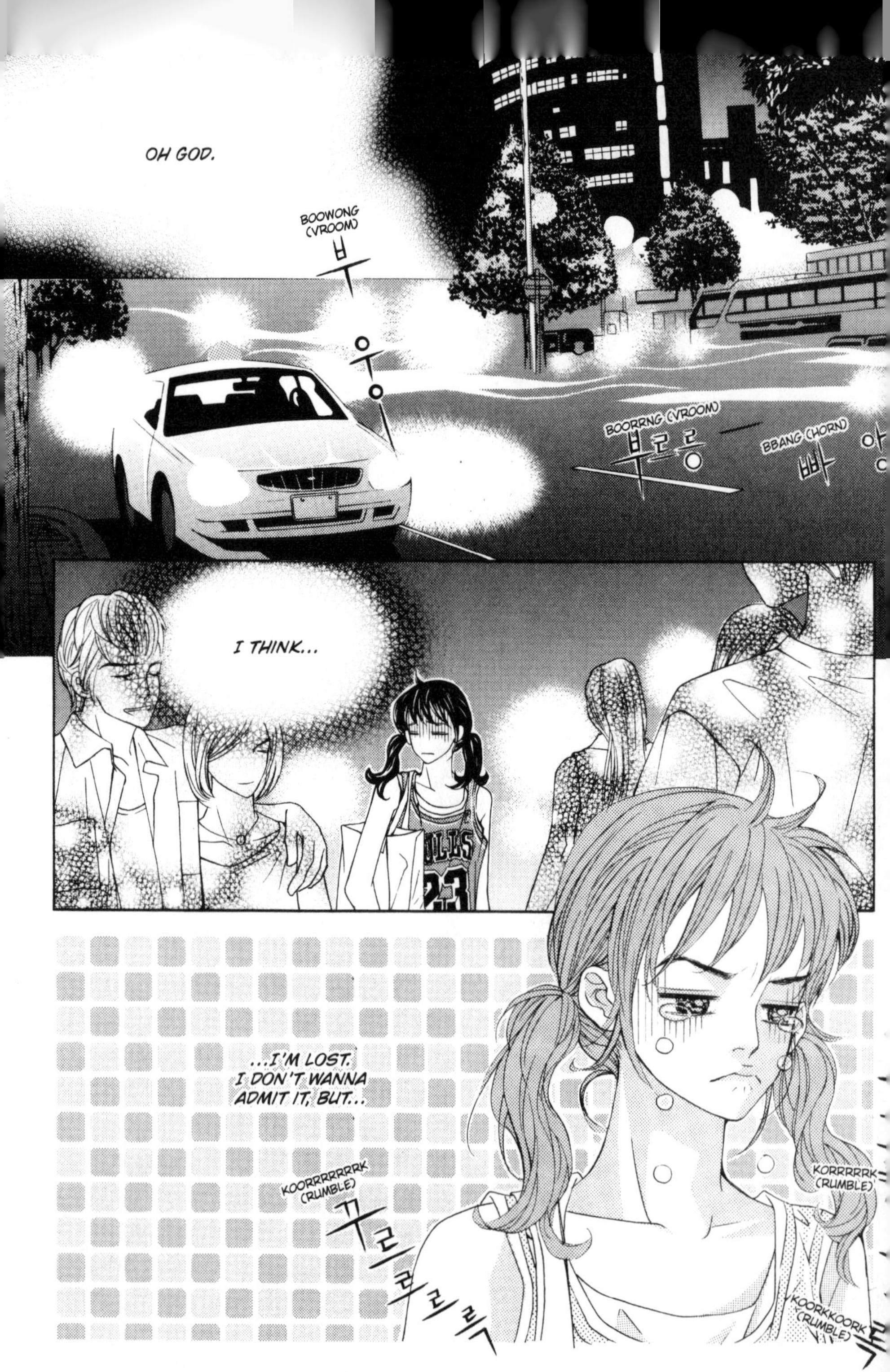
OH GOD.
BOOWONG (VROOM)
부우웅
BOORRNG (VROOM)
부르릉
BBANG (HORN)
빠앙
I THINK...
...I'M LOST. I DON'T WANNA ADMIT IT, BUT...
KOORRRRRRRK (RUMBLE)
꾸르르르륵
KORRRRRK (RUMBLE)
KOORKKOORK (RUMBLE)

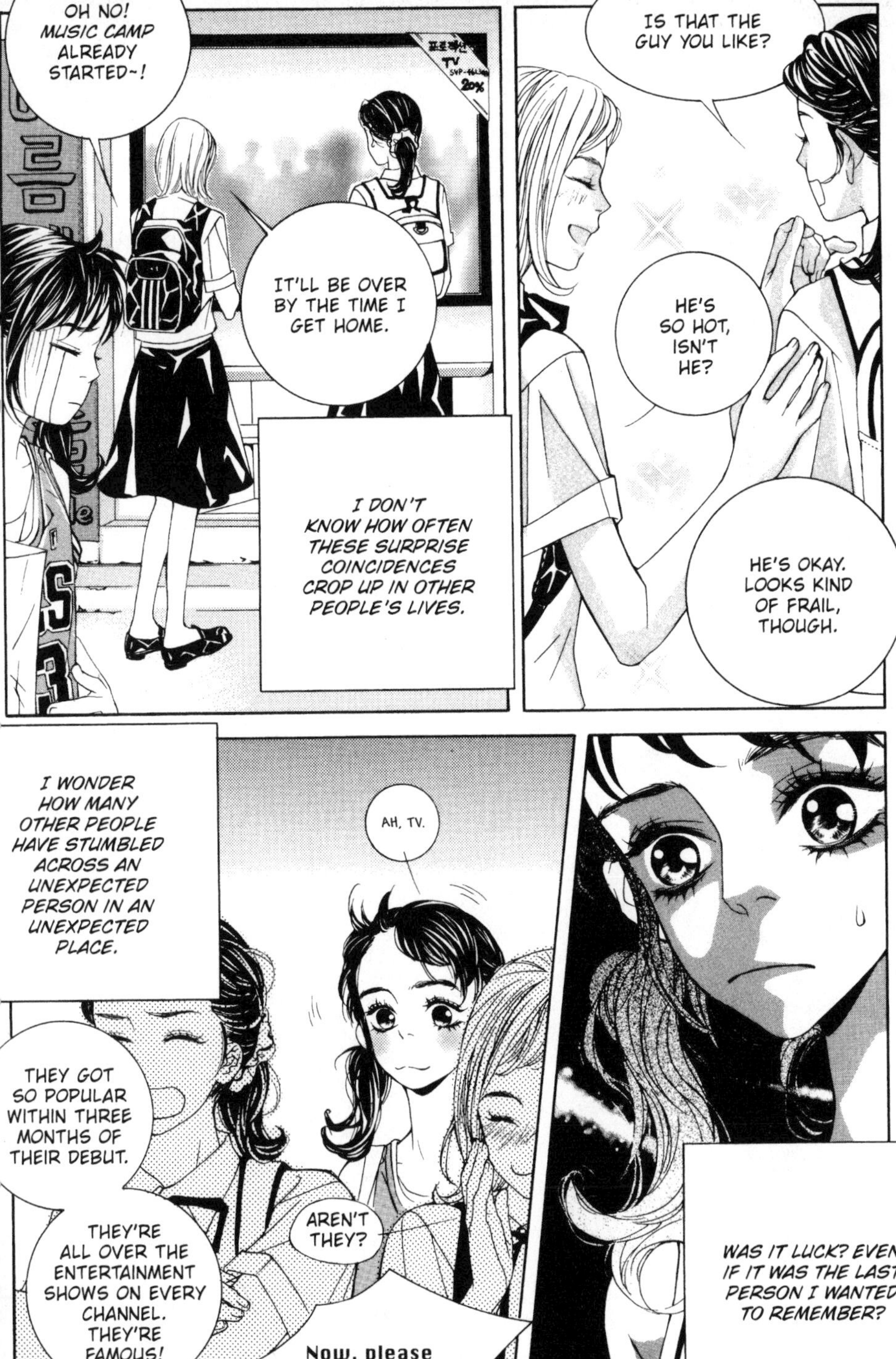
OH NO! MUSIC CAMP ALREADY STARTED~!
IT'LL BE OVER BY THE TIME I GET HOME.
I DON'T KNOW HOW OFTEN THESE SURPRISE COINCIDENCES CROP UP IN OTHER PEOPLE'S LIVES.
IS THAT THE GUY YOU LIKE?
HE'S SO HOT, ISN'T HE?
HE'S OKAY. LOOKS KIND OF FRAIL, THOUGH.
I WONDER HOW MANY OTHER PEOPLE HAVE STUMBLED ACROSS AN UNEXPECTED PERSON IN AN UNEXPECTED PLACE.
AH, TV.
THEY GOT SO POPULAR WITHIN THREE MONTHS OF THEIR DEBUT.
THEY'RE ALL OVER THE ENTERTAINMENT SHOWS ON EVERY CHANNEL. THEY'RE FAMOUS!
AREN'T THEY?
Now, please introduce yourselves~.
WAS IT LUCK? EVEN IF IT WAS THE LAST PERSON I WANTED TO REMEMBER?

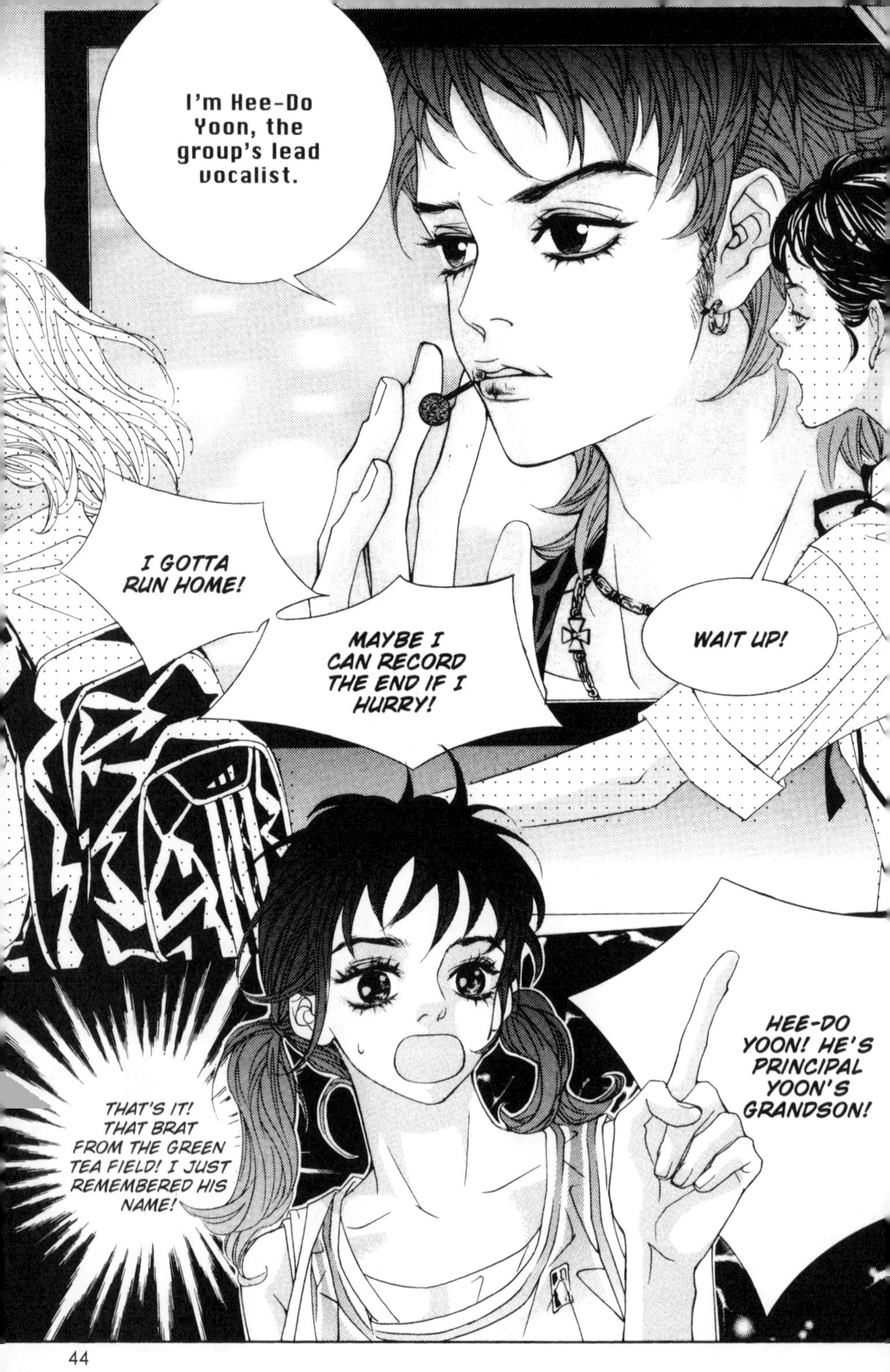
I'm Hee-Do Yoon, the group's lead vocalist.
I GOTTA RUN HOME!
MAYBE I CAN RECORD THE END IF I HURRY!
WAIT UP!
THAT'S IT! THAT BRAT FROM THE GREEN TEA FIELD! I JUST REMEMBERED HIS NAME!
HEE-DO YOON! HE'S PRINCIPAL YOON'S GRANDSON!

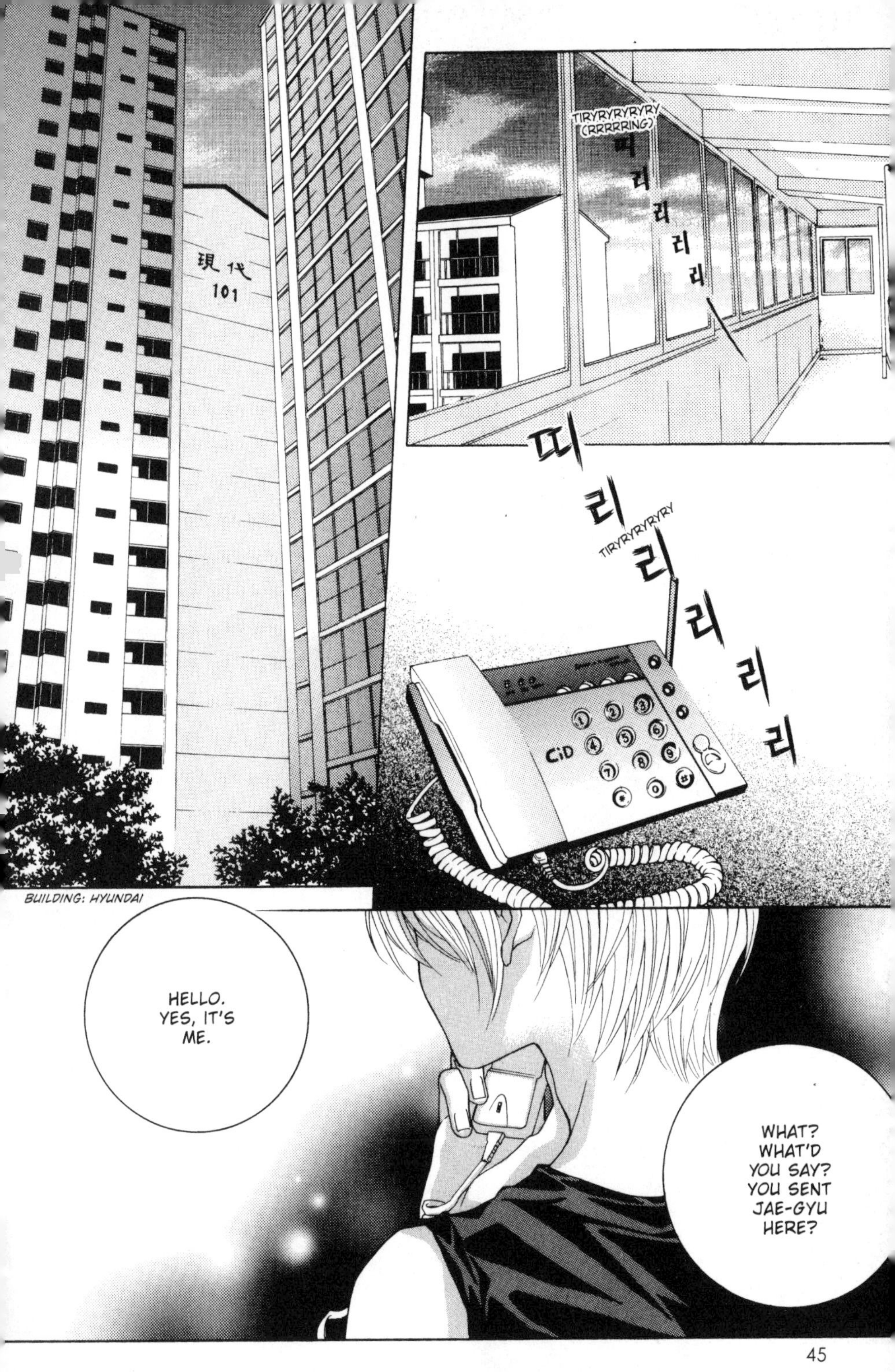

現代
101
BUILDING: HYUNDAI
TIRYRYRYRYRY
(RRRRRING)
띠리리리리
띠리리리리리
TIRYRYRYRYRY
CiD
HELLO. YES, IT'S ME.
WHAT? WHAT'D YOU SAY? YOU SENT JAE-GYU HERE?

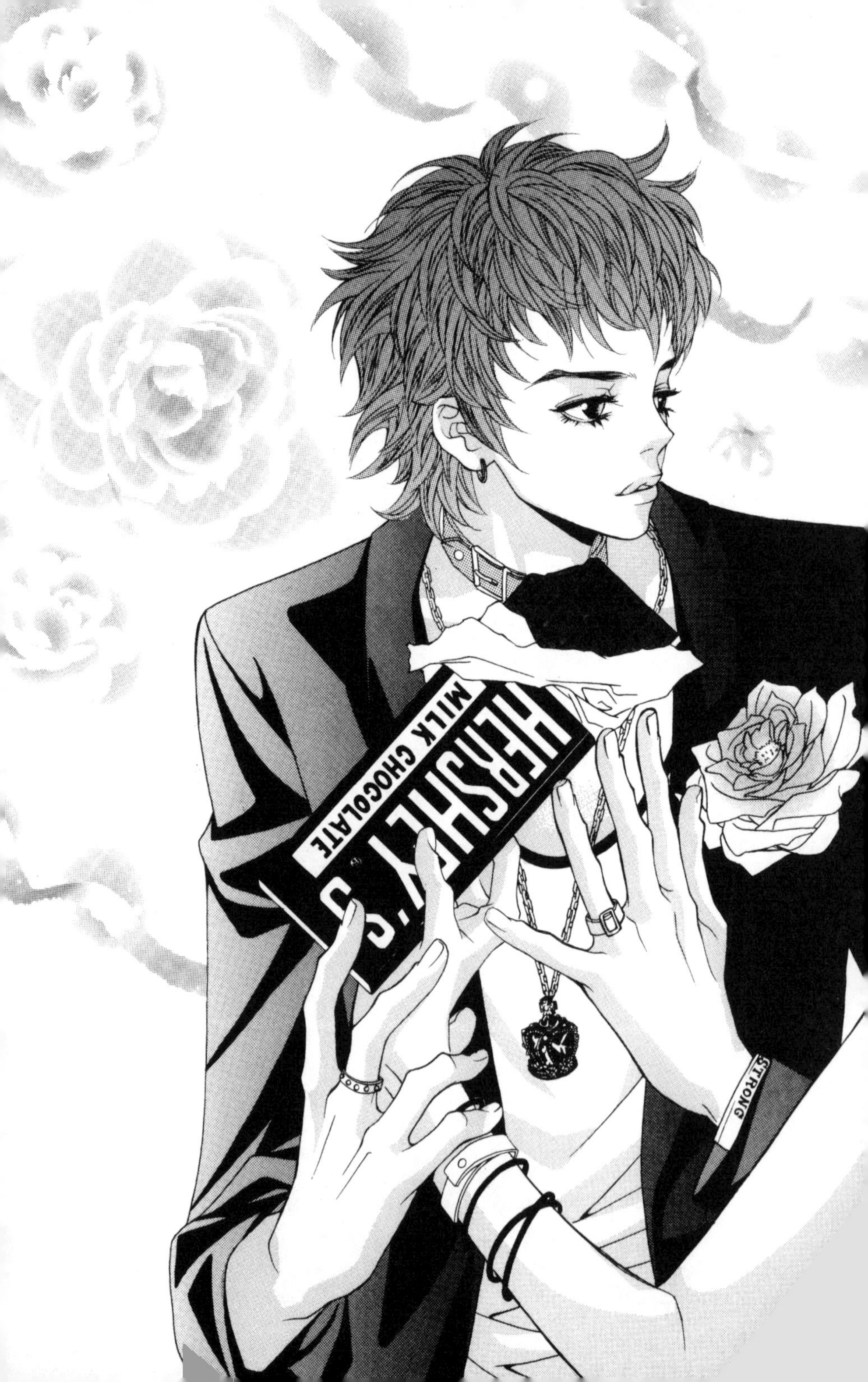
HERSHEY'S
MILK CHOCOLATE
STRONG

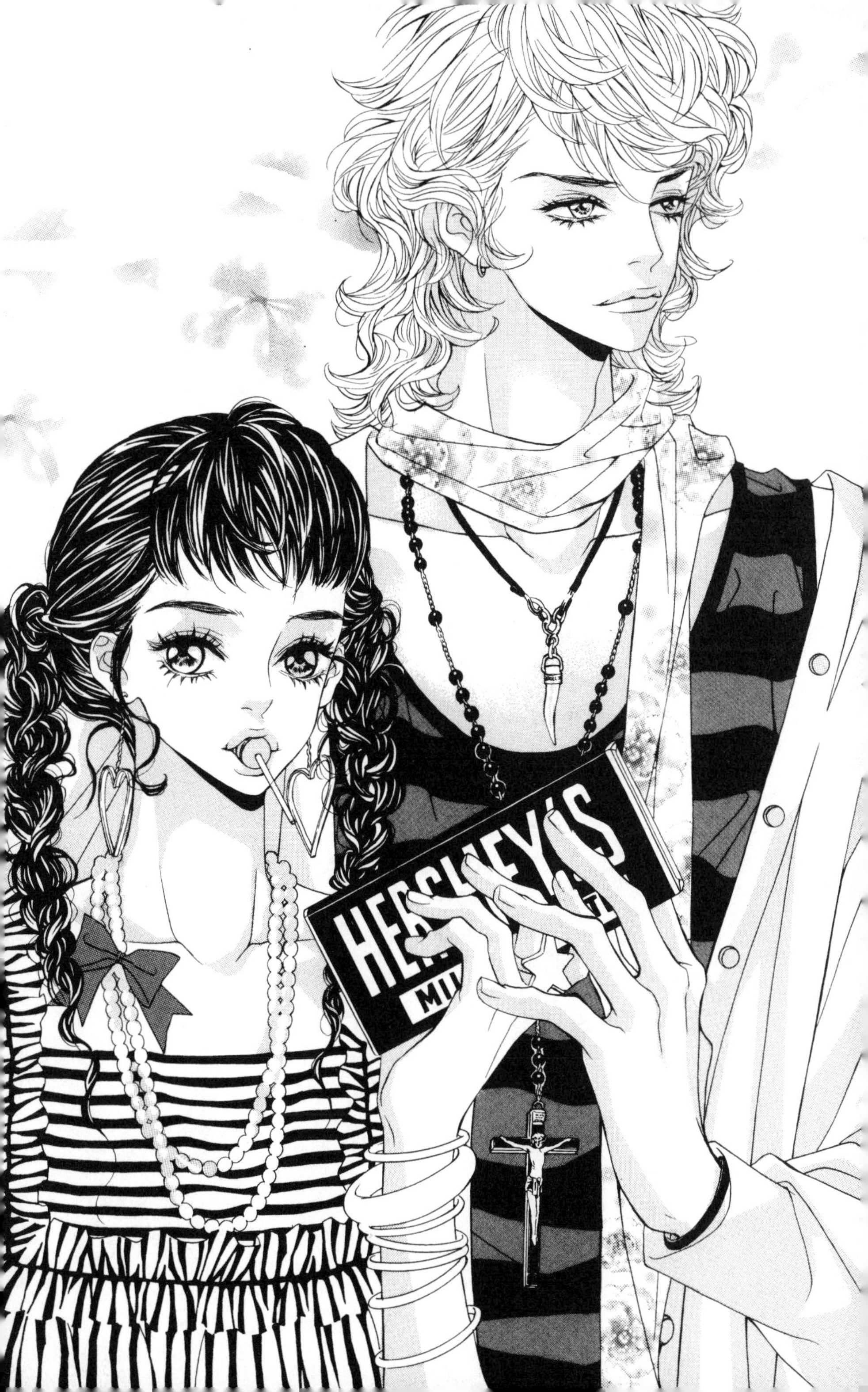

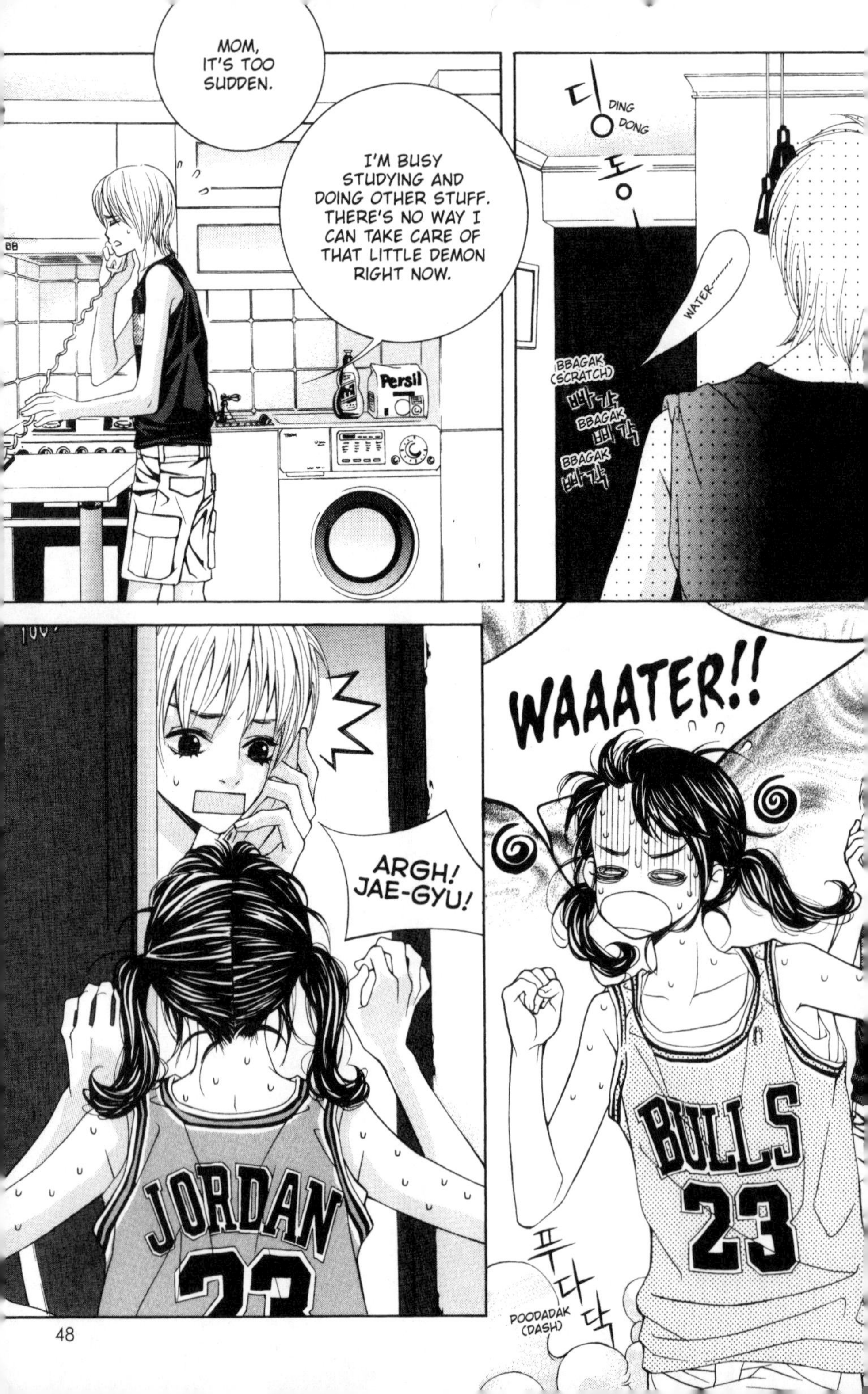
MOM, IT'S TOO SUDDEN.
I'M BUSY STUDYING AND DOING OTHER STUFF. THERE'S NO WAY I CAN TAKE CARE OF THAT LITTLE DEMON RIGHT NOW.
Persil
디
ING DONG
동
WATER------
BBAGAK (SCRATCH)
빠각
BBAGAK
빠각
BBAGAK
빠각
ARGH! JAE-GYU!
WAAATER!!
BULLS
23
JORDAN
푸다닥
POODADAK (DASH)

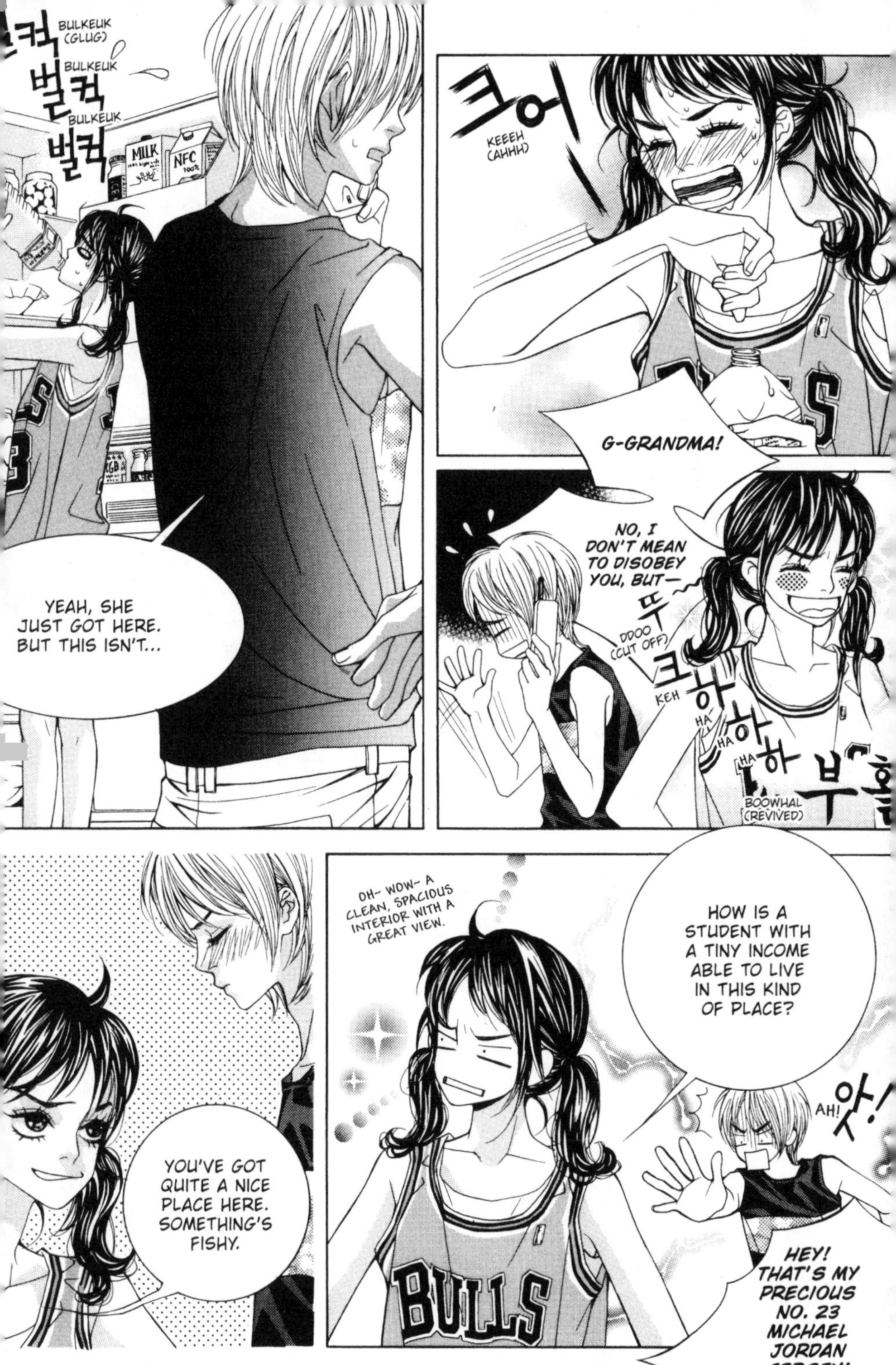
BULKEUK (GLUG)
BULKEUK
벌컥
BULKEUK
벌컥
YEAH, SHE JUST GOT HERE. BUT THIS ISN'T...
크어
KEEEH (AHHH)
G-GRANDMA!
NO, I DON'T MEAN TO DISOBEY YOU, BUT—
뚜
DDOO (CUT OFF)
크하하하
KEH HA HA HA
부활
BOOWHAL (REVIVED)
YOU'VE GOT QUITE A NICE PLACE HERE. SOMETHING'S FISHY.
OH~ WOW~ A CLEAN, SPACIOUS INTERIOR WITH A GREAT VIEW.
HOW IS A STUDENT WITH A TINY INCOME ABLE TO LIVE IN THIS KIND OF PLACE?
AH! 앗!
HEY! THAT'S MY PRECIOUS NO. 23 MICHAEL JORDAN JERSEY!

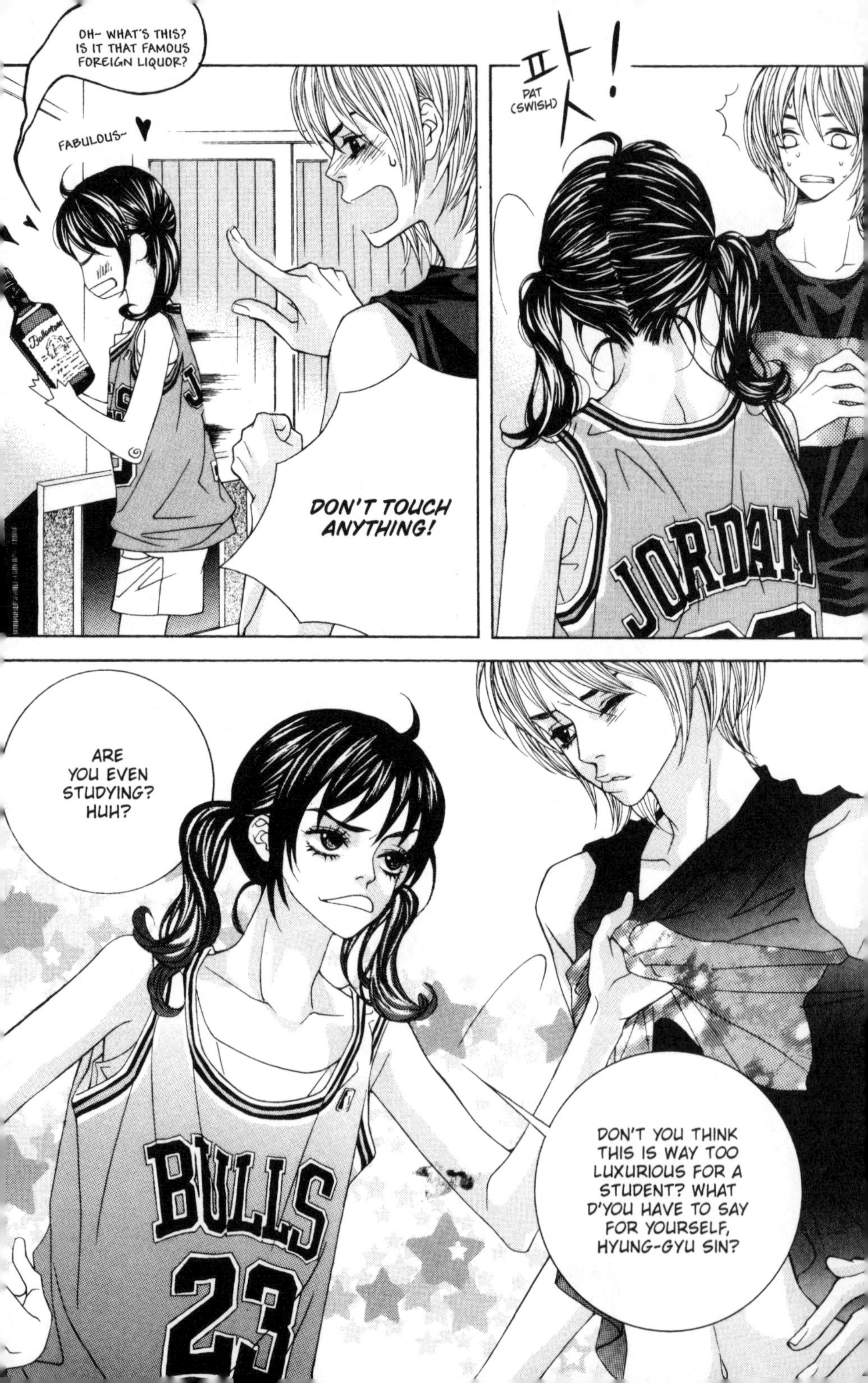
OH~ WHAT'S THIS? IS IT THAT FAMOUS FOREIGN LIQUOR?
FABULOUS~
DON'T TOUCH ANYTHING!
ㅍㅏㅅ! PAT (SWISH)
ARE YOU EVEN STUDYING? HUH?
DON'T YOU THINK THIS IS WAY TOO LUXURIOUS FOR A STUDENT? WHAT D'YOU HAVE TO SAY FOR YOURSELF, HYUNG-GYU SIN?

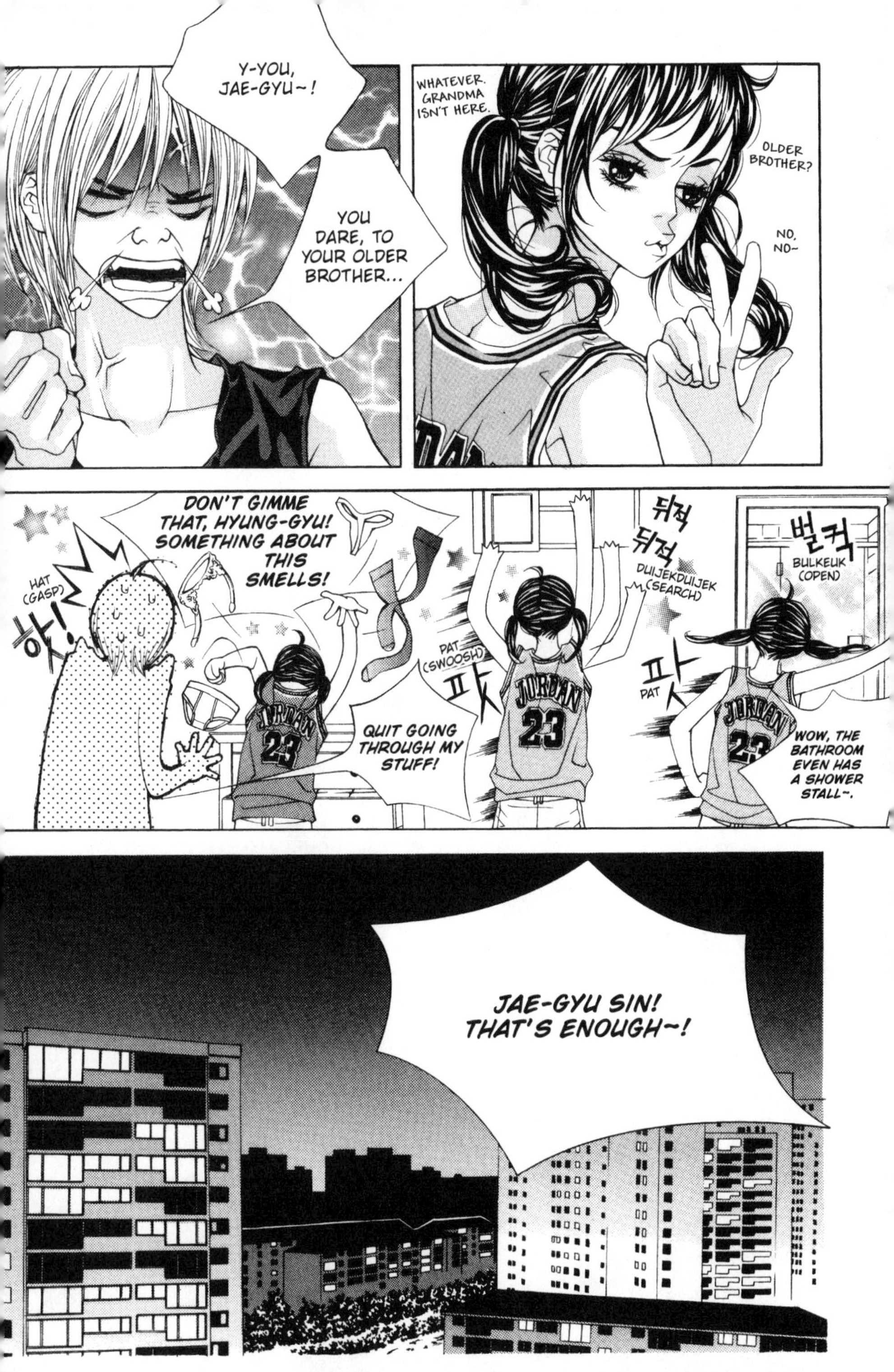
Y-YOU, JAE-GYU~!
YOU DARE, TO YOUR OLDER BROTHER...
WHATEVER. GRANDMA ISN'T HERE.
OLDER BROTHER?
NO, NO~
HAT (GASP)
핫!
DON'T GIMME THAT, HYUNG-GYU! SOMETHING ABOUT THIS SMELLS!
QUIT GOING THROUGH MY STUFF!
뒤적 뒤적
DUIJEKDUIJEK (SEARCH)
팟
PAT (SWOOSH)
팟
PAT
벌컥
BULKEUK (OPEN)
WOW, THE BATHROOM EVEN HAS A SHOWER STALL~.
JAE-GYU SIN! THAT'S ENOUGH~!

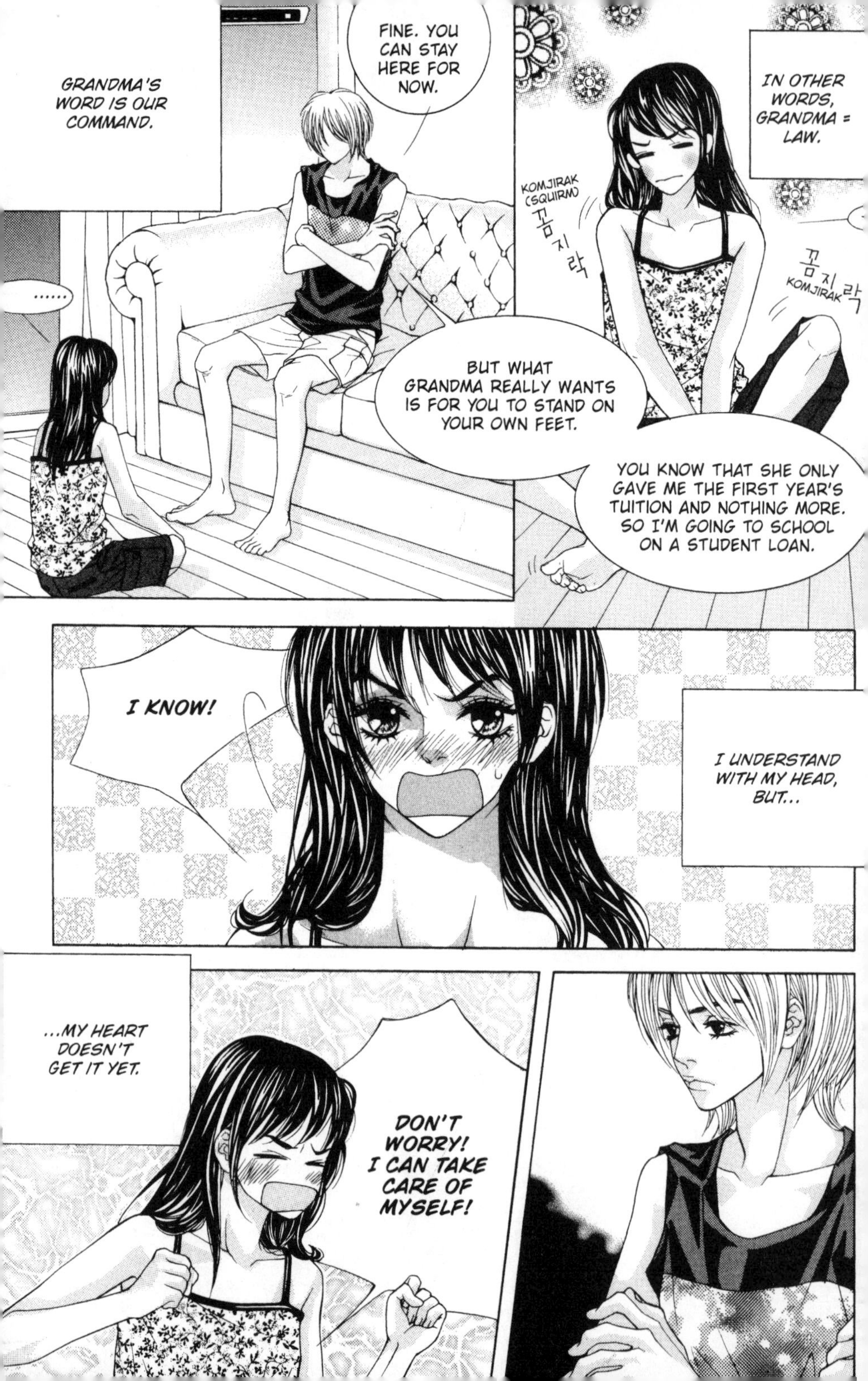
GRANDMA'S WORD IS OUR COMMAND.
FINE. YOU CAN STAY HERE FOR NOW.
......
IN OTHER WORDS, GRANDMA = LAW.
KOMJIRAK (SQUIRM)
꼼지락
꼼지락
KOMJIRAK
BUT WHAT GRANDMA REALLY WANTS IS FOR YOU TO STAND ON YOUR OWN FEET.
YOU KNOW THAT SHE ONLY GAVE ME THE FIRST YEAR'S TUITION AND NOTHING MORE. SO I'M GOING TO SCHOOL ON A STUDENT LOAN.
I KNOW!
I UNDERSTAND WITH MY HEAD, BUT...
...MY HEART DOESN'T GET IT YET.
DON'T WORRY! I CAN TAKE CARE OF MYSELF!

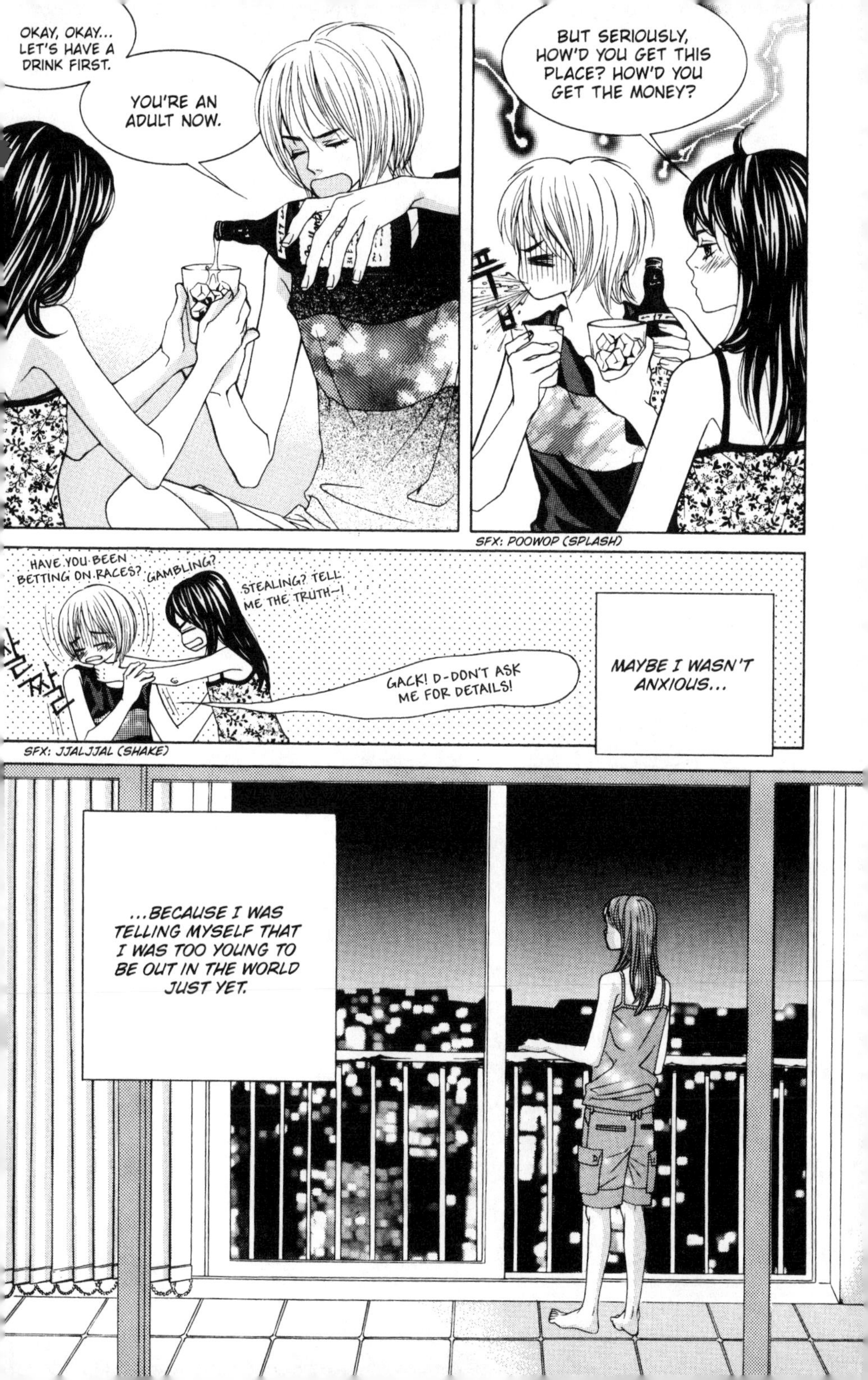
OKAY, OKAY... LET'S HAVE A DRINK FIRST.
YOU'RE AN ADULT NOW.
BUT SERIOUSLY, HOW'D YOU GET THIS PLACE? HOW'D YOU GET THE MONEY?
SFX: POOWOP (SPLASH)
HAVE YOU BEEN BETTING ON RACES?
GAMBLING?
STEALING? TELL ME THE TRUTH~!
GACK! D-DON'T ASK ME FOR DETAILS!
SFX: JJALJJAL (SHAKE)
MAYBE I WASN'T ANXIOUS...
...BECAUSE I WAS TELLING MYSELF THAT I WAS TOO YOUNG TO BE OUT IN THE WORLD JUST YET.

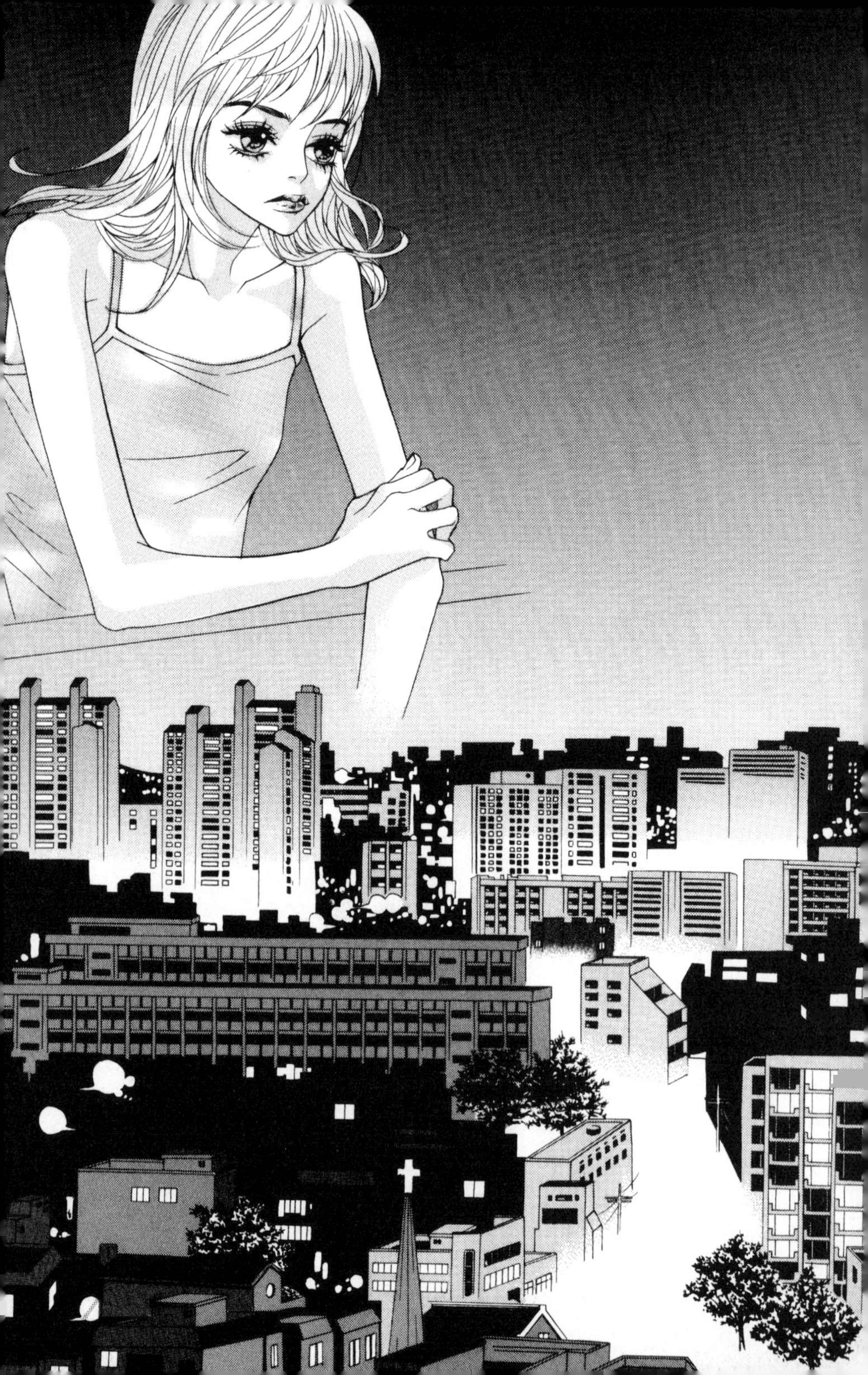

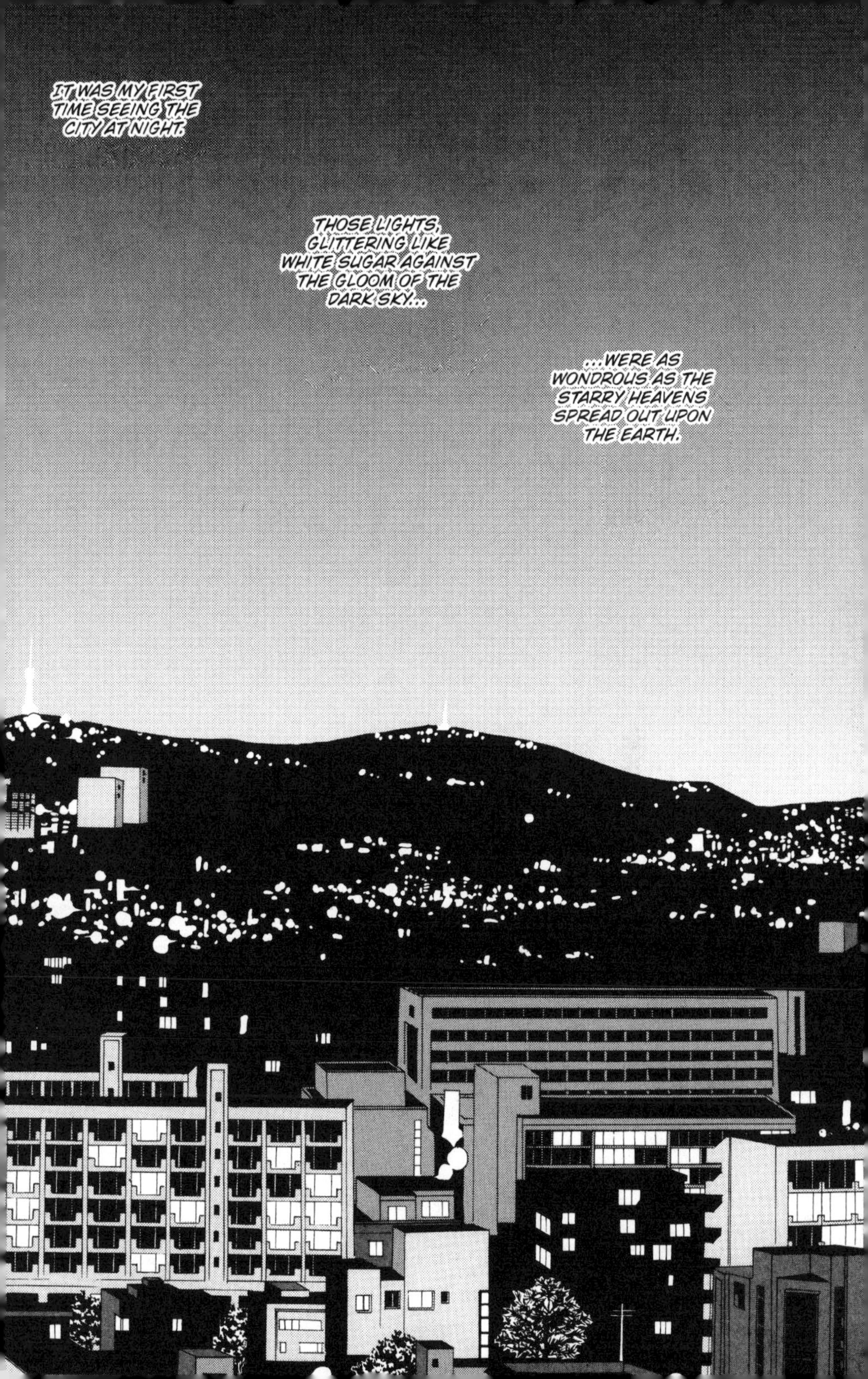
IT WAS MY FIRST TIME SEEING THE CITY AT NIGHT.
THOSE LIGHTS, GLITTERING LIKE WHITE SUGAR AGAINST THE GLOOM OF THE DARK SKY...
...WERE AS WONDROUS AS THE STARRY HEAVENS SPREAD OUT UPON THE EARTH.

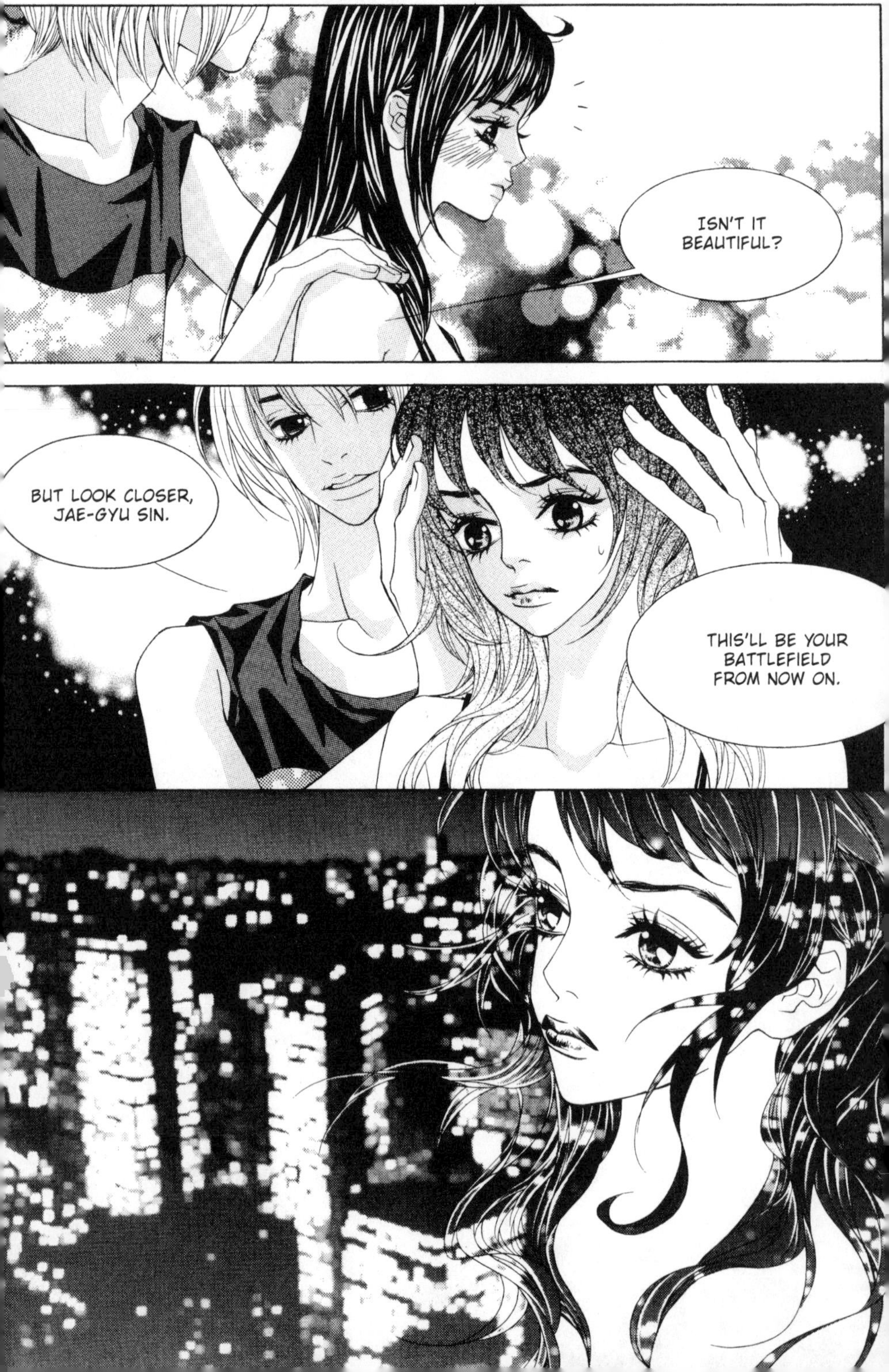
ISN'T IT BEAUTIFUL?
BUT LOOK CLOSER, JAE-GYU SIN.
THIS'LL BE YOUR BATTLEFIELD FROM NOW ON.

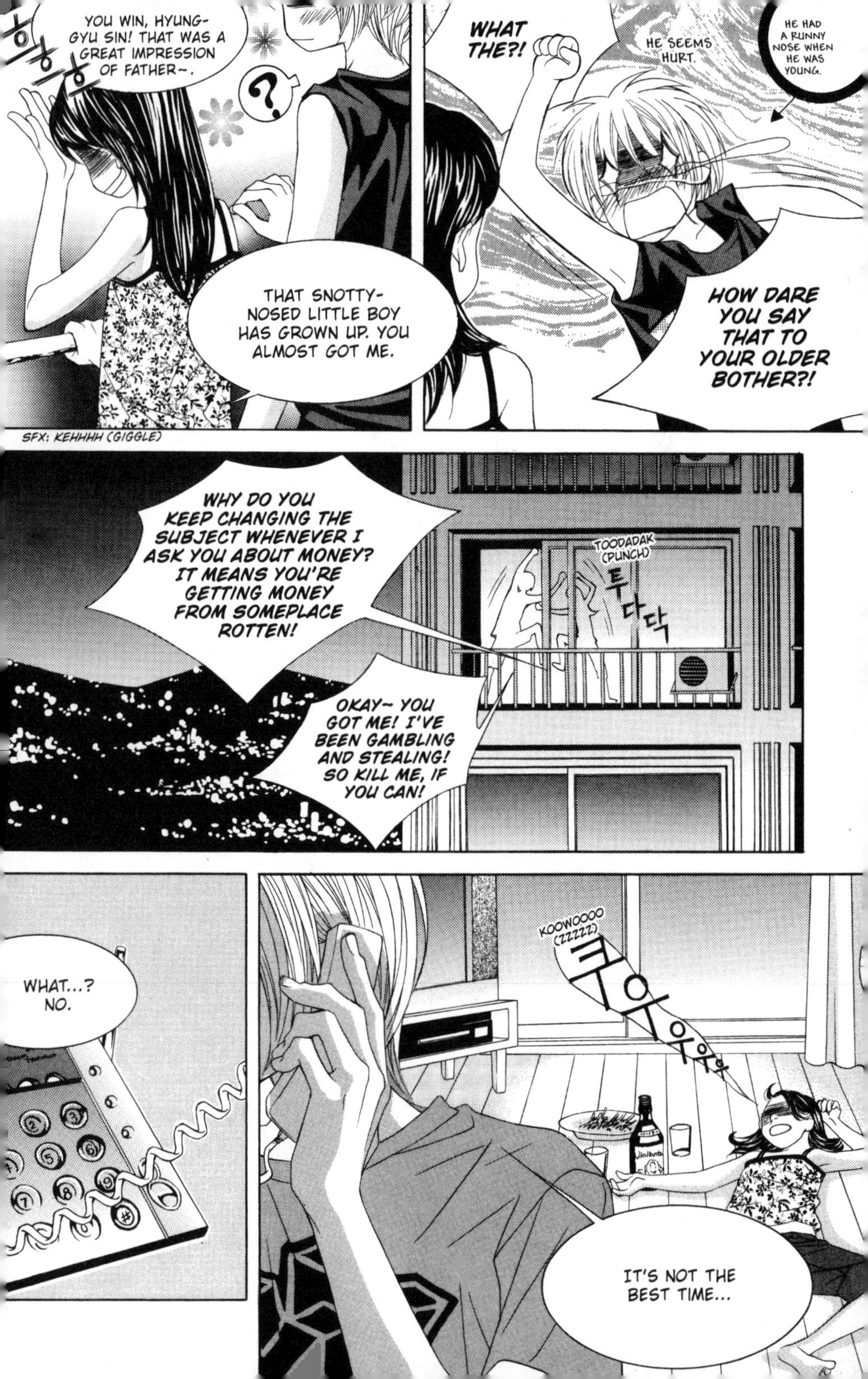

흐흐흐
YOU WIN, HYUNG-GYU SIN! THAT WAS A GREAT IMPRESSION OF FATHER~.
?
THAT SNOTTY-NOSED LITTLE BOY HAS GROWN UP. YOU ALMOST GOT ME.
WHAT THE?!
HE SEEMS HURT.
HE HAD A RUNNY NOSE WHEN HE WAS YOUNG.
HOW DARE YOU SAY THAT TO YOUR OLDER BOTHER?!
SFX: KEHHHH (GIGGLE)
WHY DO YOU KEEP CHANGING THE SUBJECT WHENEVER I ASK YOU ABOUT MONEY? IT MEANS YOU'RE GETTING MONEY FROM SOMEPLACE ROTTEN!
TOODADAK (PUNCH)
투다닥
OKAY~ YOU GOT ME! I'VE BEEN GAMBLING AND STEALING! SO KILL ME, IF YOU CAN!
WHAT...? NO.
KOOWOOOO (ZZZZZ)
쿠우우우
IT'S NOT THE BEST TIME...

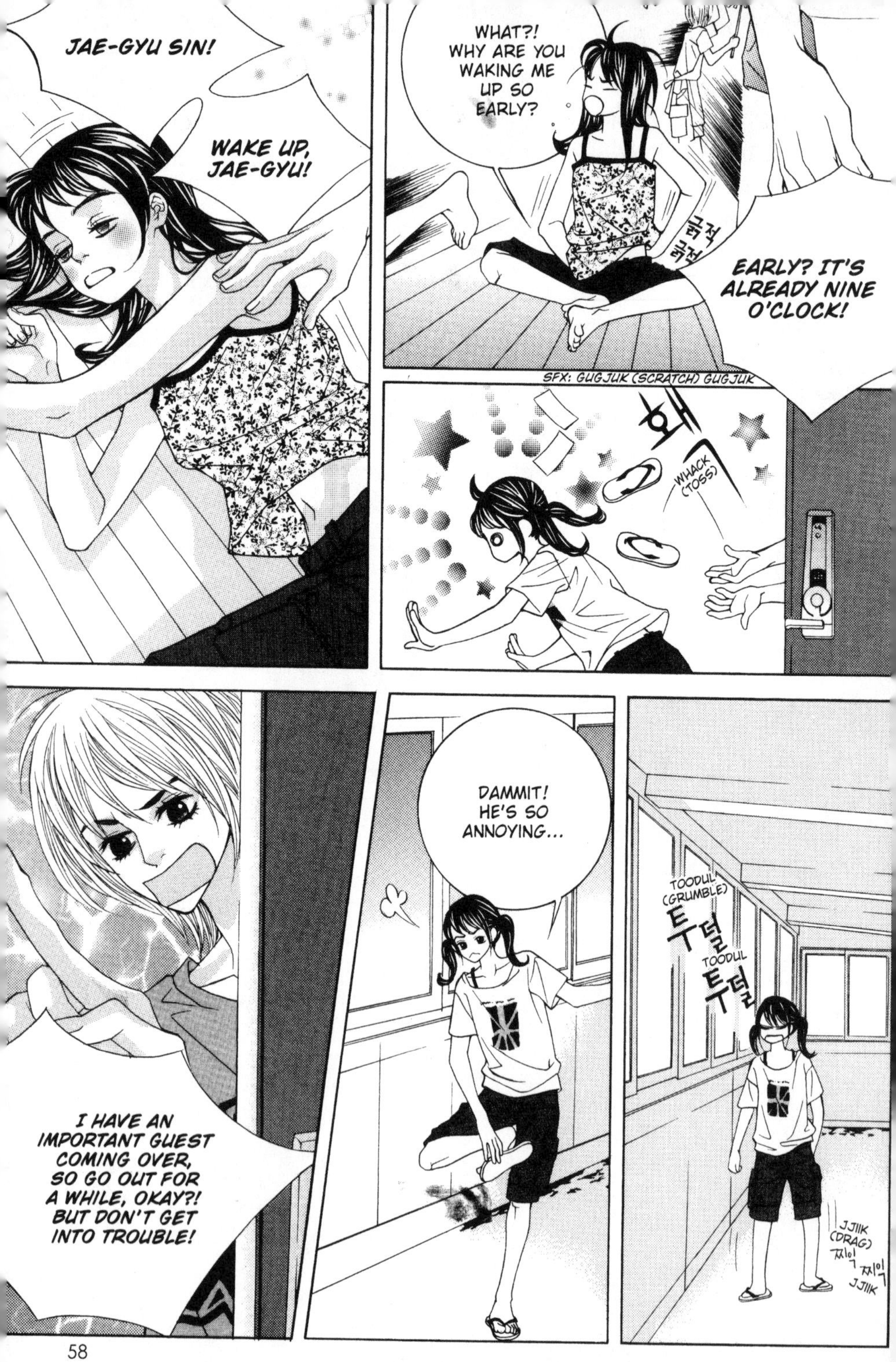
JAE-GYU SIN!
WAKE UP, JAE-GYU!
WHAT?! WHY ARE YOU WAKING ME UP SO EARLY?
EARLY? IT'S ALREADY NINE O'CLOCK!
SFX: GUGJUK (SCRATCH) GUGJUK
WHACK (TOSS)
I HAVE AN IMPORTANT GUEST COMING OVER, SO GO OUT FOR A WHILE, OKAY?! BUT DON'T GET INTO TROUBLE!
DAMMIT! HE'S SO ANNOYING...
TOODUL (GRUMBLE)
투덜
TOODUL
투덜
JJIIK (DRAG)
찌익 찌익
JJIIK

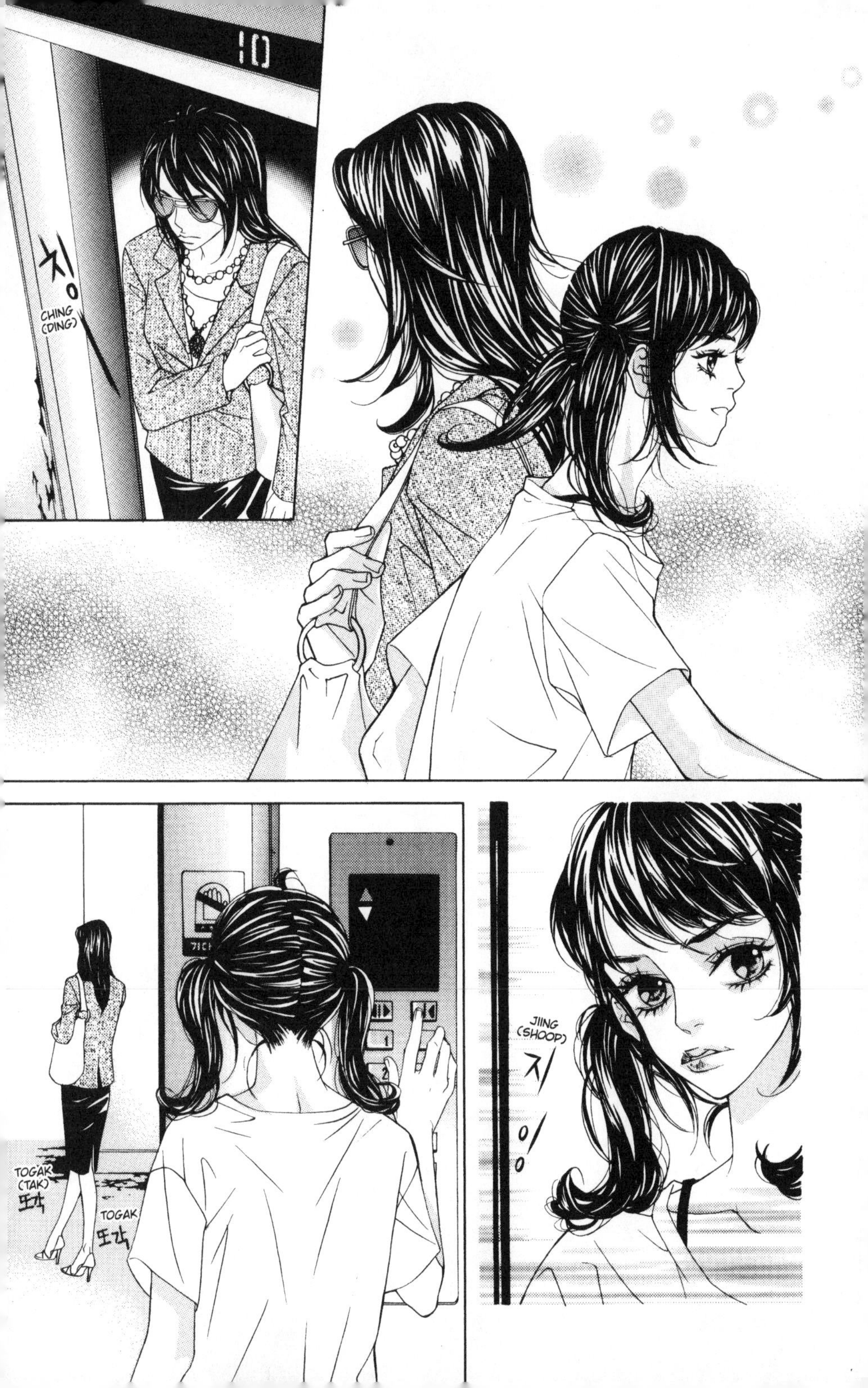
10
징
CHING (DING)
TOGAK (TAK)
또각
TOGAK
또각
JIING (SHOOP)
지잉

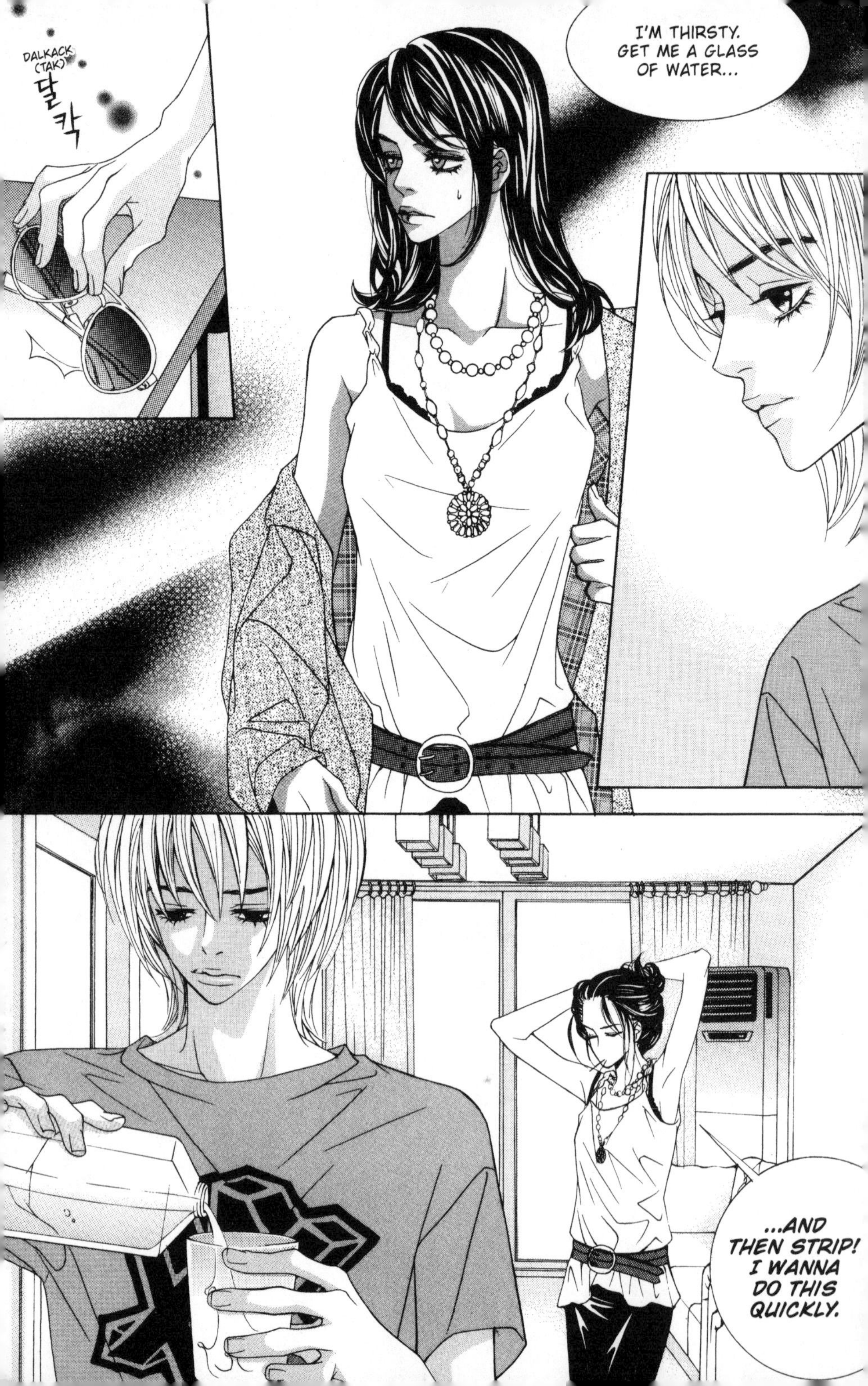
DALKACK (TAK)
달칵
I'M THIRSTY. GET ME A GLASS OF WATER...
...AND THEN STRIP! I WANNA DO THIS QUICKLY.

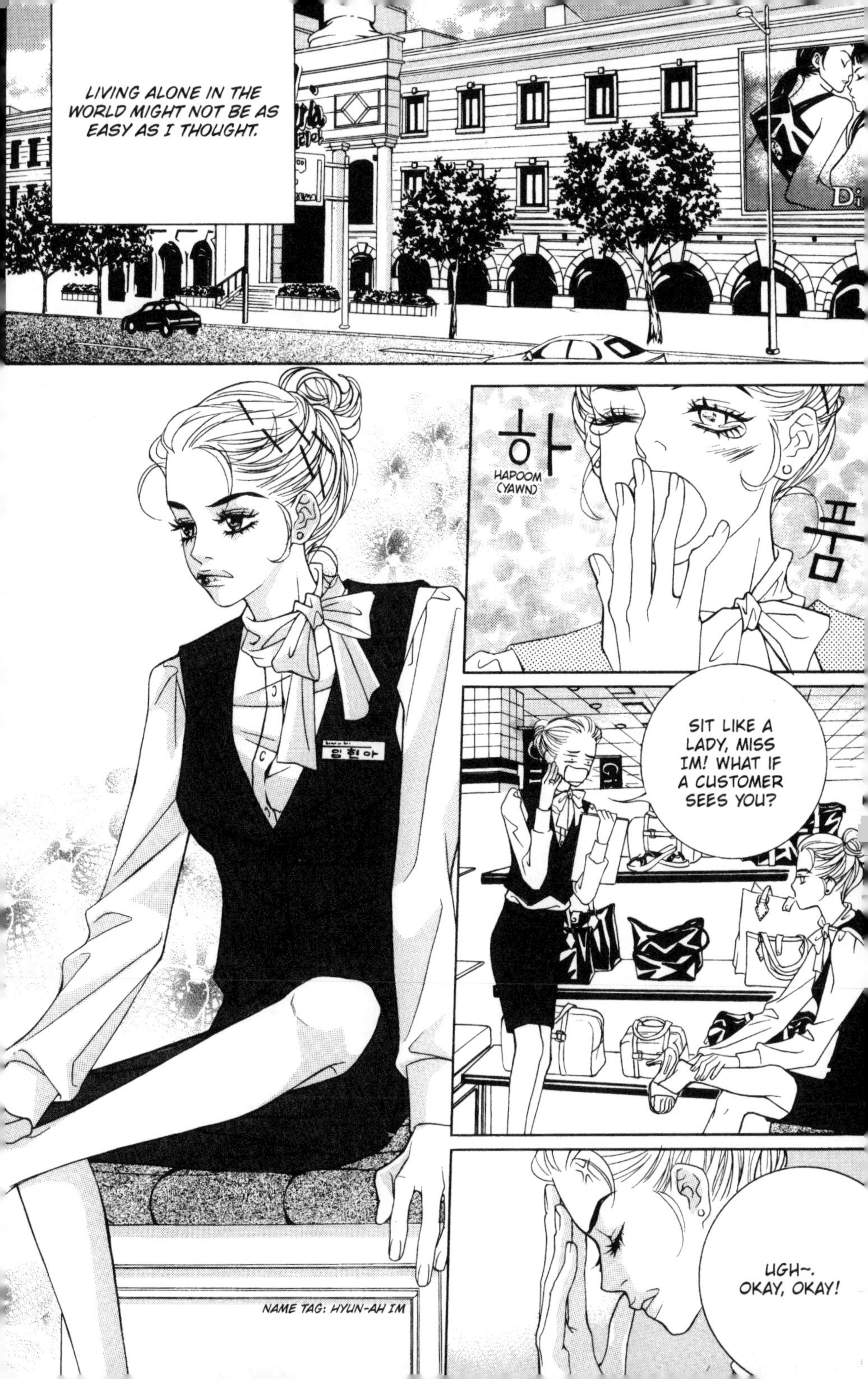
LIVING ALONE IN THE WORLD MIGHT NOT BE AS EASY AS I THOUGHT.
NAME TAG: HYUN-AH IM
하
품
HAPOOM (YAWN)
SIT LIKE A LADY, MISS IM! WHAT IF A CUSTOMER SEES YOU?
UGH~. OKAY, OKAY!

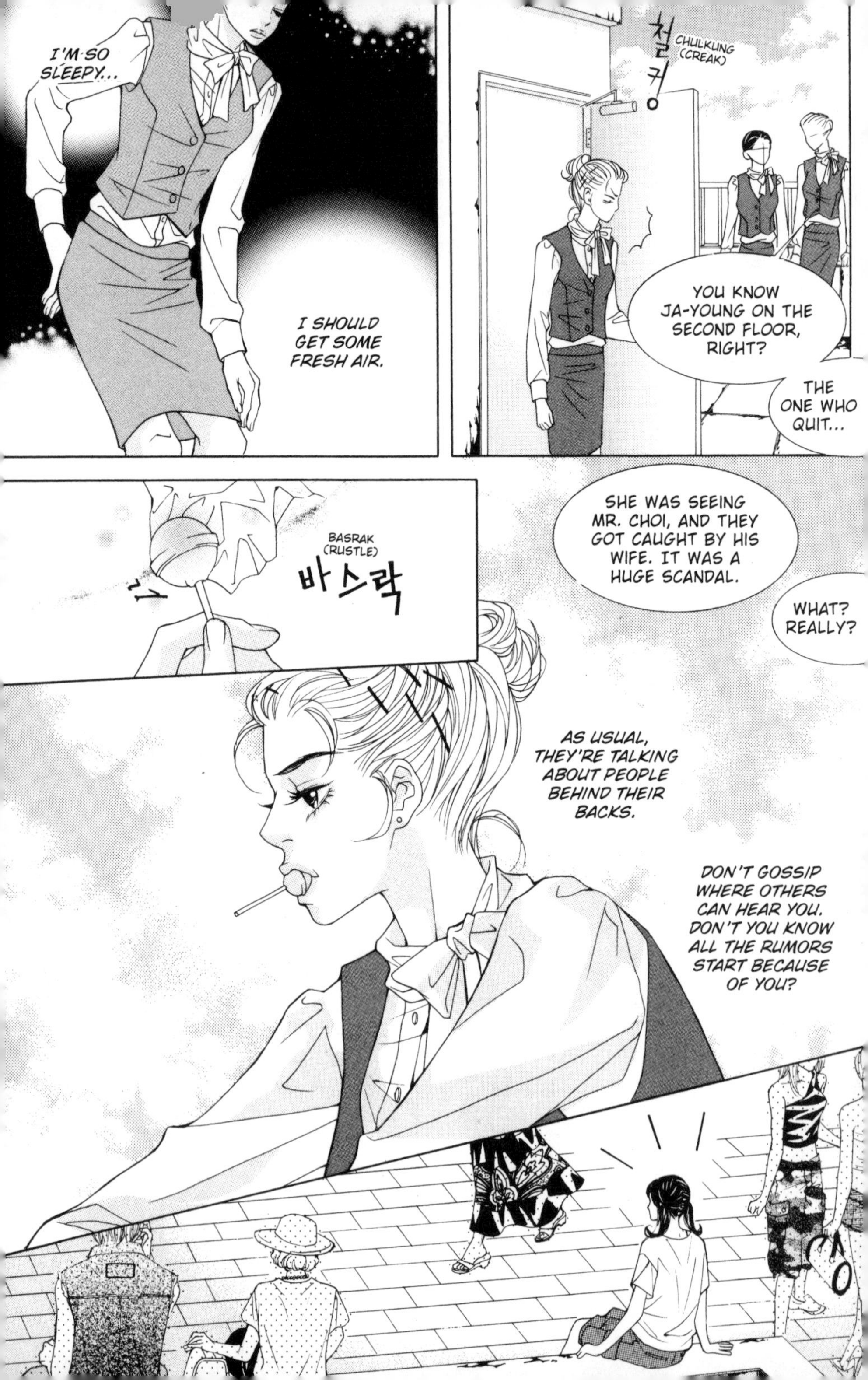
I'M SO SLEEPY...
I SHOULD GET SOME FRESH AIR.
철컥!
CHULKUNG (CREAK)
YOU KNOW JA-YOUNG ON THE SECOND FLOOR, RIGHT?
THE ONE WHO QUIT...
바스락
BASRAK (RUSTLE)
SHE WAS SEEING MR. CHOI, AND THEY GOT CAUGHT BY HIS WIFE. IT WAS A HUGE SCANDAL.
WHAT? REALLY?
AS USUAL, THEY'RE TALKING ABOUT PEOPLE BEHIND THEIR BACKS.
DON'T GOSSIP WHERE OTHERS CAN HEAR YOU. DON'T YOU KNOW ALL THE RUMORS START BECAUSE OF YOU?

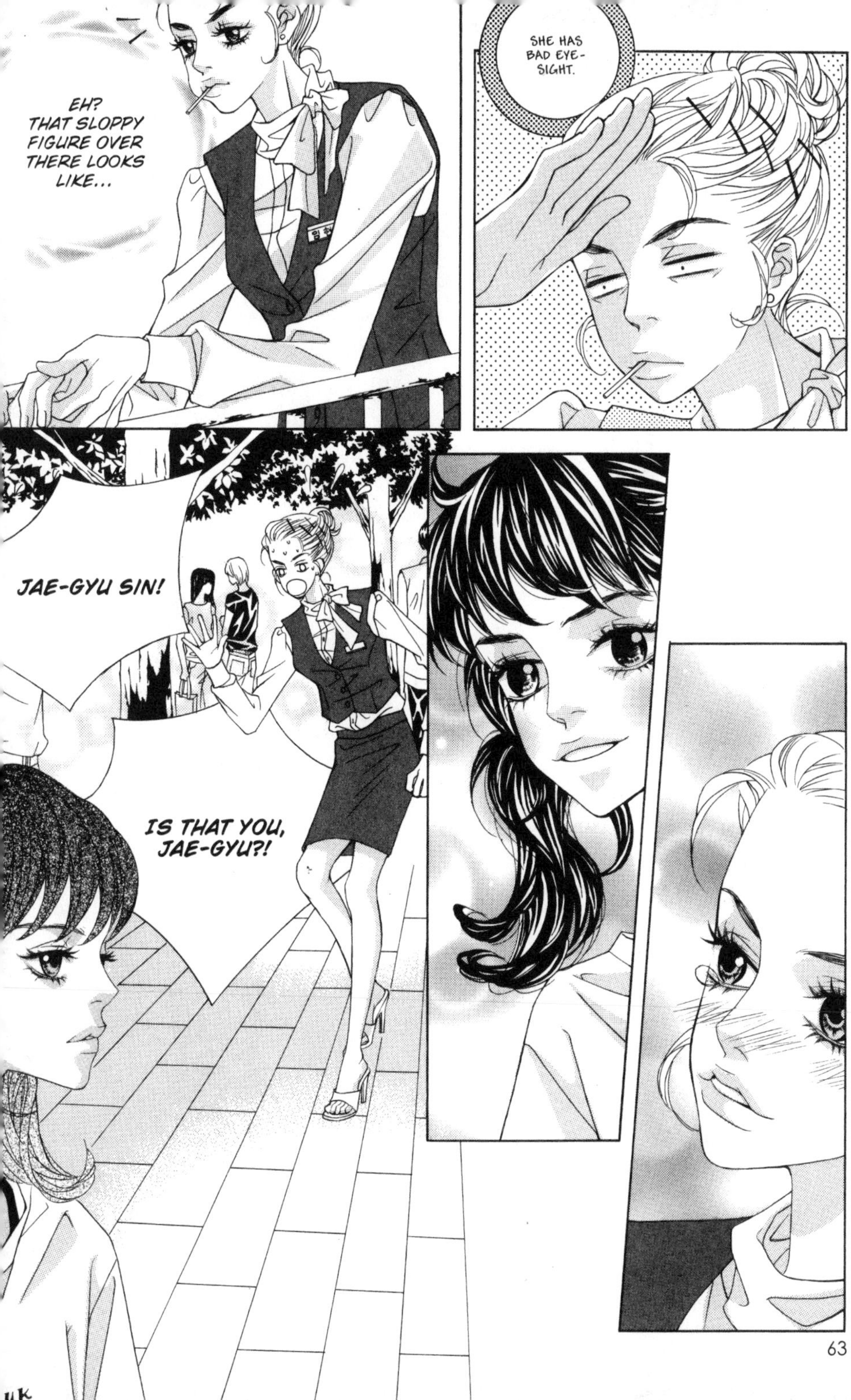
EH? THAT SLOPPY FIGURE OVER THERE LOOKS LIKE...
SHE HAS BAD EYE-SIGHT.
JAE-GYU SIN!
IS THAT YOU, JAE-GYU?!

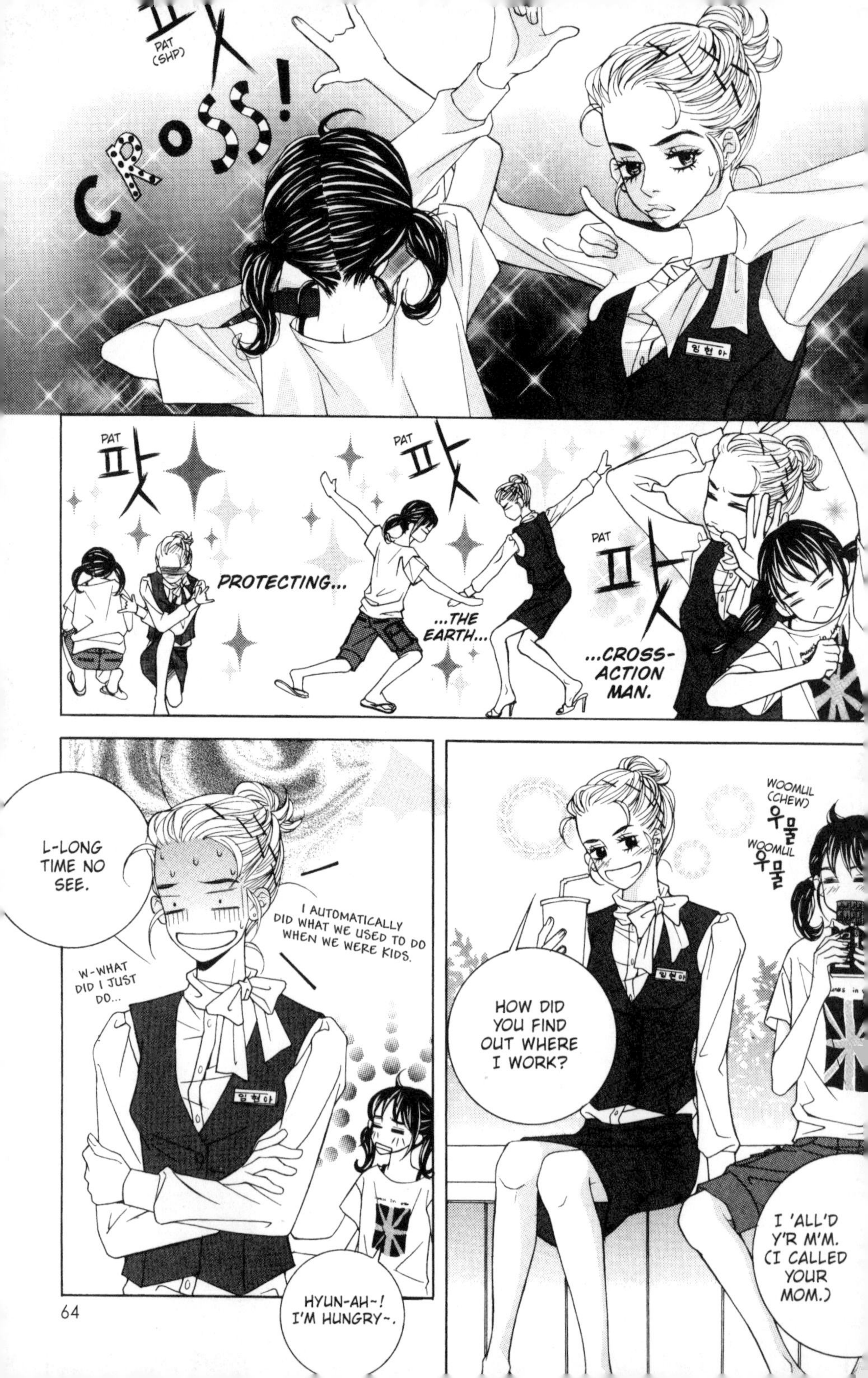
PAT (SHP)
CROSS!
PAT
팟
PAT
팟
PROTECTING...
...THE EARTH...
PAT
팟
...CROSS-ACTION MAN.
L-LONG TIME NO SEE.
I AUTOMATICALLY DID WHAT WE USED TO DO WHEN WE WERE KIDS.
W-WHAT DID I JUST DO...
HYUN-AH~! I'M HUNGRY~.
WOOMUL (CHEW)
우물
WOOMUL
우물
HOW DID YOU FIND OUT WHERE I WORK?
I 'ALL'D Y'R M'M. (I CALLED YOUR MOM.)

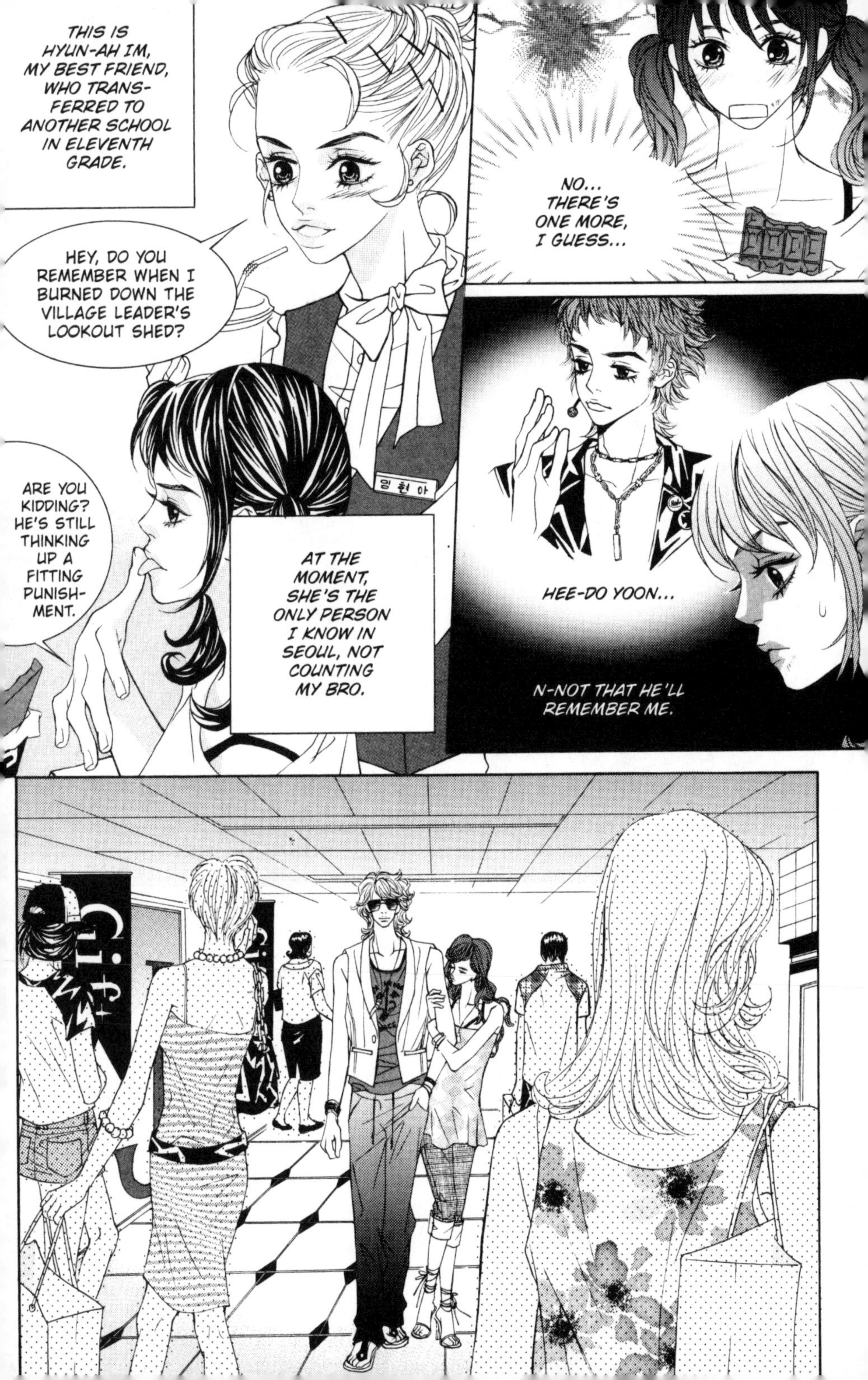
THIS IS HYUN-AH IM, MY BEST FRIEND, WHO TRANS-FERRED TO ANOTHER SCHOOL IN ELEVENTH GRADE.
HEY, DO YOU REMEMBER WHEN I BURNED DOWN THE VILLAGE LEADER'S LOOKOUT SHED?
ARE YOU KIDDING? HE'S STILL THINKING UP A FITTING PUNISH-MENT.
AT THE MOMENT, SHE'S THE ONLY PERSON I KNOW IN SEOUL, NOT COUNTING MY BRO.
NO... THERE'S ONE MORE, I GUESS...
HEE-DO YOON...
N-NOT THAT HE'LL REMEMBER ME.

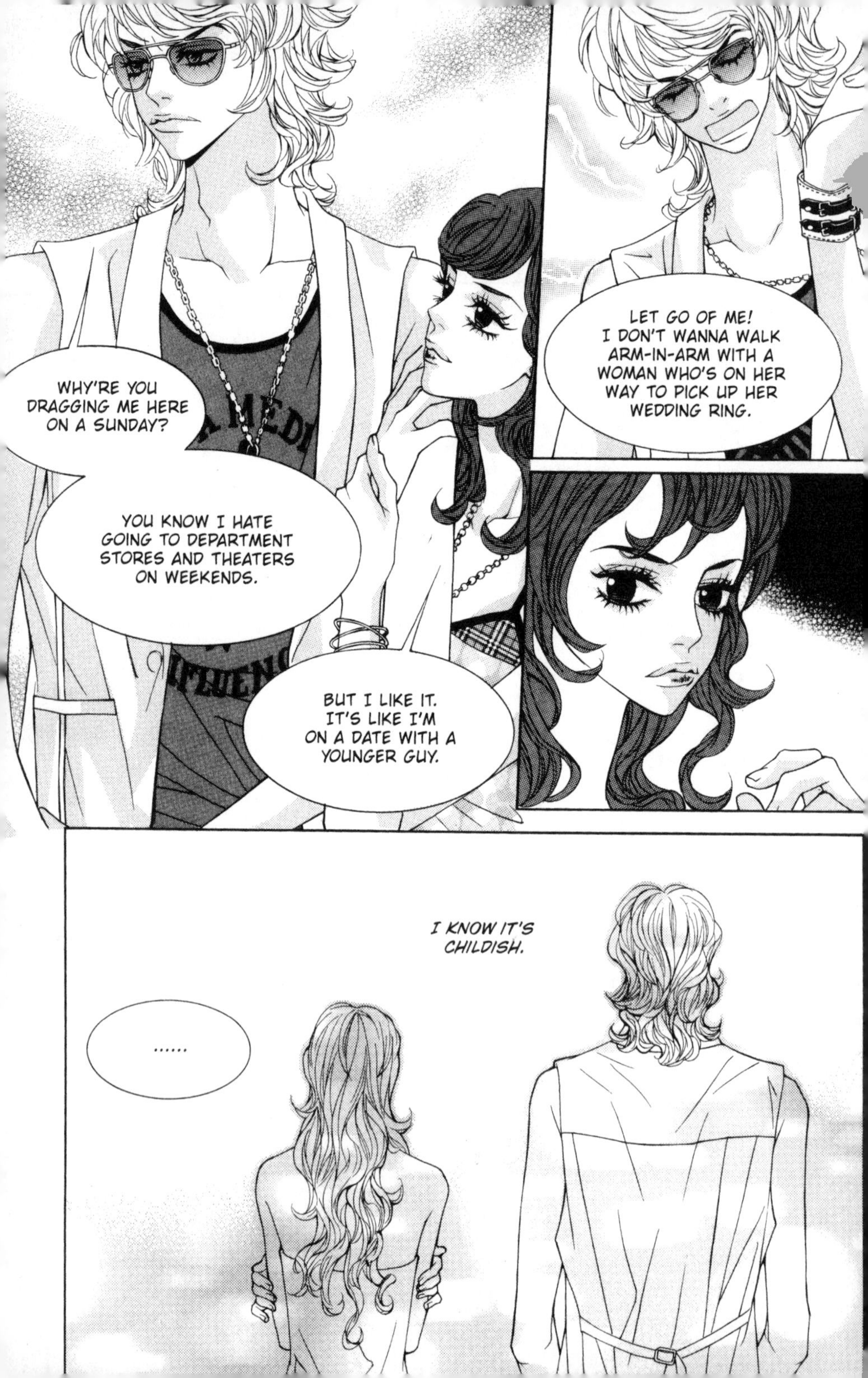
WHY'RE YOU DRAGGING ME HERE ON A SUNDAY?
YOU KNOW I HATE GOING TO DEPARTMENT STORES AND THEATERS ON WEEKENDS.
BUT I LIKE IT. IT'S LIKE I'M ON A DATE WITH A YOUNGER GUY.
LET GO OF ME! I DON'T WANNA WALK ARM-IN-ARM WITH A WOMAN WHO'S ON HER WAY TO PICK UP HER WEDDING RING.
I KNOW IT'S CHILDISH.
......

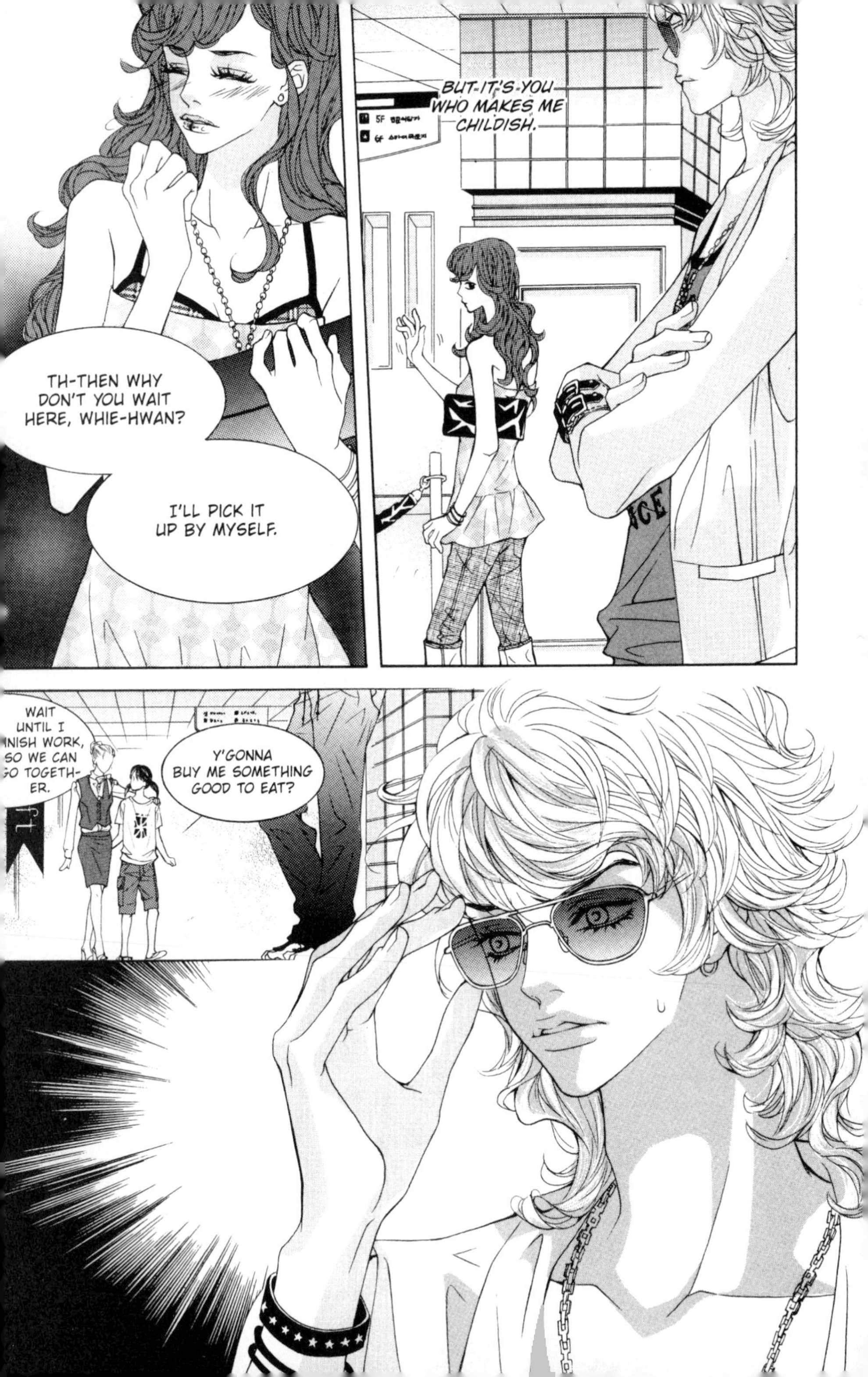
TH-THEN WHY DON'T YOU WAIT HERE, WHIE-HWAN?
I'LL PICK IT UP BY MYSELF.
5F
6F
BUT IT'S YOU WHO MAKES ME CHILDISH.
WAIT UNTIL I INISH WORK, SO WE CAN GO TOGETH-ER.
Y'GONNA BUY ME SOMETHING GOOD TO EAT?

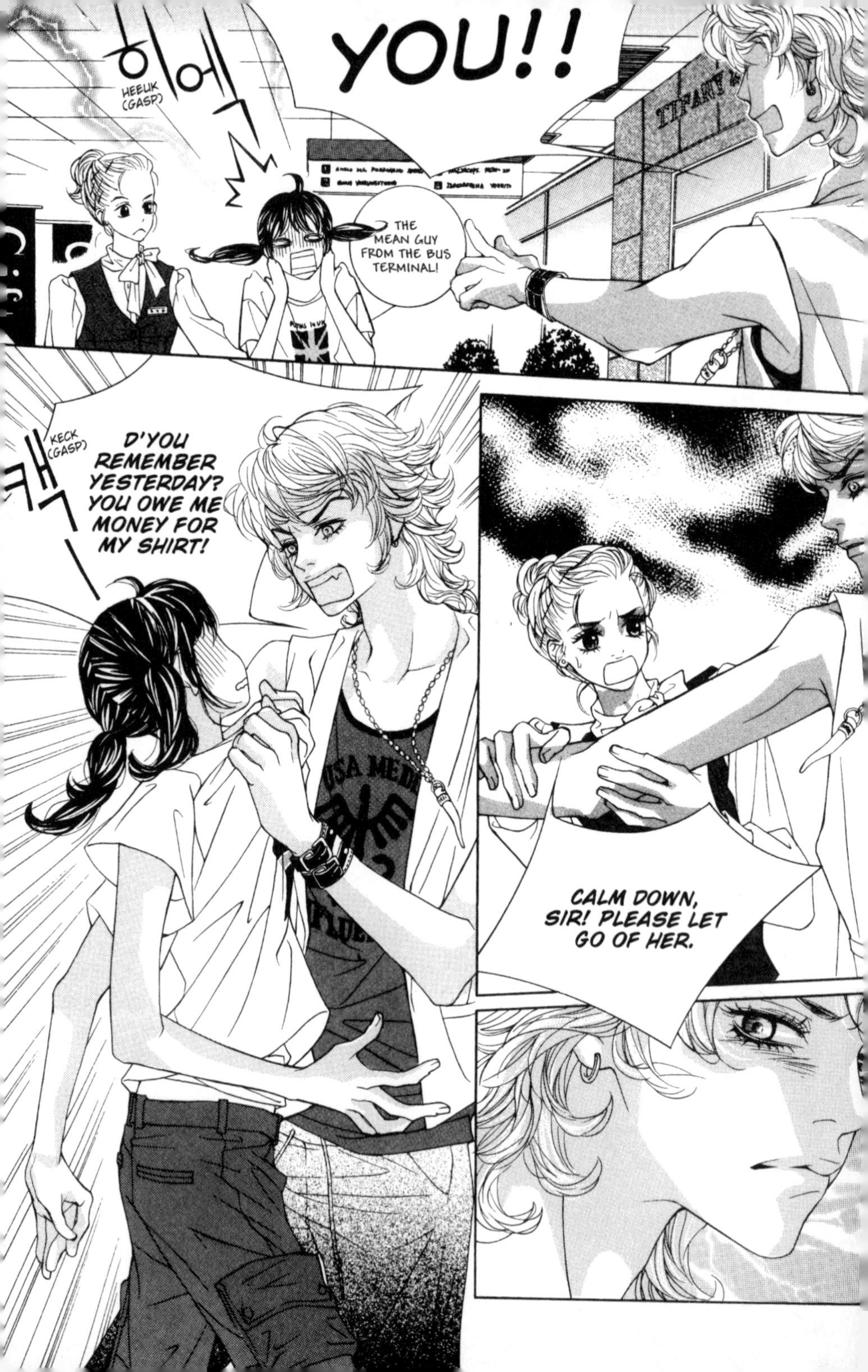
히에ㄱ
HEEUK (GASP)
YOU!!
THE MEAN GUY FROM THE BUS TERMINAL!
캑
KECK (GASP)
D'YOU REMEMBER YESTERDAY? YOU OWE ME MONEY FOR MY SHIRT!
CALM DOWN, SIR! PLEASE LET GO OF HER.

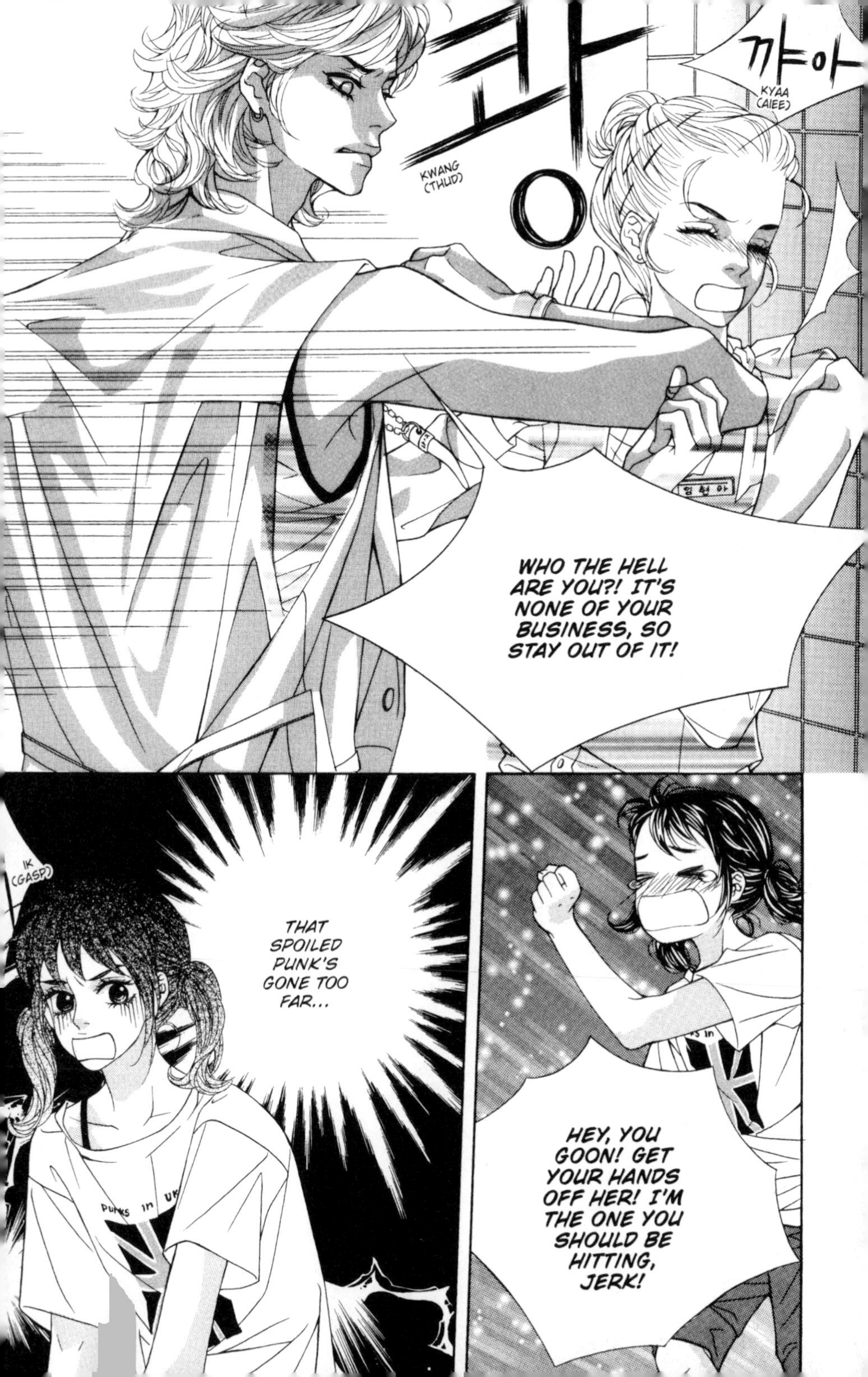
쾅
KWANG (THUD)
꺄아
KYAA (AIEE)
WHO THE HELL ARE YOU?! IT'S NONE OF YOUR BUSINESS, SO STAY OUT OF IT!
IK (GASP)
THAT SPOILED PUNK'S GONE TOO FAR...
PUNKS IN UK
HEY, YOU GOON! GET YOUR HANDS OFF HER! I'M THE ONE YOU SHOULD BE HITTING, JERK!

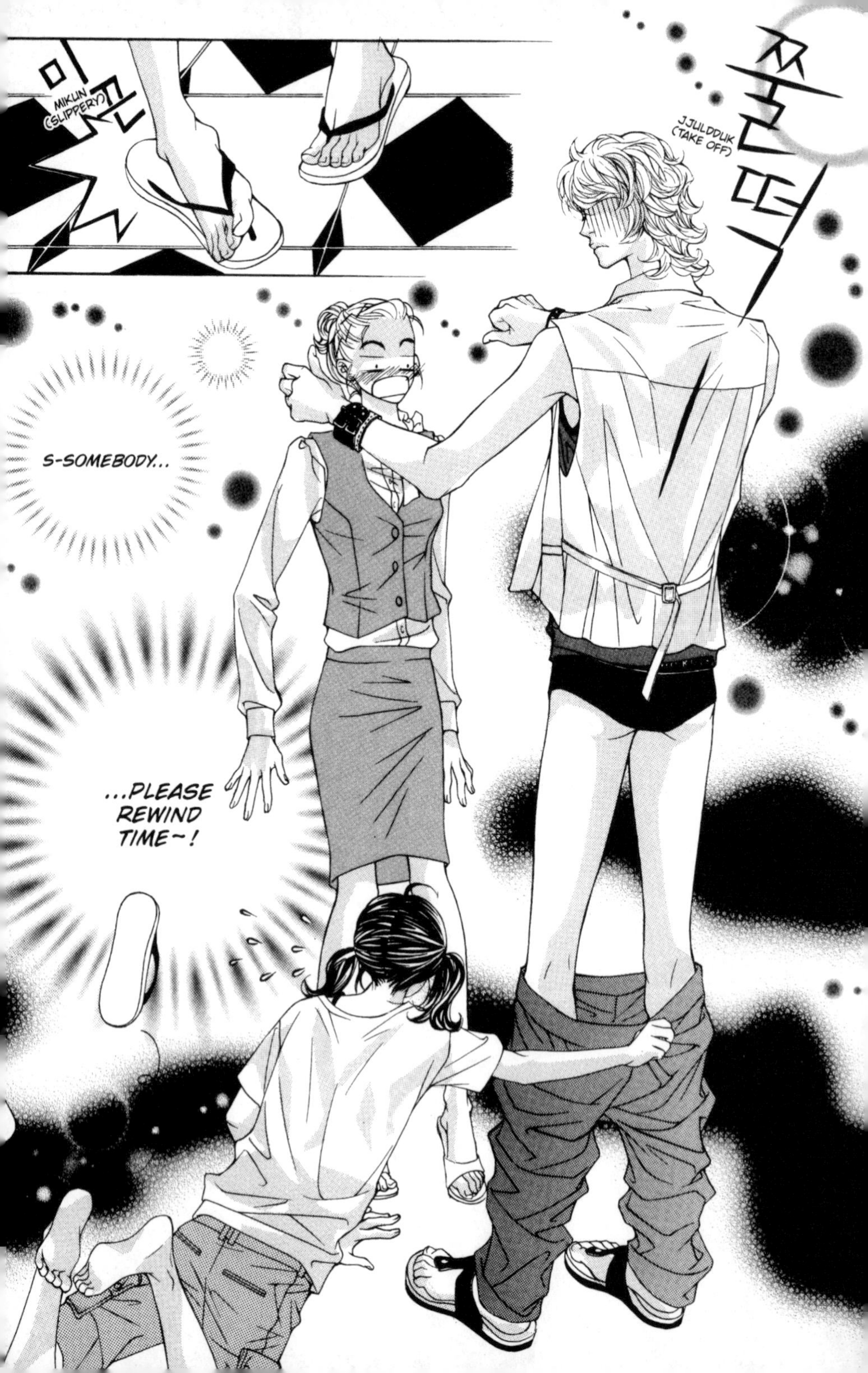
미끈
MIKUN (SLIPPERY)
쭐떡
JJULDDUK (TAKE OFF)
S-SOMEBODY...
...PLEASE REWIND TIME~!

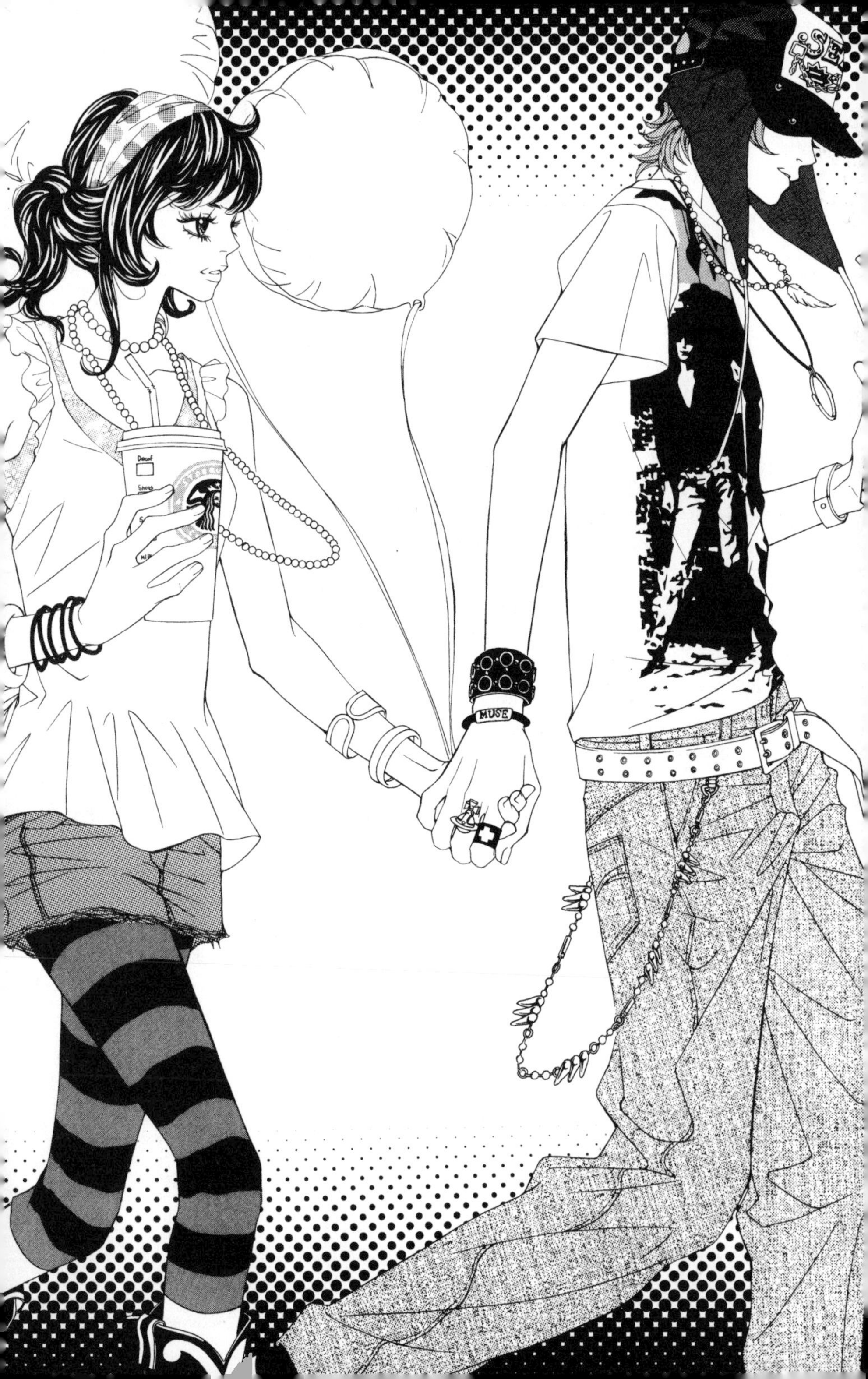
Decaf
Shots
MUSE

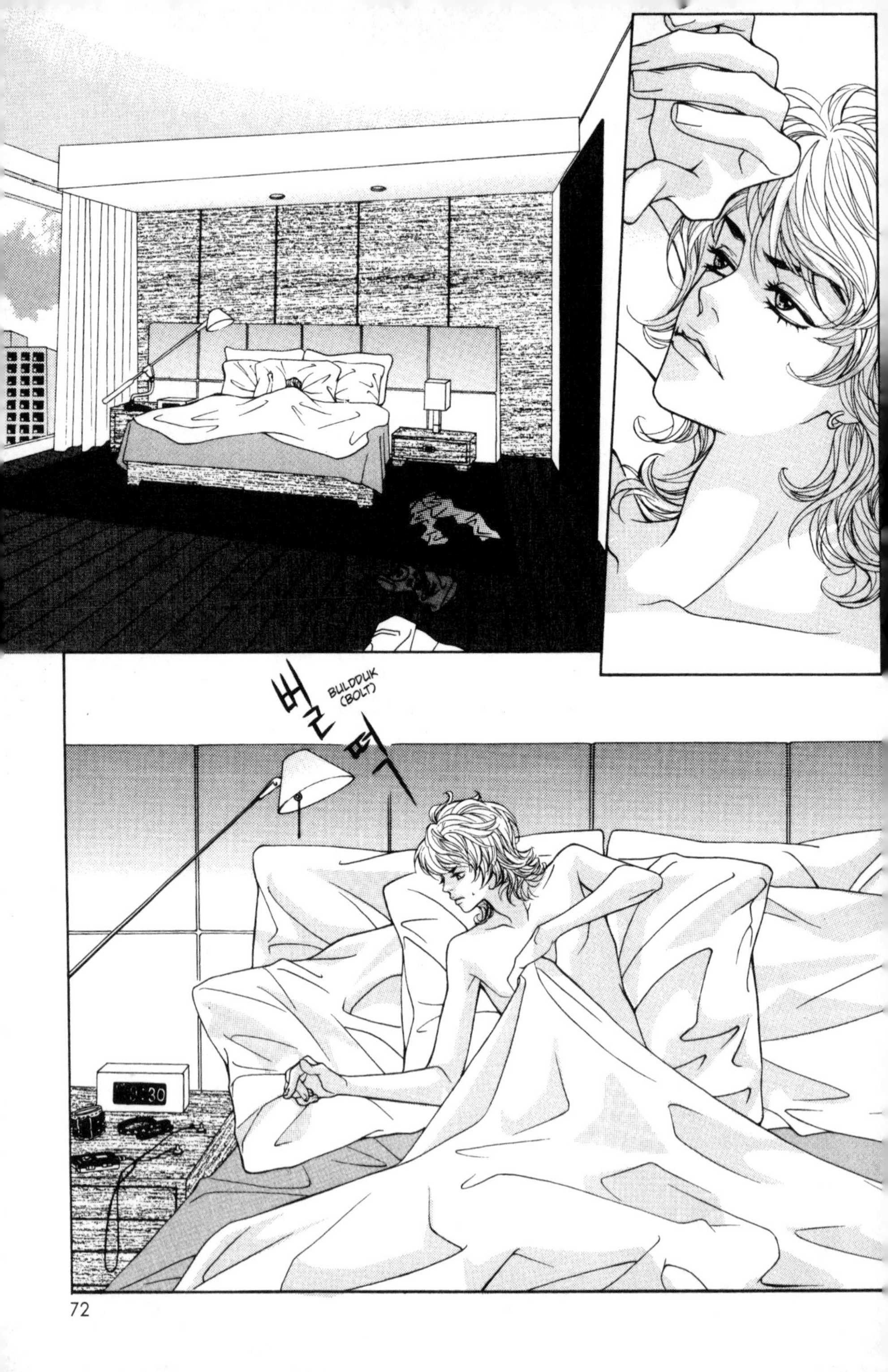
벌떡
BULDDUK (BOLT)

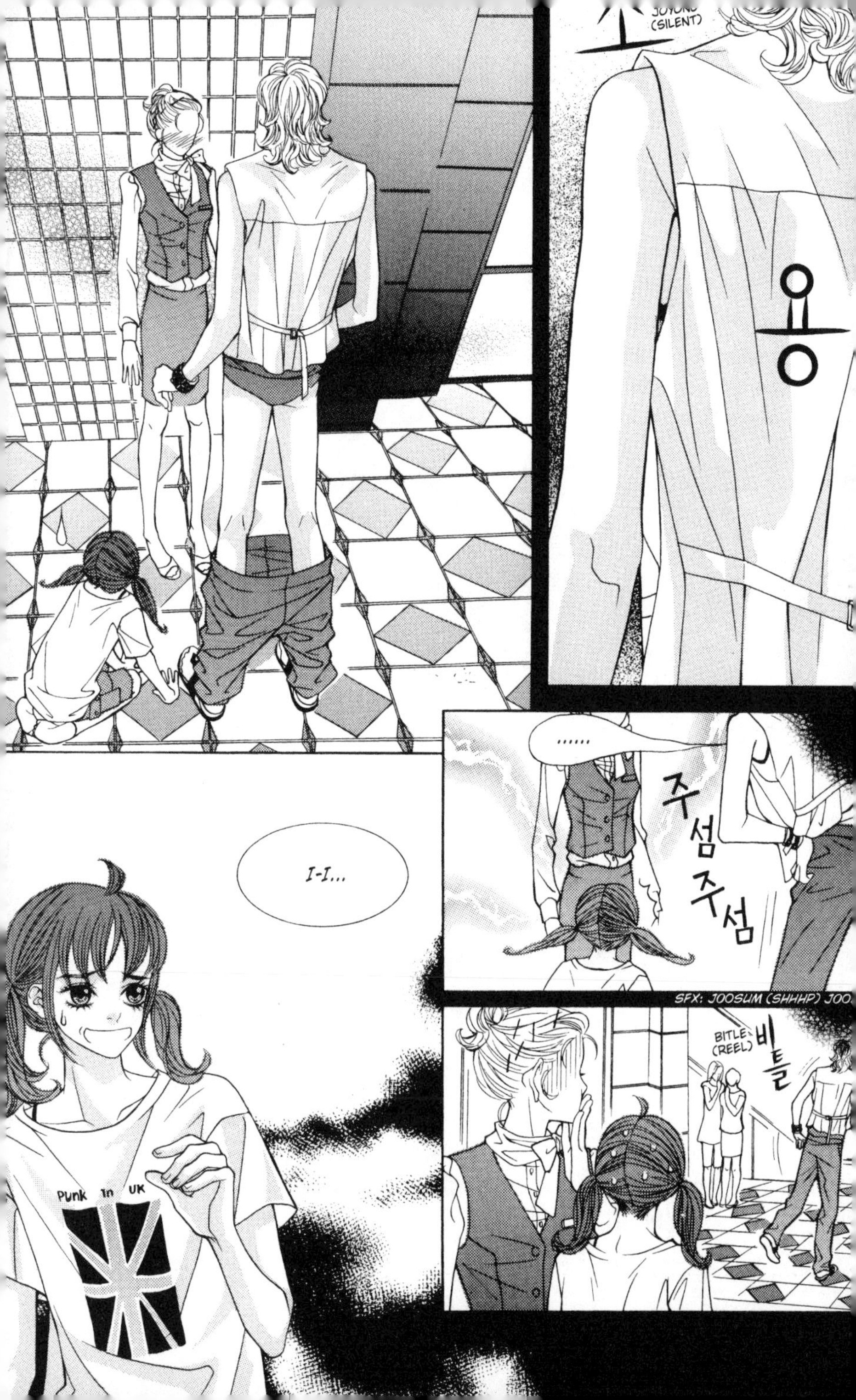
JOYUNG (SILENT)
용
I-I...
......
주섬주섬
SFX: JOOSUM (SHHHP) JOO
BITLE (REEL)
비틀

I-I DIDN'T M-MEAN TO...

IT WAS LIKE NO ONE COULD SPEAK.

THAT REALLY... WASN'T MY INTENTION.

비틀 BITLE (REEL)

I CAN HEAR... WHAT YOU'RE THINKING...

음 MWA
화 HA
화 HA
화 HA

카 KYA
하 HA
하 HA
하 HA

WE ALL SAW YOUR SKIVVIES~!

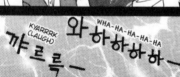

까르륵— KYARRRK (LAUGH)
와하하하하— WHA-HA-HA-HA-HA

WHY DON'T YOU LAUGH OUT LOUD, EVIL DEMONS?!

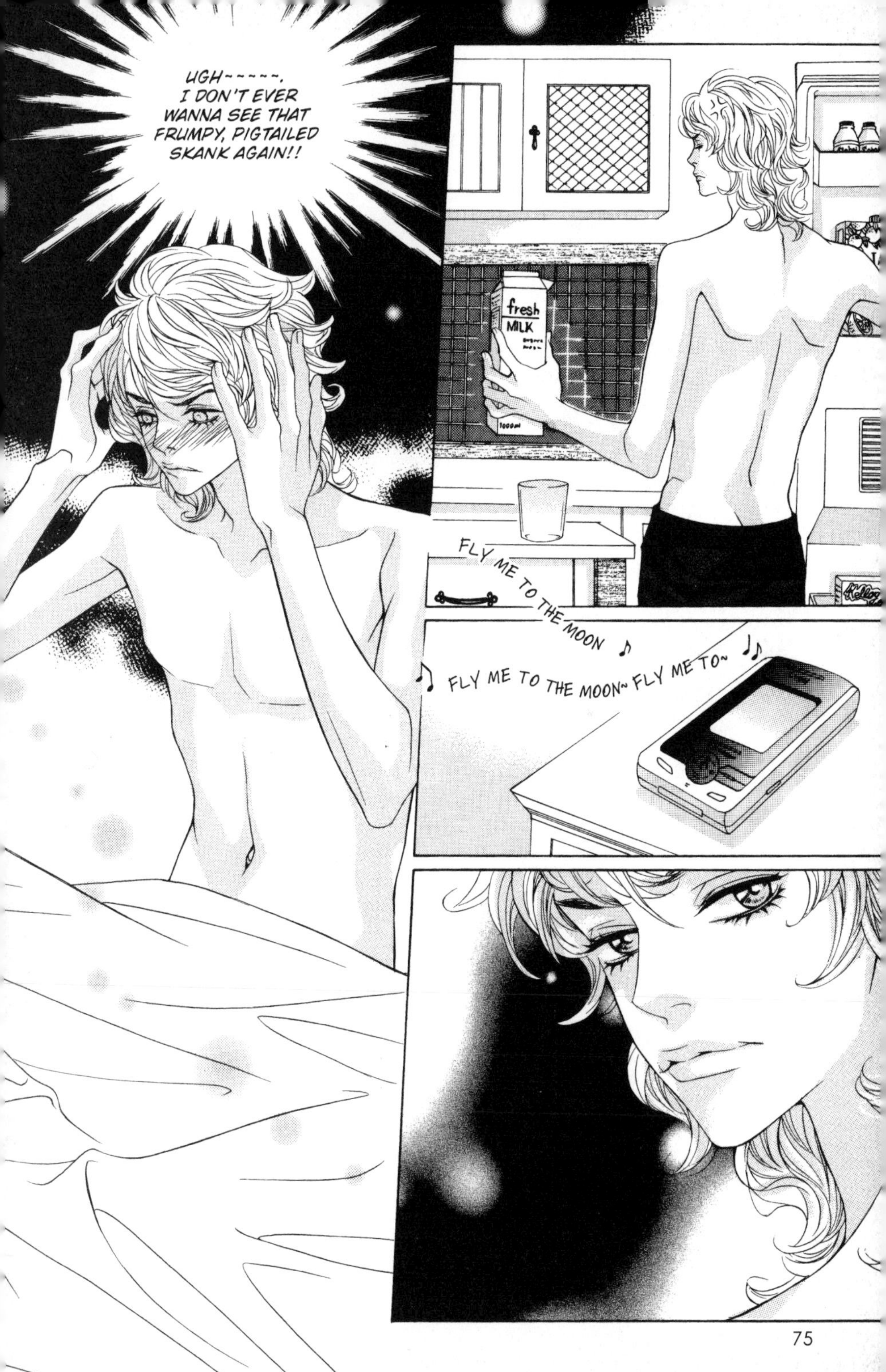
UGH~~~~~. I DON'T EVER WANNA SEE THAT FRUMPY, PIGTAILED SKANK AGAIN!!
fresh MILK
FLY ME TO THE MOON ♪
♪ FLY ME TO THE MOON~ FLY ME TO~ ♪

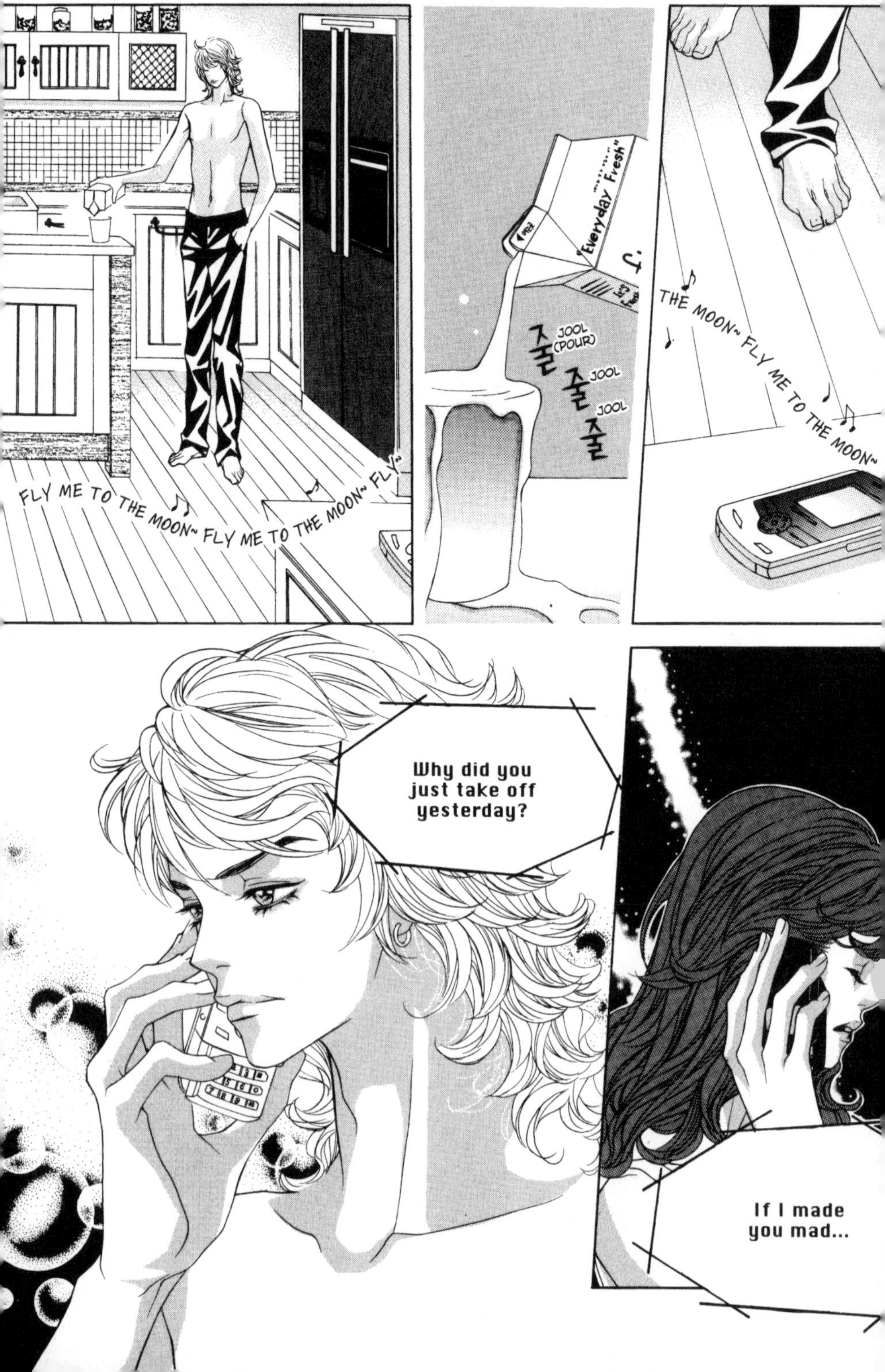
FLY ME TO THE MOON~ FLY ME TO THE MOON~ FLY~
"Everyday Fresh"
줄 JOOL (POUR)
줄 JOOL
줄 JOOL
THE MOON~ FLY ME TO THE MOON~
Why did you just take off yesterday?
If I made you mad...

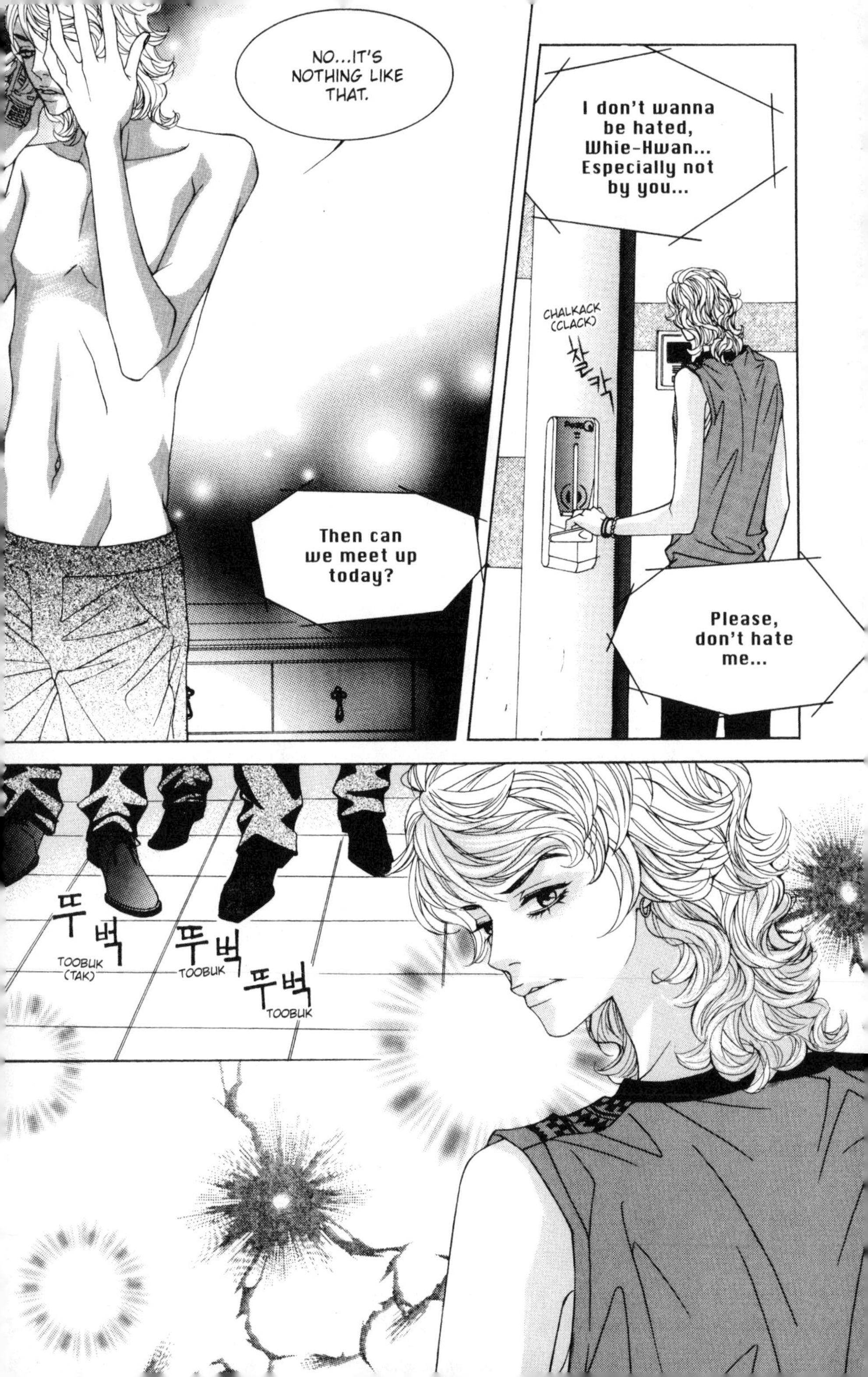
NO...IT'S NOTHING LIKE THAT.
Then can we meet up today?
I don't wanna be hated, Whie-Hwan... Especially not by you...
CHALKACK (CLACK)
찰칵
Please, don't hate me...
뚜벅
TOOBUK (TAK)
뚜벅
TOOBUK
뚜벅
TOOBUK

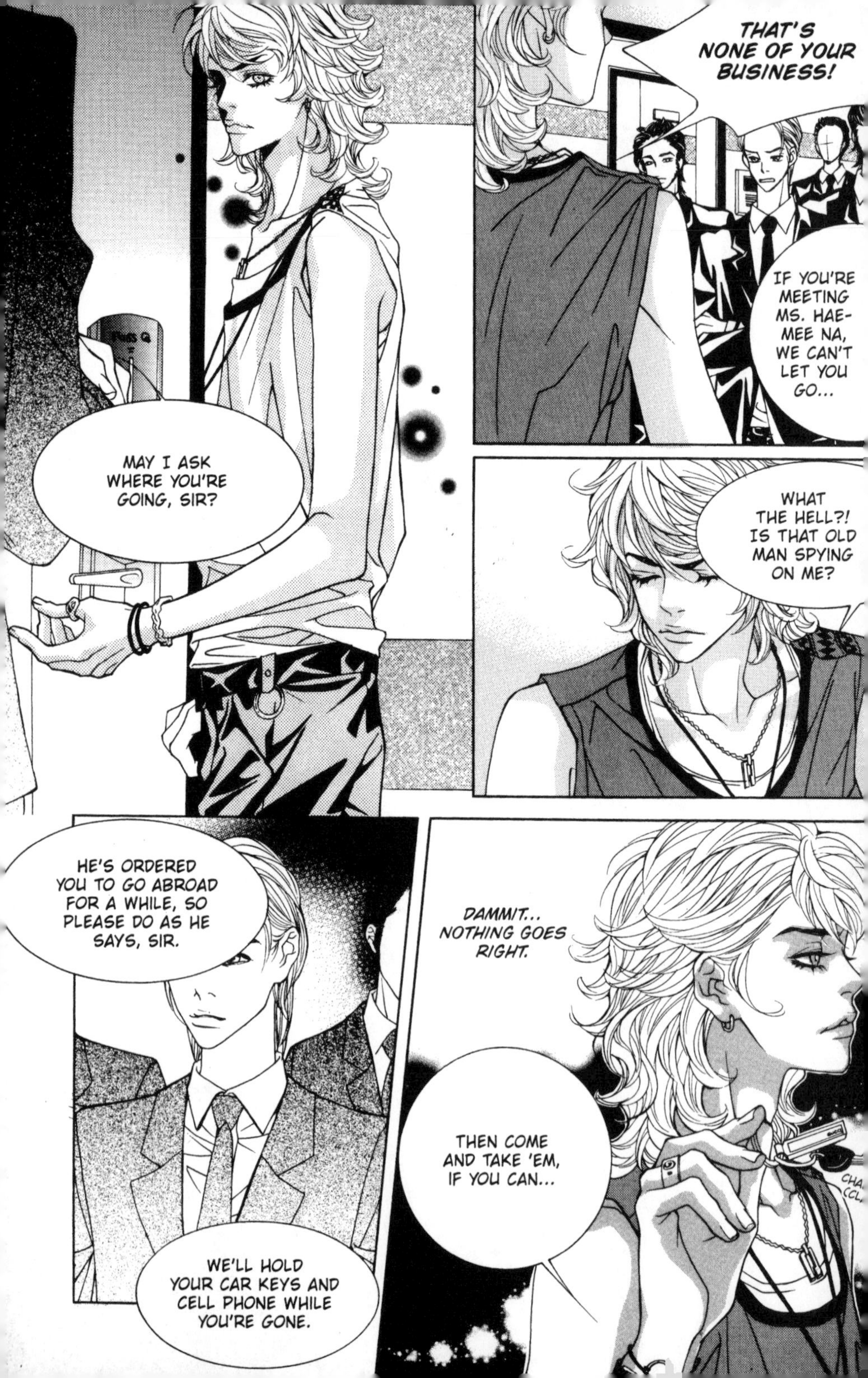
MAY I ASK WHERE YOU'RE GOING, SIR?
THAT'S NONE OF YOUR BUSINESS!
IF YOU'RE MEETING MS. HAE-MEE NA, WE CAN'T LET YOU GO...
WHAT THE HELL?! IS THAT OLD MAN SPYING ON ME?
HE'S ORDERED YOU TO GO ABROAD FOR A WHILE, SO PLEASE DO AS HE SAYS, SIR.
WE'LL HOLD YOUR CAR KEYS AND CELL PHONE WHILE YOU'RE GONE.
DAMMIT... NOTHING GOES RIGHT.
THEN COME AND TAKE 'EM, IF YOU CAN...

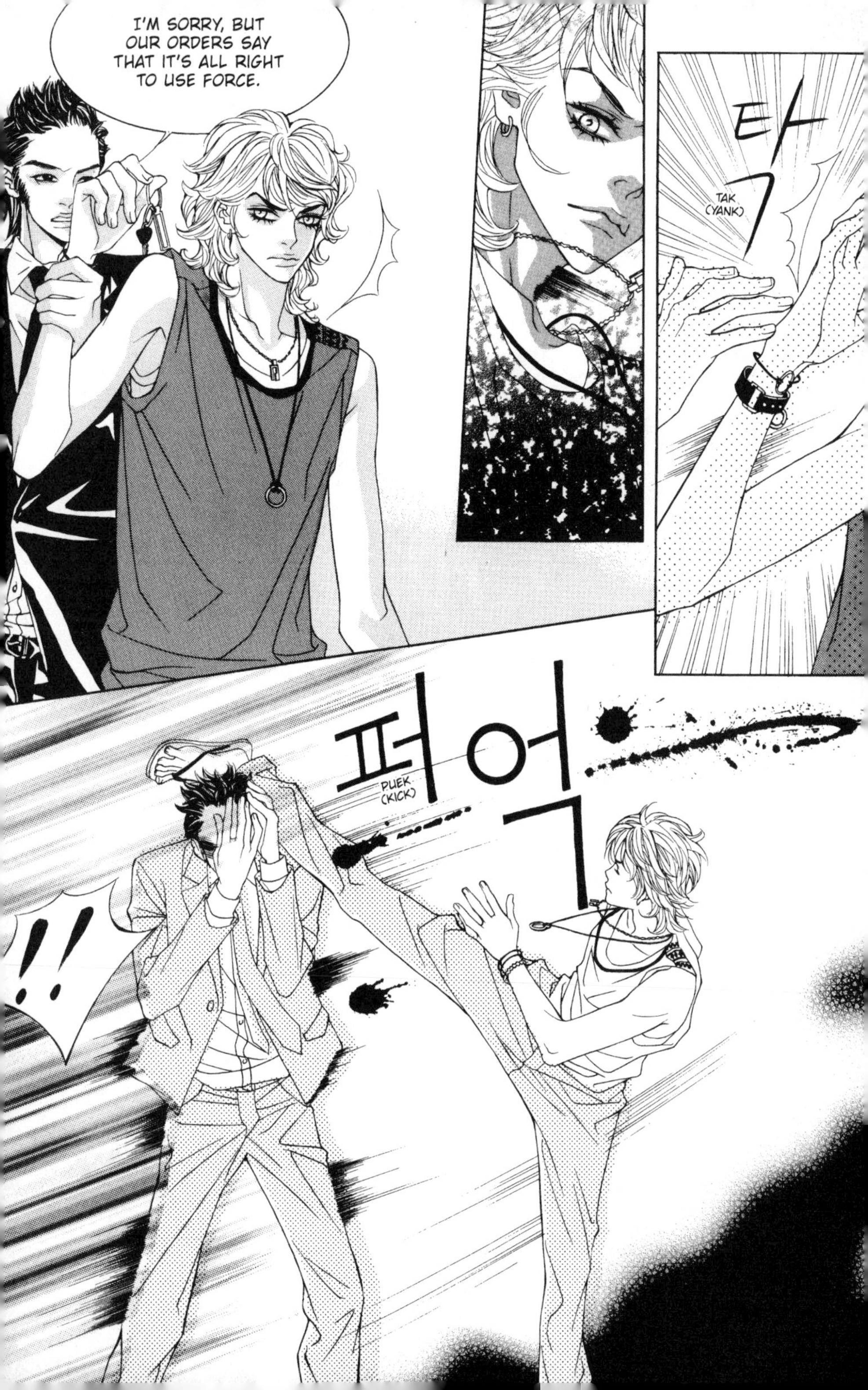
I'M SORRY, BUT OUR ORDERS SAY THAT IT'S ALL RIGHT TO USE FORCE.
탁
TAK (YANK)
!!
퍼억
PUEK (KICK)

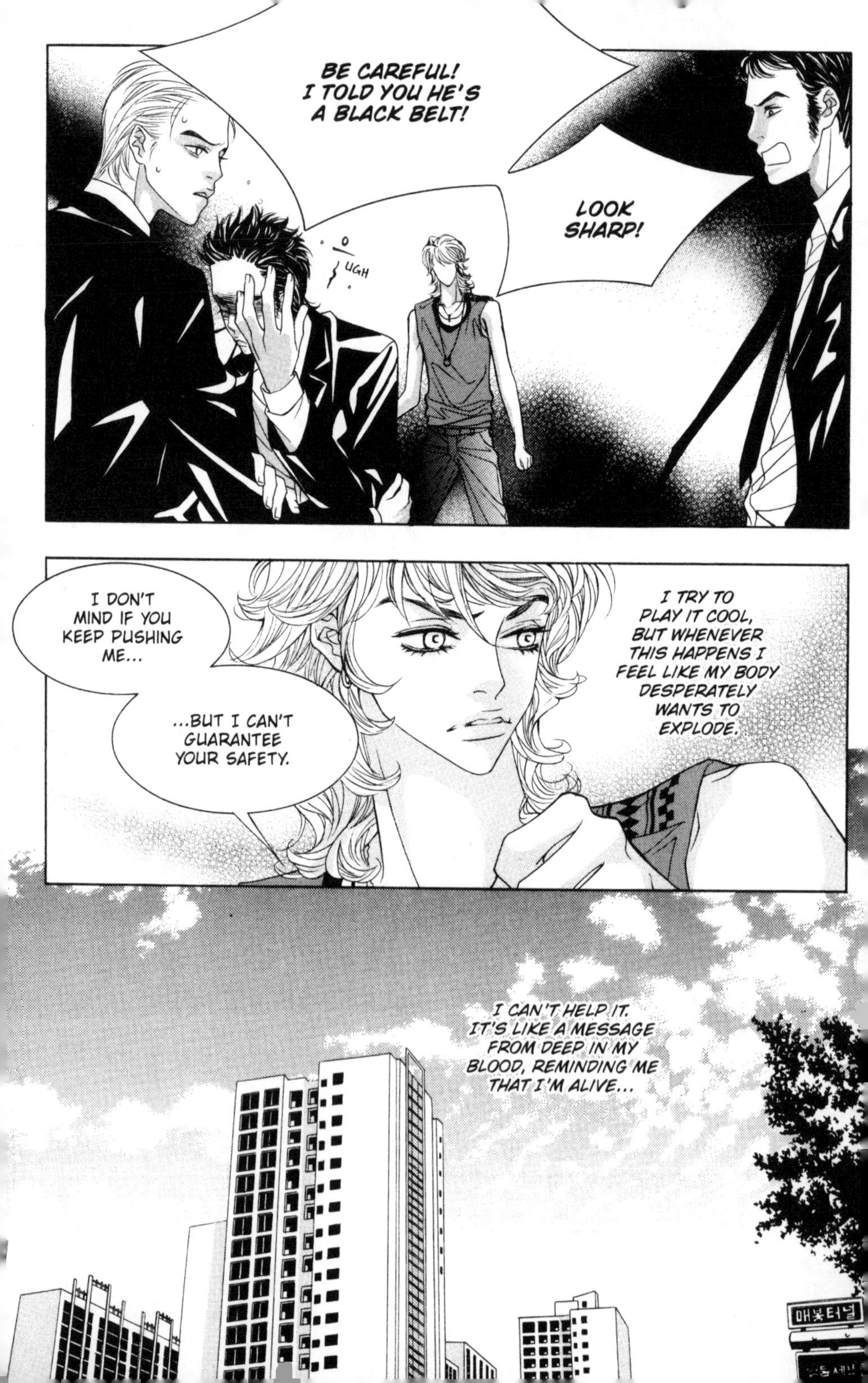
BE CAREFUL! I TOLD YOU HE'S A BLACK BELT!
UGH
LOOK SHARP!
I DON'T MIND IF YOU KEEP PUSHING ME...
...BUT I CAN'T GUARANTEE YOUR SAFETY.
I TRY TO PLAY IT COOL, BUT WHENEVER THIS HAPPENS I FEEL LIKE MY BODY DESPERATELY WANTS TO EXPLODE.
I CAN'T HELP IT. IT'S LIKE A MESSAGE FROM DEEP IN MY BLOOD, REMINDING ME THAT I'M ALIVE...
매봉터널

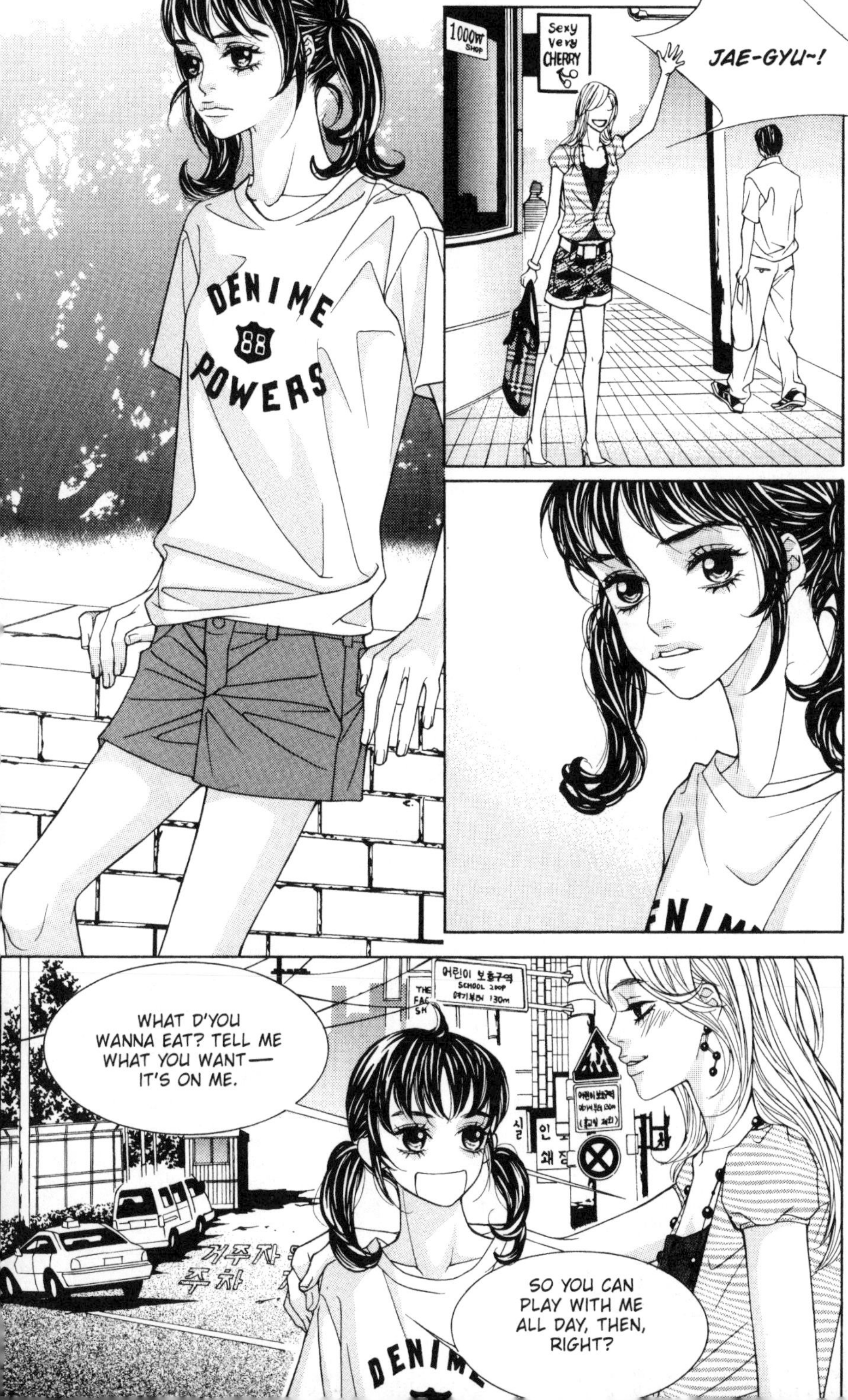
DENIME
88
POWERS
1000₩
SHOP
Sexy
Very
CHERRY
JAE-GYU~!
어린이 보호구역
WHAT D'YOU WANNA EAT? TELL ME WHAT YOU WANT— IT'S ON ME.
SO YOU CAN PLAY WITH ME ALL DAY, THEN, RIGHT?

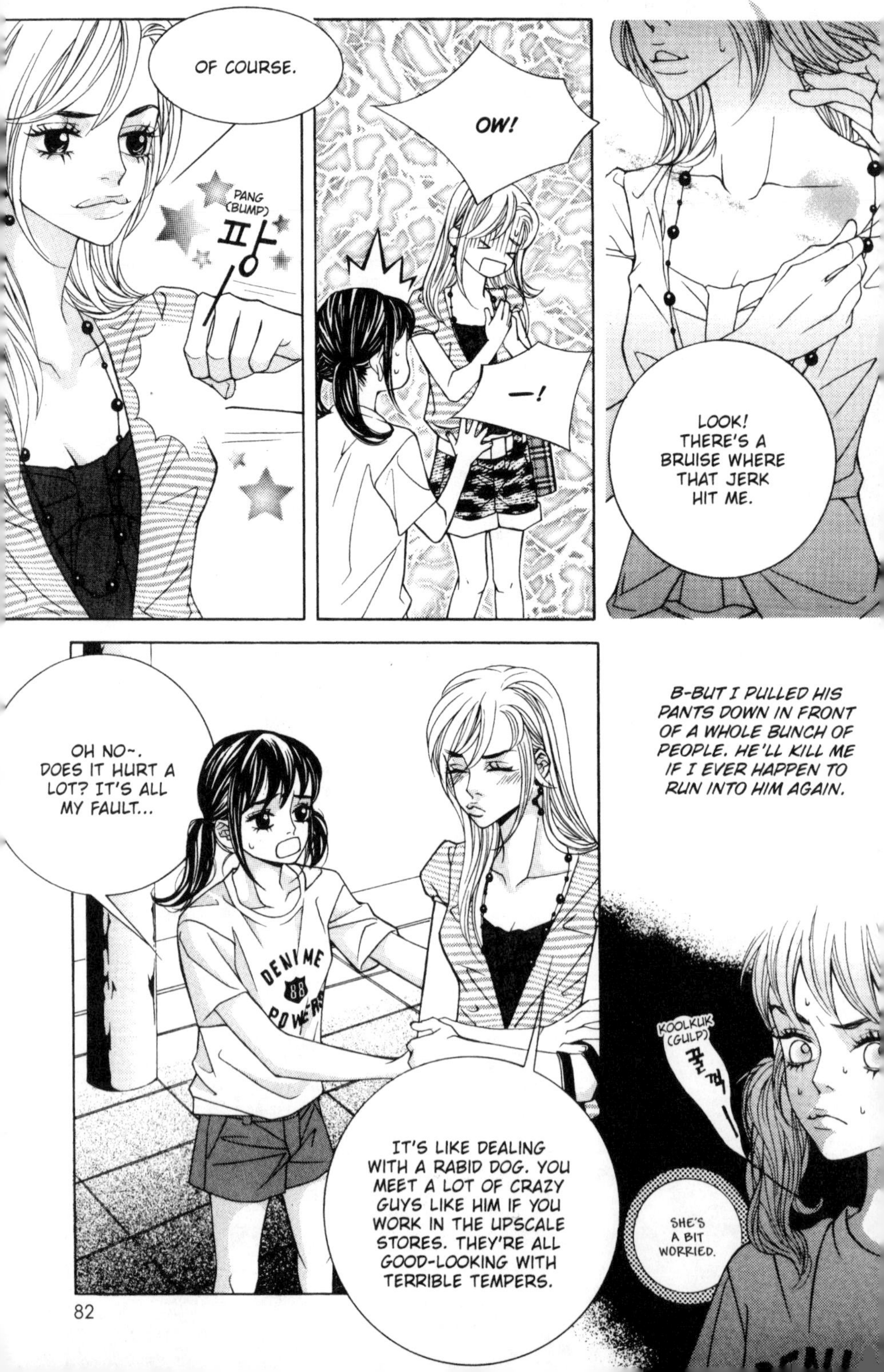
OF COURSE.
PANG (BUMP)
팡
OW!
—!
LOOK! THERE'S A BRUISE WHERE THAT JERK HIT ME.
OH NO~. DOES IT HURT A LOT? IT'S ALL MY FAULT...
IT'S LIKE DEALING WITH A RABID DOG. YOU MEET A LOT OF CRAZY GUYS LIKE HIM IF YOU WORK IN THE UPSCALE STORES. THEY'RE ALL GOOD-LOOKING WITH TERRIBLE TEMPERS.
B-BUT I PULLED HIS PANTS DOWN IN FRONT OF A WHOLE BUNCH OF PEOPLE. HE'LL KILL ME IF I EVER HAPPEN TO RUN INTO HIM AGAIN.
KOOLKUK (GULP)
꿀꺽
SHE'S A BIT WORRIED.

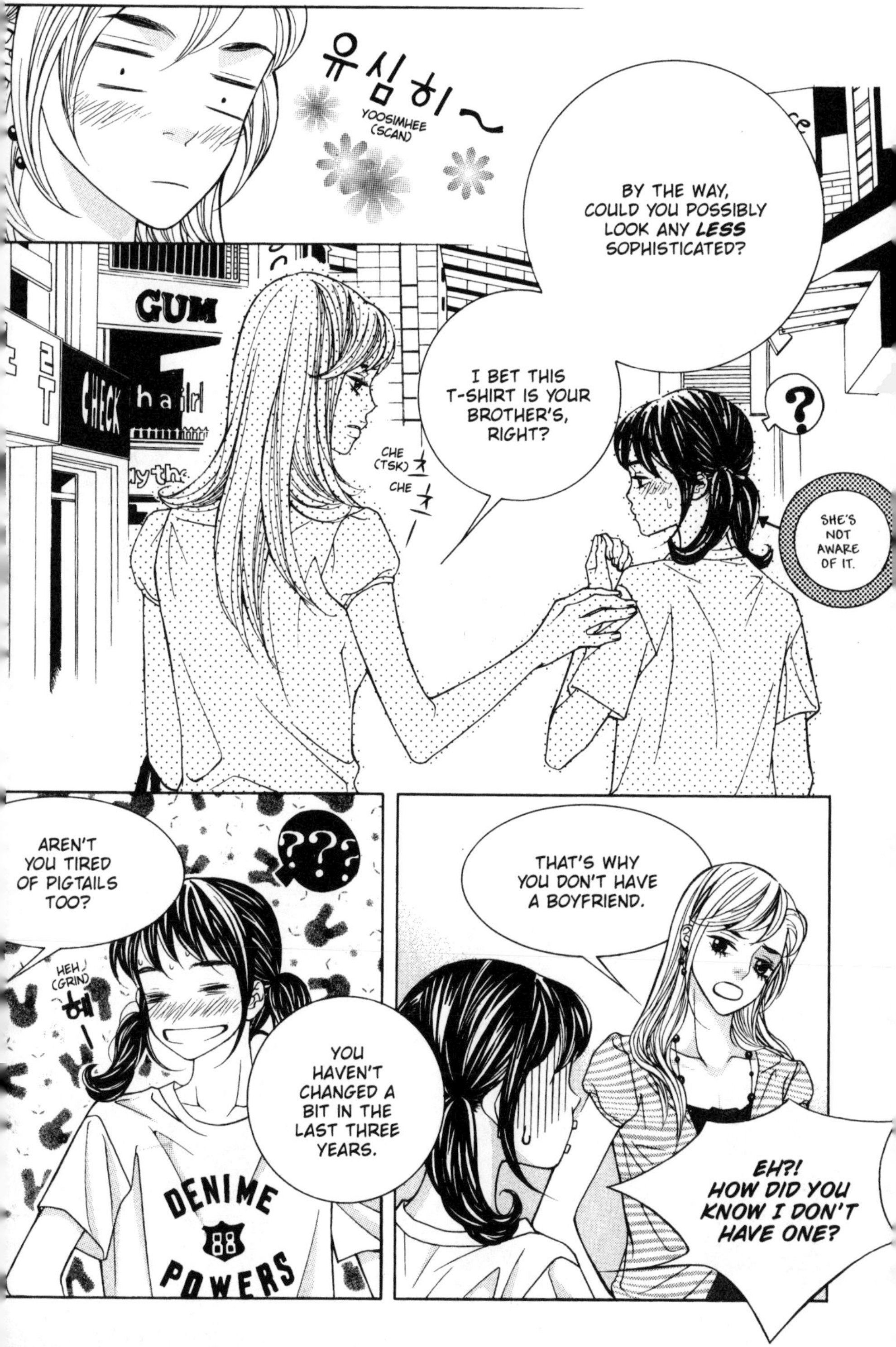
유심히~
YOOSIMHEE (SCAN)
BY THE WAY, COULD YOU POSSIBLY LOOK ANY *LESS* SOPHISTICATED?
GUM
CHECK
I BET THIS T-SHIRT IS YOUR BROTHER'S, RIGHT?
CHE (TSK) 체
CHE 체
?
SHE'S NOT AWARE OF IT.
AREN'T YOU TIRED OF PIGTAILS TOO?
???
HEH (GRIN) 헤
YOU HAVEN'T CHANGED A BIT IN THE LAST THREE YEARS.
DENIME 88 POWERS
THAT'S WHY YOU DON'T HAVE A BOYFRIEND.
EH?! HOW DID YOU KNOW I DON'T HAVE ONE?

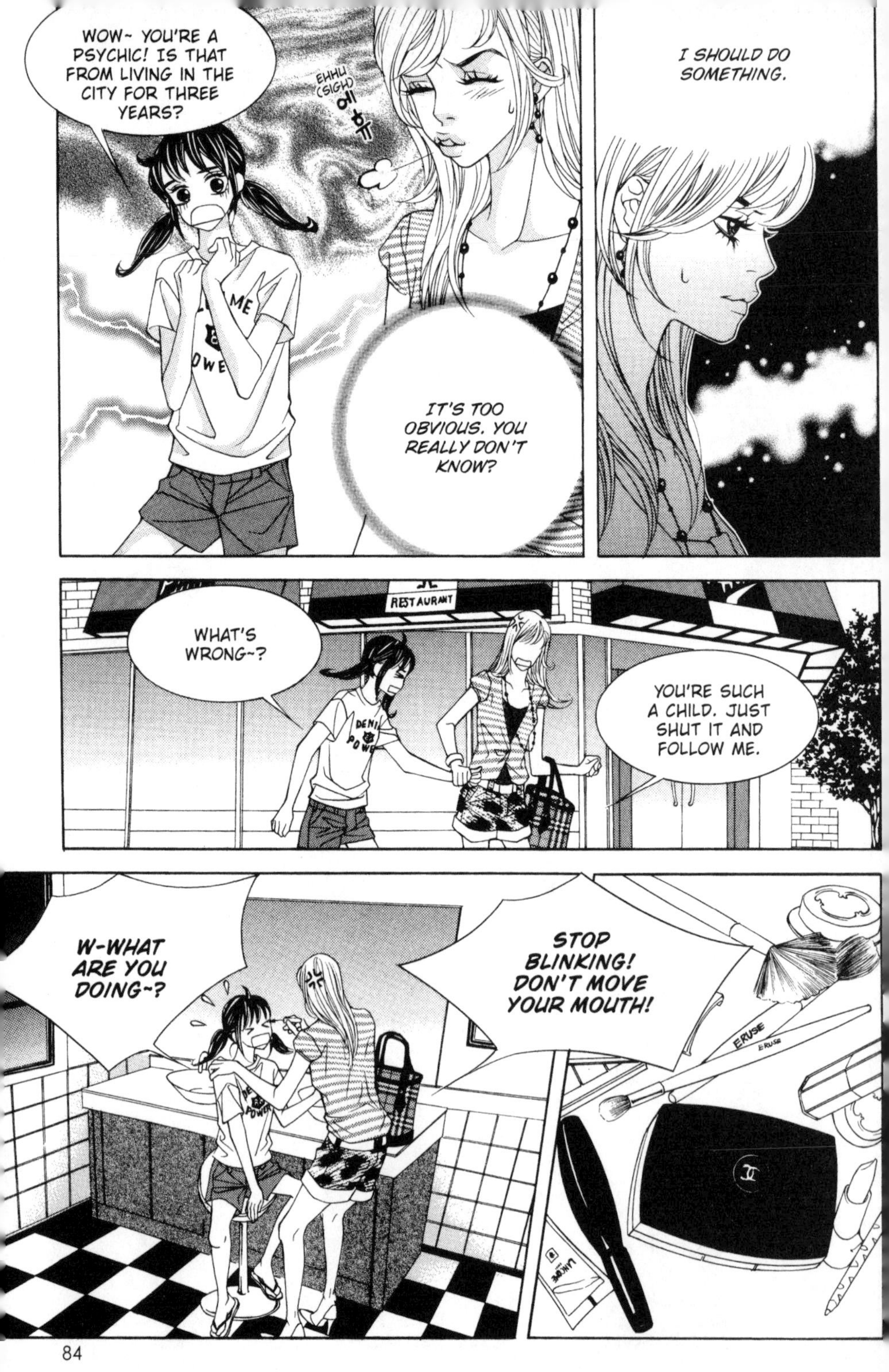
WOW~ YOU'RE A PSYCHIC! IS THAT FROM LIVING IN THE CITY FOR THREE YEARS?
EHHU (SIGH)
에휴
IT'S TOO OBVIOUS. YOU REALLY DON'T KNOW?
I SHOULD DO SOMETHING.
RESTAURANT
WHAT'S WRONG~?
YOU'RE SUCH A CHILD. JUST SHUT IT AND FOLLOW ME.
W-WHAT ARE YOU DOING~?
STOP BLINKING! DON'T MOVE YOUR MOUTH!

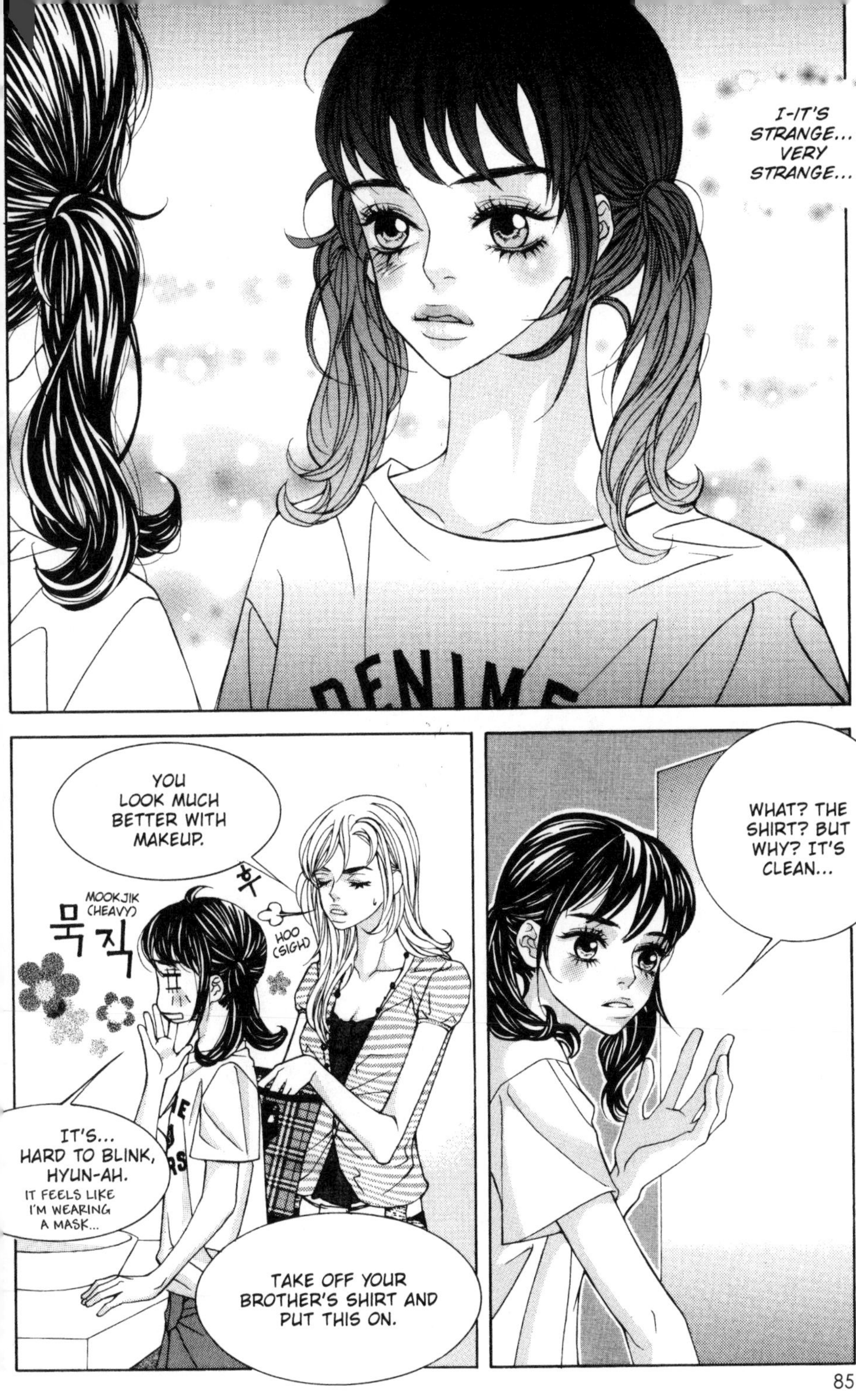
I-IT'S STRANGE... VERY STRANGE...
YOU LOOK MUCH BETTER WITH MAKEUP.
묵직
MOOKJIK (HEAVY)
후
HOO (SIGH)
IT'S... HARD TO BLINK, HYUN-AH.
IT FEELS LIKE I'M WEARING A MASK...
TAKE OFF YOUR BROTHER'S SHIRT AND PUT THIS ON.
WHAT? THE SHIRT? BUT WHY? IT'S CLEAN...

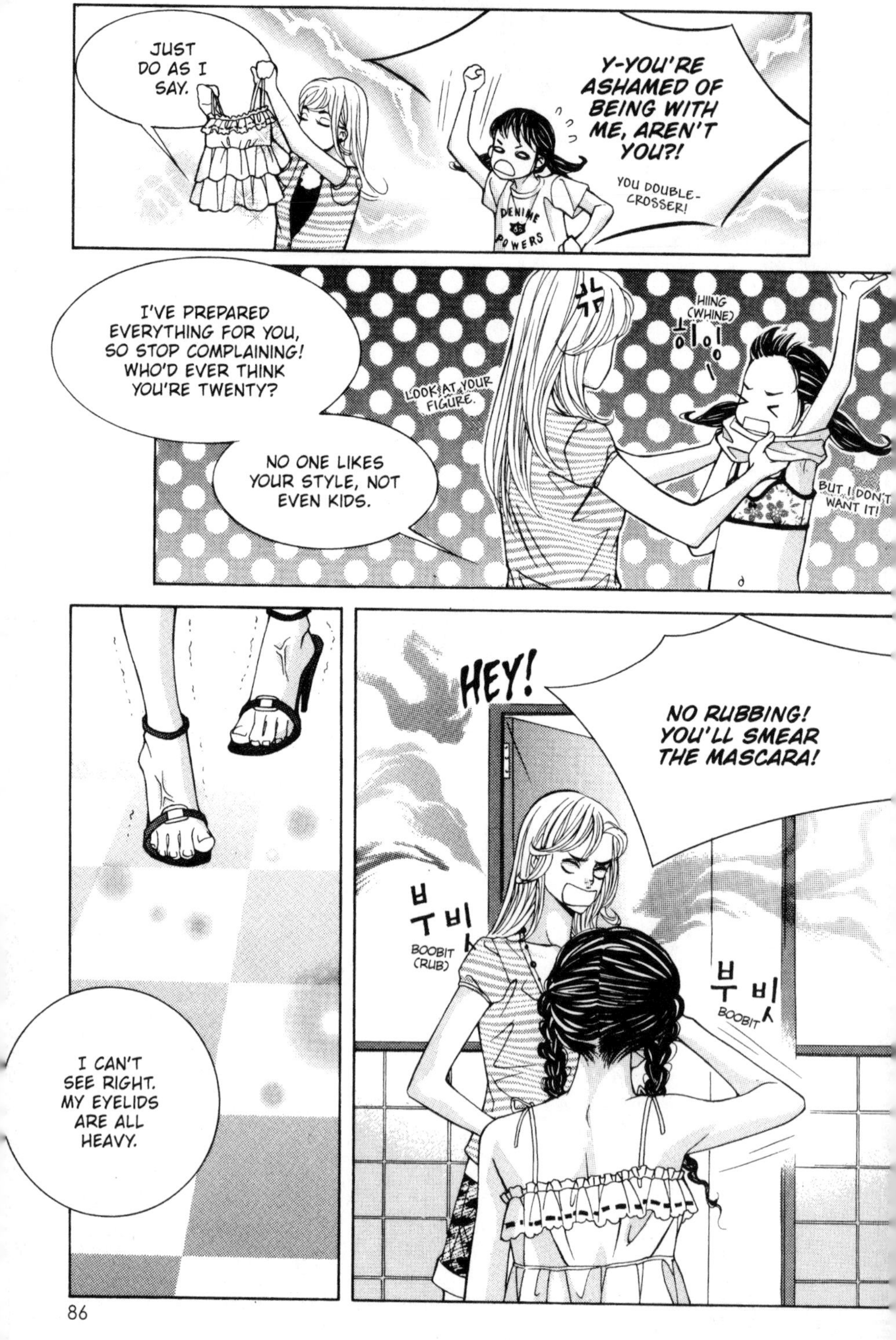
JUST DO AS I SAY.
Y-YOU'RE ASHAMED OF BEING WITH ME, AREN'T YOU?!
YOU DOUBLE-CROSSER!
DENIM POWERS
I'VE PREPARED EVERYTHING FOR YOU, SO STOP COMPLAINING! WHO'D EVER THINK YOU'RE TWENTY?
LOOK AT YOUR FIGURE.
NO ONE LIKES YOUR STYLE, NOT EVEN KIDS.
HIING (WHINE)
히잉
BUT I DON'T WANT IT!
I CAN'T SEE RIGHT. MY EYELIDS ARE ALL HEAVY.
HEY!
NO RUBBING! YOU'LL SMEAR THE MASCARA!
부빗
BOOBIT (RUB)
부빗
BOOBIT

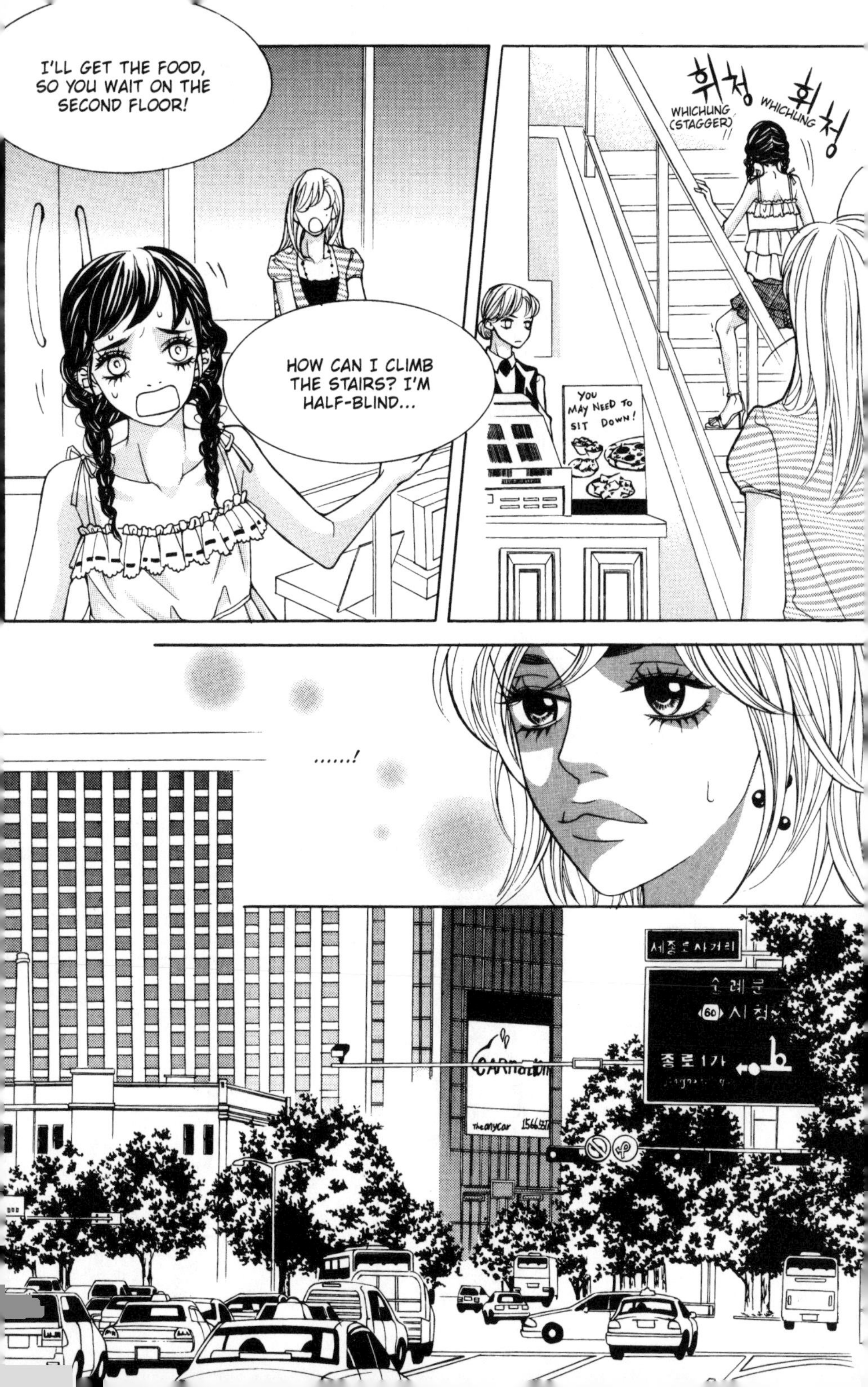
I'LL GET THE FOOD, SO YOU WAIT ON THE SECOND FLOOR!
HOW CAN I CLIMB THE STAIRS? I'M HALF-BLIND...
휘청 휘청
WHICHUNG (STAGGER)
WHICHUNG
YOU MAY NEED TO SIT DOWN!
......!
시청
종로1가

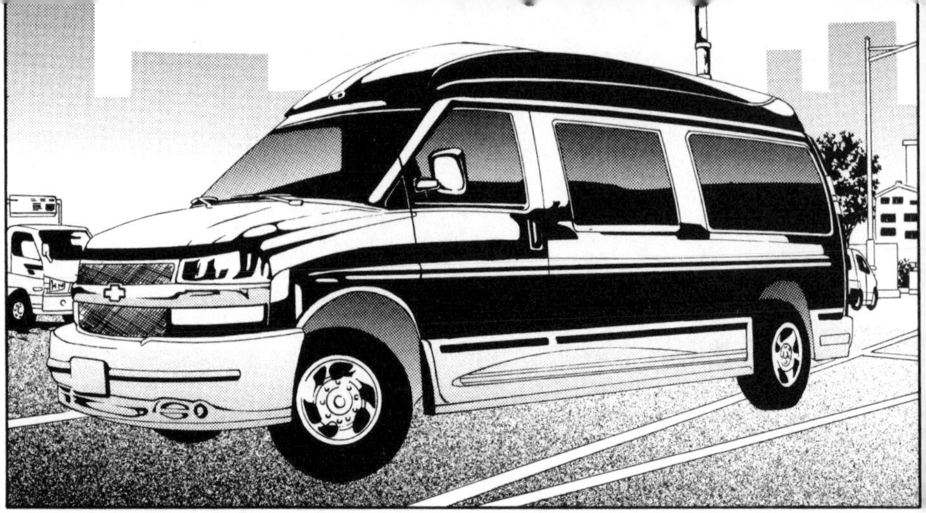

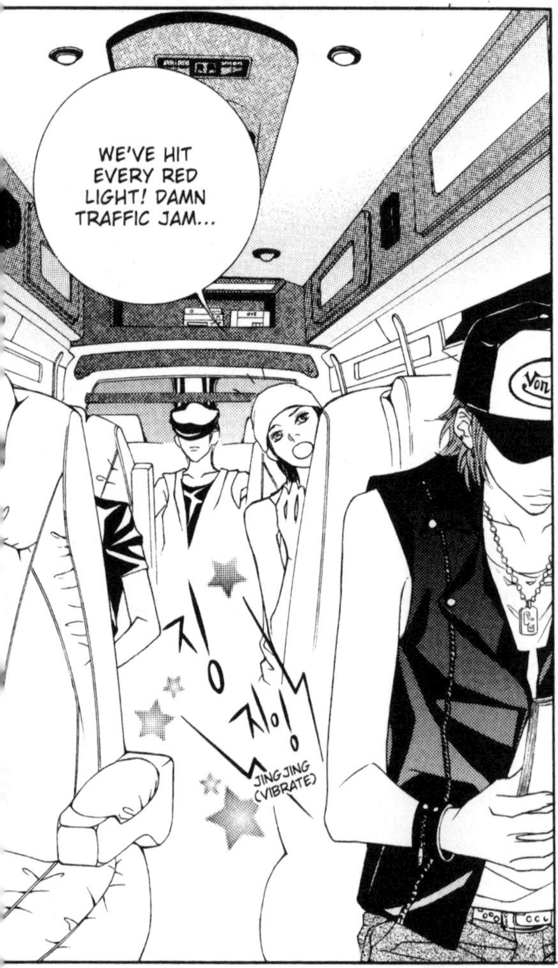
WE'VE HIT EVERY RED LIGHT! DAMN TRAFFIC JAM...
JING JING (VIBRATE)

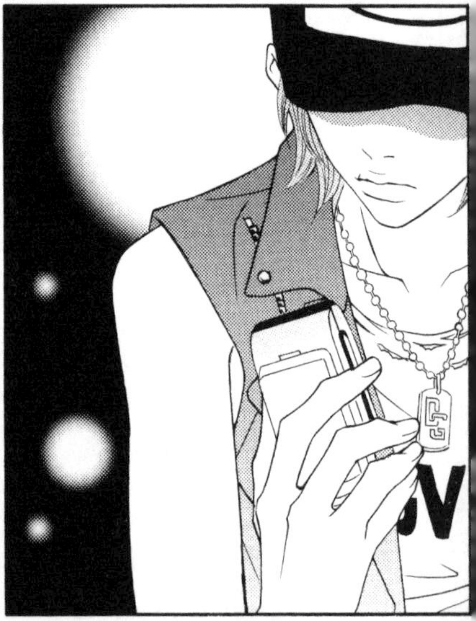

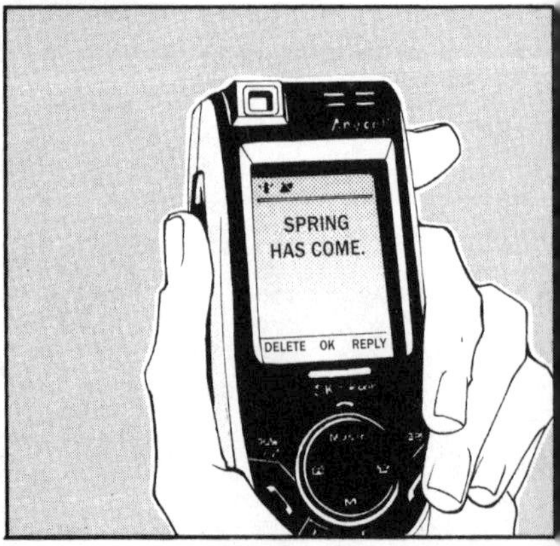
SPRING HAS COME.
DELETE OK REPLY

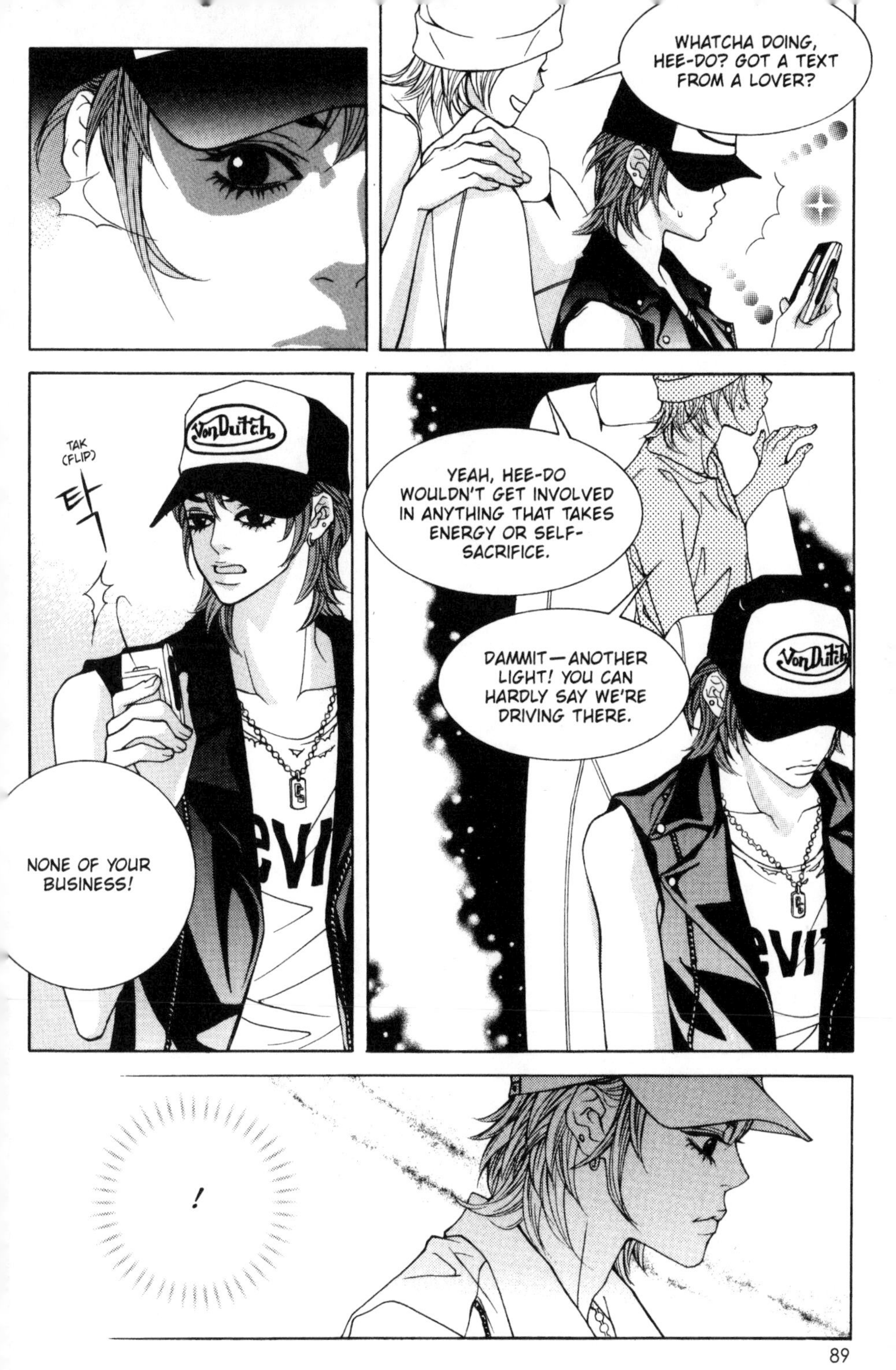
WHATCHA DOING, HEE-DO? GOT A TEXT FROM A LOVER?
TAK (FLIP)
NONE OF YOUR BUSINESS!
YEAH, HEE-DO WOULDN'T GET INVOLVED IN ANYTHING THAT TAKES ENERGY OR SELF-SACRIFICE.
DAMMIT—ANOTHER LIGHT! YOU CAN HARDLY SAY WE'RE DRIVING THERE.
!

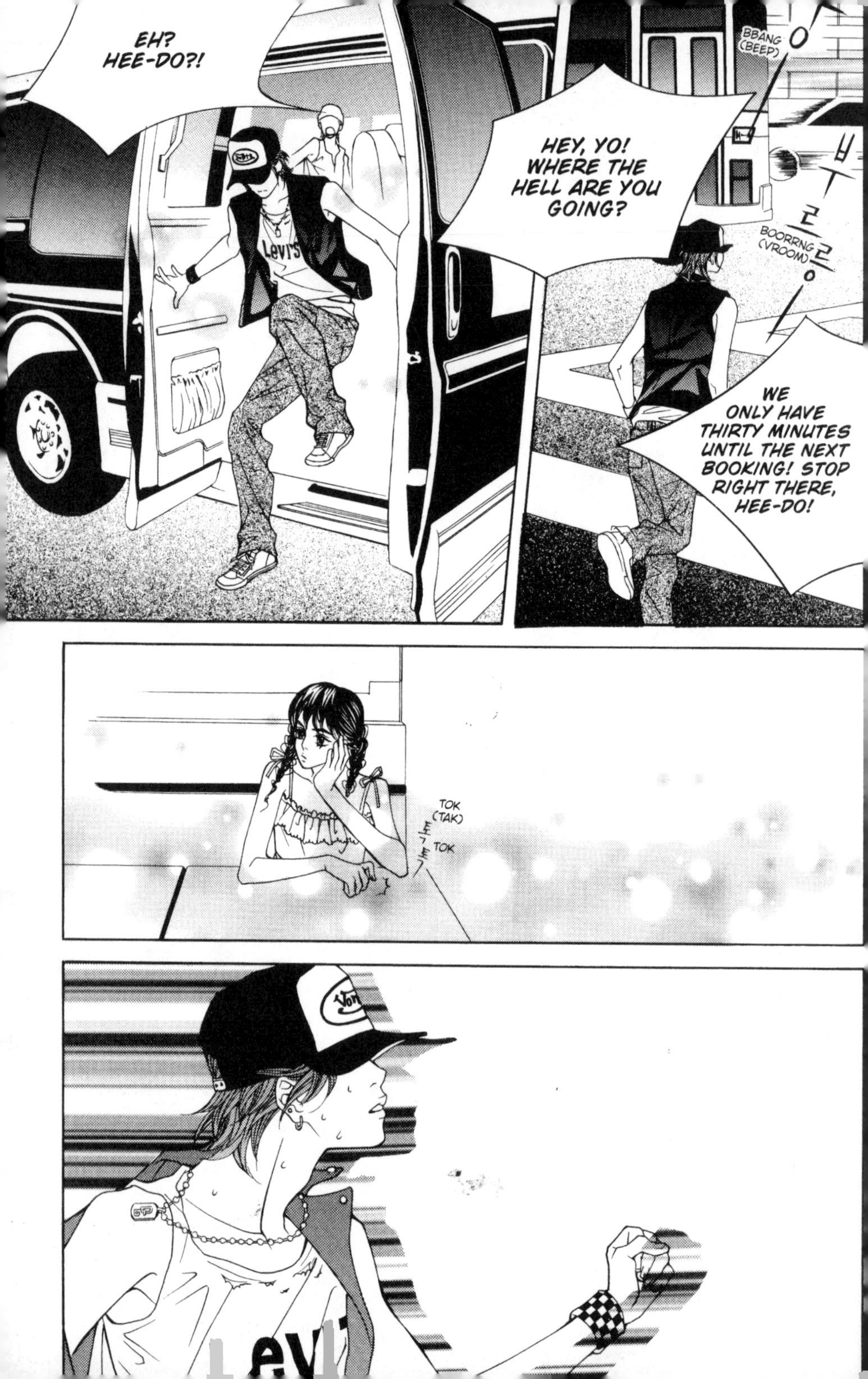

EH? HEE-DO?!
BBANG (BEEP)
HEY, YO! WHERE THE HELL ARE YOU GOING?
BOORRNG (VROOM)
WE ONLY HAVE THIRTY MINUTES UNTIL THE NEXT BOOKING! STOP RIGHT THERE, HEE-DO!
TOK (TAK)
TOK

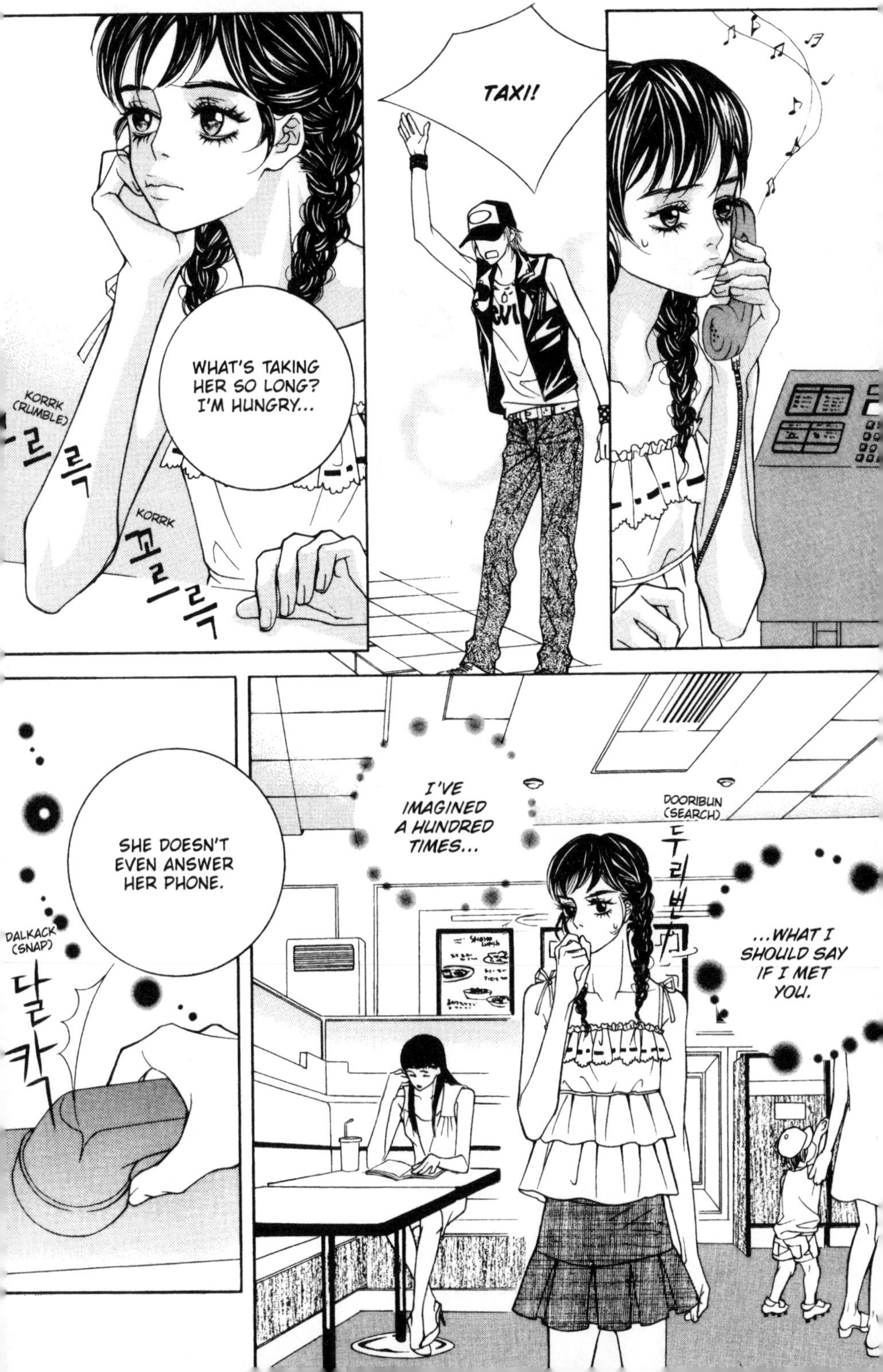
WHAT'S TAKING HER SO LONG? I'M HUNGRY...
KORRK (RUMBLE)
그르륵
KORRK
꼬르륵
TAXI!
SHE DOESN'T EVEN ANSWER HER PHONE.
DALKACK (SNAP)
달칵
I'VE IMAGINED A HUNDRED TIMES...
DOORIBUN (SEARCH)
두리번
...WHAT I SHOULD SAY IF I MET YOU.

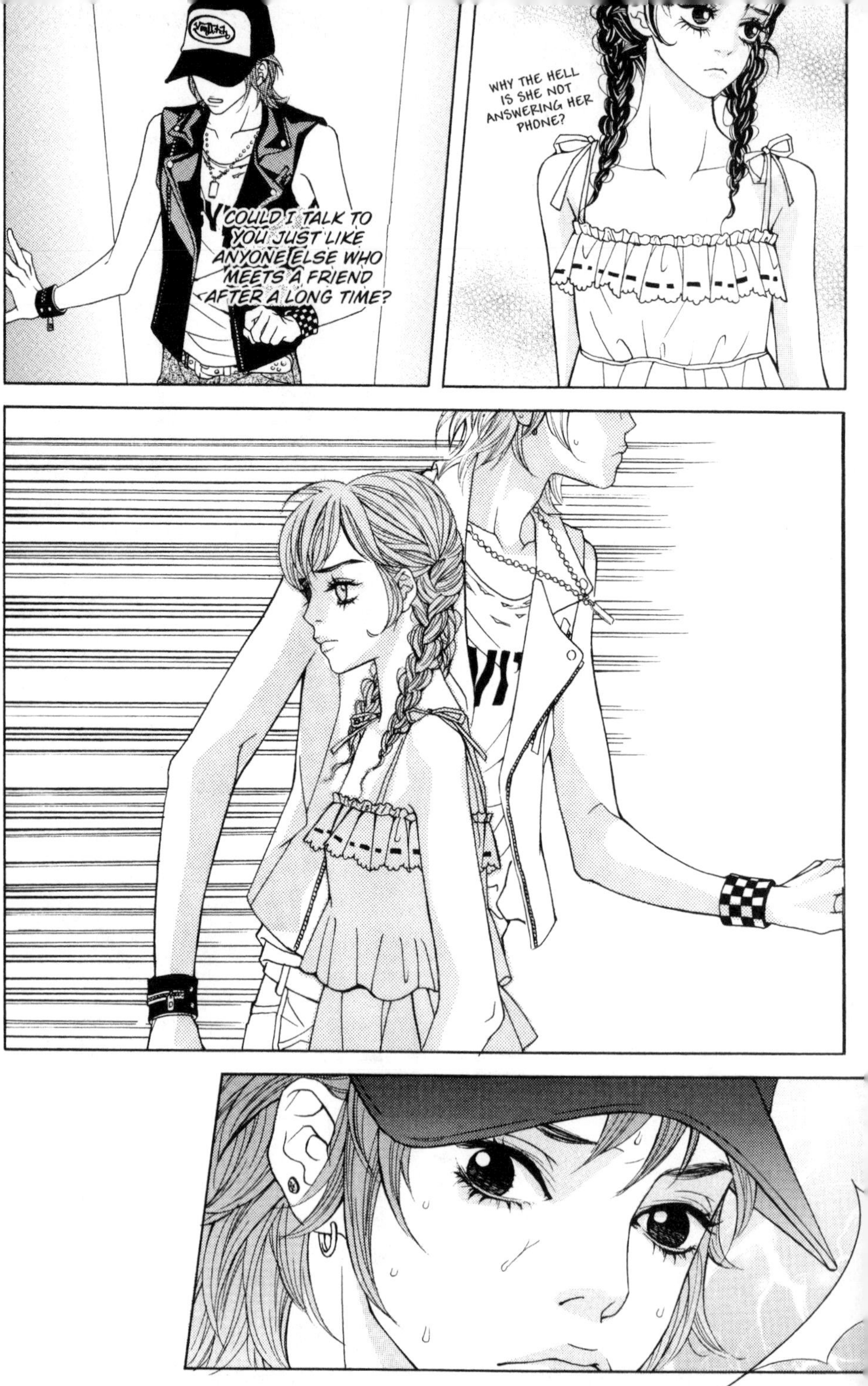
COULD I TALK TO YOU JUST LIKE ANYONE ELSE WHO MEETS A FRIEND AFTER A LONG TIME?
WHY THE HELL IS SHE NOT ANSWERING HER PHONE?

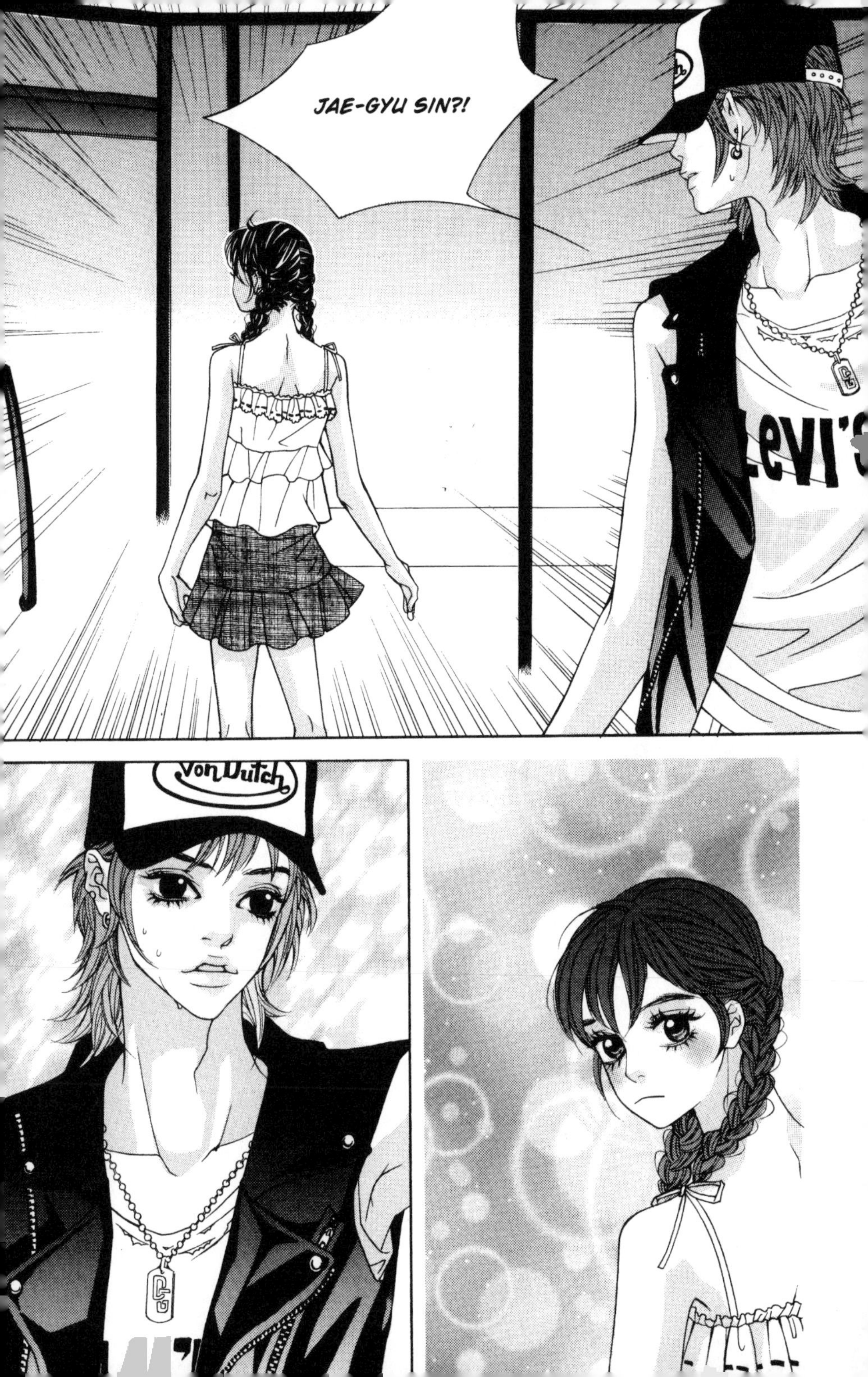
JAE-GYU SIN?!
Levi's
Von Dutch

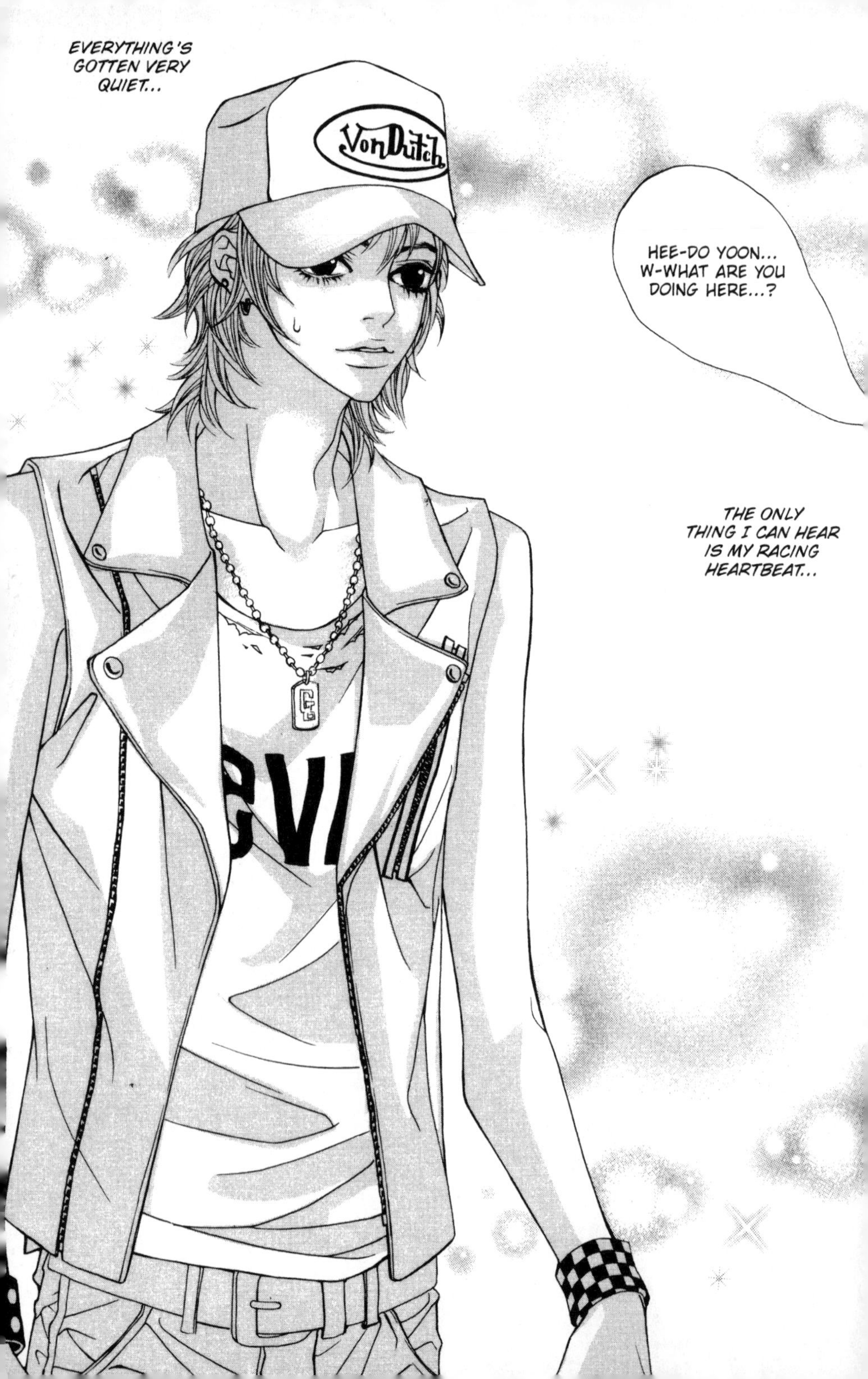
EVERYTHING'S GOTTEN VERY QUIET...
HEE-DO YOON... W-WHAT ARE YOU DOING HERE...?
THE ONLY THING I CAN HEAR IS MY RACING HEARTBEAT...

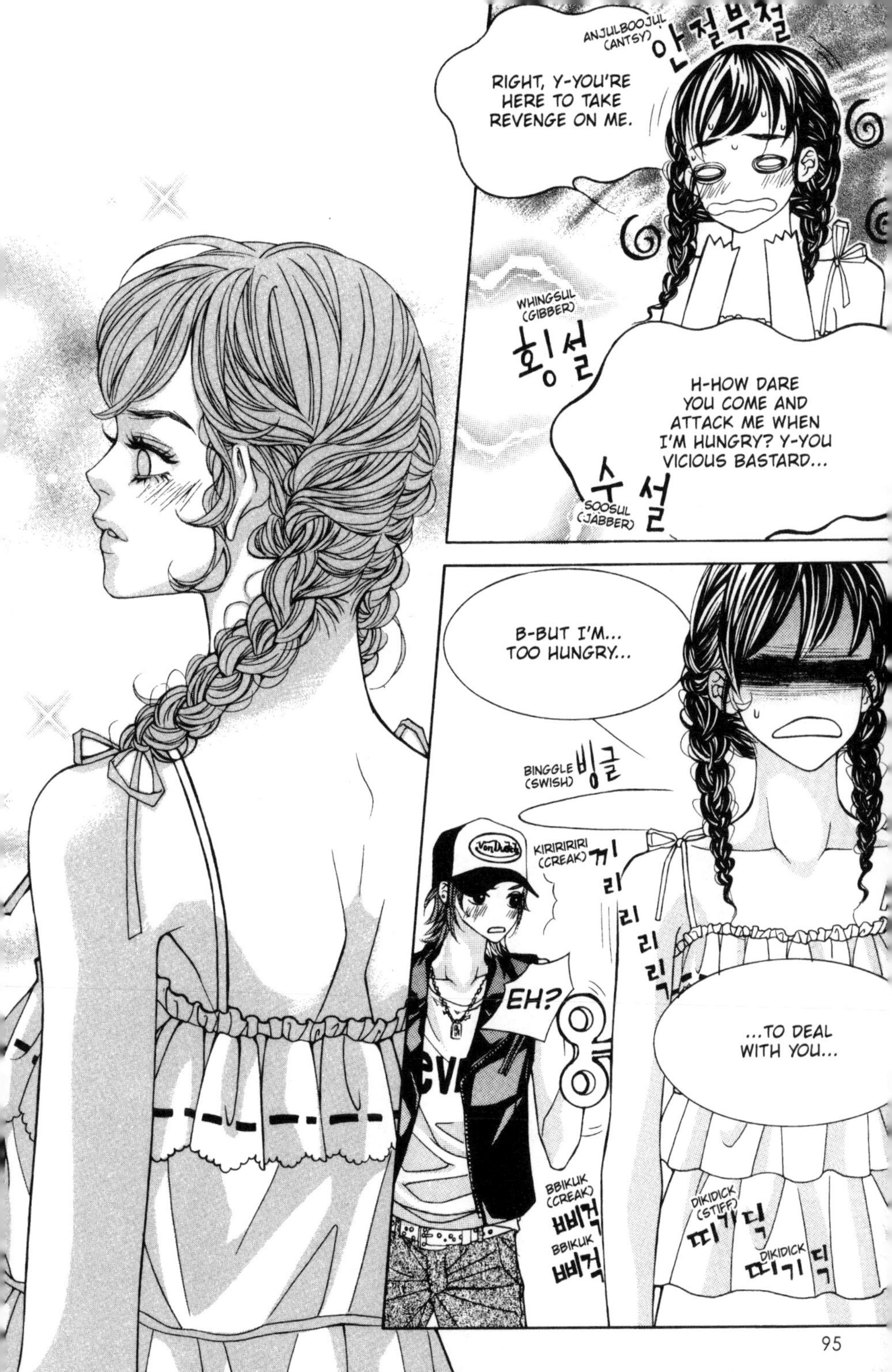
ANJULBOOJUL (ANTSY) 안절부절
RIGHT, Y-YOU'RE HERE TO TAKE REVENGE ON ME.
WHINGSUL (GIBBER) 횡설
H-HOW DARE YOU COME AND ATTACK ME WHEN I'M HUNGRY? Y-YOU VICIOUS BASTARD...
SOOSUL (JABBER) 수설
B-BUT I'M... TOO HUNGRY...
BINGGLE (SWISH) 빙글
KIRIRIRIRI (CREAK) 끼리리리릭
EH?
...TO DEAL WITH YOU...
BBIKUK (CREAK) 삐걱
BBIKUK 삐걱
DIKIDICK (STIFF) 띠기딕
DIKIDICK 띠기딕

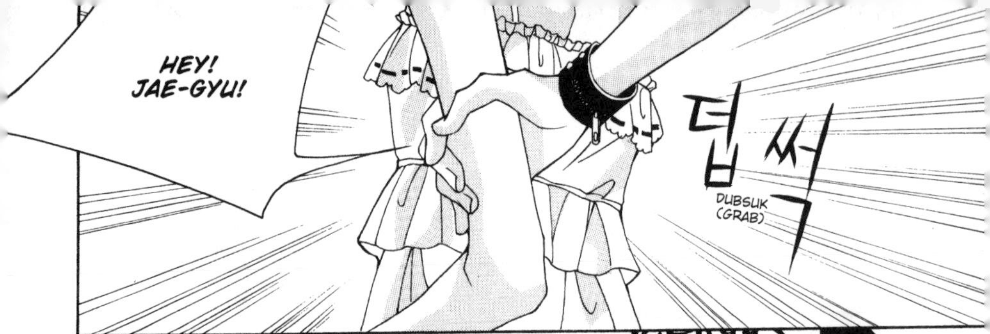
HEY! JAE-GYU!
덥썩
DUBSUK (GRAB)
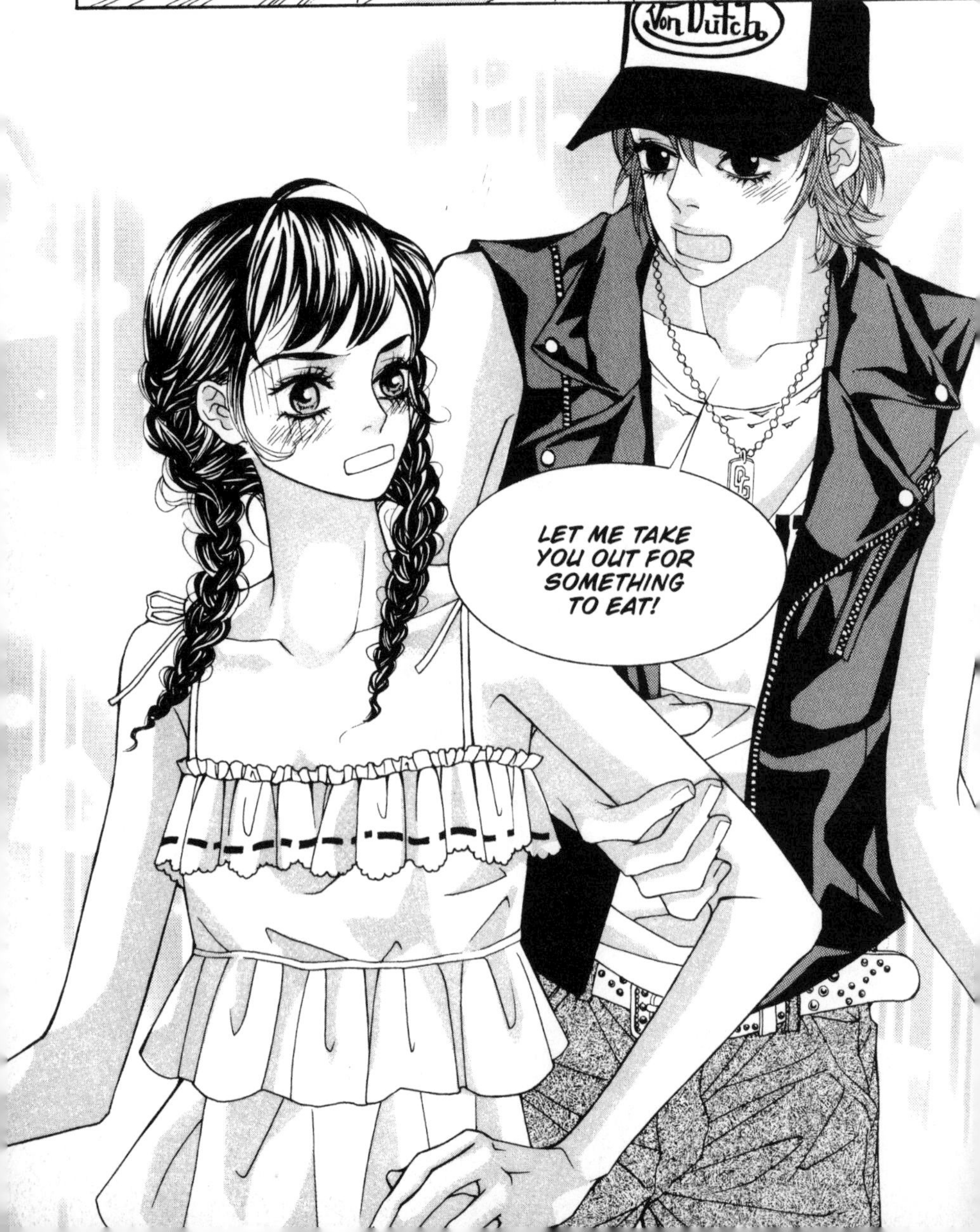
LET ME TAKE YOU OUT FOR SOMETHING TO EAT!

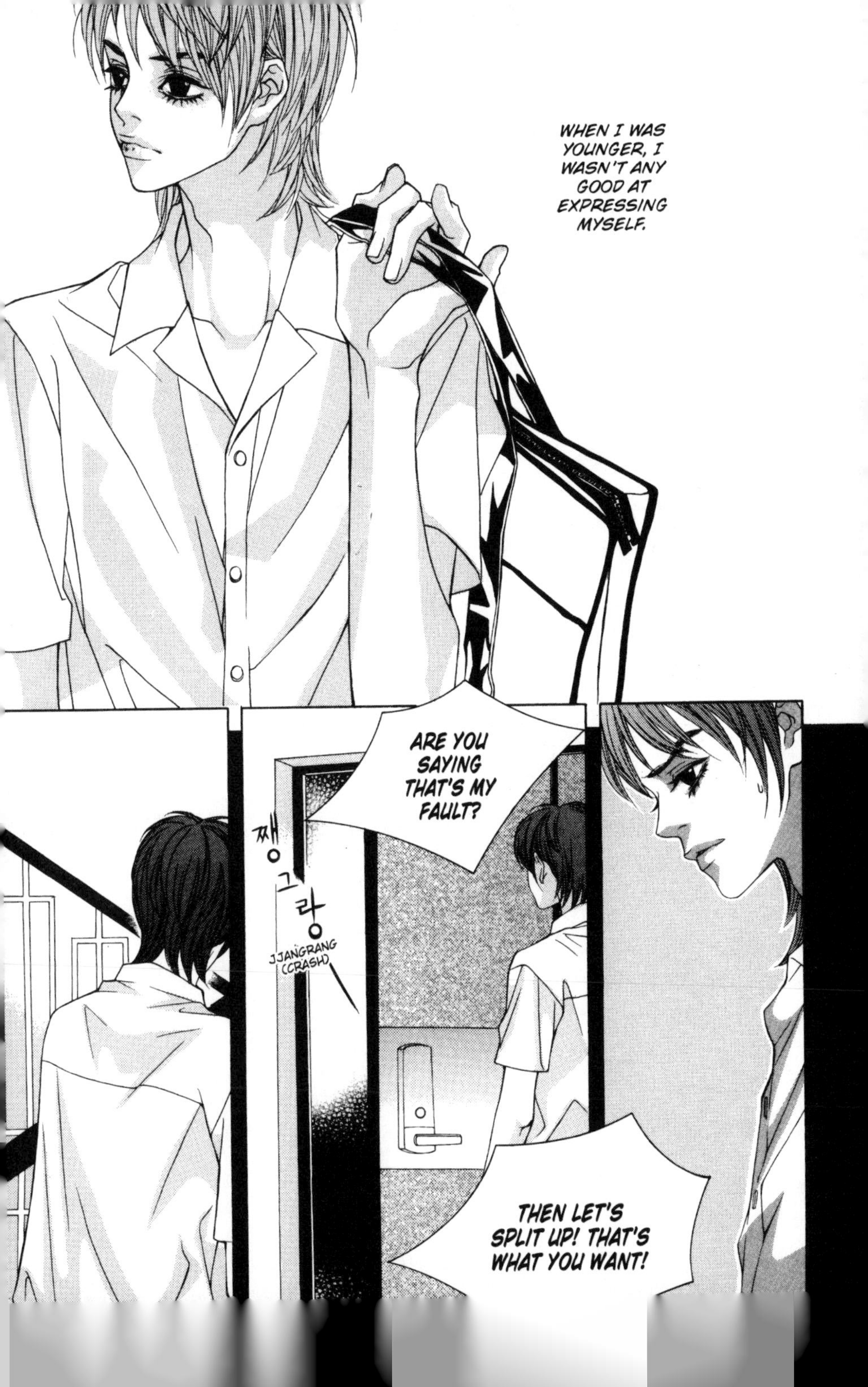
WHEN I WAS YOUNGER, I WASN'T ANY GOOD AT EXPRESSING MYSELF.
ARE YOU SAYING THAT'S MY FAULT?
짱그랑
JJANGRANG (CRASH)
THEN LET'S SPLIT UP! THAT'S WHAT YOU WANT!

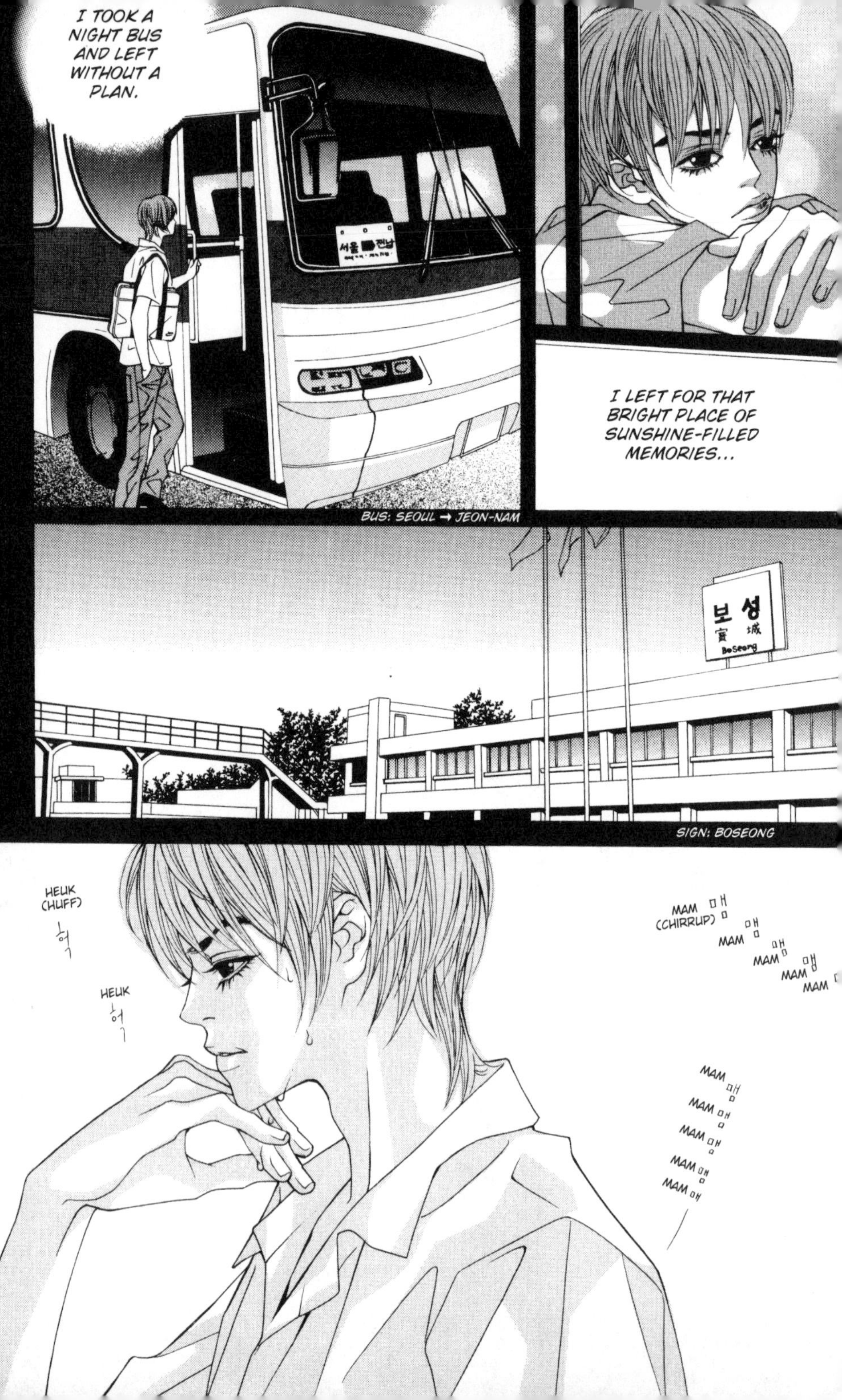
I TOOK A NIGHT BUS AND LEFT WITHOUT A PLAN.
서울 전남
BUS: SEOUL → JEON-NAM
I LEFT FOR THAT BRIGHT PLACE OF SUNSHINE-FILLED MEMORIES...
보성
寶城
Boseong
SIGN: BOSEONG
HEUK (HUFF)
헉
HEUK
헉
MAM (CHIRRUP)
MAM
MAM
MAM
MAM
MAM
MAM
MAM
MAM
MAM

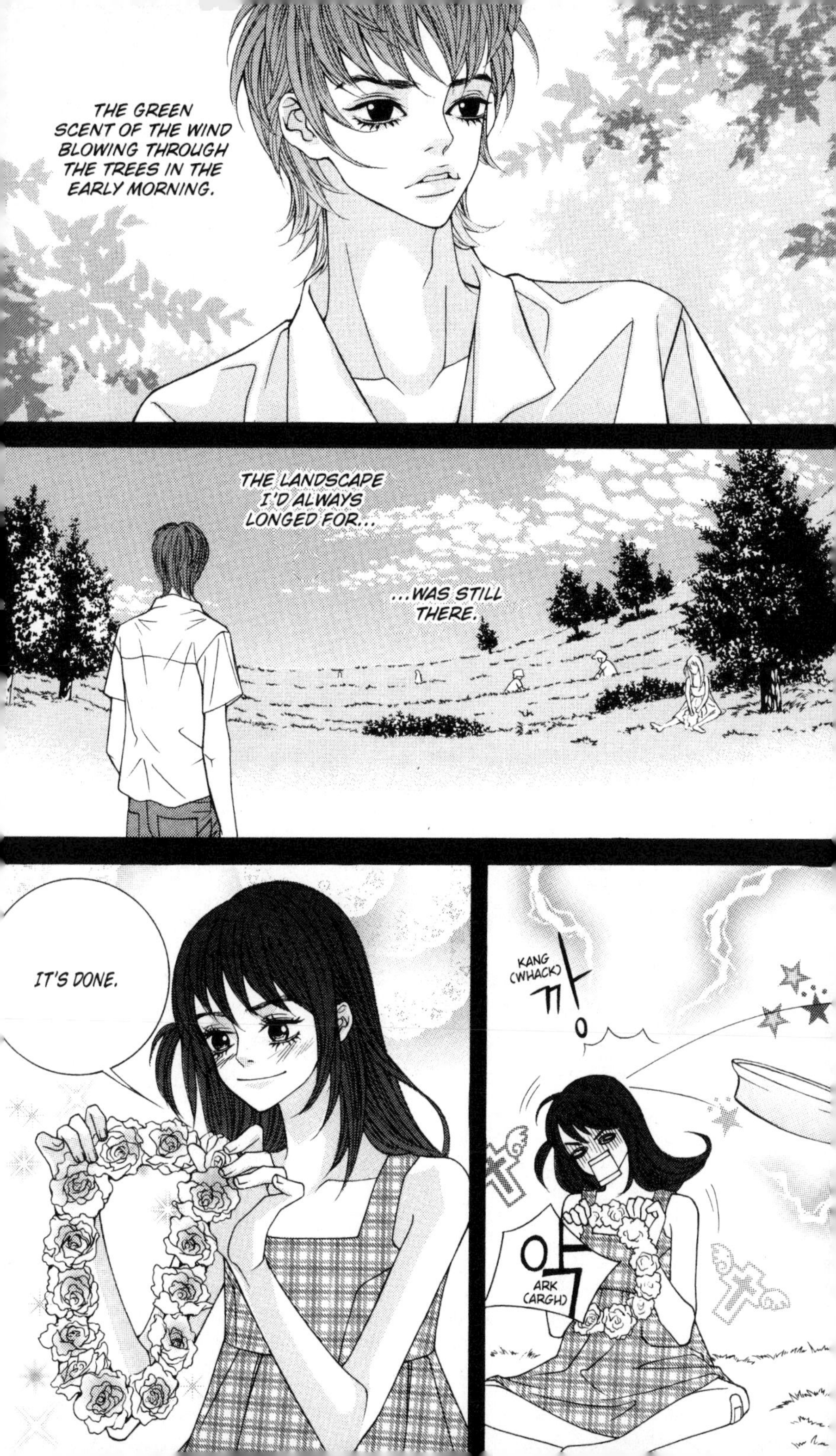
THE GREEN SCENT OF THE WIND BLOWING THROUGH THE TREES IN THE EARLY MORNING.
THE LANDSCAPE I'D ALWAYS LONGED FOR...
...WAS STILL THERE.
IT'S DONE.
KANG (WHACK)
까
ARK (ARGH)
악

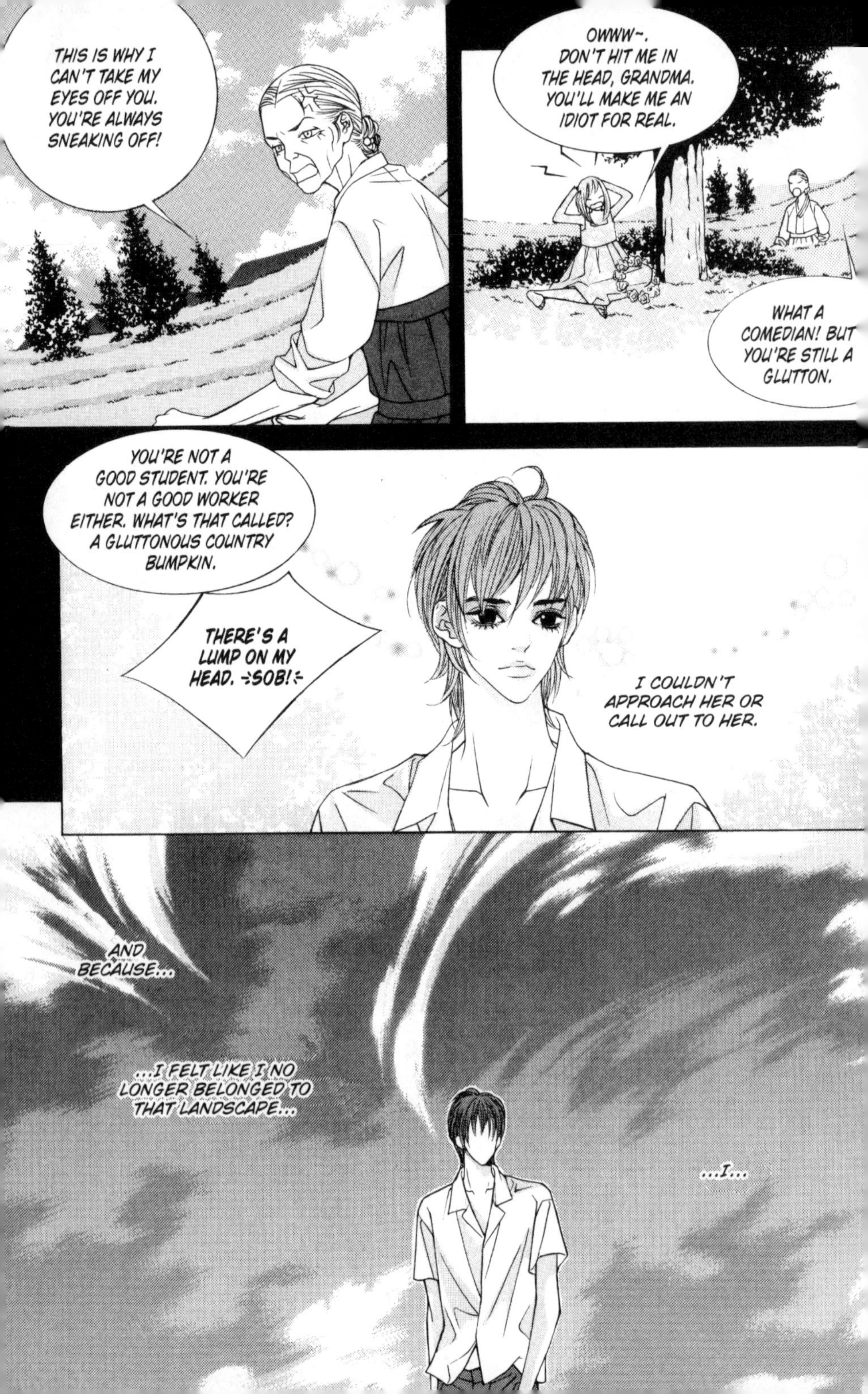
THIS IS WHY I CAN'T TAKE MY EYES OFF YOU. YOU'RE ALWAYS SNEAKING OFF!
OWWW~. DON'T HIT ME IN THE HEAD, GRANDMA. YOU'LL MAKE ME AN IDIOT FOR REAL.
WHAT A COMEDIAN! BUT YOU'RE STILL A GLUTTON.
YOU'RE NOT A GOOD STUDENT. YOU'RE NOT A GOOD WORKER EITHER. WHAT'S THAT CALLED? A GLUTTONOUS COUNTRY BUMPKIN.
THERE'S A LUMP ON MY HEAD. -SOB!-
I COULDN'T APPROACH HER OR CALL OUT TO HER.
AND BECAUSE...
...I FELT LIKE I NO LONGER BELONGED TO THAT LANDSCAPE...
...I...

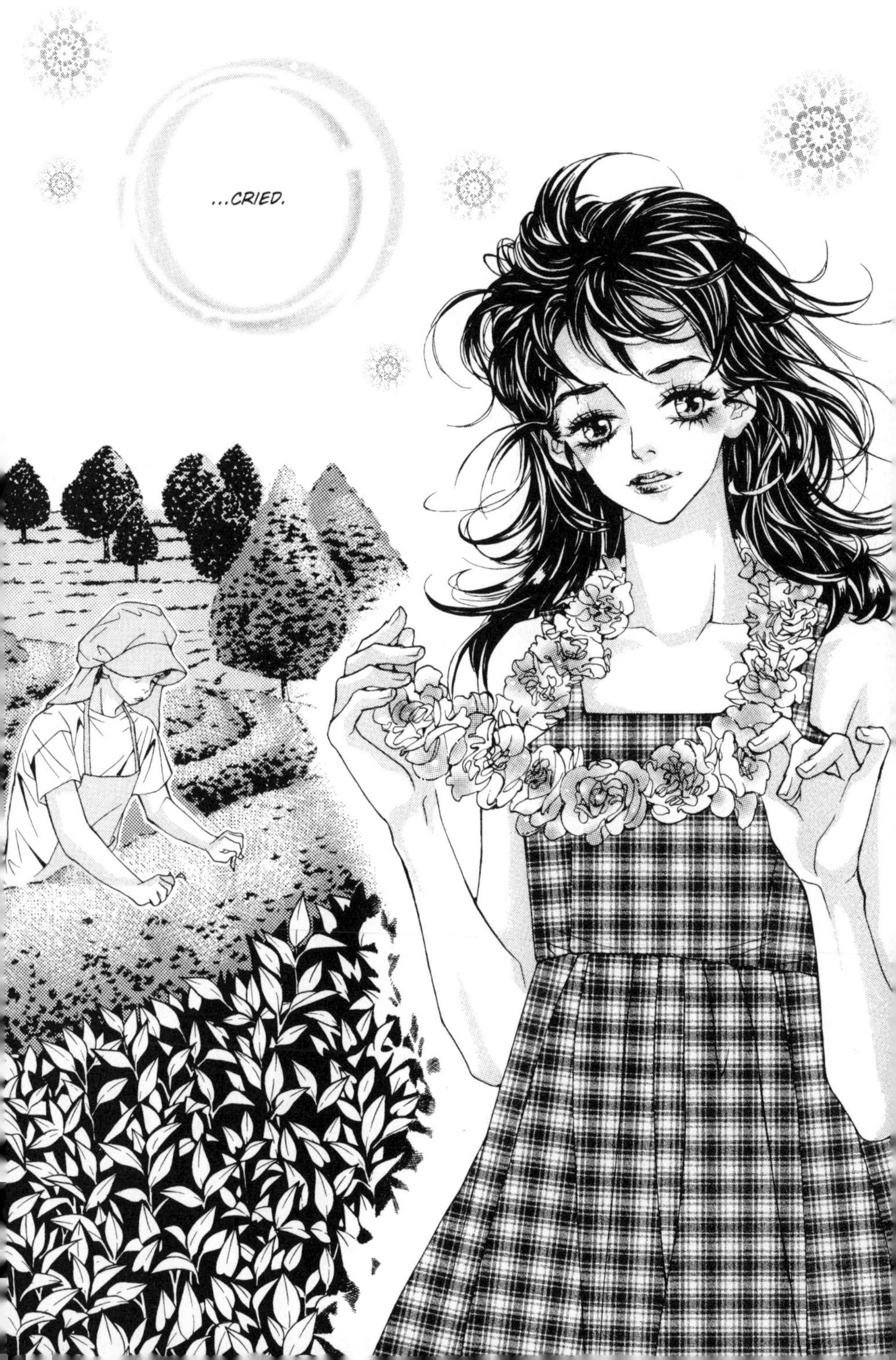
...CRIED.

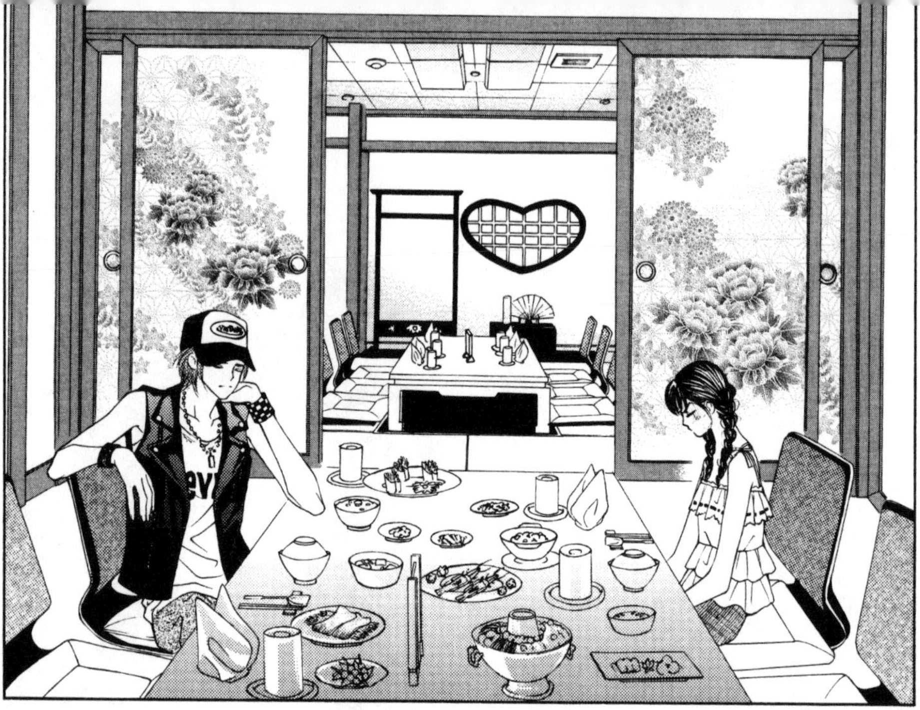

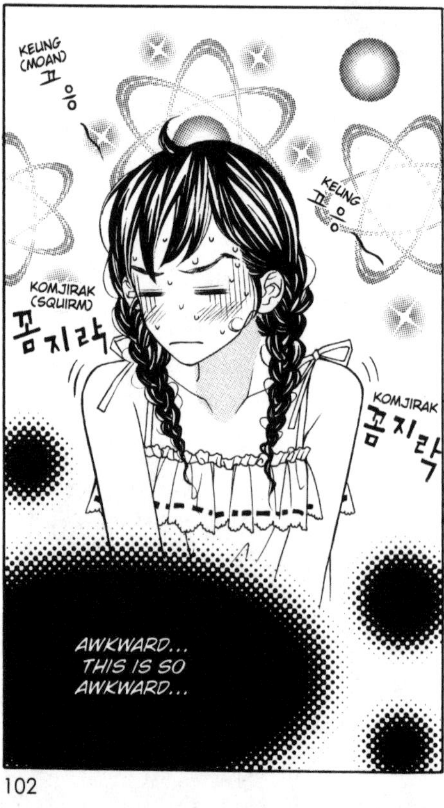
KELING (MOAN)
끄응
KELING
끄응
KOMJIRAK (SQUIRM)
꼼지락
KOMJIRAK
꼼지락
AWKWARD... THIS IS SO AWKWARD...

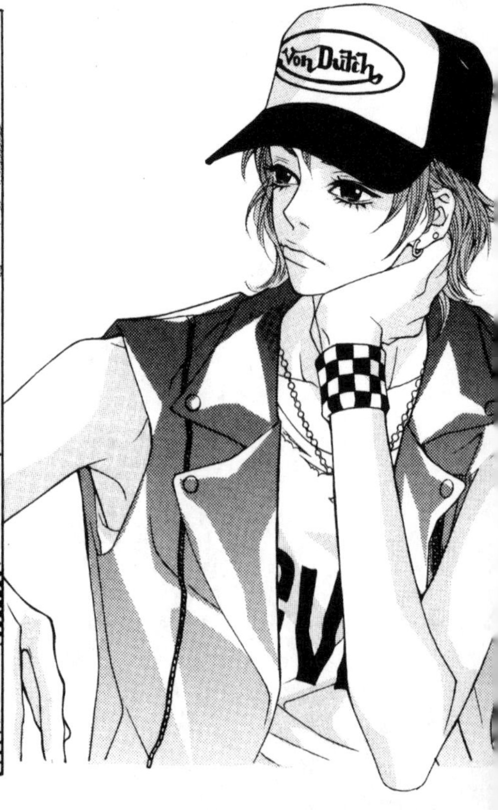
Von Dutch

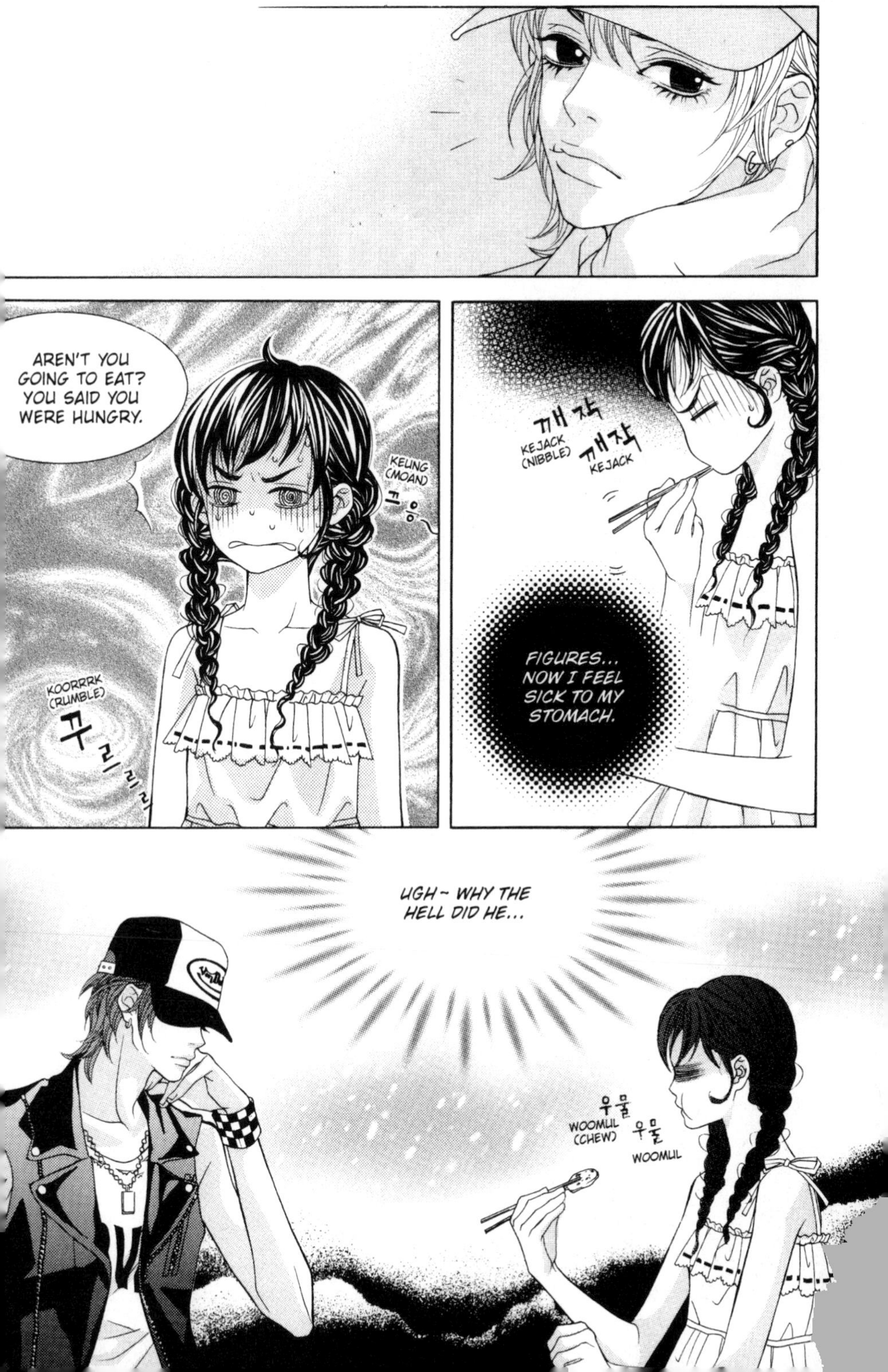
AREN'T YOU GOING TO EAT? YOU SAID YOU WERE HUNGRY.
KEUNG (MOAN)
KOORRRK (RUMBLE)
깨작
KEJACK (NIBBLE)
깨작
KEJACK
FIGURES... NOW I FEEL SICK TO MY STOMACH.
UGH~ WHY THE HELL DID HE...
우물
WOOMUL (CHEW)
우물
WOOMUL

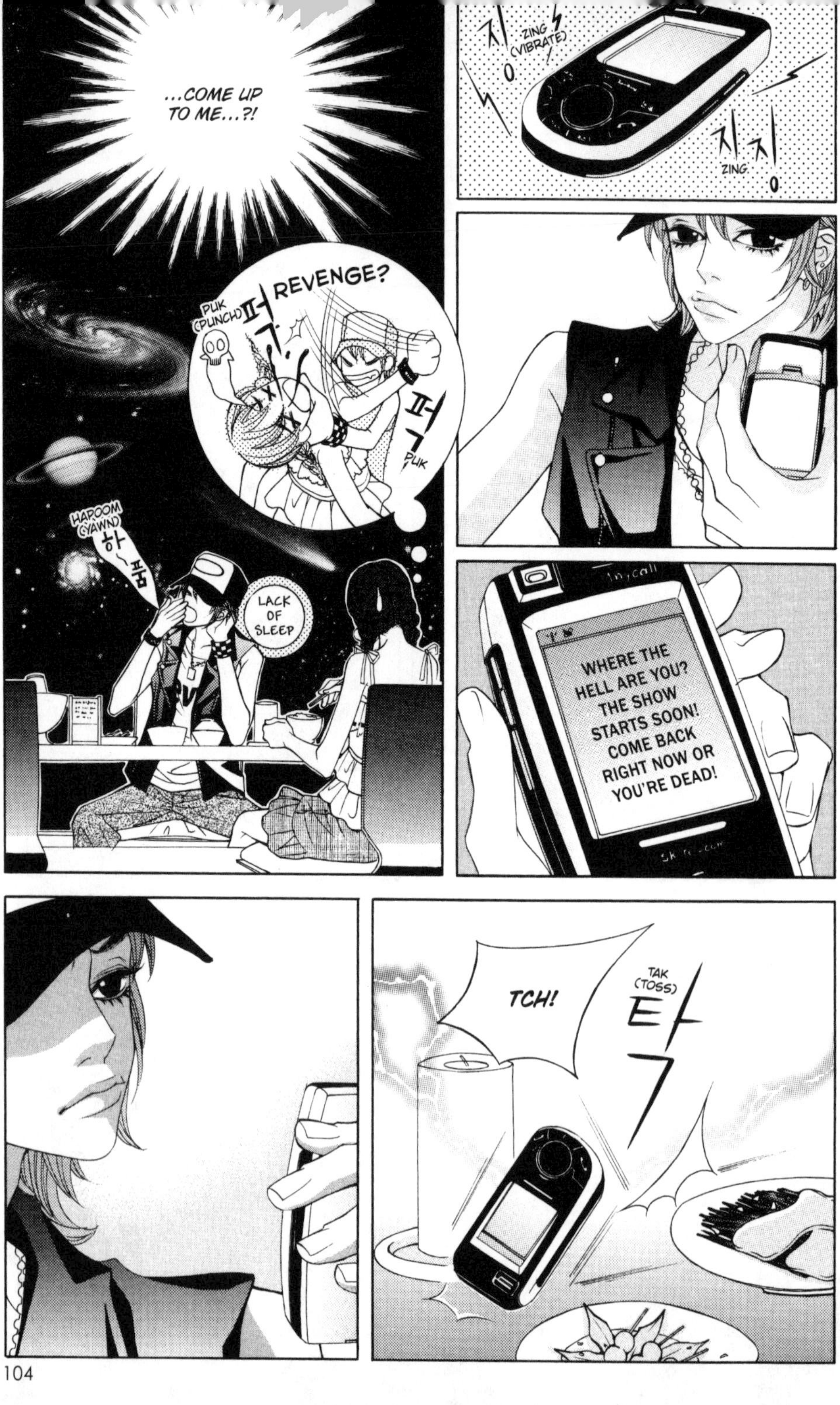
...COME UP TO ME...?!
REVENGE?
PUK (PUNCH)
퍽
퍽
PUK
HAPOOM (YAWN)
하~품
LACK OF SLEEP
ZING (VIBRATE)
ZING
WHERE THE HELL ARE YOU? THE SHOW STARTS SOON! COME BACK RIGHT NOW OR YOU'RE DEAD!
TCH!
TAK (TOSS)
탁

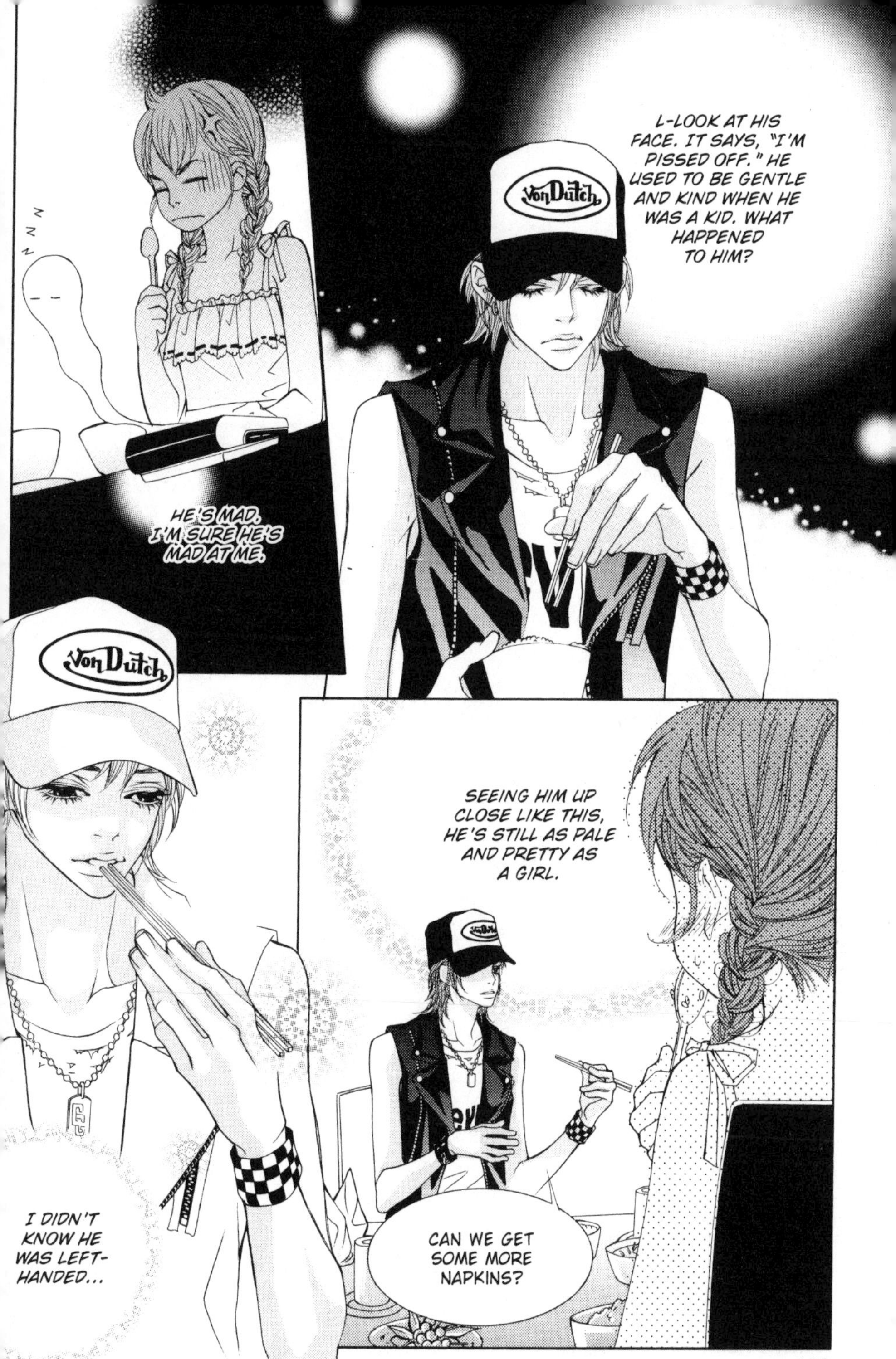
L-LOOK AT HIS FACE. IT SAYS, "I'M PISSED OFF." HE USED TO BE GENTLE AND KIND WHEN HE WAS A KID. WHAT HAPPENED TO HIM?
HE'S MAD. I'M SURE HE'S MAD AT ME.
SEEING HIM UP CLOSE LIKE THIS, HE'S STILL AS PALE AND PRETTY AS A GIRL.
I DIDN'T KNOW HE WAS LEFT-HANDED...
CAN WE GET SOME MORE NAPKINS?

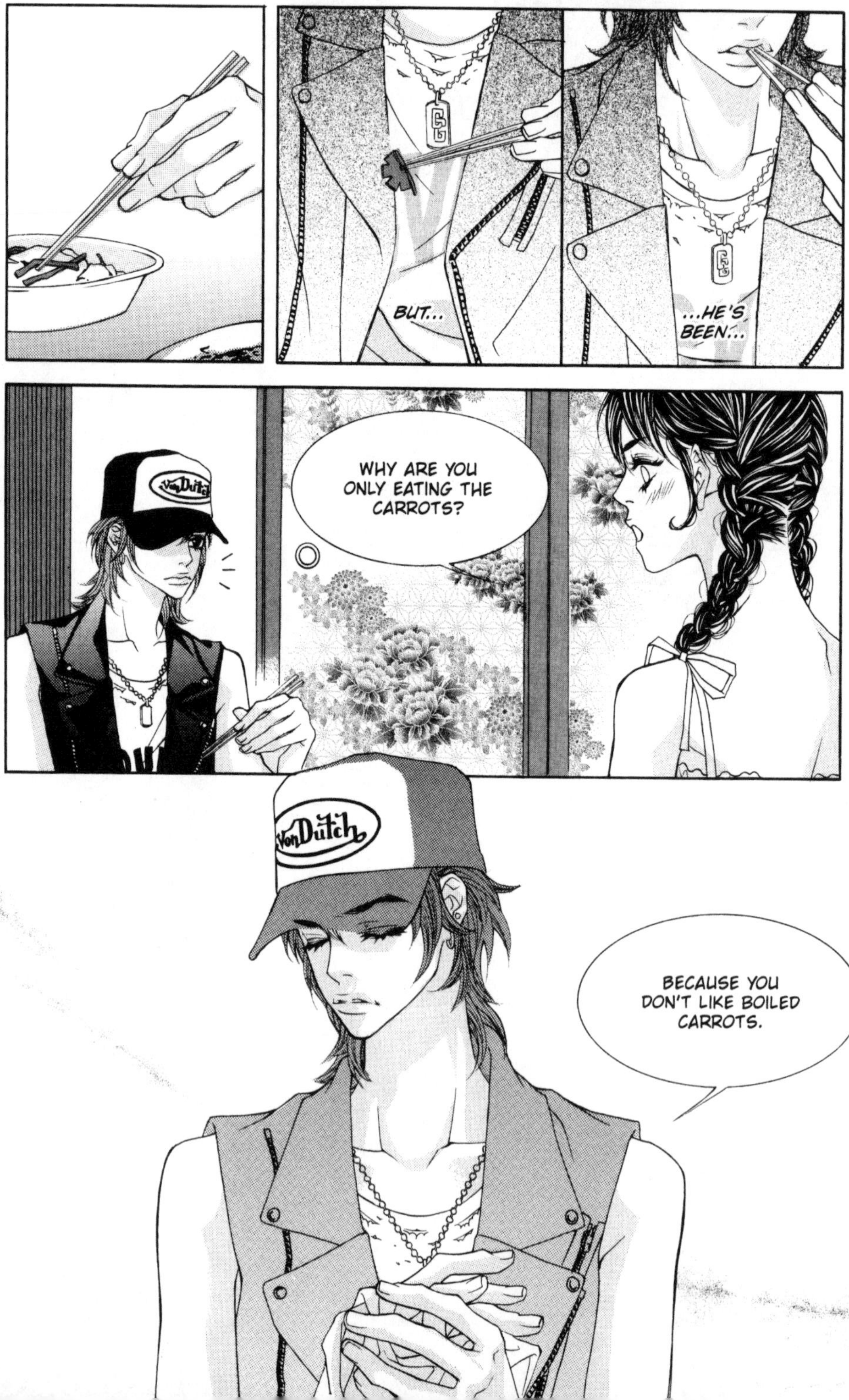
BUT...
...HE'S BEEN...
WHY ARE YOU ONLY EATING THE CARROTS?
BECAUSE YOU DON'T LIKE BOILED CARROTS.

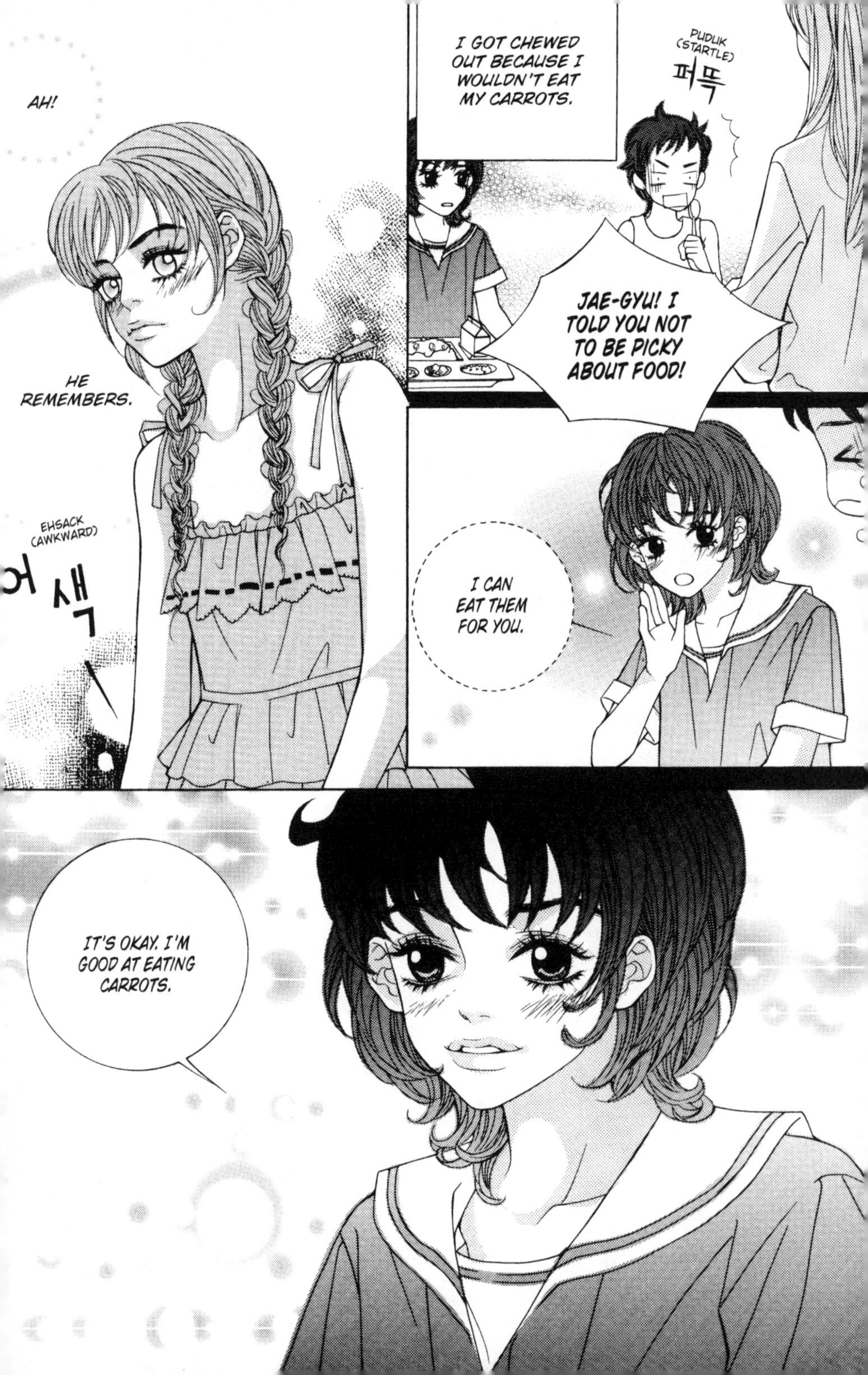
AH!
HE REMEMBERS.
EHSACK (AWKWARD)
어색
I GOT CHEWED OUT BECAUSE I WOULDN'T EAT MY CARROTS.
PUDUK (STARTLE)
퍼뜩
JAE-GYU! I TOLD YOU NOT TO BE PICKY ABOUT FOOD!
I CAN EAT THEM FOR YOU.
IT'S OKAY. I'M GOOD AT EATING CARROTS.

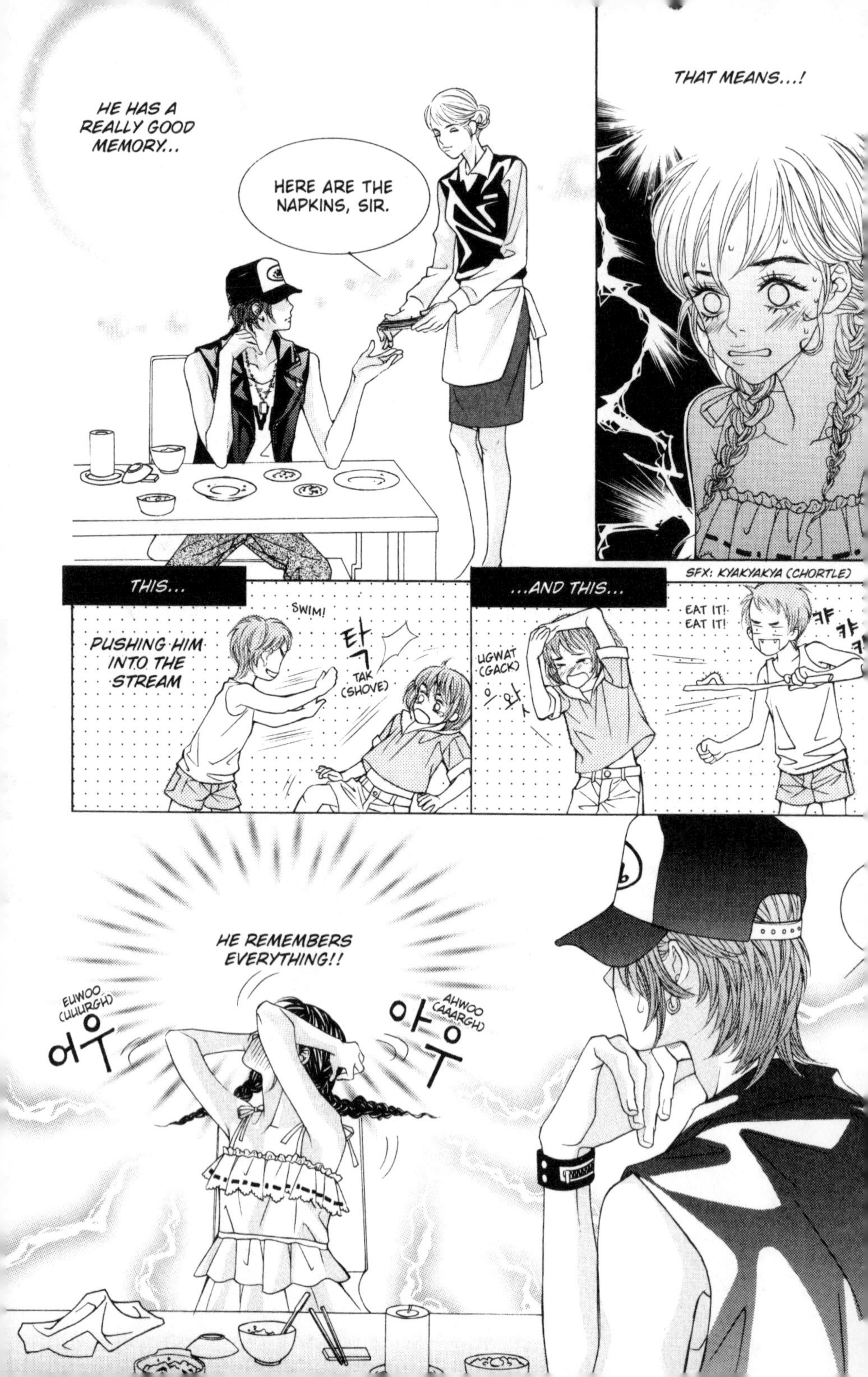
HE HAS A REALLY GOOD MEMORY...
HERE ARE THE NAPKINS, SIR.
THAT MEANS...!
THIS...
PUSHING HIM INTO THE STREAM
SWIM!
탁
TAK (SHOVE)
SFX: KYAKYAKYA (CHORTLE)
...AND THIS...
UGWAT (GACK)
EAT IT! EAT IT!
HE REMEMBERS EVERYTHING!!
EUWOO (UHHURGH)
어우
AHWOO (CAAARGH)
아우

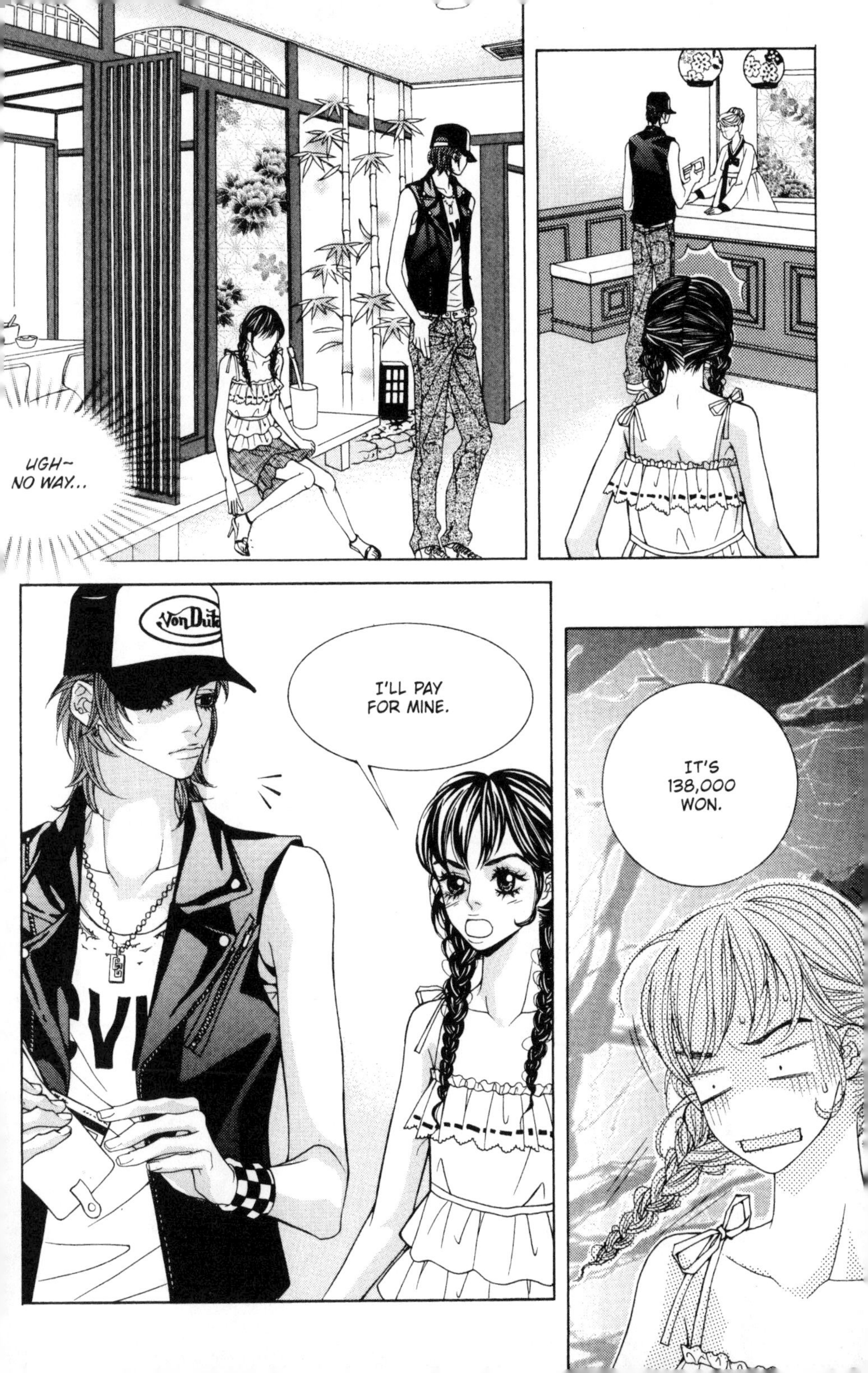
UGH~ NO WAY...
I'LL PAY FOR MINE.
IT'S 138,000 WON.

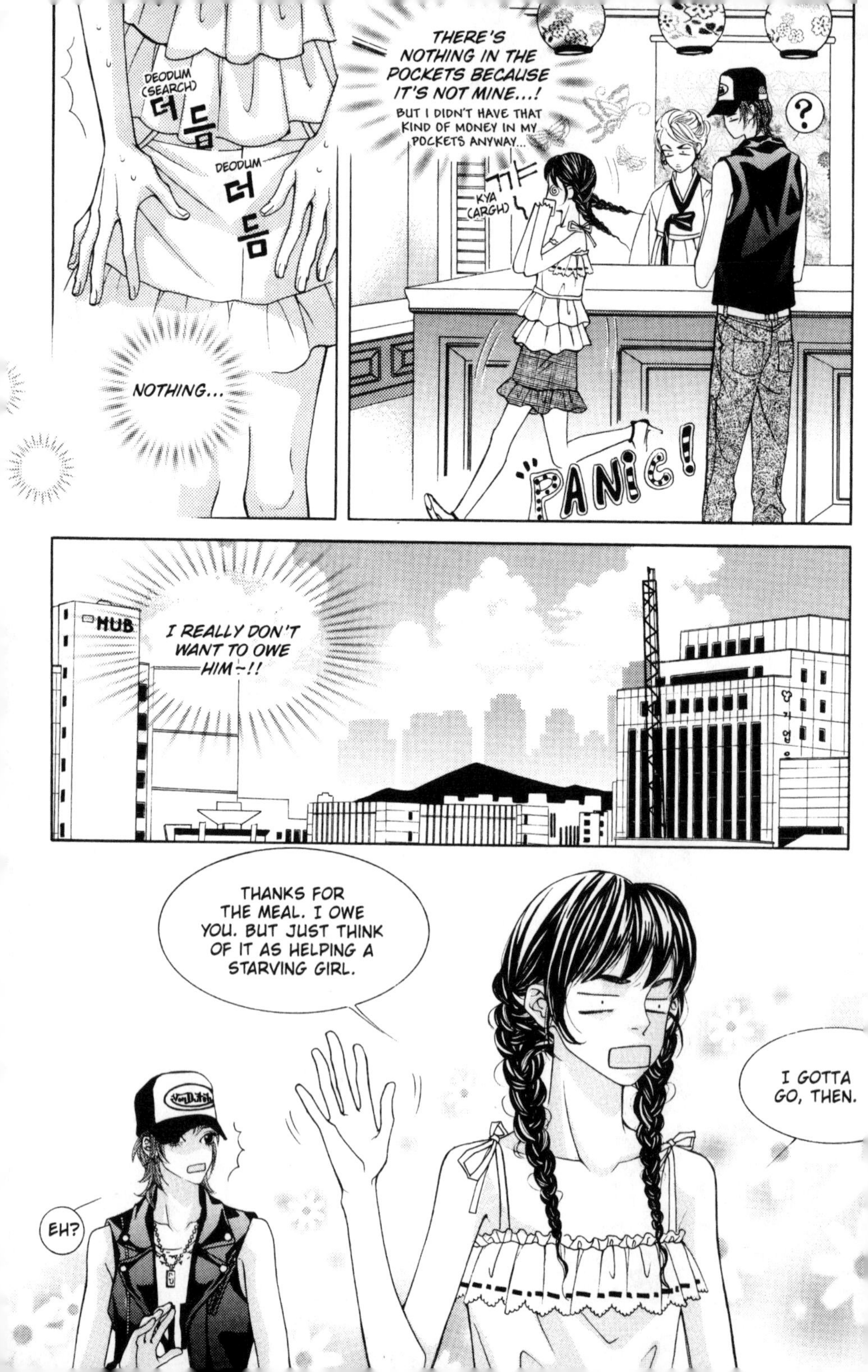
DEODUM (SEARCH)
더듬
DEODUM
더듬
NOTHING...
THERE'S NOTHING IN THE POCKETS BECAUSE IT'S NOT MINE...!
BUT I DIDN'T HAVE THAT KIND OF MONEY IN MY POCKETS ANYWAY...
KYA (ARGH)
?
PANIC!
HUB
I REALLY DON'T WANT TO OWE HIM~!!
THANKS FOR THE MEAL. I OWE YOU. BUT JUST THINK OF IT AS HELPING A STARVING GIRL.
I GOTTA GO, THEN.
EH?

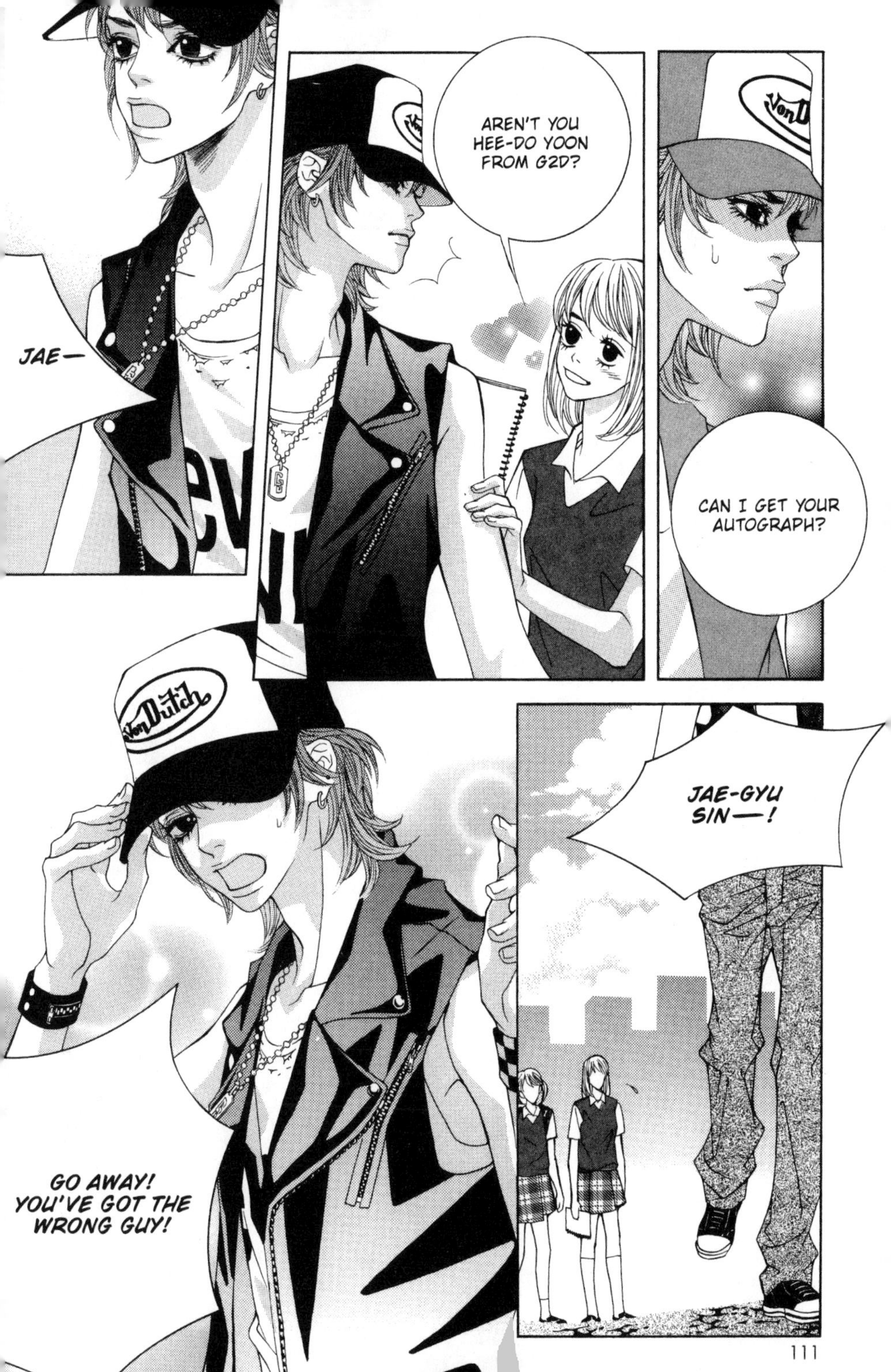
JAE—
AREN'T YOU HEE-DO YOON FROM G2D?
CAN I GET YOUR AUTOGRAPH?
GO AWAY! YOU'VE GOT THE WRONG GUY!
JAE-GYU SIN—!

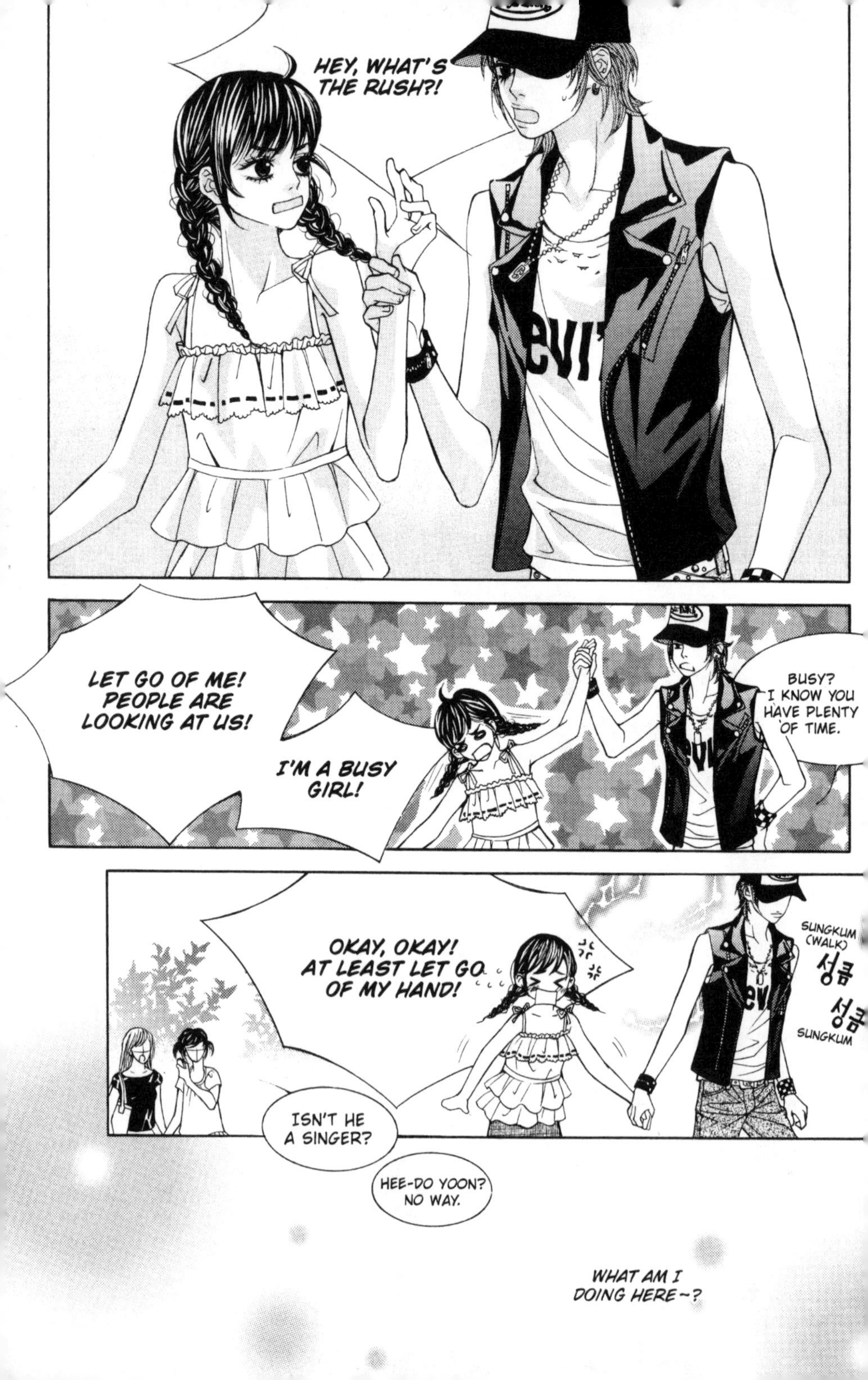
HEY, WHAT'S THE RUSH?!
LET GO OF ME! PEOPLE ARE LOOKING AT US!
I'M A BUSY GIRL!
BUSY? I KNOW YOU HAVE PLENTY OF TIME.
OKAY, OKAY! AT LEAST LET GO OF MY HAND!
SUNGKUM (WALK)
성큼
성큼
SUNGKUM
ISN'T HE A SINGER?
HEE-DO YOON? NO WAY.
WHAT AM I DOING HERE~?

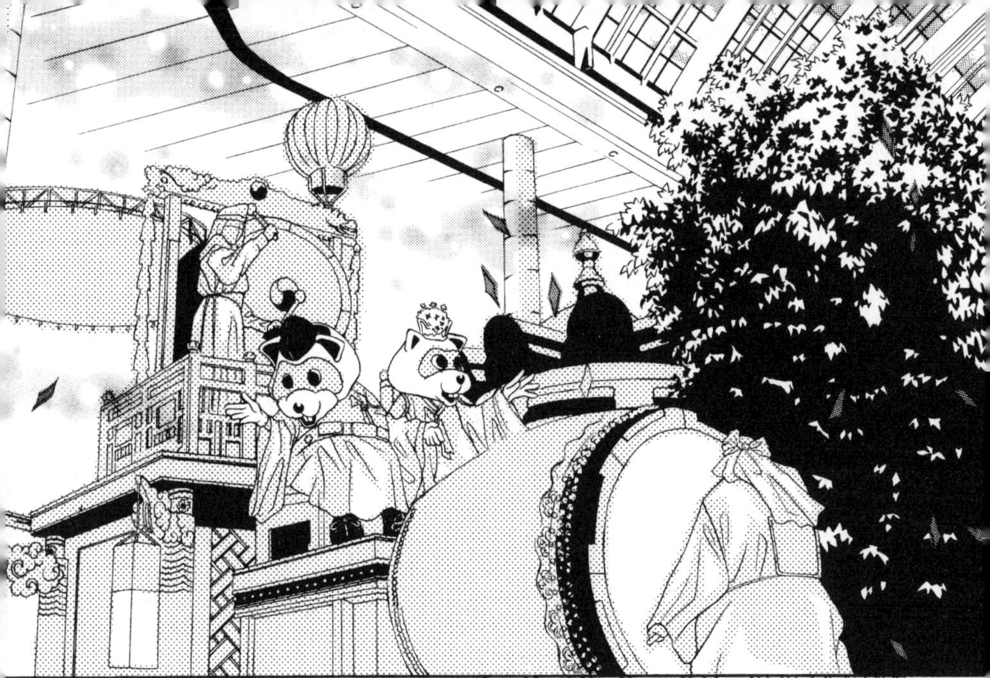
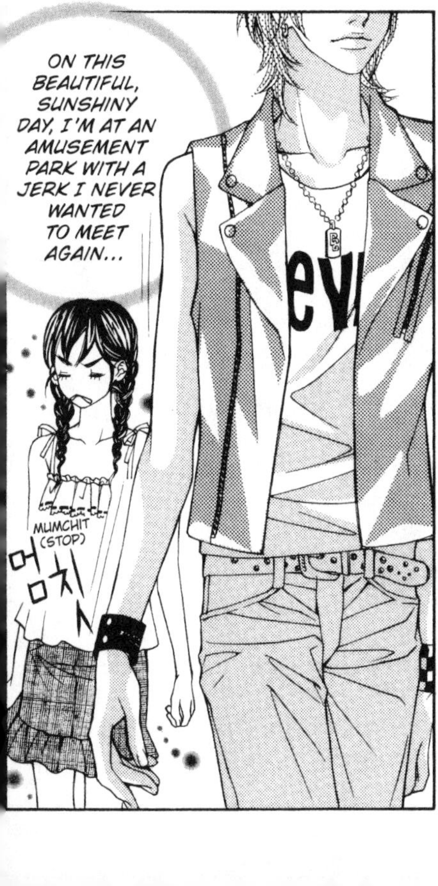
ON THIS BEAUTIFUL, SUNSHINY DAY, I'M AT AN AMUSEMENT PARK WITH A JERK I NEVER WANTED TO MEET AGAIN...
MUMCHIT (STOP)
멈칫
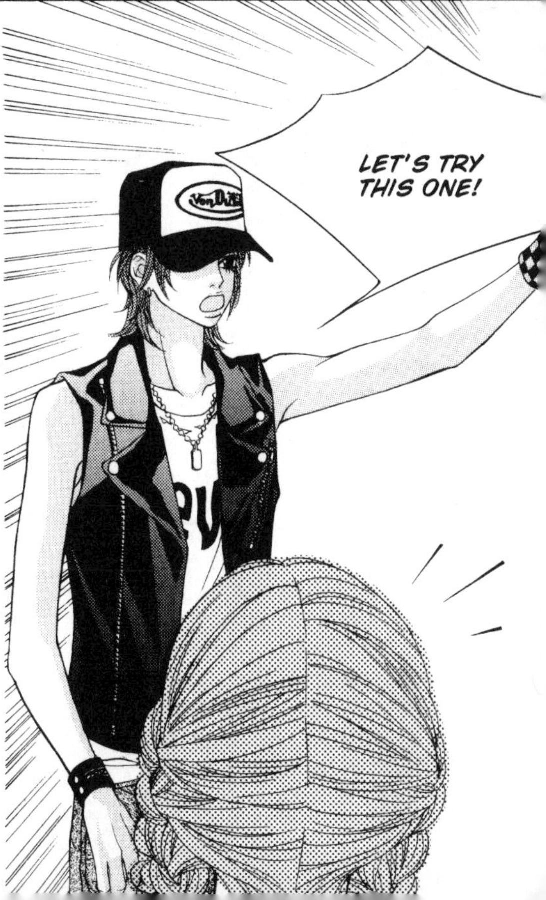
LET'S TRY THIS ONE!

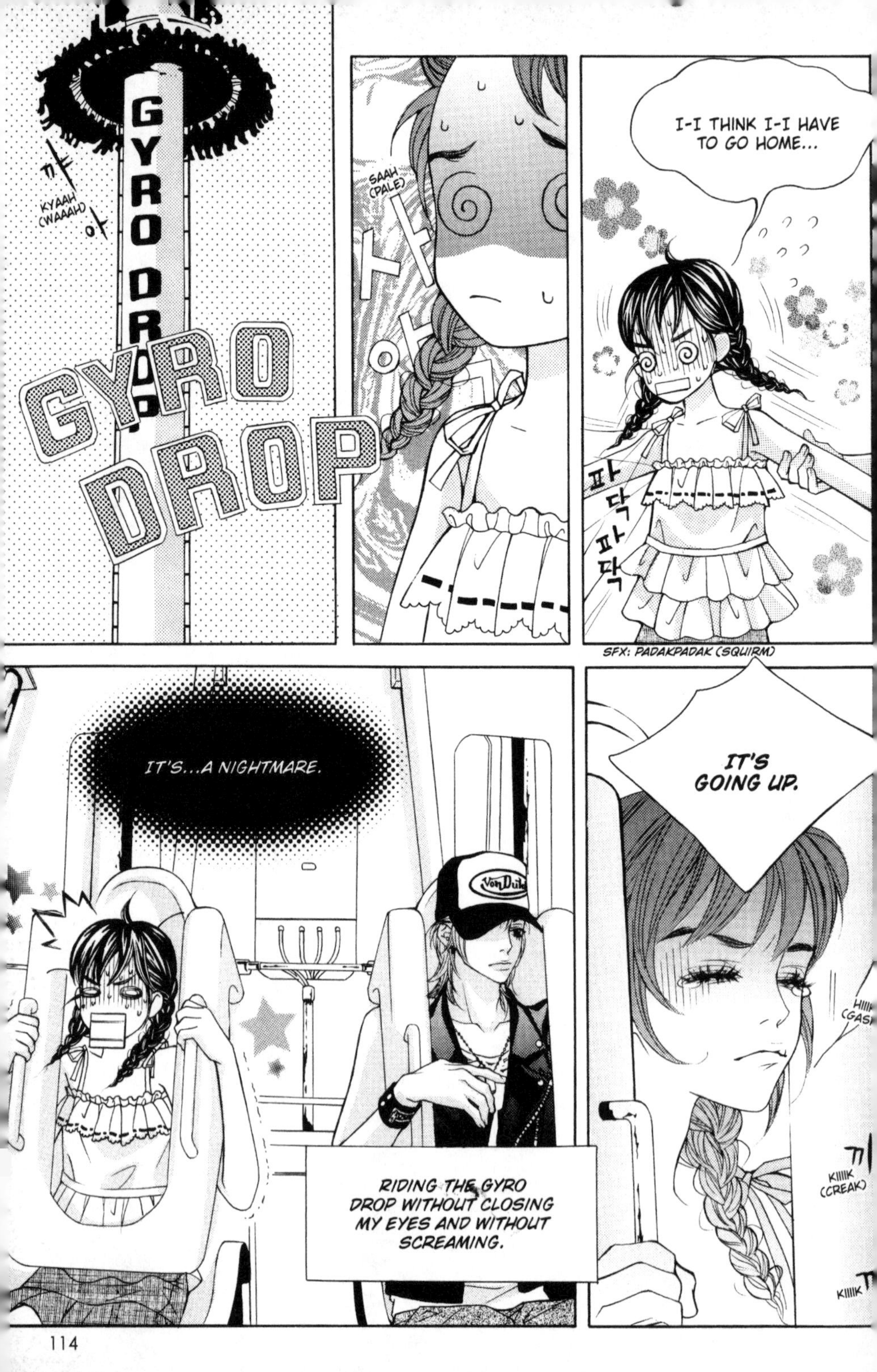
KYAAH (WAAAH)
GYRO DROP
GYRO DROP
SAAH (PALE)
I-I THINK I-I HAVE TO GO HOME...
파닥 파닥
SFX: PADAKPADAK (SQUIRM)
IT'S...A NIGHTMARE.
RIDING THE GYRO DROP WITHOUT CLOSING MY EYES AND WITHOUT SCREAMING.
IT'S GOING UP.
KIIIIK (CREAK)
KIIIK

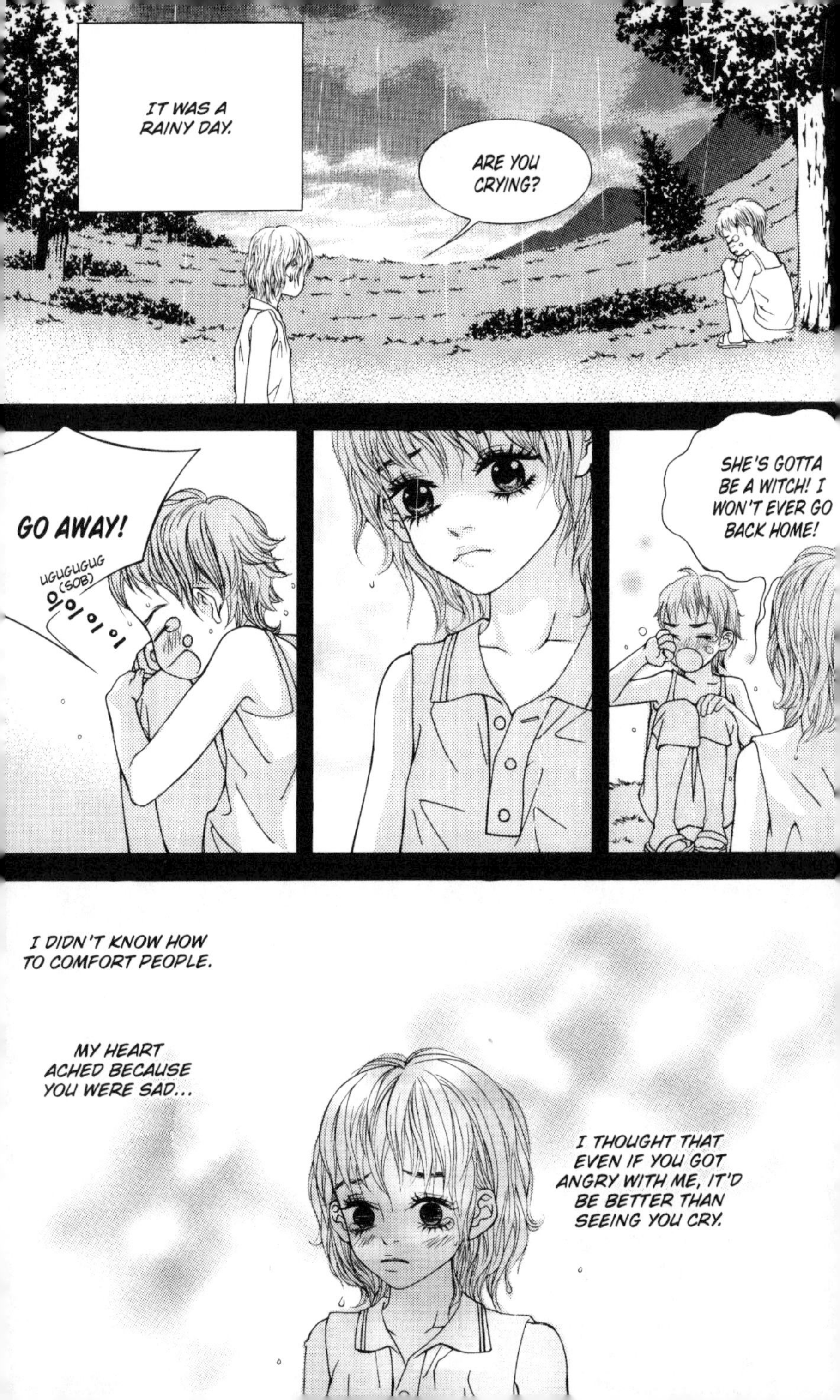
IT WAS A RAINY DAY.
ARE YOU CRYING?
GO AWAY!
UGUGUGUG (SOB)
으이이이
SHE'S GOTTA BE A WITCH! I WON'T EVER GO BACK HOME!
I DIDN'T KNOW HOW TO COMFORT PEOPLE.
MY HEART ACHED BECAUSE YOU WERE SAD...
I THOUGHT THAT EVEN IF YOU GOT ANGRY WITH ME, IT'D BE BETTER THAN SEEING YOU CRY.

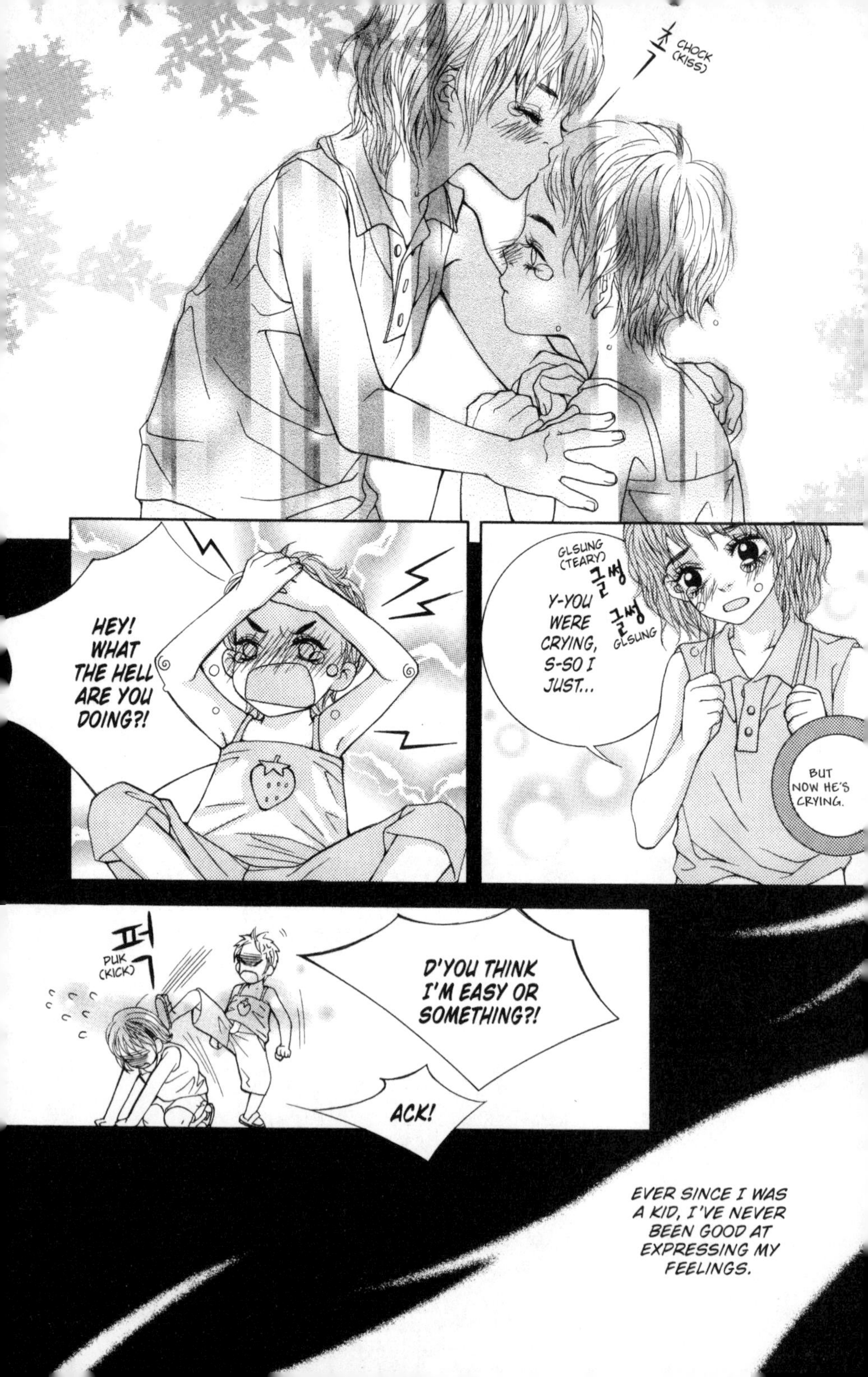

촉
CHOCK (KISS)
HEY! WHAT THE HELL ARE YOU DOING?!
글썽 글썽
GLSUNG (TEARY)
GLSUNG
Y-YOU WERE CRYING, S-SO I JUST...
BUT NOW HE'S CRYING.
D'YOU THINK I'M EASY OR SOMETHING?!
퍽
PUK (KICK)
ACK!
EVER SINCE I WAS A KID, I'VE NEVER BEEN GOOD AT EXPRESSING MY FEELINGS.

IF ONLY THERE WERE SOME WAY TO COMMUNICATE HOW I FEEL DIRECTLY, WITHOUT SPEAKING...

우웨에에에

WOOWEEHHHK (BLEEARGH)

YOU ASKED FOR IT!

HEY! HEE-DO YOON!

?

WHO TOLD YOU?!

YOU WEREN'T THERE BY CHANCE, WERE YOU? YOU PLANNED ALL THIS TO GET YOUR REVENGE ON ME, DIDN'T YOU?!

YES, BUT I... CAN'T TELL YOU WHO TOLD ME. FOR SECURITY REASONS.

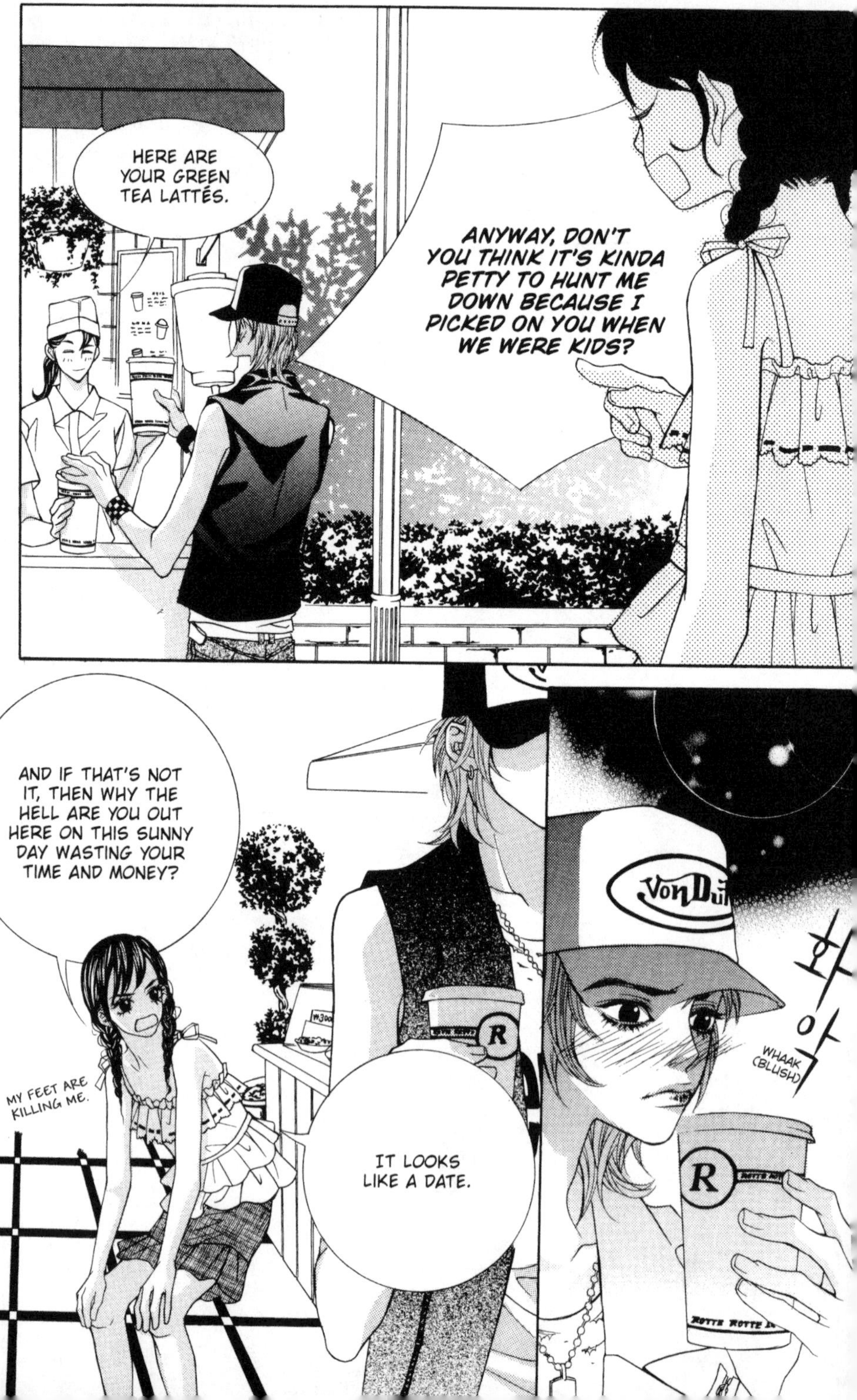
HERE ARE YOUR GREEN TEA LATTÉS.
ANYWAY, DON'T YOU THINK IT'S KINDA PETTY TO HUNT ME DOWN BECAUSE I PICKED ON YOU WHEN WE WERE KIDS?
AND IF THAT'S NOT IT, THEN WHY THE HELL ARE YOU OUT HERE ON THIS SUNNY DAY WASTING YOUR TIME AND MONEY?
MY FEET ARE KILLING ME.
IT LOOKS LIKE A DATE.
WHAAK (BLUSH)

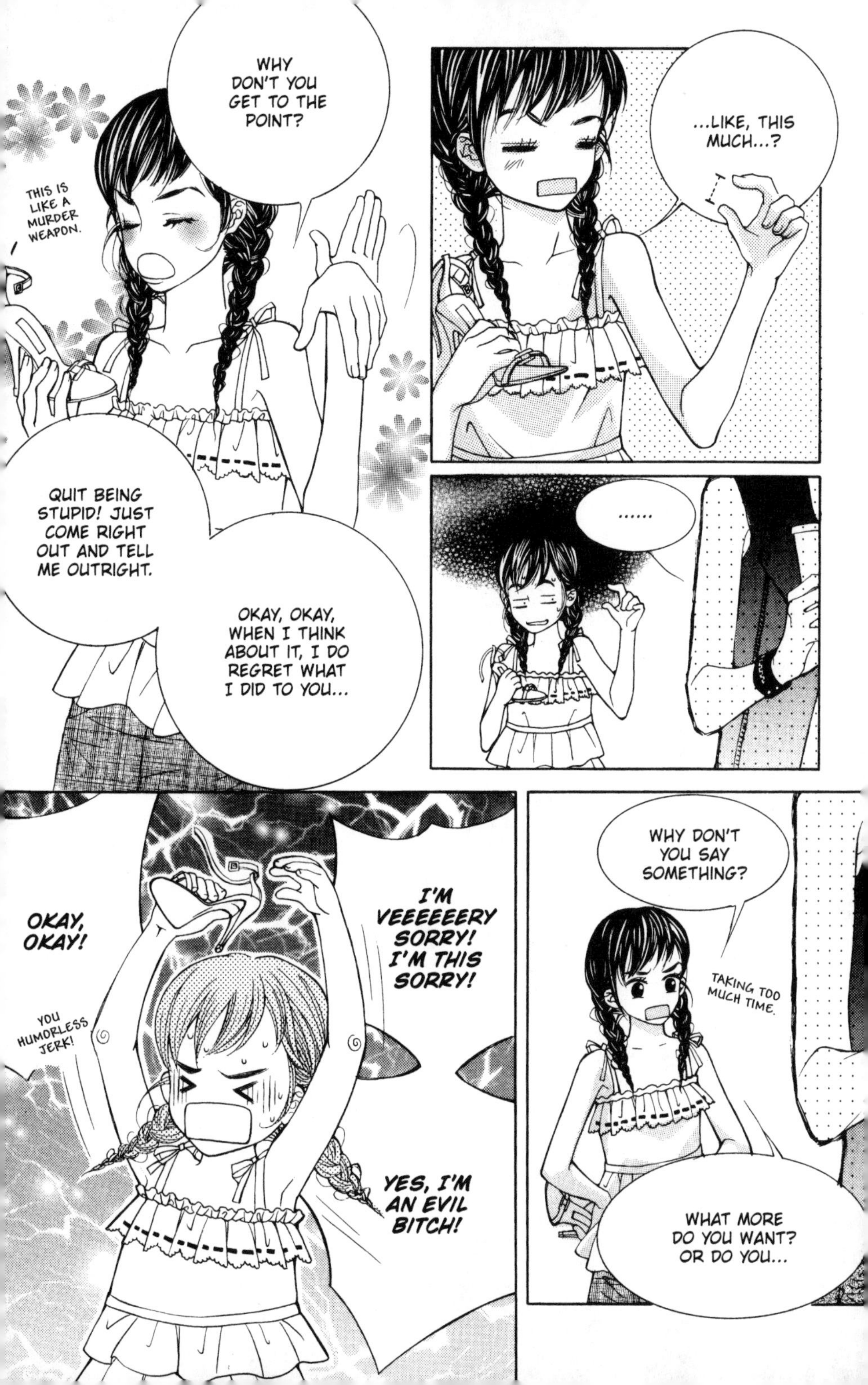
WHY DON'T YOU GET TO THE POINT?
THIS IS LIKE A MURDER WEAPON.
QUIT BEING STUPID! JUST COME RIGHT OUT AND TELL ME OUTRIGHT.
OKAY, OKAY, WHEN I THINK ABOUT IT, I DO REGRET WHAT I DID TO YOU...
...LIKE, THIS MUCH...?
......
OKAY, OKAY!
YOU HUMORLESS JERK!
I'M VEEEEEERY SORRY! I'M THIS SORRY!
YES, I'M AN EVIL BITCH!
WHY DON'T YOU SAY SOMETHING?
TAKING TOO MUCH TIME.
WHAT MORE DO YOU WANT? OR DO YOU...

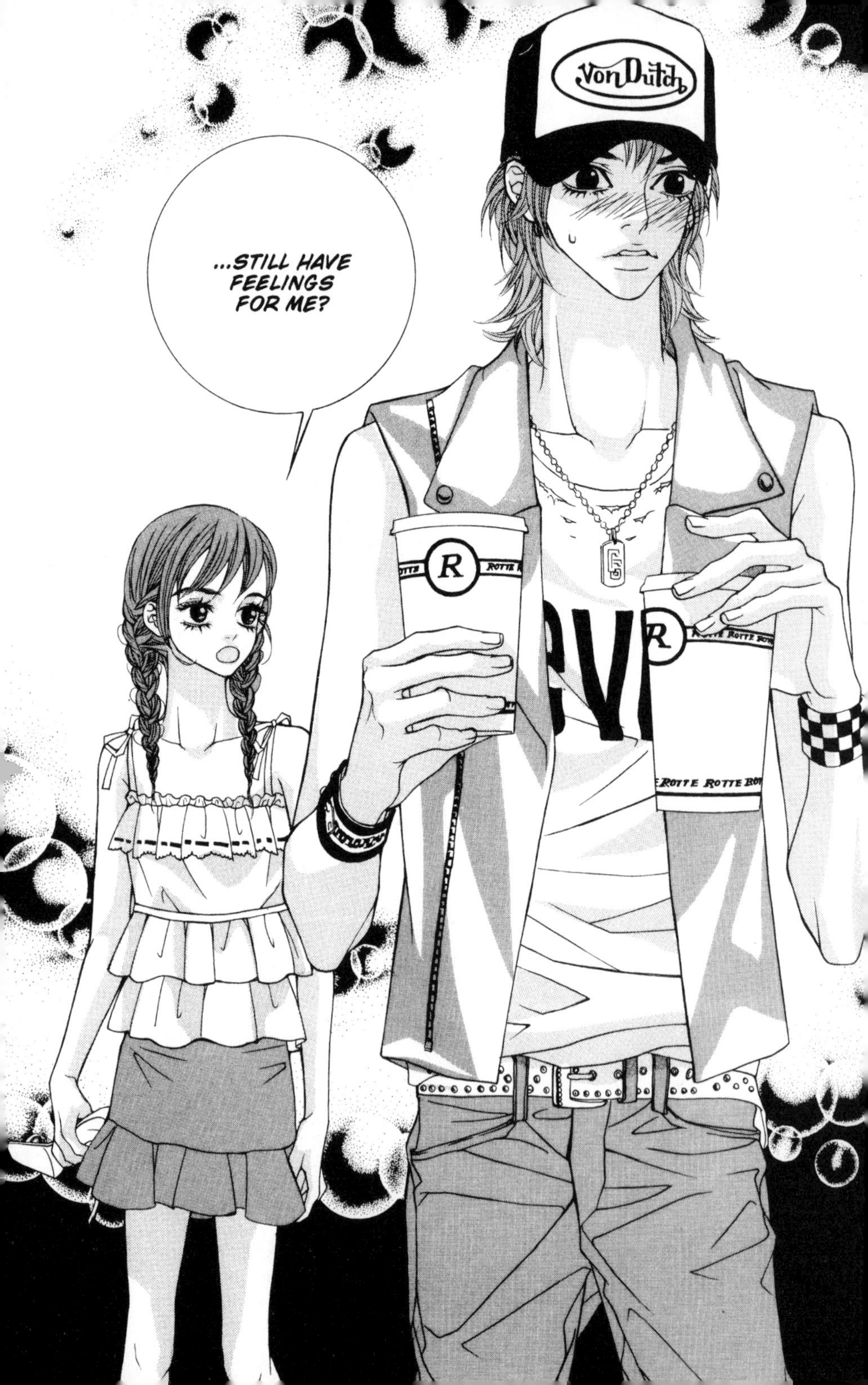
...STILL HAVE FEELINGS FOR ME?
Von Dutch

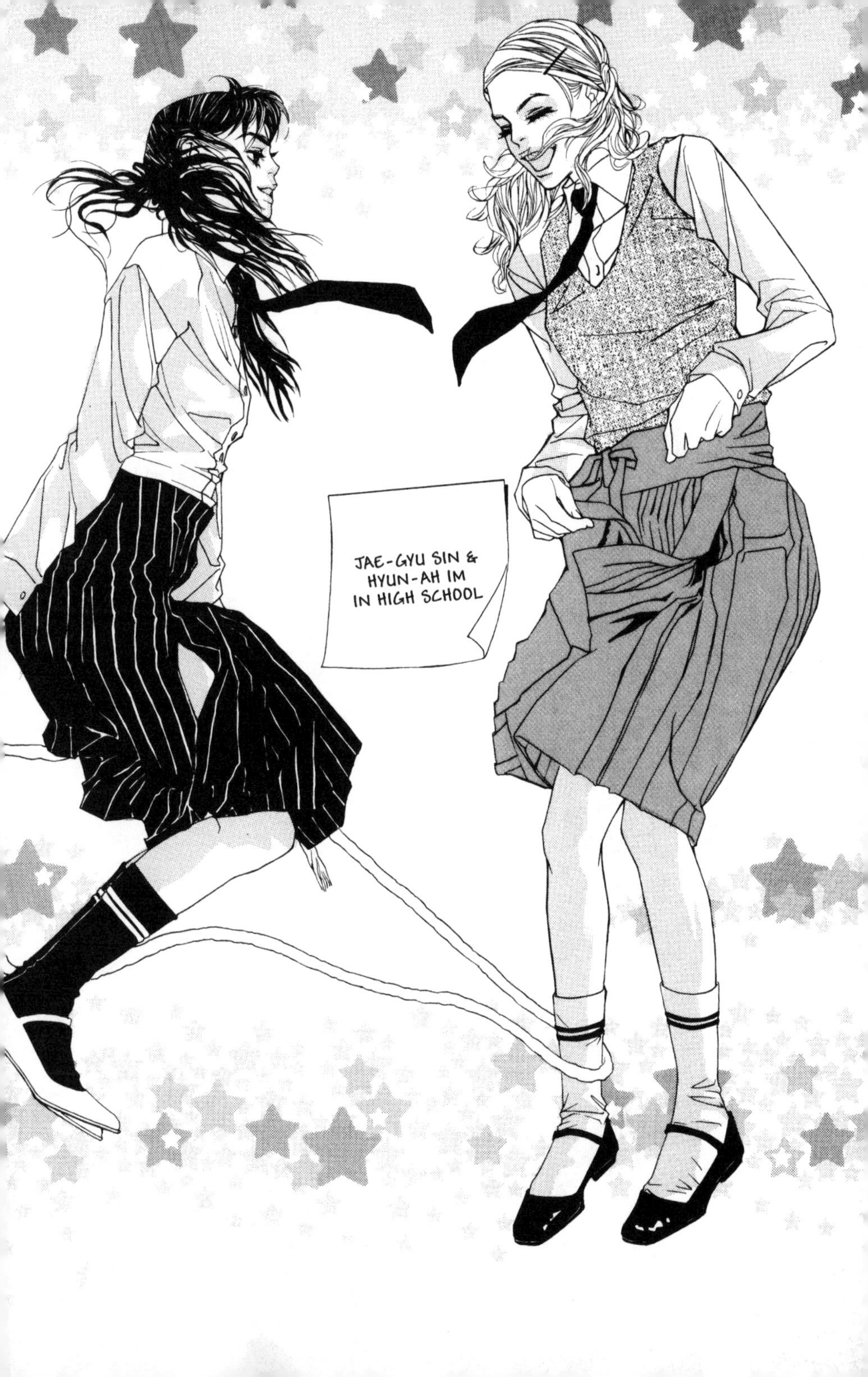
JAE-GYU SIN &
HYUN-AH IM
IN HIGH SCHOOL

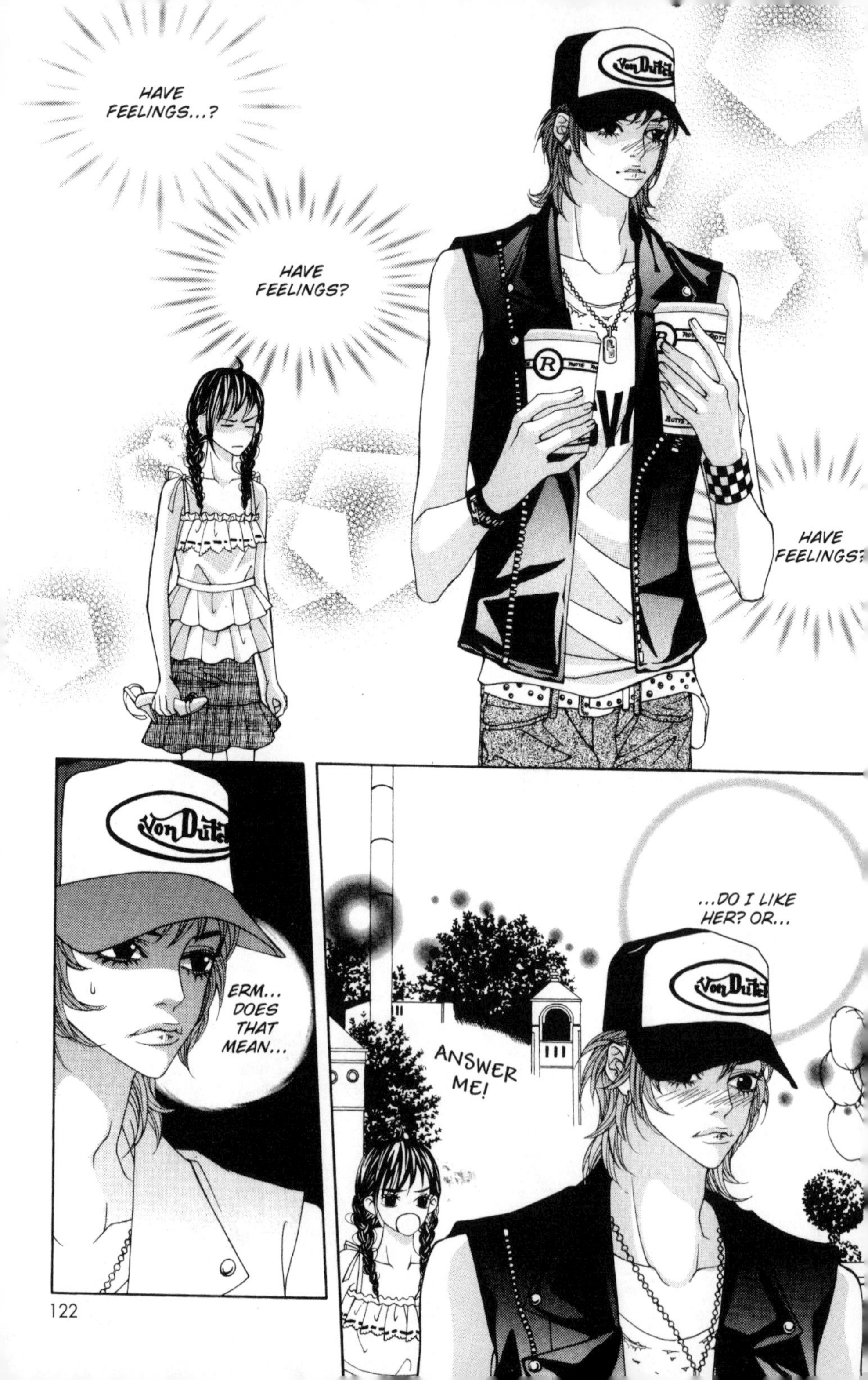
HAVE FEELINGS...?
HAVE FEELINGS?
HAVE FEELINGS?
ERM... DOES THAT MEAN...
...DO I LIKE HER? OR...
ANSWER ME!

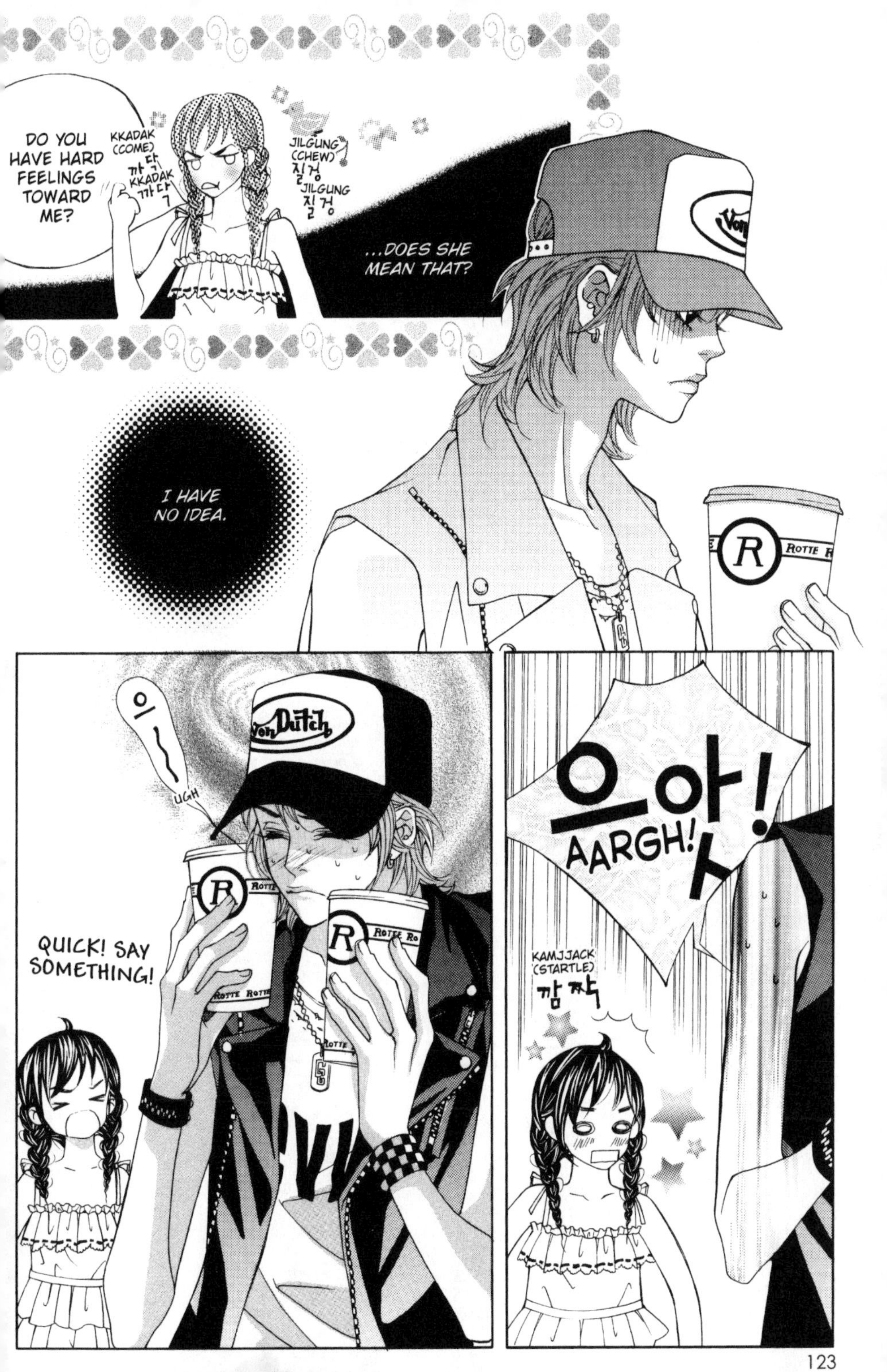
DO YOU HAVE HARD FEELINGS TOWARD ME?
KKADAK (COME)
까닥
KKADAK
까닥
JILGUNG (CHEW)
질겅
JILGUNG
질겅
...DOES SHE MEAN THAT?
I HAVE NO IDEA.
으~
UGH
Von Dutch
ROTTE
QUICK! SAY SOMETHING!
으악!
AARGH!
KAMJJACK (STARTLE)
깜짝

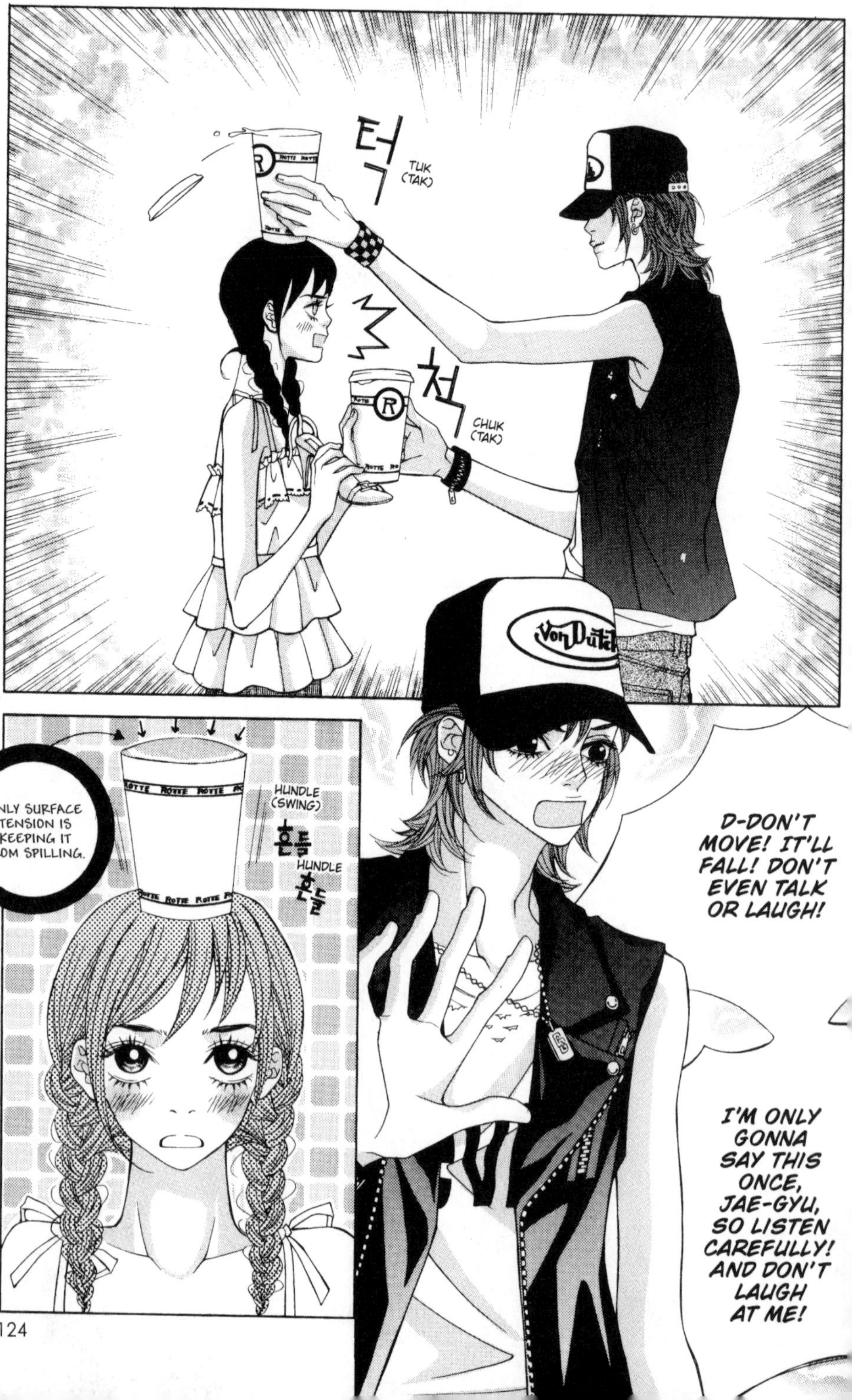

턱
TUK (TAK)
척
CHUK (TAK)
ONLY SURFACE TENSION IS KEEPING IT FROM SPILLING.
HUNDLE (SWING)
흔들
HUNDLE
흔들
D-DON'T MOVE! IT'LL FALL! DON'T EVEN TALK OR LAUGH!
I'M ONLY GONNA SAY THIS ONCE, JAE-GYU, SO LISTEN CAREFULLY! AND DON'T LAUGH AT ME!

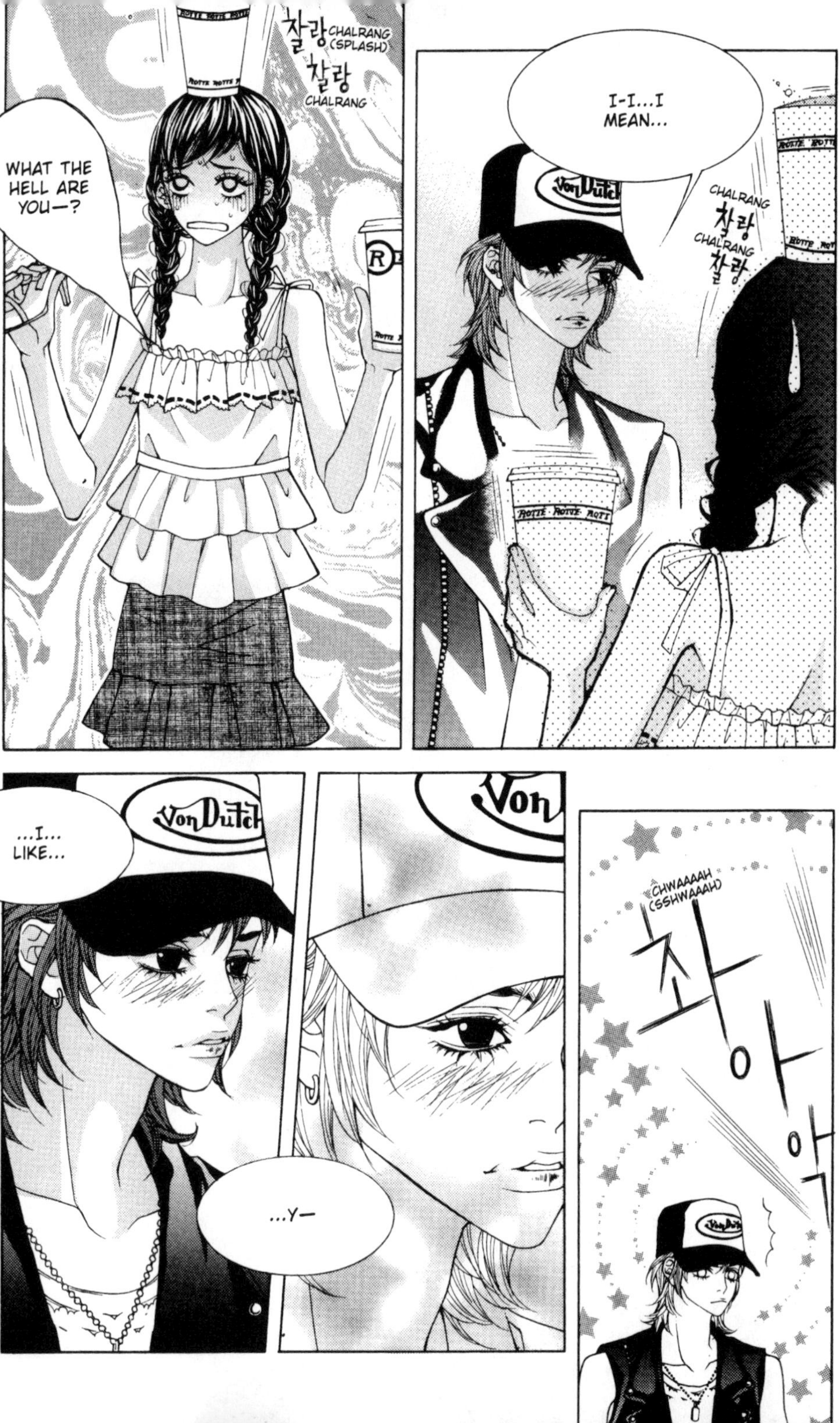
찰랑 CHALRANG (SPLASH)
찰랑 CHALRANG
WHAT THE HELL ARE YOU—?
I-I...I MEAN...
CHALRANG 찰랑
CHALRANG 찰랑
...I... LIKE...
...Y—
CHWAAAAH (SSHWAAAH)
촤아아악

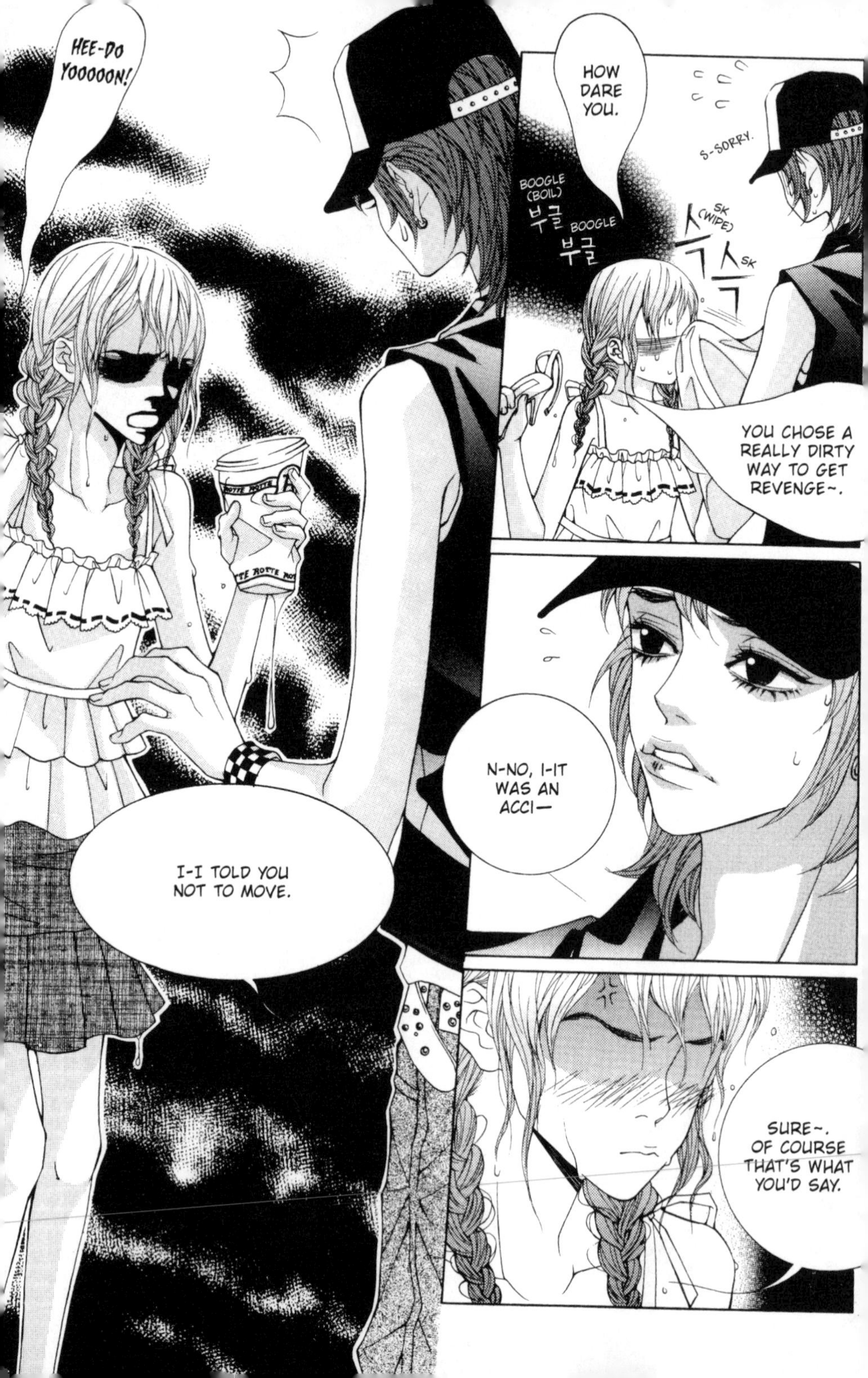
HEE-DO YOOOOON!
I-I TOLD YOU NOT TO MOVE.
HOW DARE YOU.
BOOGLE (BOIL) 부글 BOOGLE 부글
S-SORRY.
SK (WIPE) 슥 SK 슥
YOU CHOSE A REALLY DIRTY WAY TO GET REVENGE~.
N-NO, I-IT WAS AN ACCI—
SURE~. OF COURSE THAT'S WHAT YOU'D SAY.

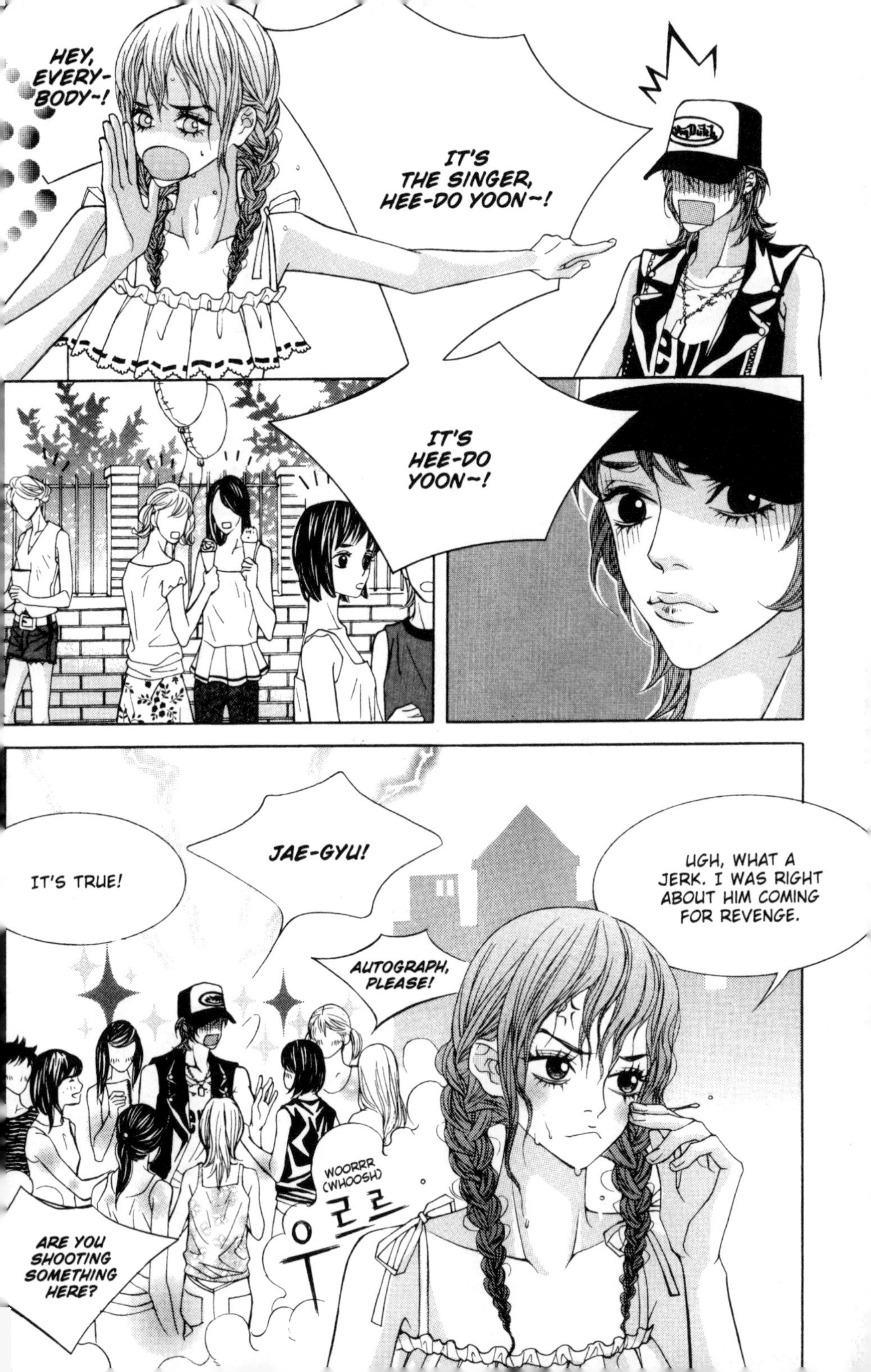
HEY, EVERY-BODY~!
IT'S THE SINGER, HEE-DO YOON~!
IT'S HEE-DO YOON~!
IT'S TRUE!
JAE-GYU!
AUTOGRAPH, PLEASE!
UGH, WHAT A JERK. I WAS RIGHT ABOUT HIM COMING FOR REVENGE.
WOORRR (WHOOSH)
우르르
ARE YOU SHOOTING SOMETHING HERE?

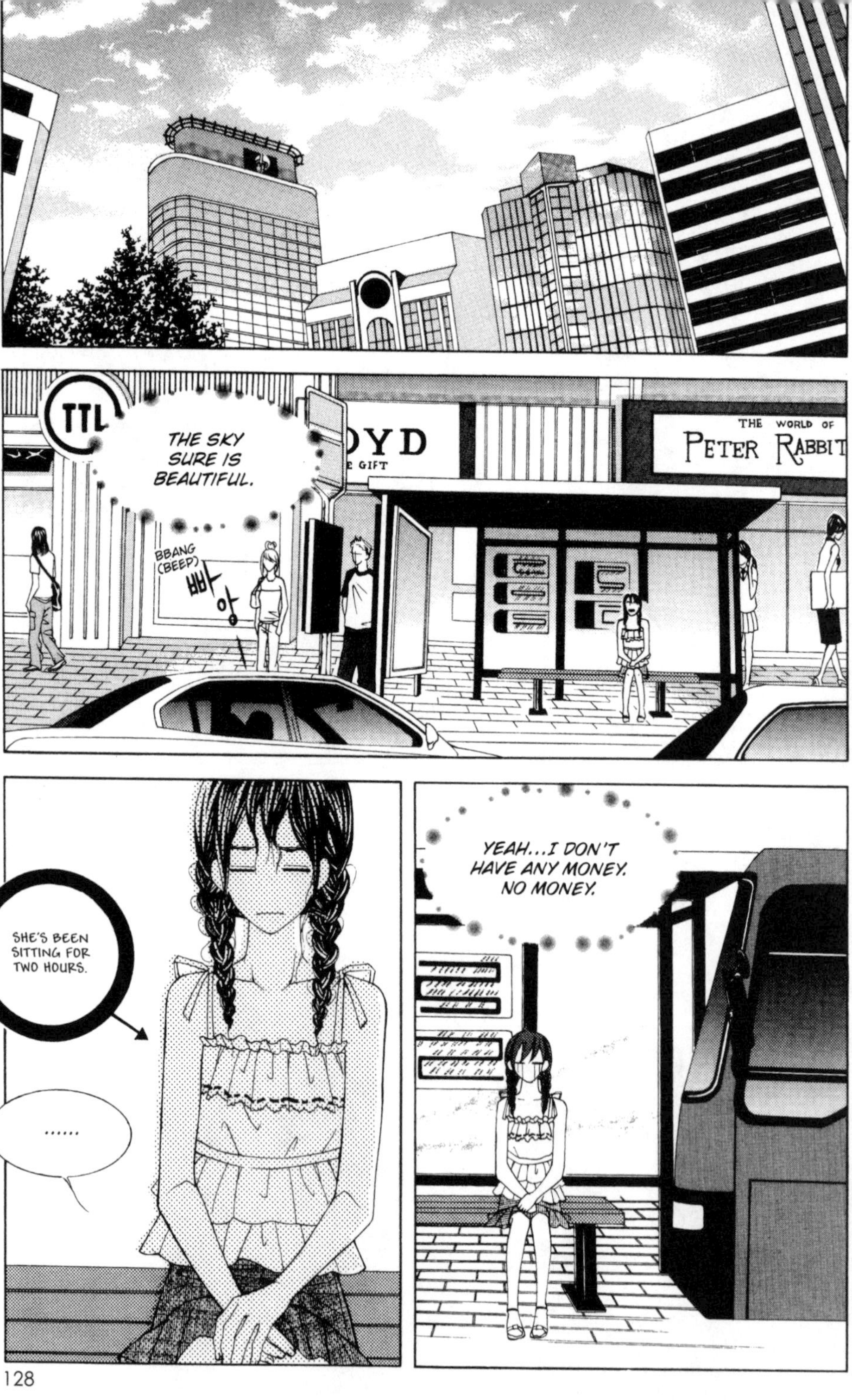
TTL
THE SKY SURE IS BEAUTIFUL.
OYD
E GIFT
THE WORLD OF PETER RABBIT
BBANG (BEEP)
SHE'S BEEN SITTING FOR TWO HOURS.
......
YEAH...I DON'T HAVE ANY MONEY. NO MONEY.

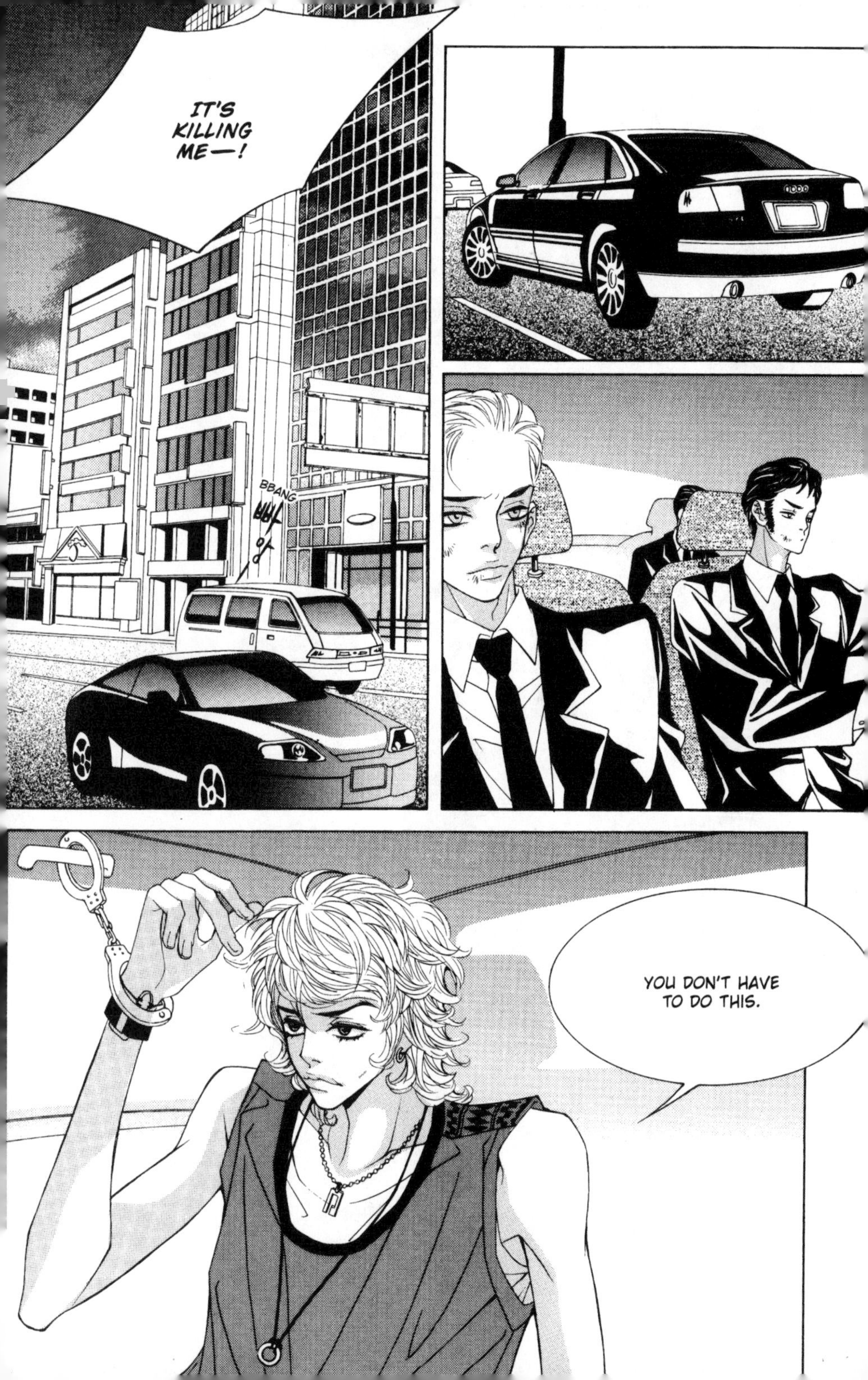
IT'S KILLING ME—!
BBANG
YOU DON'T HAVE TO DO THIS.

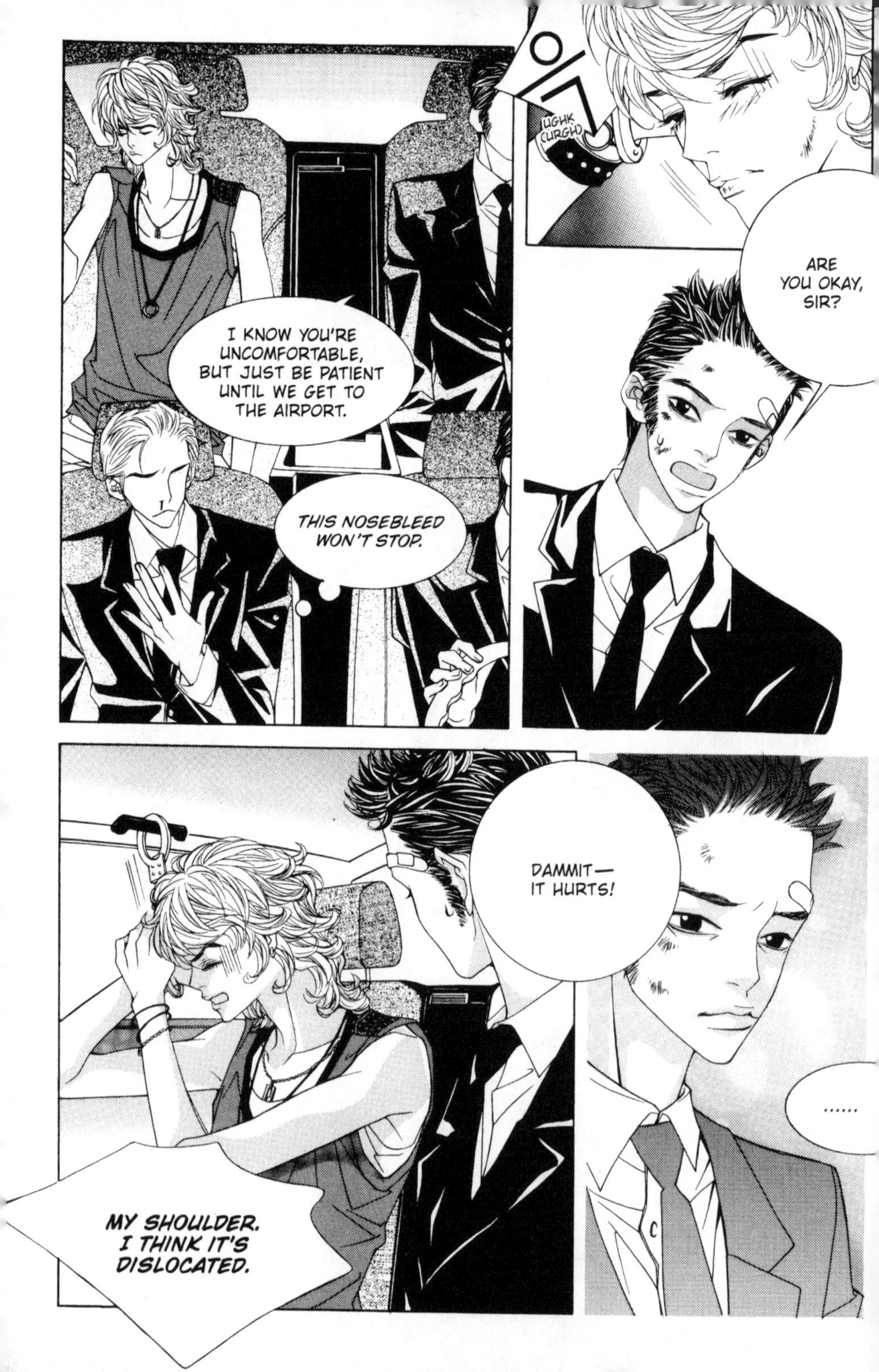
I KNOW YOU'RE UNCOMFORTABLE, BUT JUST BE PATIENT UNTIL WE GET TO THE AIRPORT.
THIS NOSEBLEED WON'T STOP.
UGHK (URGH)
ARE YOU OKAY, SIR?
DAMMIT— IT HURTS!
MY SHOULDER. I THINK IT'S DISLOCATED.
......

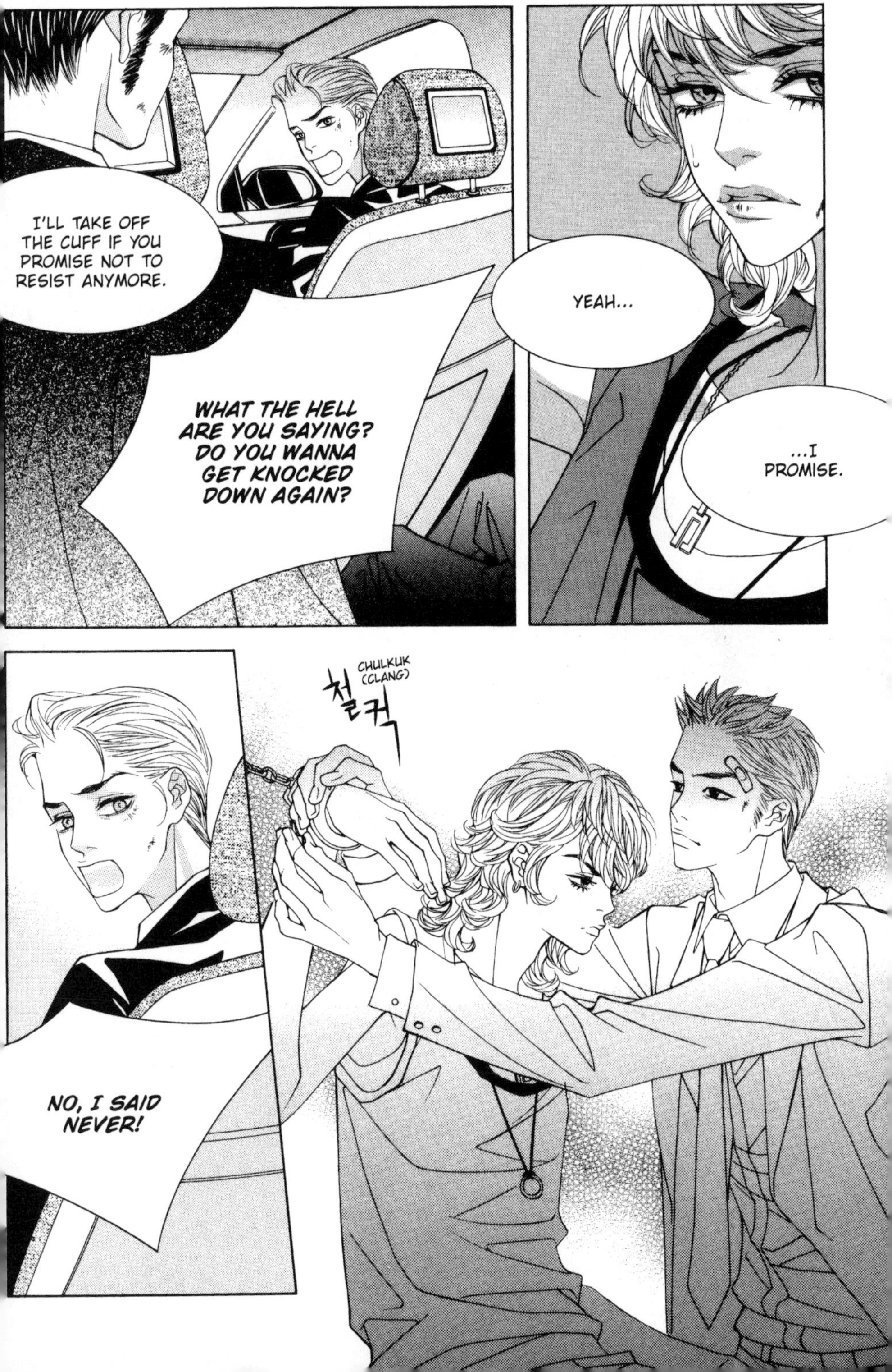
I'LL TAKE OFF THE CUFF IF YOU PROMISE NOT TO RESIST ANYMORE.
WHAT THE HELL ARE YOU SAYING? DO YOU WANNA GET KNOCKED DOWN AGAIN?
YEAH...
...I PROMISE.
NO, I SAID NEVER!
철컥
CHULKUK (CLANG)

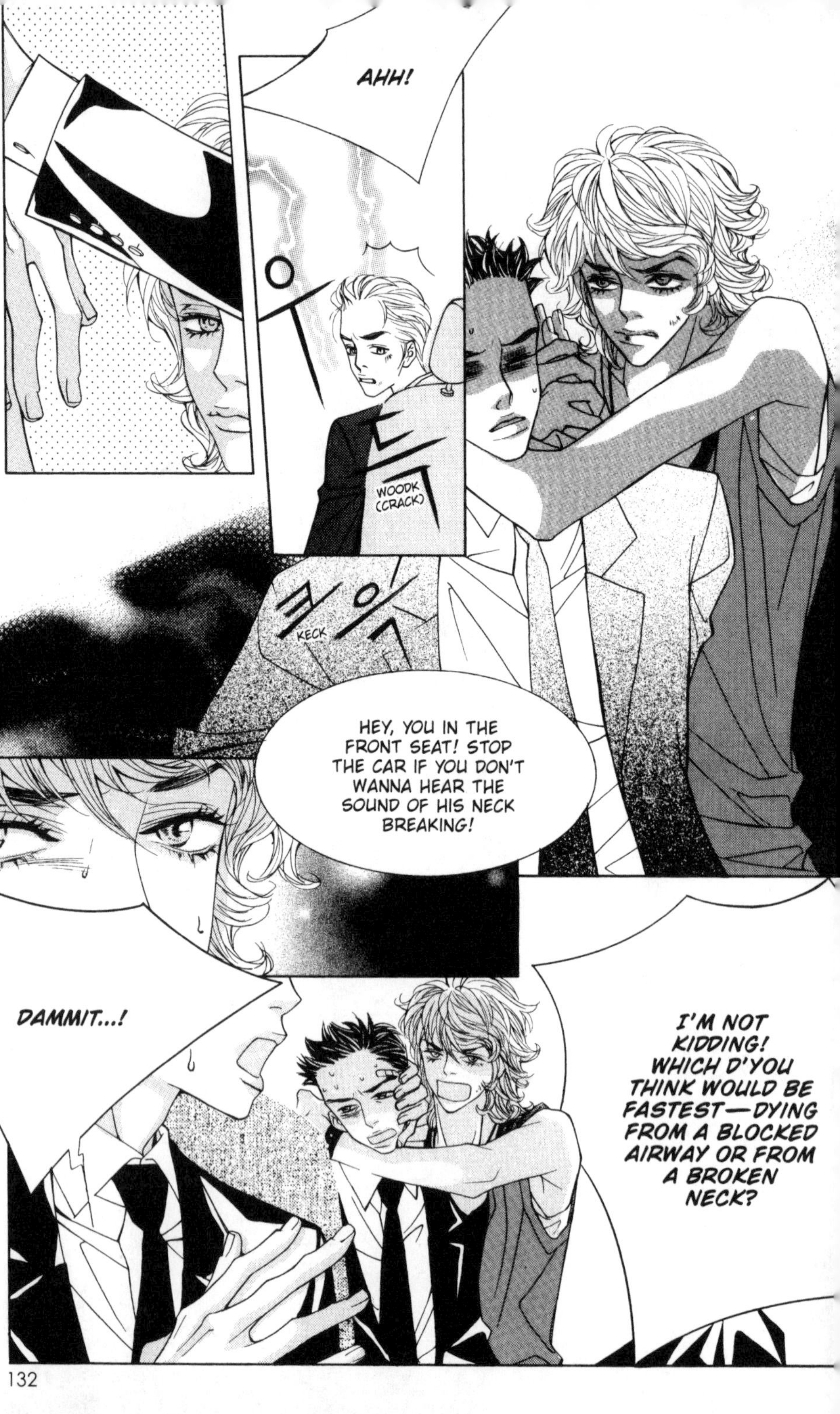
AHH!
WOODK (CRACK)
KECK
HEY, YOU IN THE FRONT SEAT! STOP THE CAR IF YOU DON'T WANNA HEAR THE SOUND OF HIS NECK BREAKING!
DAMMIT...!
I'M NOT KIDDING! WHICH D'YOU THINK WOULD BE FASTEST—DYING FROM A BLOCKED AIRWAY OR FROM A BROKEN NECK?

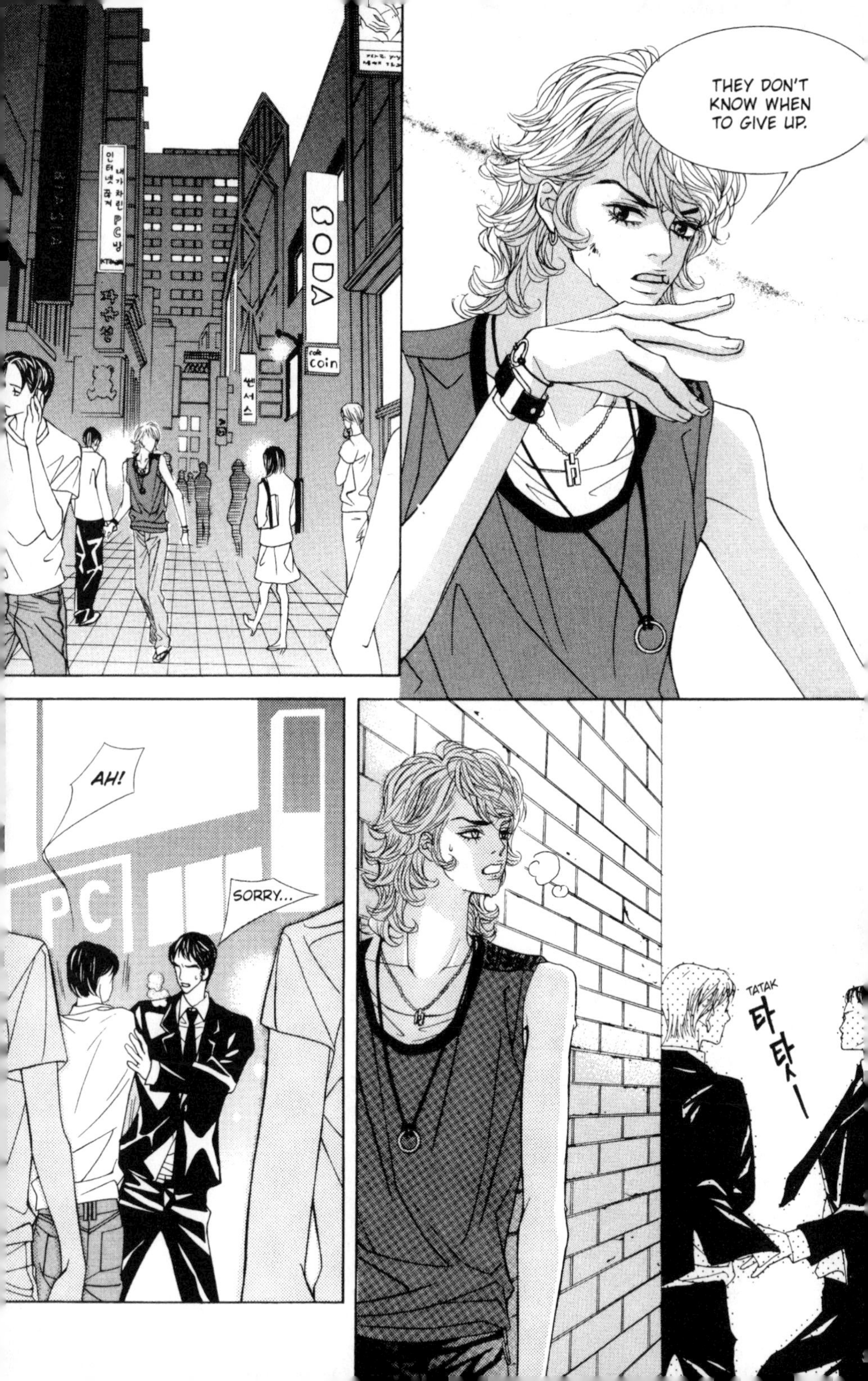
SODA
coin
센서스
THEY DON'T KNOW WHEN TO GIVE UP.
AH!
PC
SORRY...
TATAK
타탁

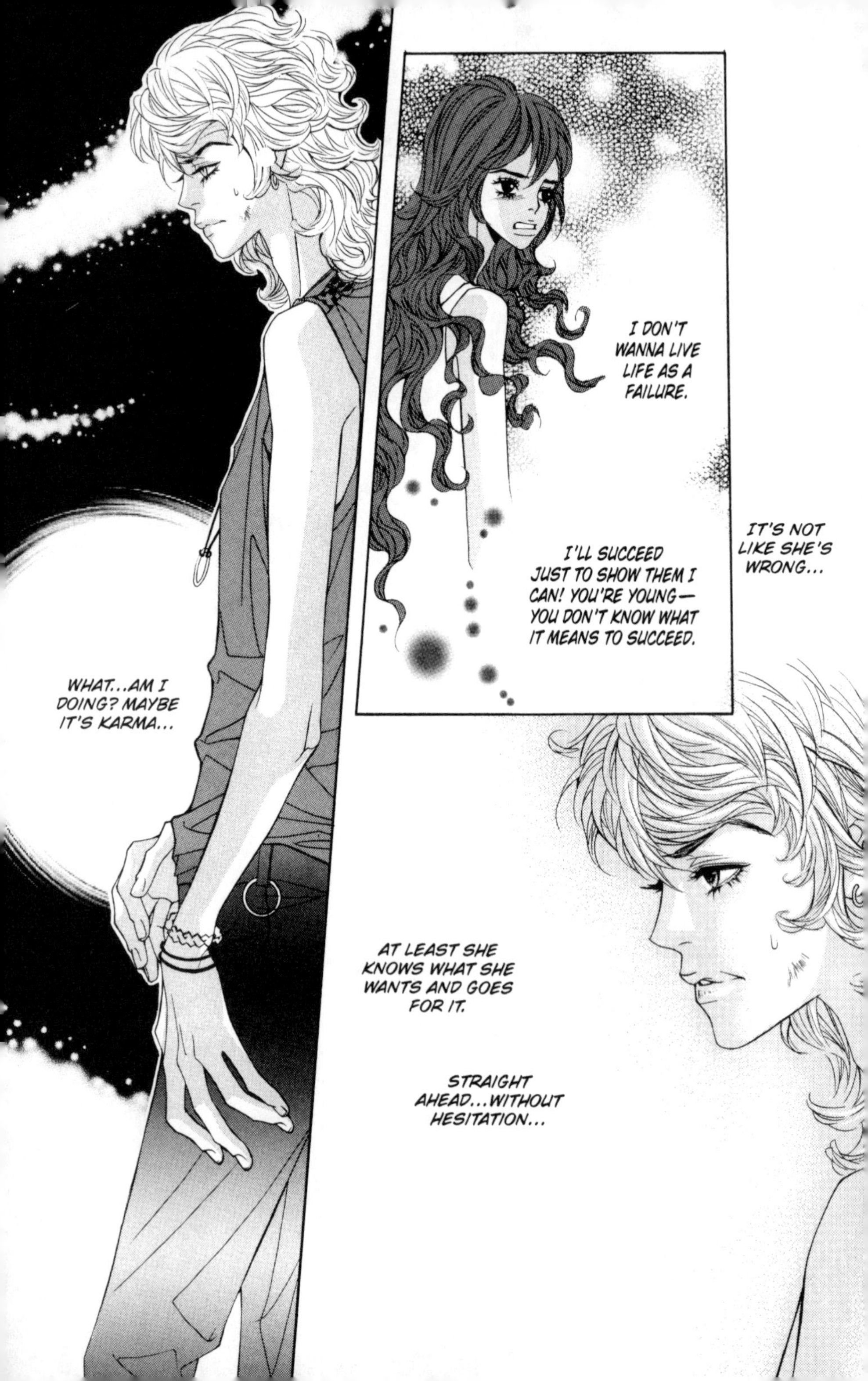
WHAT...AM I DOING? MAYBE IT'S KARMA...
I DON'T WANNA LIVE LIFE AS A FAILURE.
I'LL SUCCEED JUST TO SHOW THEM I CAN! YOU'RE YOUNG—YOU DON'T KNOW WHAT IT MEANS TO SUCCEED.
IT'S NOT LIKE SHE'S WRONG...
AT LEAST SHE KNOWS WHAT SHE WANTS AND GOES FOR IT.
STRAIGHT AHEAD...WITHOUT HESITATION...

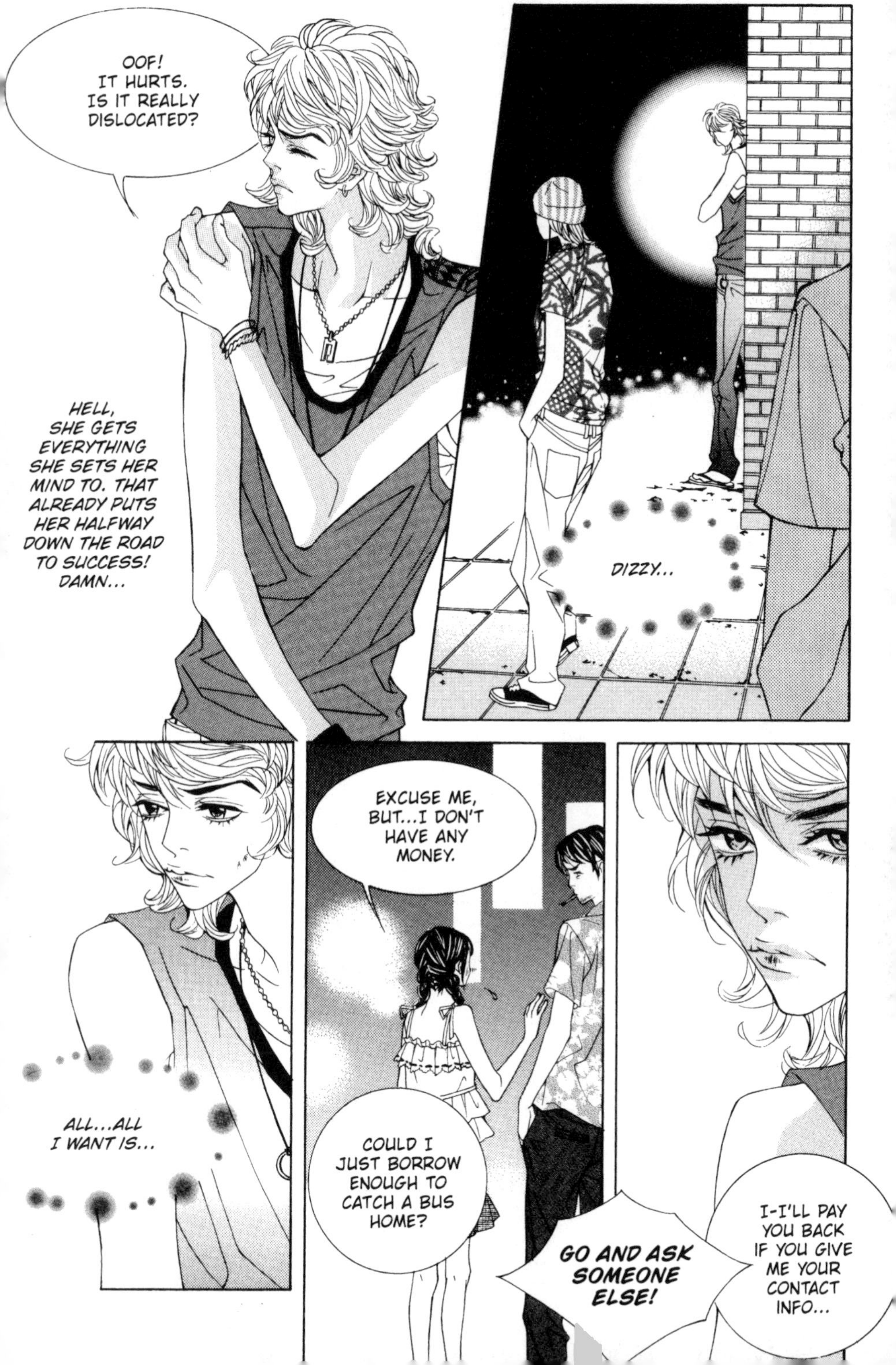
OOF! IT HURTS. IS IT REALLY DISLOCATED?
HELL, SHE GETS EVERYTHING SHE SETS HER MIND TO. THAT ALREADY PUTS HER HALFWAY DOWN THE ROAD TO SUCCESS! DAMN...
DIZZY...
ALL...ALL I WANT IS...
EXCUSE ME, BUT...I DON'T HAVE ANY MONEY.
COULD I JUST BORROW ENOUGH TO CATCH A BUS HOME?
GO AND ASK SOMEONE ELSE!
I-I'LL PAY YOU BACK IF YOU GIVE ME YOUR CONTACT INFO...

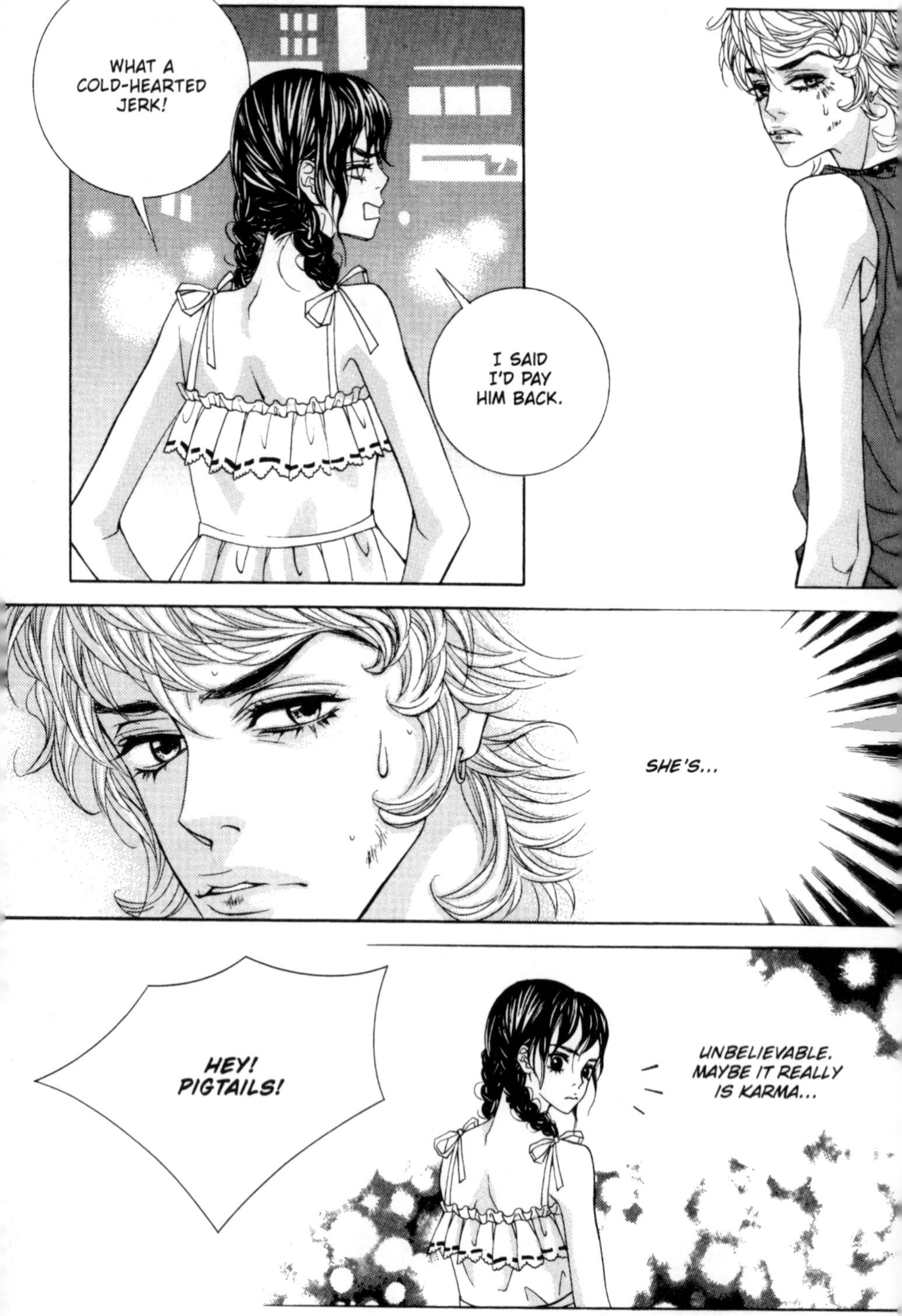
WHAT A COLD-HEARTED JERK!
I SAID I'D PAY HIM BACK.
SHE'S...
HEY! PIGTAILS!
UNBELIEVABLE. MAYBE IT REALLY IS KARMA...

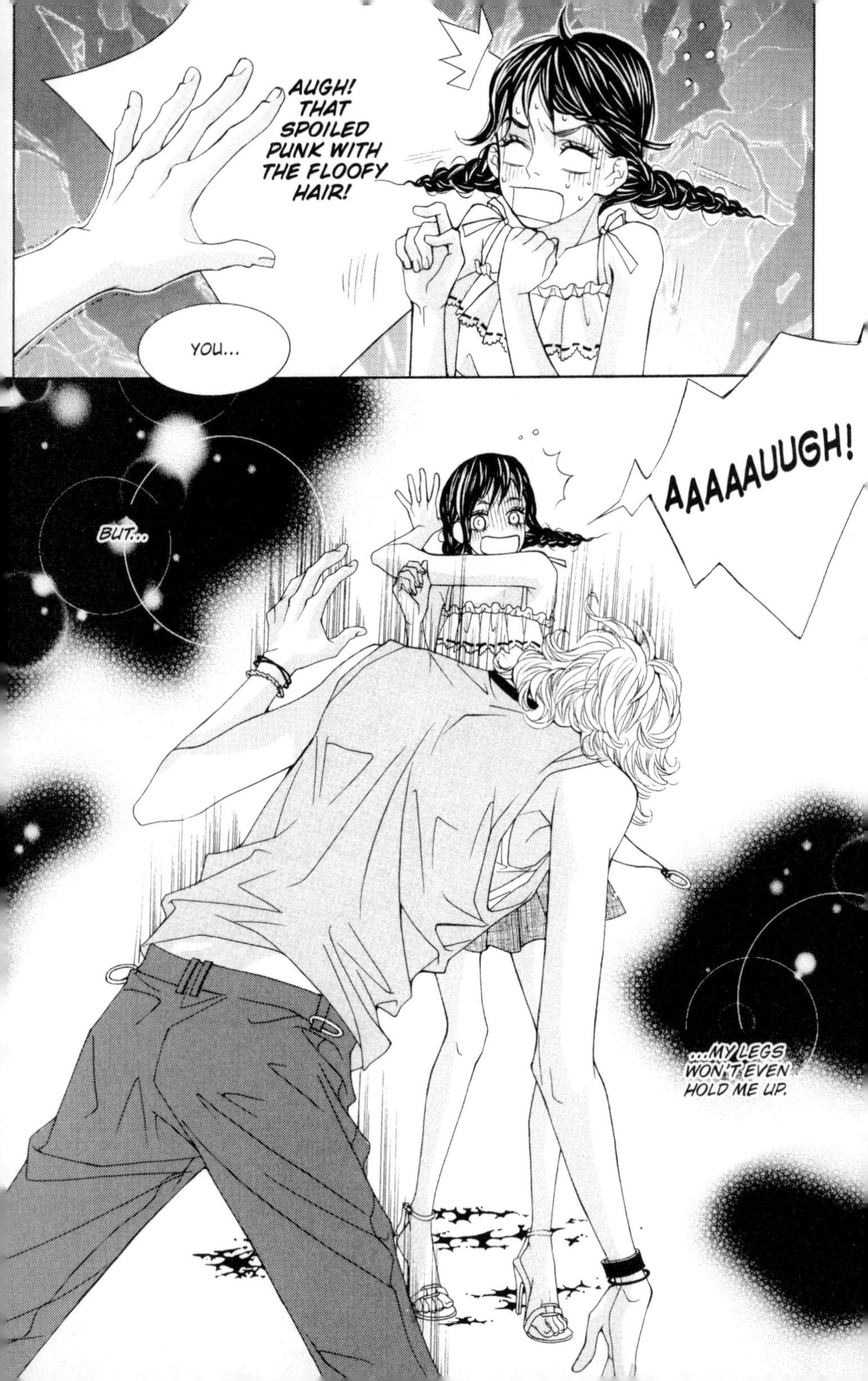
AUGH! THAT SPOILED PUNK WITH THE FLOOFY HAIR!
YOU...
BUT...
AAAAAUUGH!
...MY LEGS WON'T EVEN HOLD ME UP.

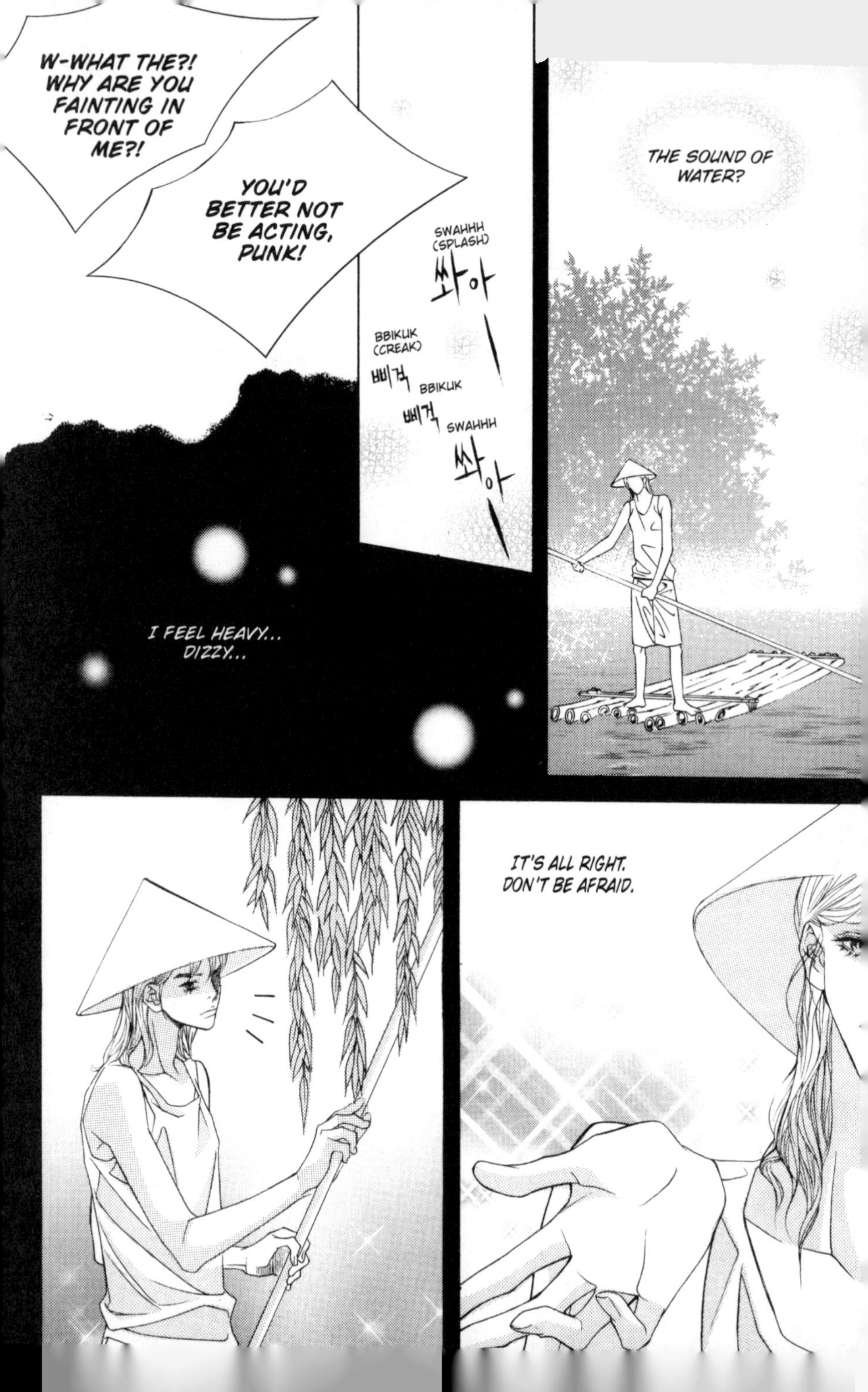
W-WHAT THE?! WHY ARE YOU FAINTING IN FRONT OF ME?!
YOU'D BETTER NOT BE ACTING, PUNK!
I FEEL HEAVY... DIZZY...
SWAHHH (SPLASH)
쏴아
BBIKUK (CREAK)
삐걱
BBIKUK
삐걱
SWAHHH
쏴아
THE SOUND OF WATER?
IT'S ALL RIGHT. DON'T BE AFRAID.

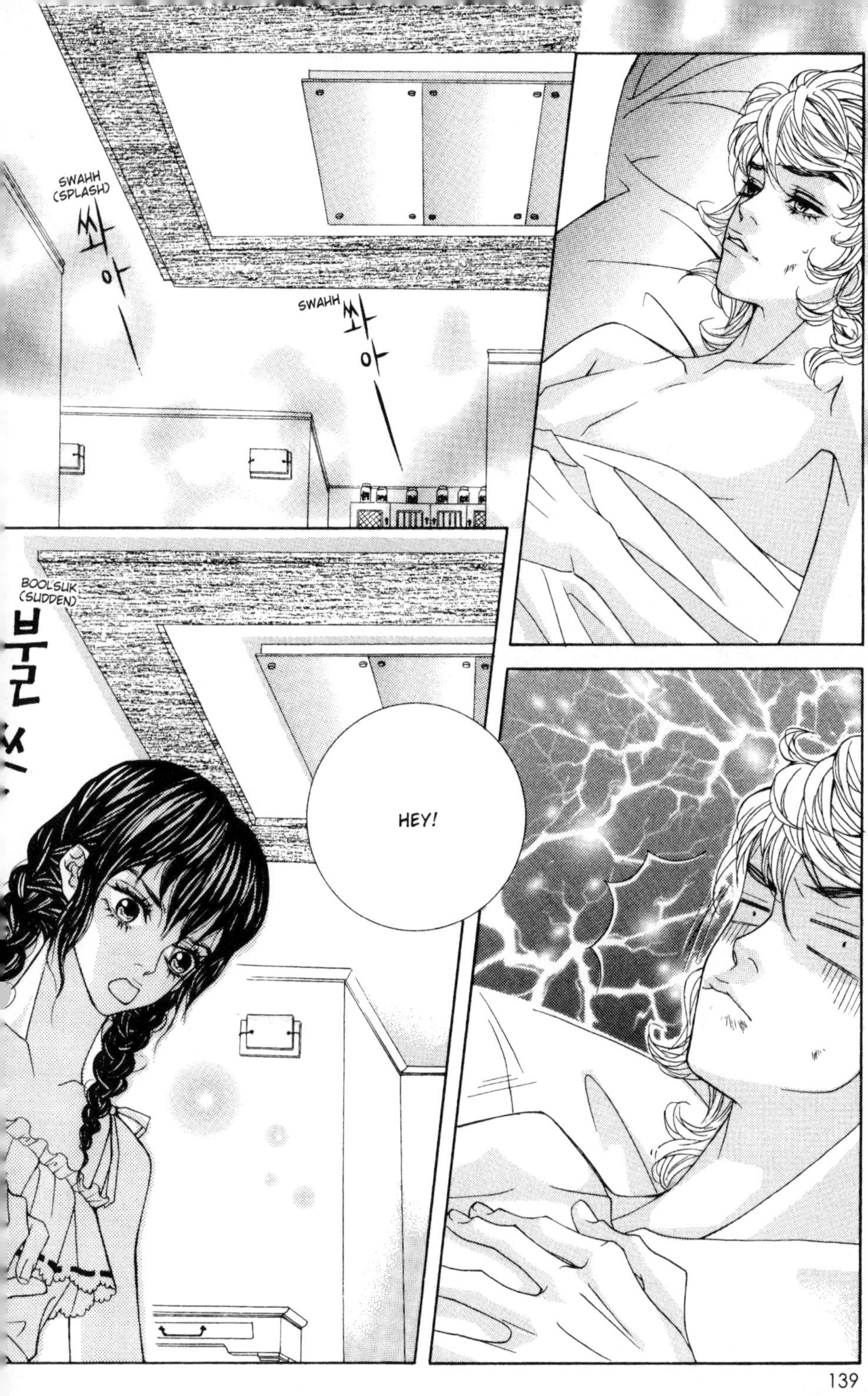
SWAHH (SPLASH)
쏴아
SWAHH
쏴아
BOOLSUK (SUDDEN)
불
HEY!

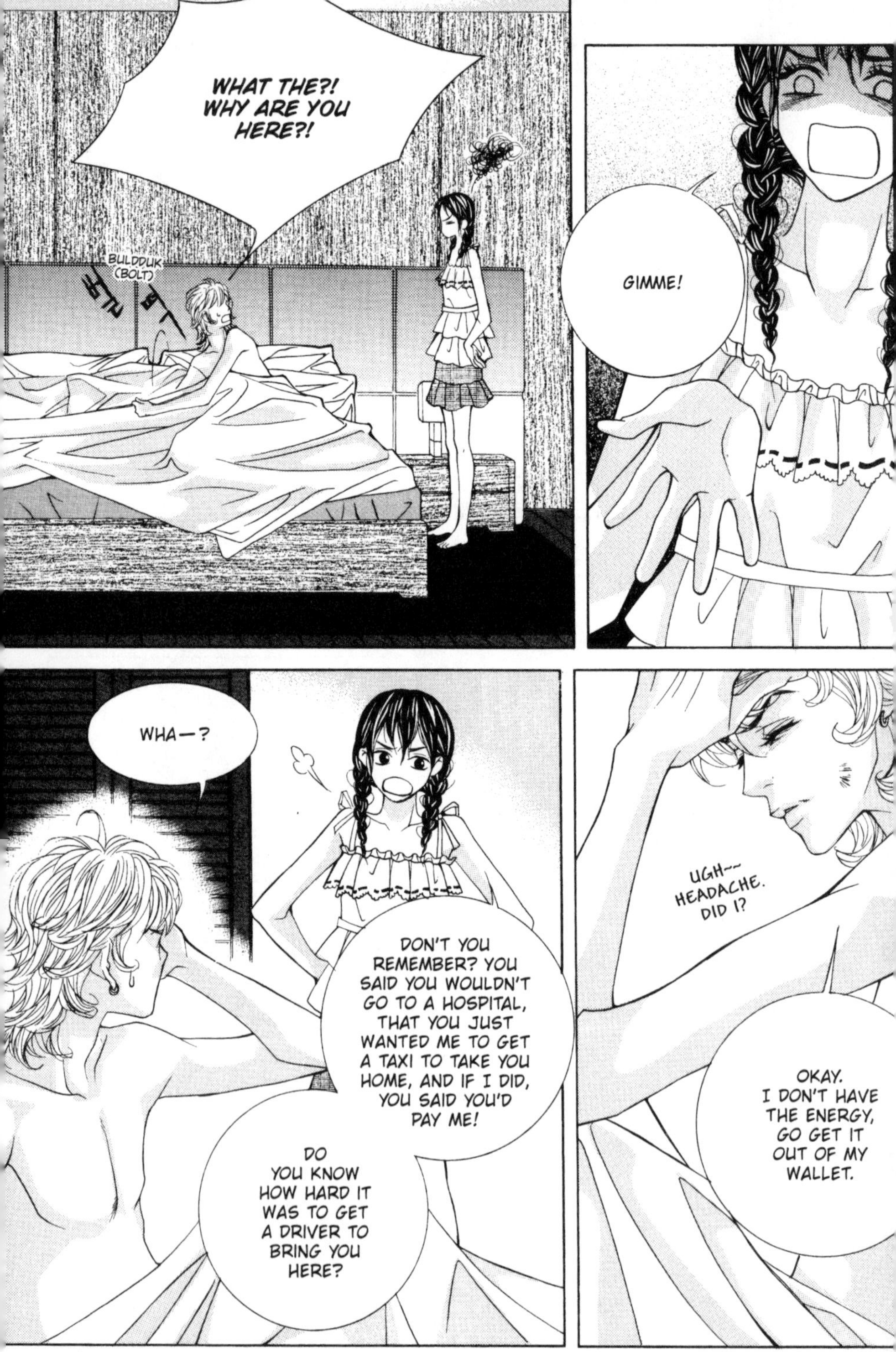
WHAT THE?! WHY ARE YOU HERE?!
BULDDUK (BOLT)
GIMME!
WHA—?
DON'T YOU REMEMBER? YOU SAID YOU WOULDN'T GO TO A HOSPITAL, THAT YOU JUST WANTED ME TO GET A TAXI TO TAKE YOU HOME, AND IF I DID, YOU SAID YOU'D PAY ME!
DO YOU KNOW HOW HARD IT WAS TO GET A DRIVER TO BRING YOU HERE?
UGH-- HEADACHE. DID I?
OKAY. I DON'T HAVE THE ENERGY, GO GET IT OUT OF MY WALLET.

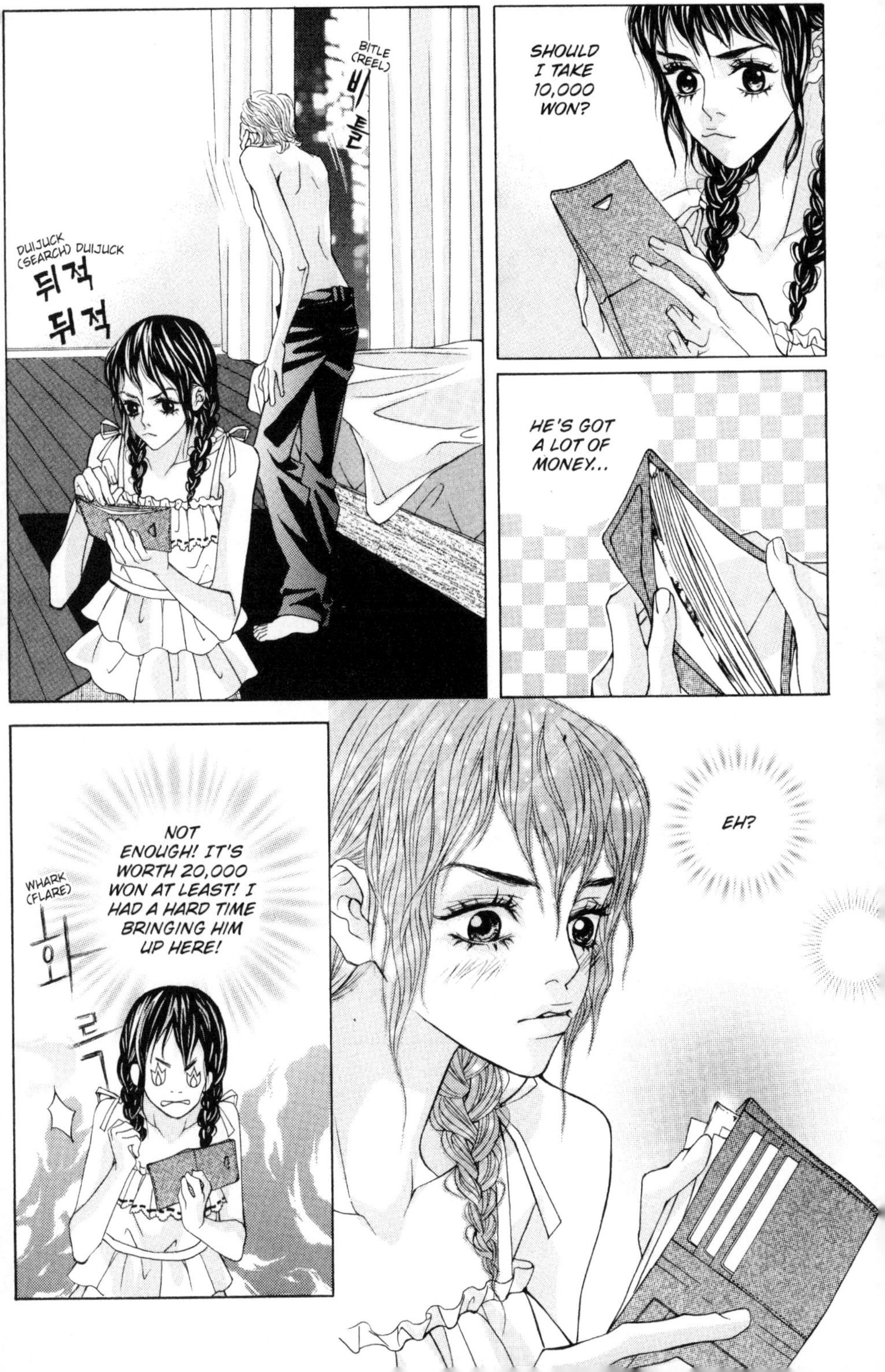
BITLE (REEL)
비틀
DUIJUCK (SEARCH) DUIJUCK
뒤적 뒤적
SHOULD I TAKE 10,000 WON?
HE'S GOT A LOT OF MONEY...
WHARK (FLARE)
화륵
NOT ENOUGH! IT'S WORTH 20,000 WON AT LEAST! I HAD A HARD TIME BRINGING HIM UP HERE!
EH?

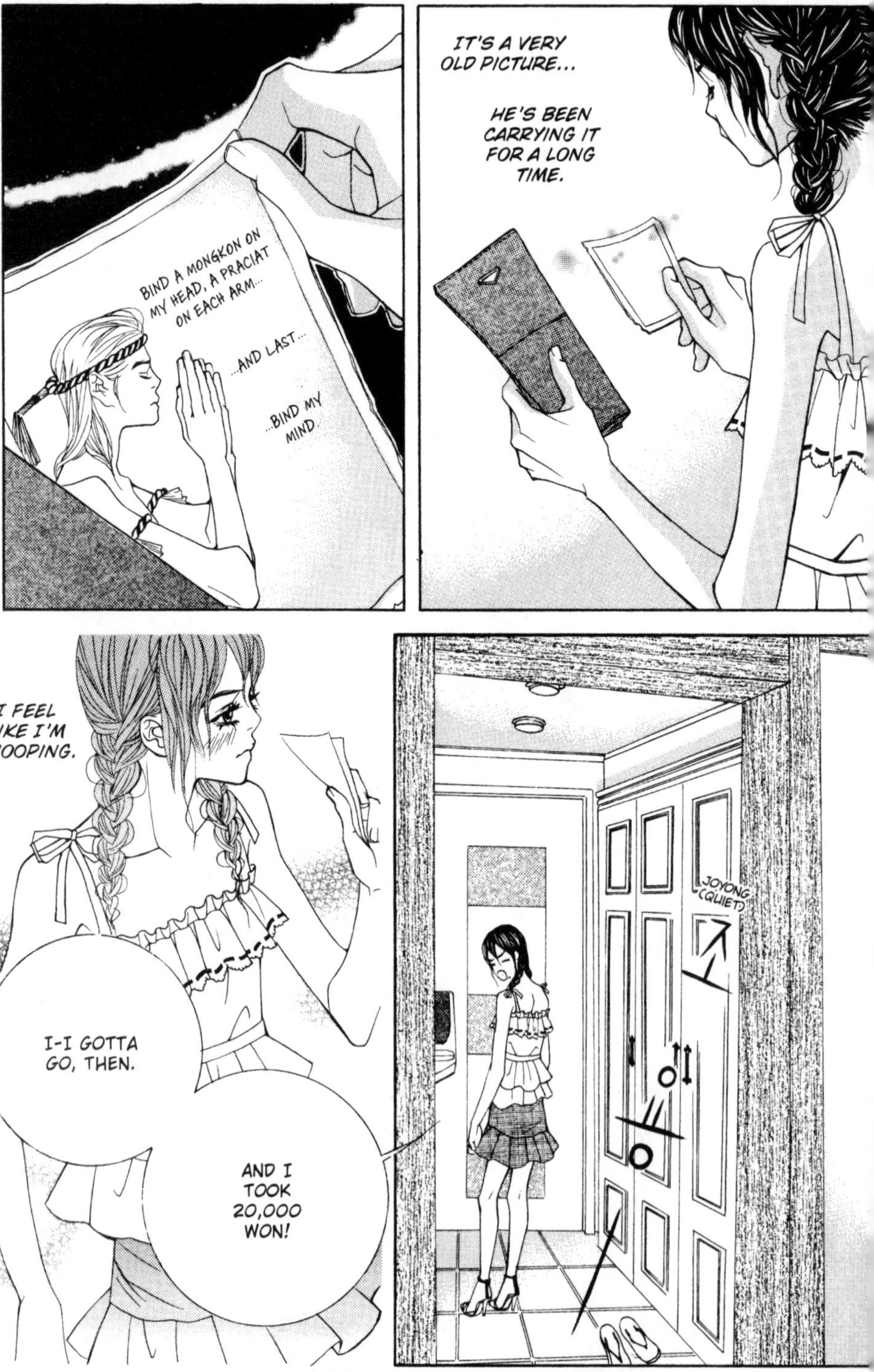
BIND A MONGKON ON MY HEAD, A PRACIAT ON EACH ARM...
...AND LAST...
...BIND MY MIND.
IT'S A VERY OLD PICTURE...
HE'S BEEN CARRYING IT FOR A LONG TIME.
I FEEL LIKE I'M SNOOPING.
I-I GOTTA GO, THEN.
AND I TOOK 20,000 WON!
JOYONG (QUIET)

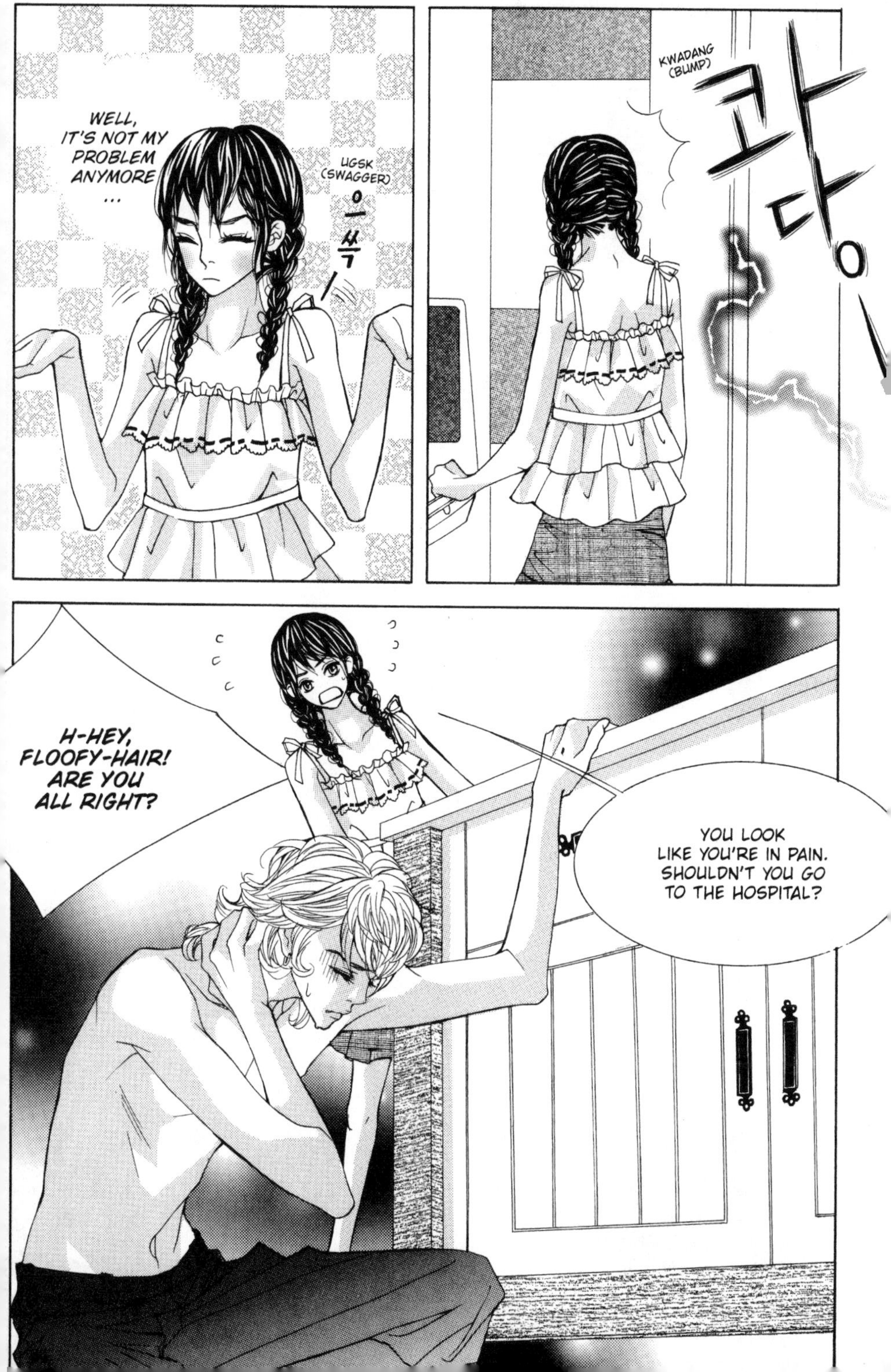
WELL, IT'S NOT MY PROBLEM ANYMORE ...
UGSK (SWAGGER)
으쓱
KWADANG (BUMP)
콰당
H-HEY, FLOOFY-HAIR! ARE YOU ALL RIGHT?
YOU LOOK LIKE YOU'RE IN PAIN. SHOULDN'T YOU GO TO THE HOSPITAL?

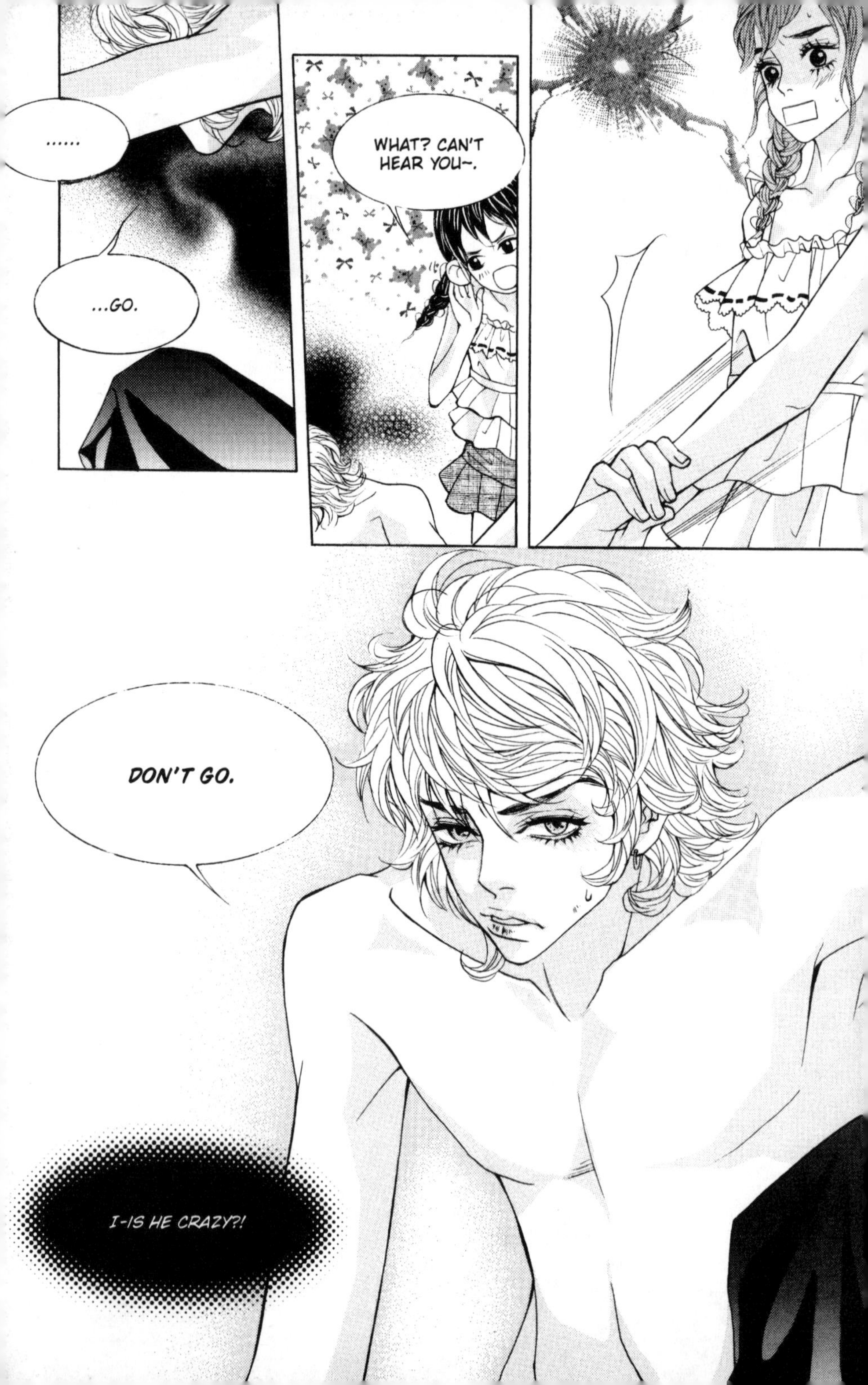
......
...GO.
WHAT? CAN'T HEAR YOU~.
DON'T GO.
I-IS HE CRAZY?!

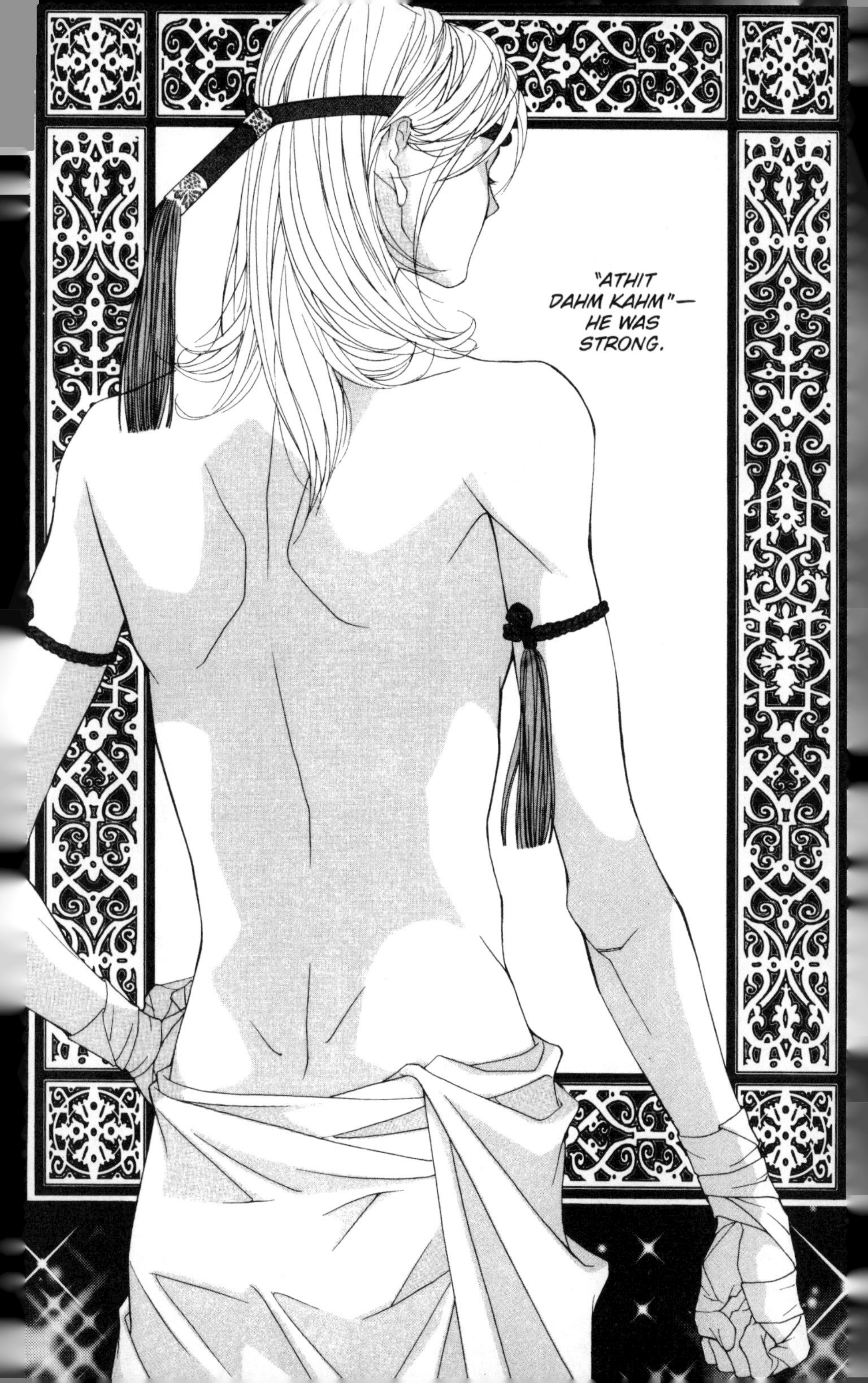
"ATHIT DAHM KAHM"—HE WAS STRONG.

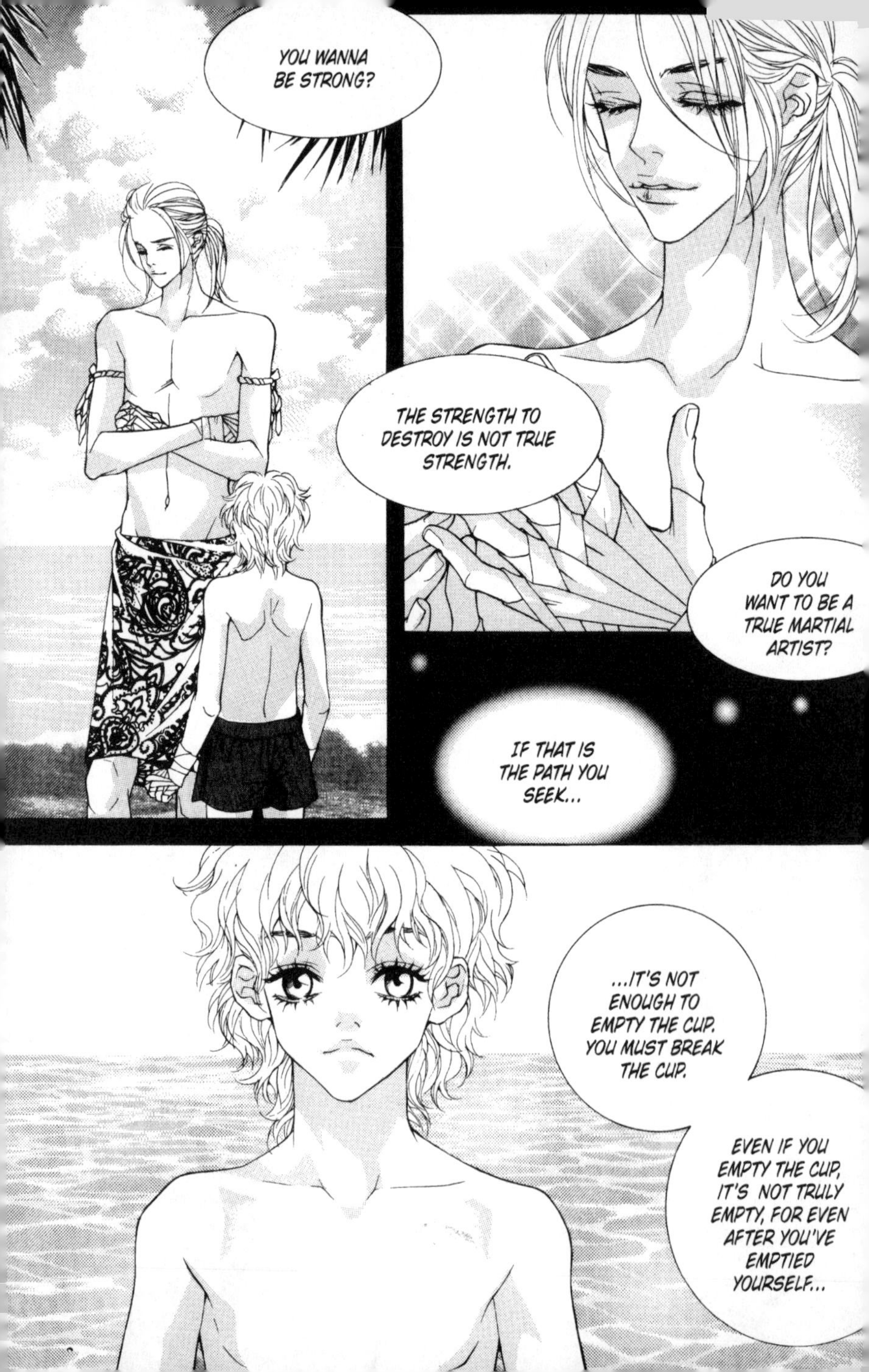
YOU WANNA BE STRONG?
THE STRENGTH TO DESTROY IS NOT TRUE STRENGTH.
DO YOU WANT TO BE A TRUE MARTIAL ARTIST?
IF THAT IS THE PATH YOU SEEK...
...IT'S NOT ENOUGH TO EMPTY THE CUP. YOU MUST BREAK THE CUP.
EVEN IF YOU EMPTY THE CUP, IT'S NOT TRULY EMPTY, FOR EVEN AFTER YOU'VE EMPTIED YOURSELF...

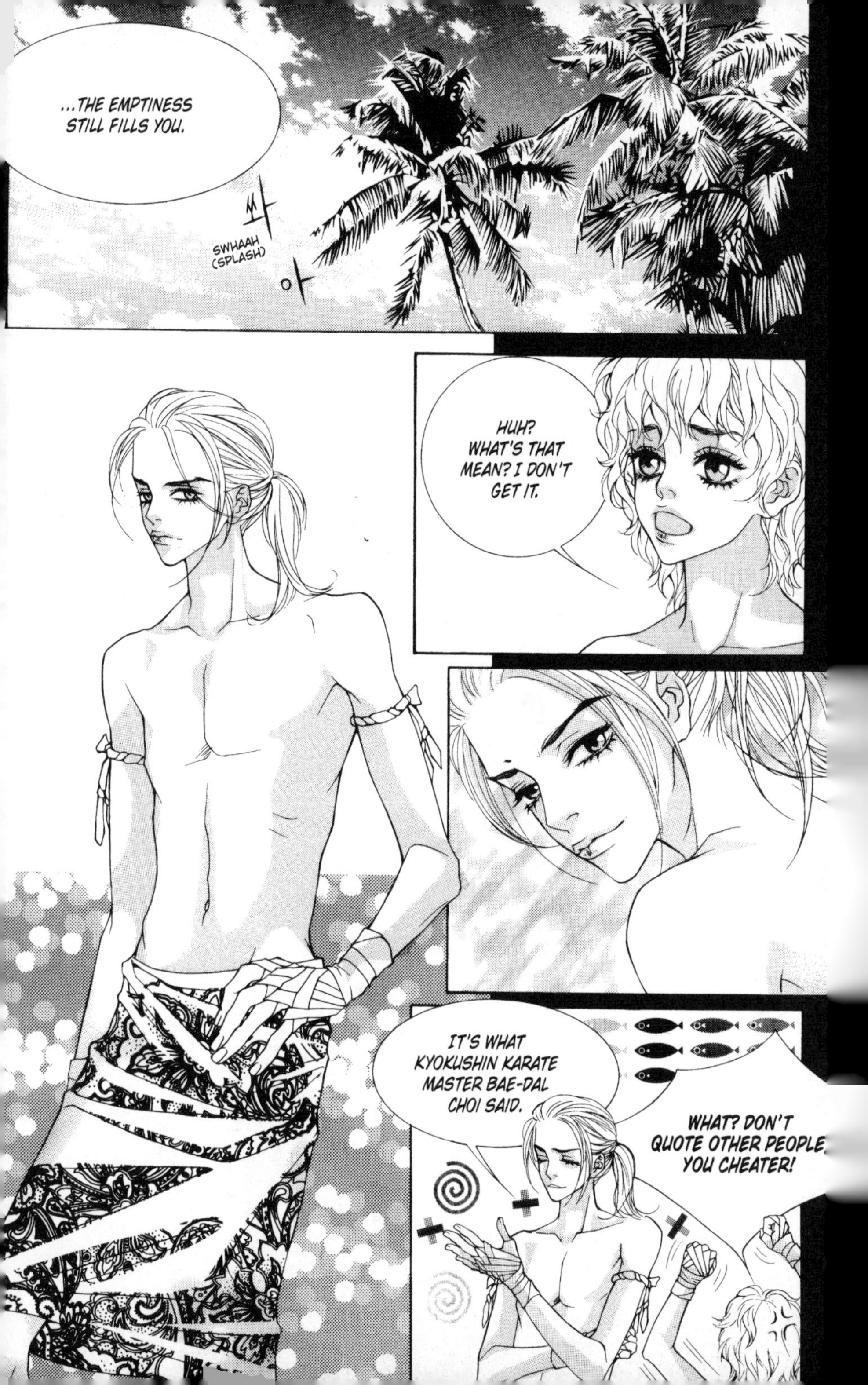
...THE EMPTINESS STILL FILLS YOU.
쏴
SWHAAH (SPLASH)
아
HUH? WHAT'S THAT MEAN? I DON'T GET IT.
IT'S WHAT KYOKUSHIN KARATE MASTER BAE-DAL CHOI SAID.
WHAT? DON'T QUOTE OTHER PEOPLE, YOU CHEATER!

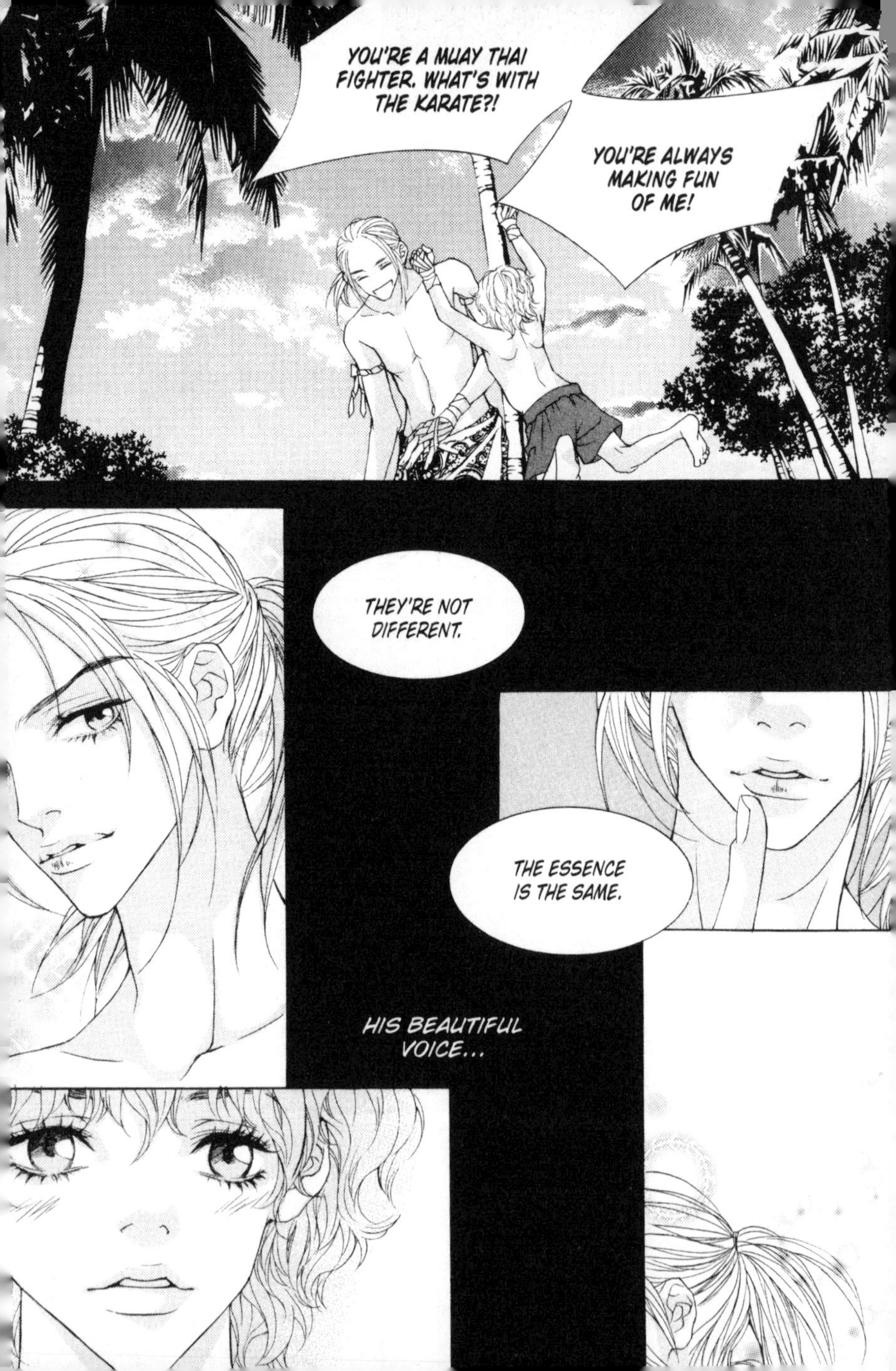
YOU'RE A MUAY THAI FIGHTER. WHAT'S WITH THE KARATE?!
YOU'RE ALWAYS MAKING FUN OF ME!
THEY'RE NOT DIFFERENT.
THE ESSENCE IS THE SAME.
HIS BEAUTIFUL VOICE...

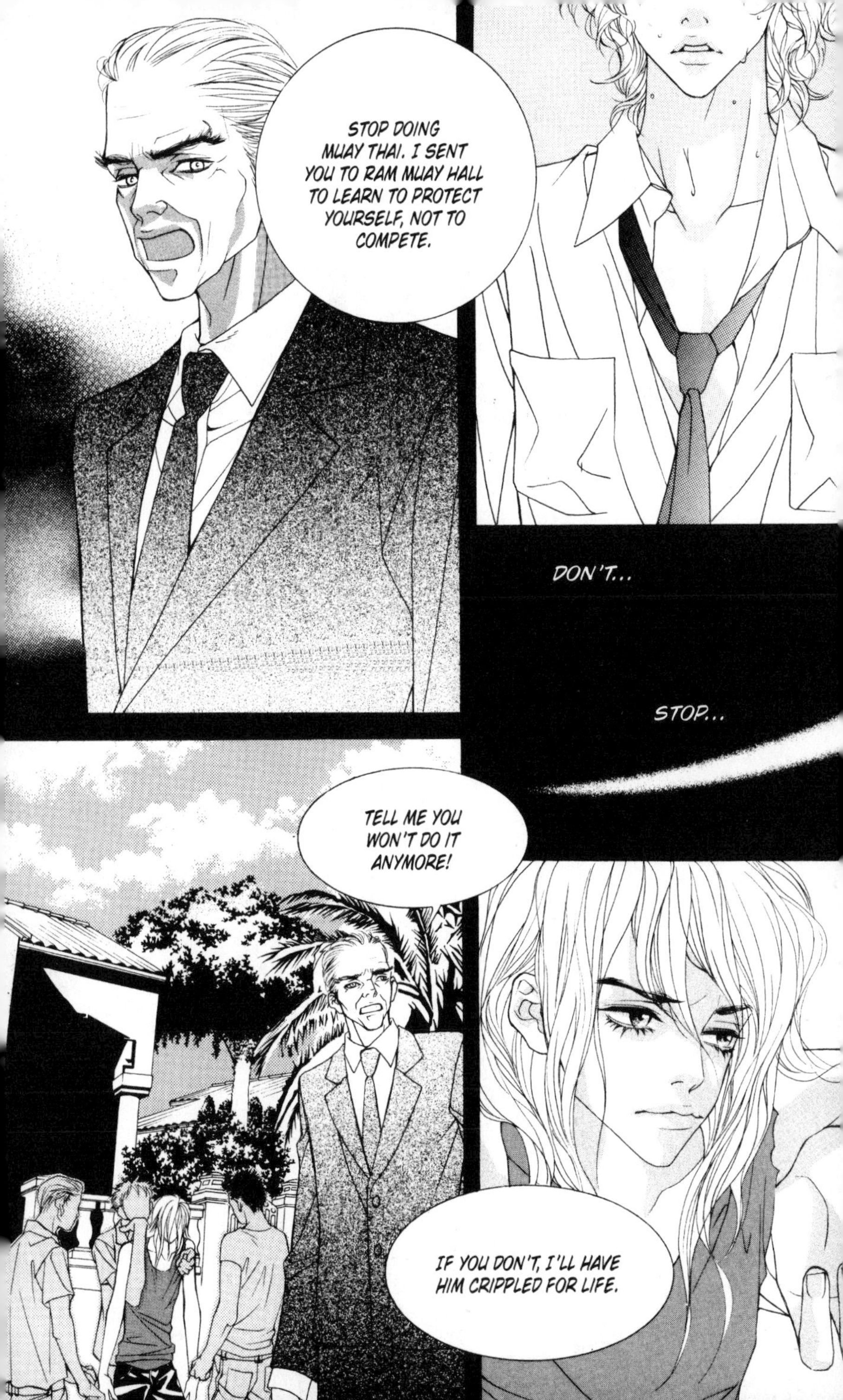
STOP DOING MUAY THAI. I SENT YOU TO RAM MUAY HALL TO LEARN TO PROTECT YOURSELF, NOT TO COMPETE.
DON'T...
STOP...
TELL ME YOU WON'T DO IT ANYMORE!
IF YOU DON'T, I'LL HAVE HIM CRIPPLED FOR LIFE.

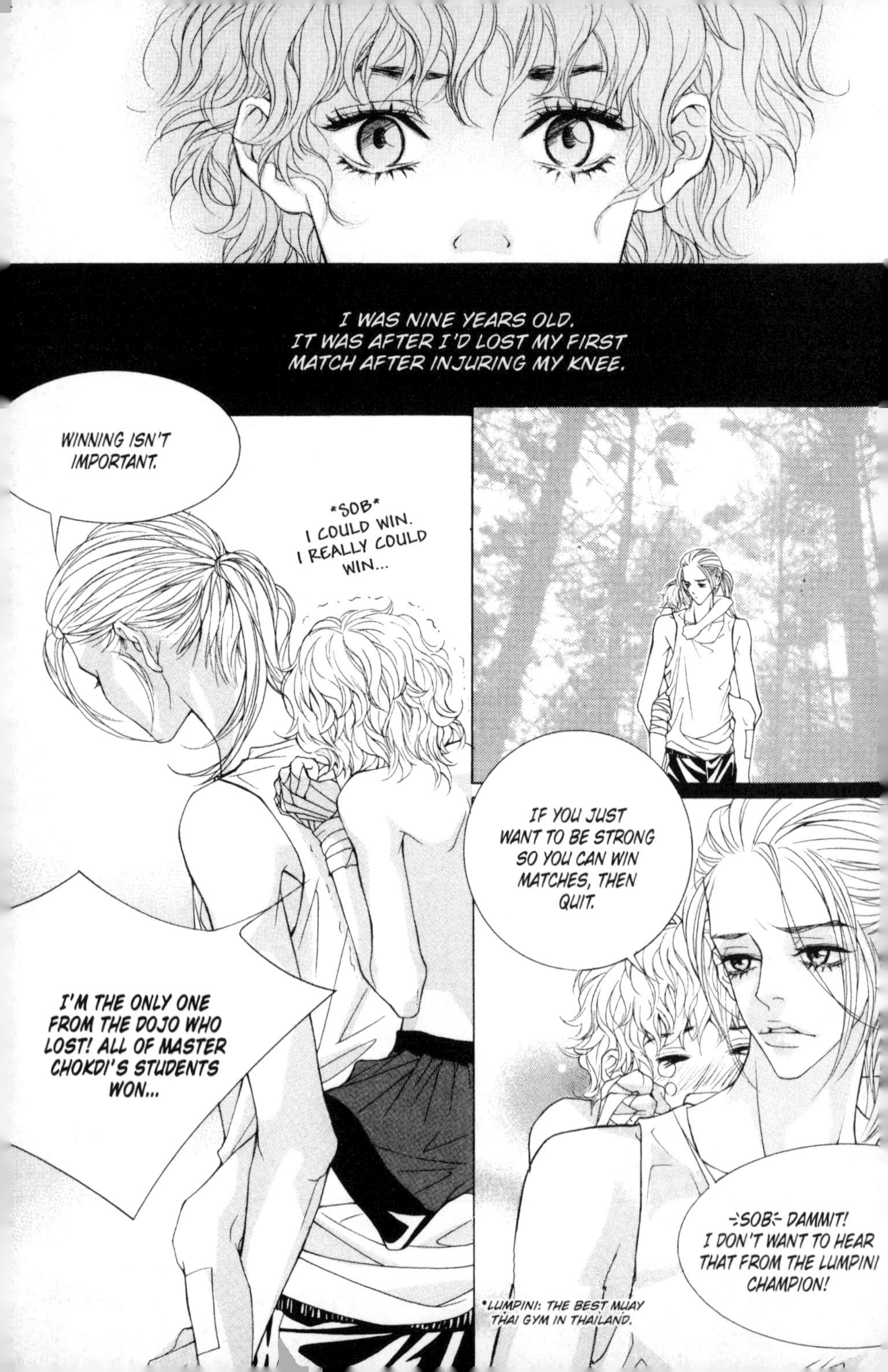
I WAS NINE YEARS OLD. IT WAS AFTER I'D LOST MY FIRST MATCH AFTER INJURING MY KNEE.
WINNING ISN'T IMPORTANT.
SOB I COULD WIN. I REALLY COULD WIN...
I'M THE ONLY ONE FROM THE DOJO WHO LOST! ALL OF MASTER CHOKDI'S STUDENTS WON...
IF YOU JUST WANT TO BE STRONG SO YOU CAN WIN MATCHES, THEN QUIT.
SOB DAMMIT! I DON'T WANT TO HEAR THAT FROM THE LUMPINI CHAMPION!
*LUMPINI: THE BEST MUAY THAI GYM IN THAILAND.

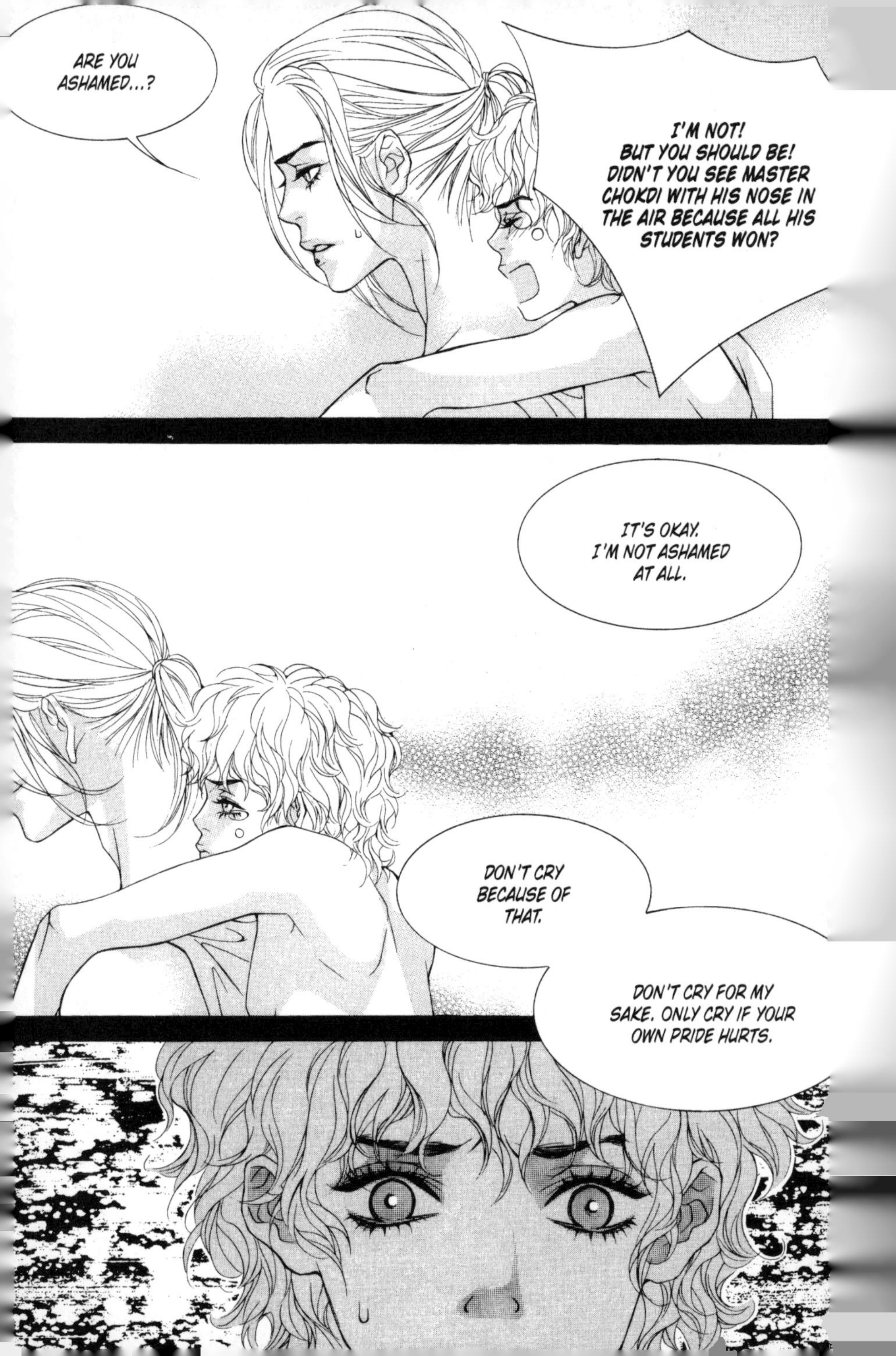
ARE YOU ASHAMED...?
I'M NOT! BUT YOU SHOULD BE! DIDN'T YOU SEE MASTER CHOKDI WITH HIS NOSE IN THE AIR BECAUSE ALL HIS STUDENTS WON?
IT'S OKAY. I'M NOT ASHAMED AT ALL.
DON'T CRY BECAUSE OF THAT.
DON'T CRY FOR MY SAKE. ONLY CRY IF YOUR OWN PRIDE HURTS.

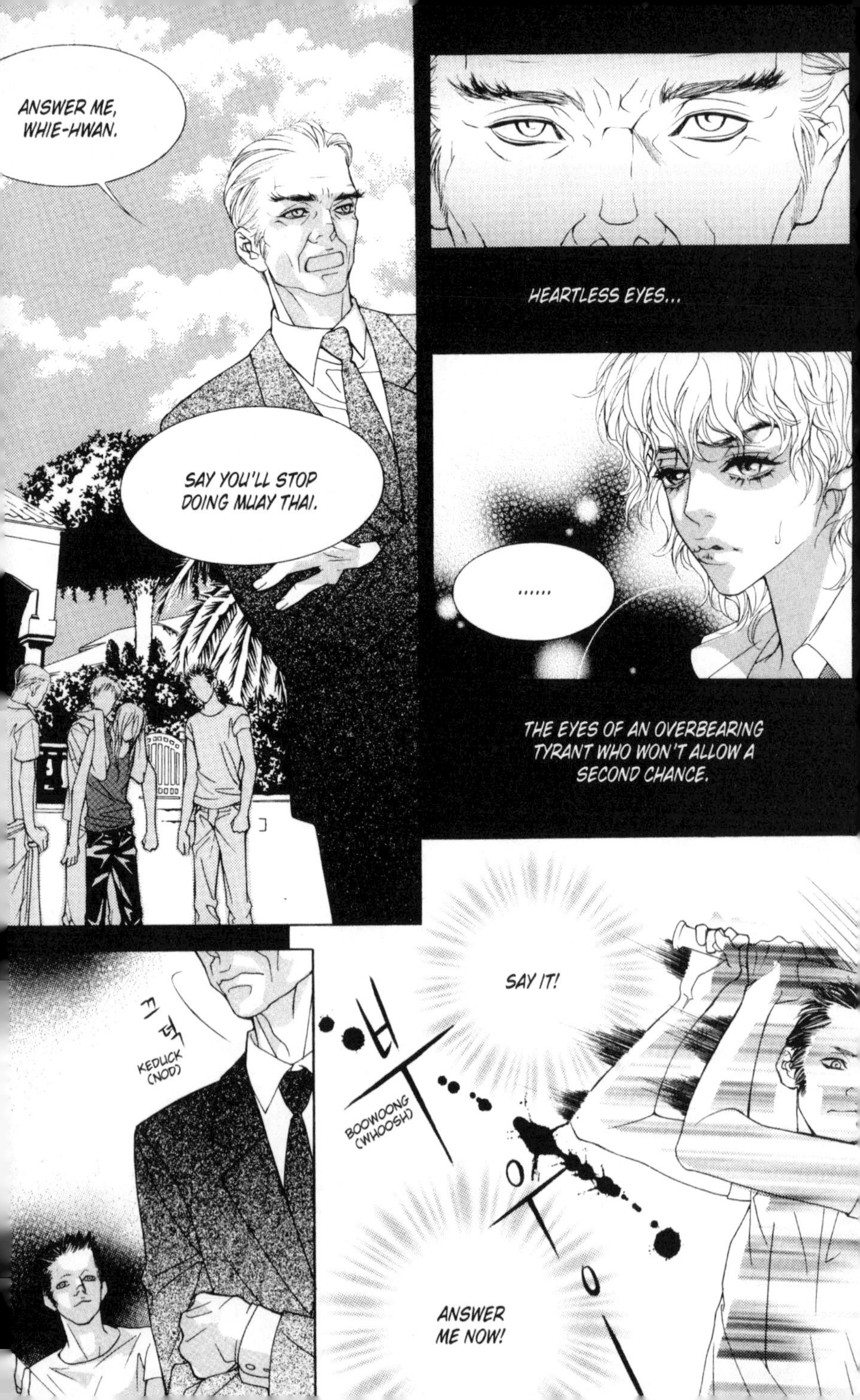
ANSWER ME, WHIE-HWAN.
SAY YOU'LL STOP DOING MUAY THAI.
HEARTLESS EYES...
......
THE EYES OF AN OVERBEARING TYRANT WHO WON'T ALLOW A SECOND CHANCE.
끄덕
KEDUCK (NOD)
SAY IT!
부웅
BOOWOONG (WHOOSH)
ANSWER ME NOW!

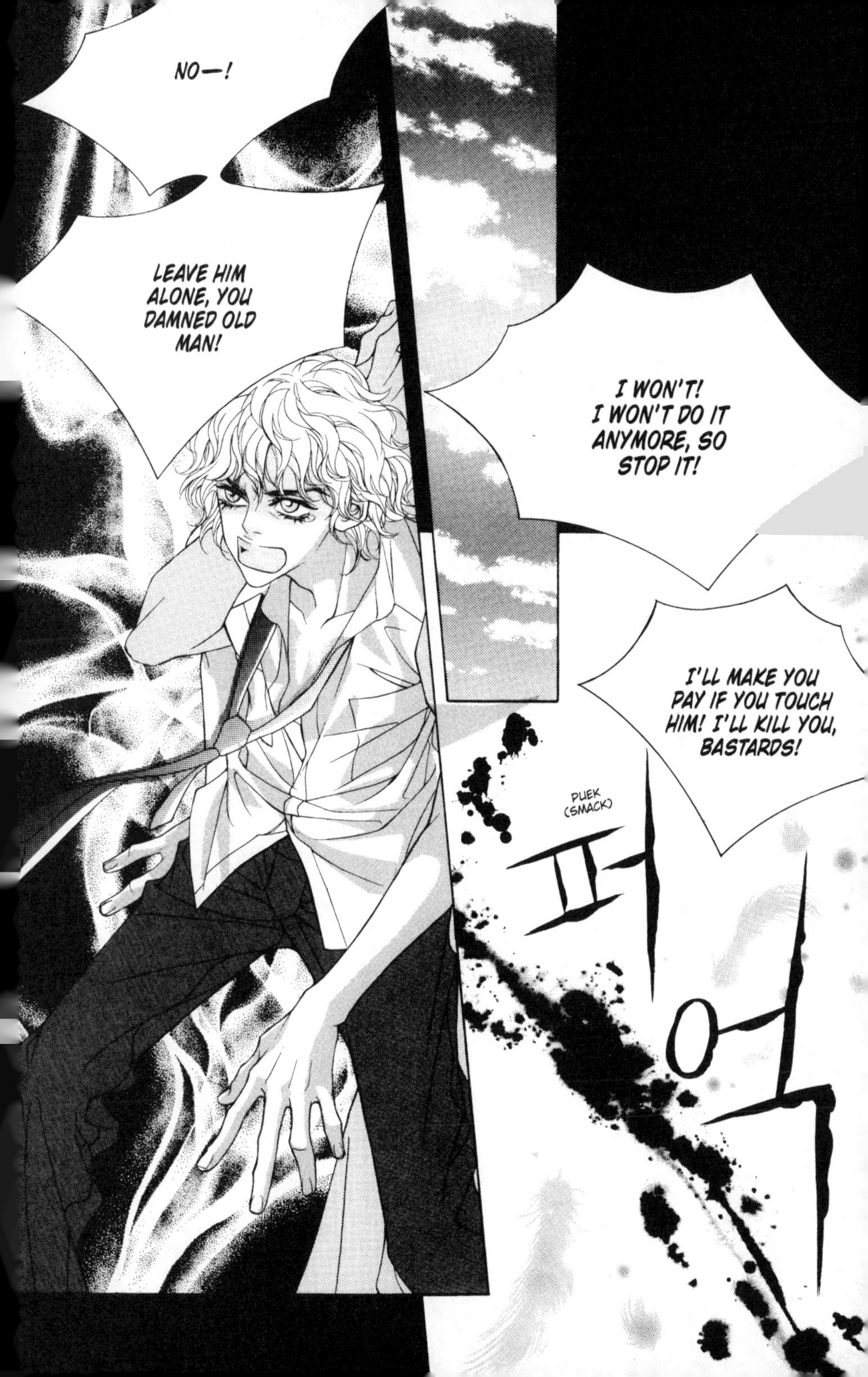
NO—!
LEAVE HIM ALONE, YOU DAMNED OLD MAN!
I WON'T! I WON'T DO IT ANYMORE, SO STOP IT!
I'LL MAKE YOU PAY IF YOU TOUCH HIM! I'LL KILL YOU, BASTARDS!
PUEK (SMACK)

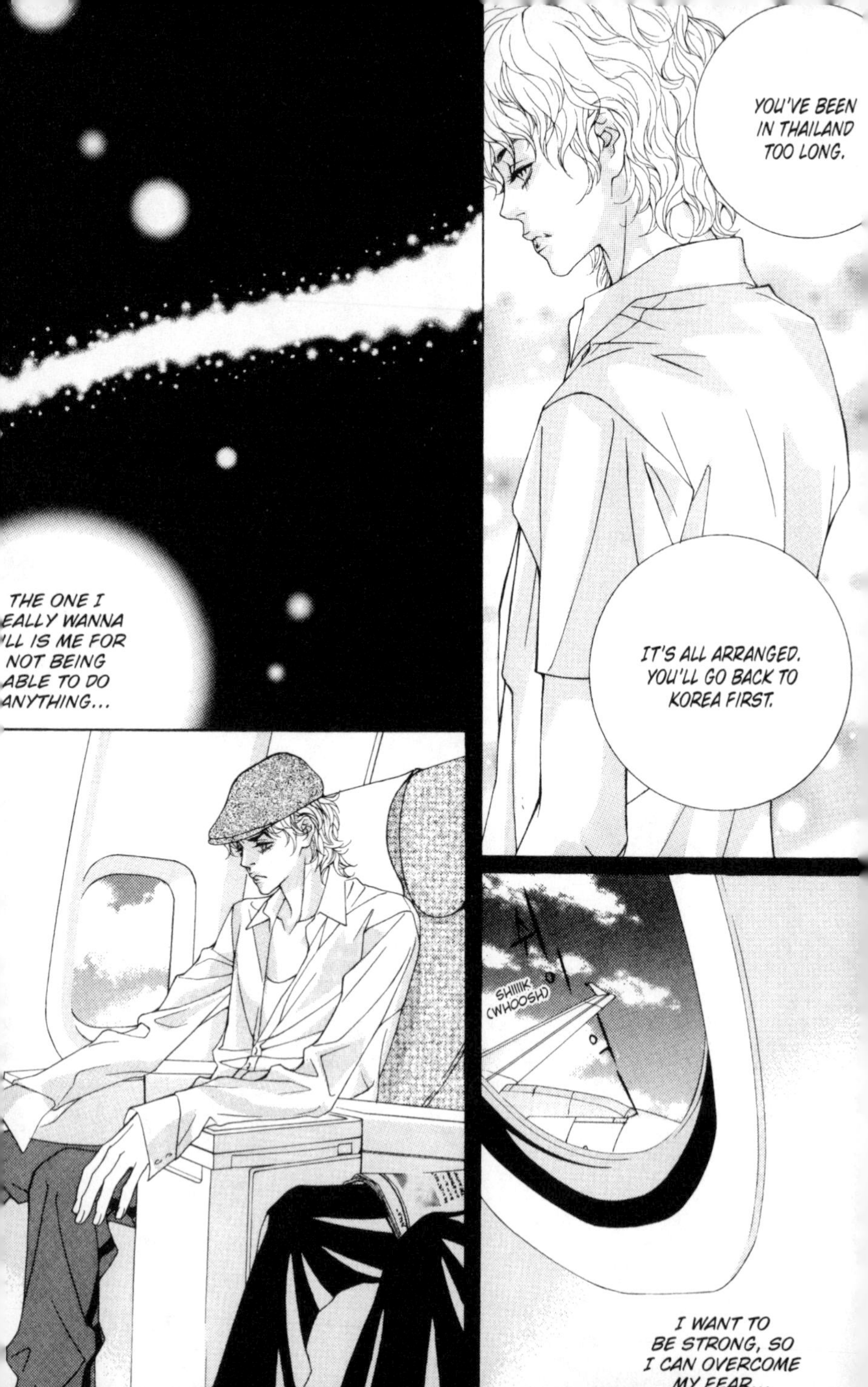
THE ONE I EALLY WANNA LL IS ME FOR NOT BEING ABLE TO DO ANYTHING...
YOU'VE BEEN IN THAILAND TOO LONG.
IT'S ALL ARRANGED. YOU'LL GO BACK TO KOREA FIRST.
SHIIIIK (WHOOSH)
I WANT TO BE STRONG, SO I CAN OVERCOME MY FEAR...

IT HURTS SO MUCH...
MORE THAN WHEN I
FAILED IN THE MATCH.
I CAN'T STAND IT...

CAN ANYTHING
HURT AS MUCH
AS THIS?

I WON'T GIVE
MY HEART TO
ANYBODY EVER
AGAIN.

HE SAID
NOT TO CRY.

I WON'T EVER CRY
AFTER THIS ONE TIME.
I WON'T EVER LOVE
ANYTHING.

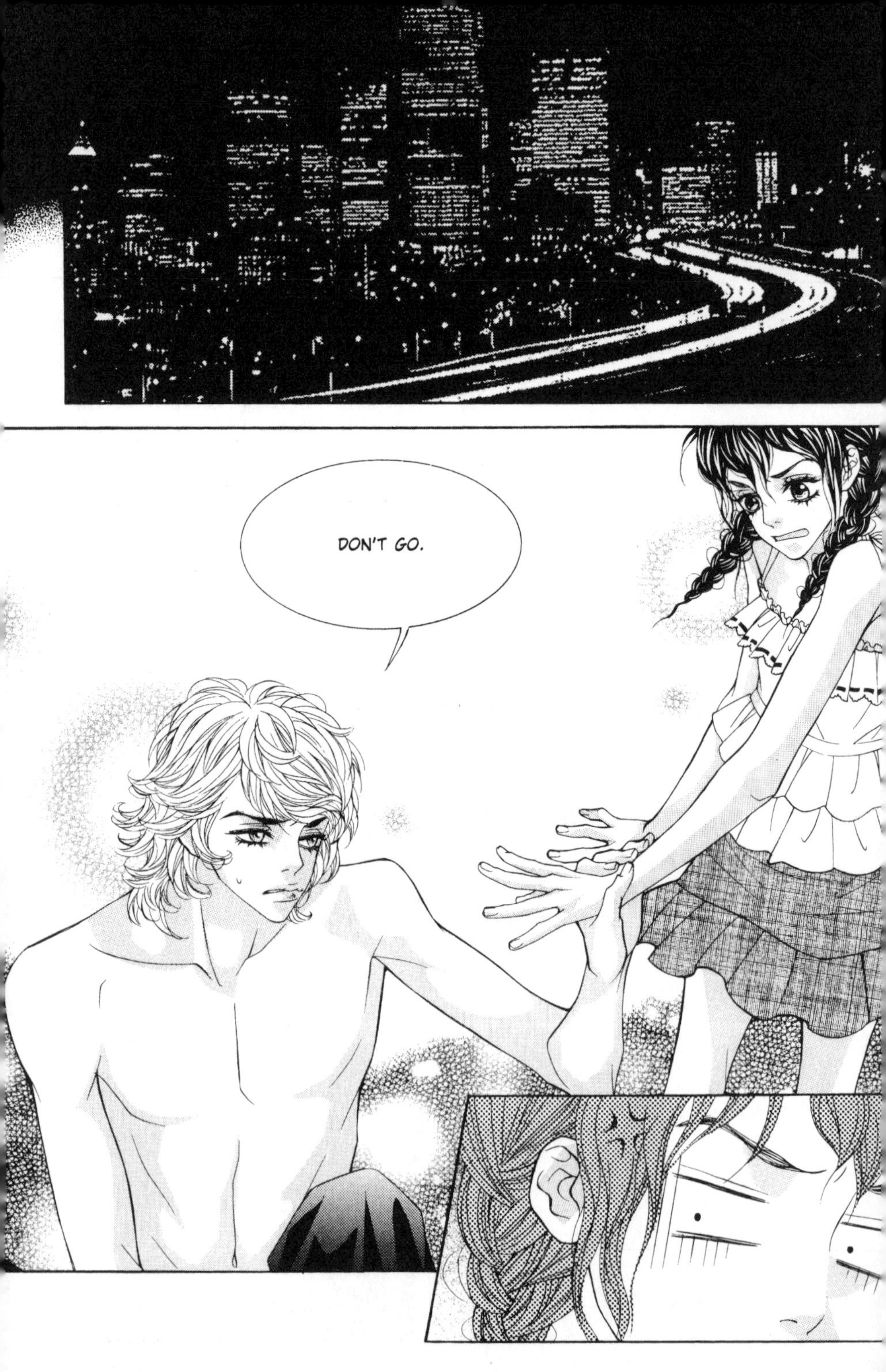
DON'T GO.

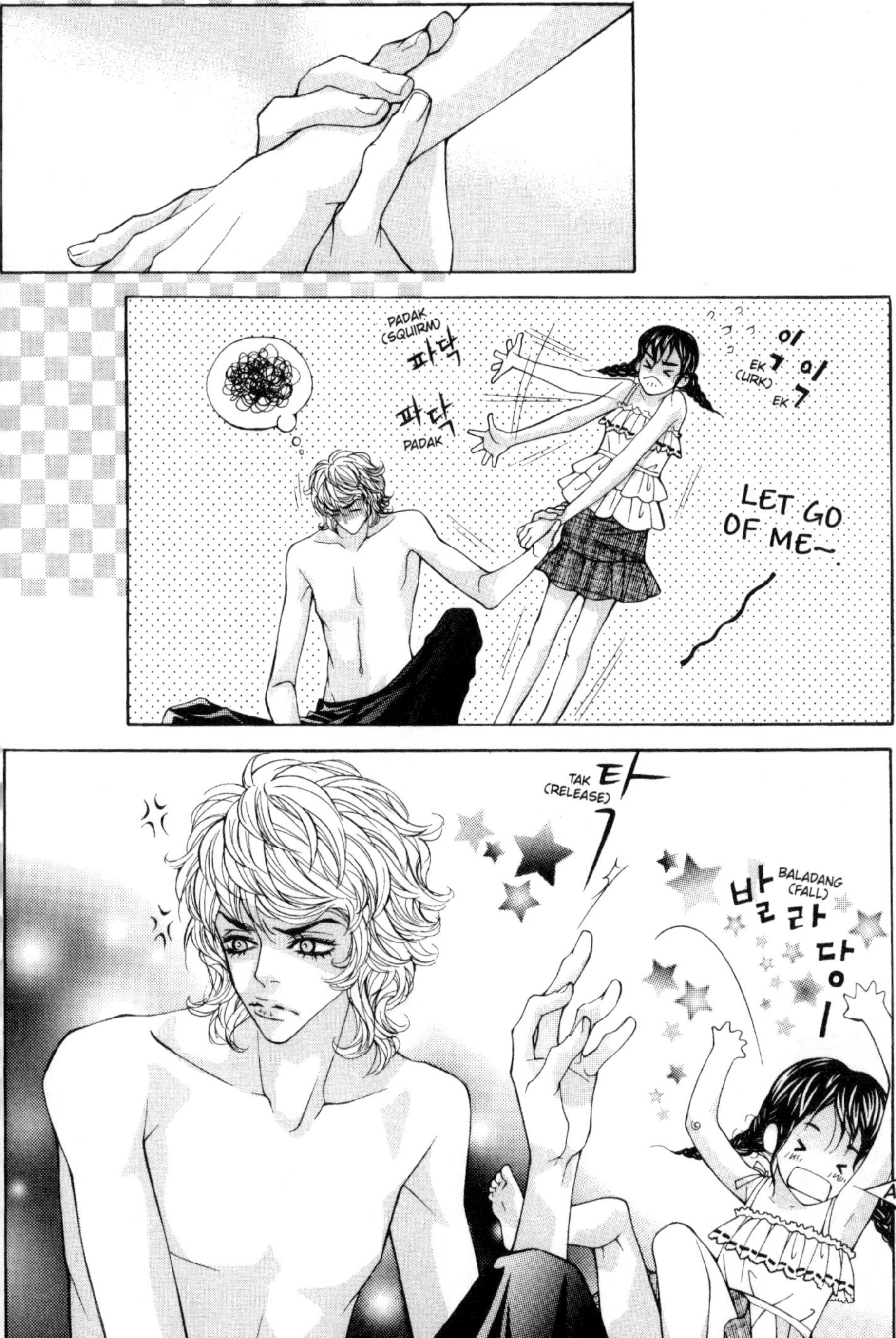
PADAK (SQUIRM)
파닥
파닥
PADAK
EK (URK)
이익
EK
이익
LET GO OF ME~.
TAK (RELEASE)
탁
BALADANG (FALL)
발라당!
AHH!

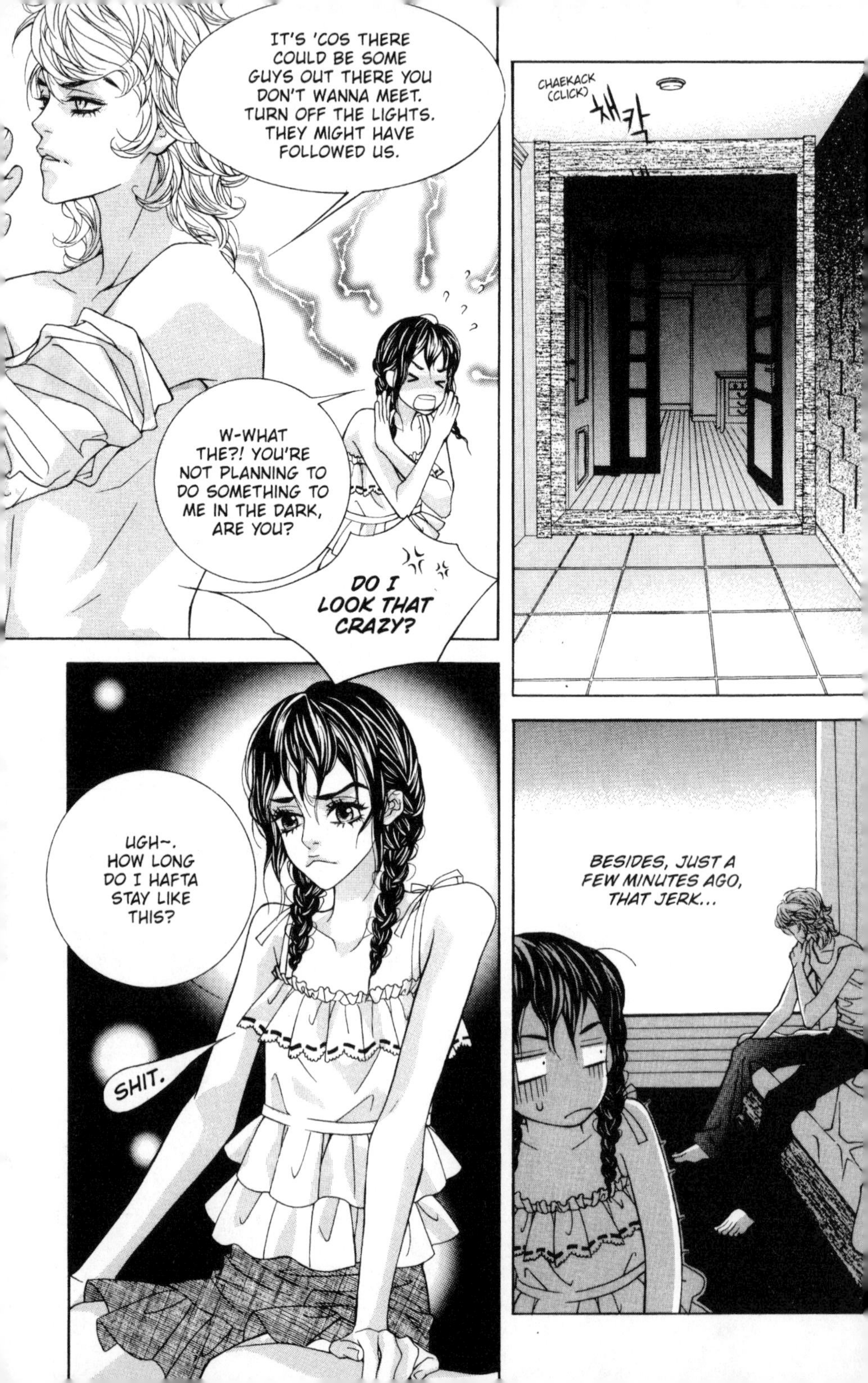
IT'S 'COS THERE COULD BE SOME GUYS OUT THERE YOU DON'T WANNA MEET. TURN OFF THE LIGHTS. THEY MIGHT HAVE FOLLOWED US.
W-WHAT THE?! YOU'RE NOT PLANNING TO DO SOMETHING TO ME IN THE DARK, ARE YOU?
DO I LOOK THAT CRAZY?
CHAEKACK (CLICK)
채칵
UGH~. HOW LONG DO I HAFTA STAY LIKE THIS?
SHIT.
BESIDES, JUST A FEW MINUTES AGO, THAT JERK...

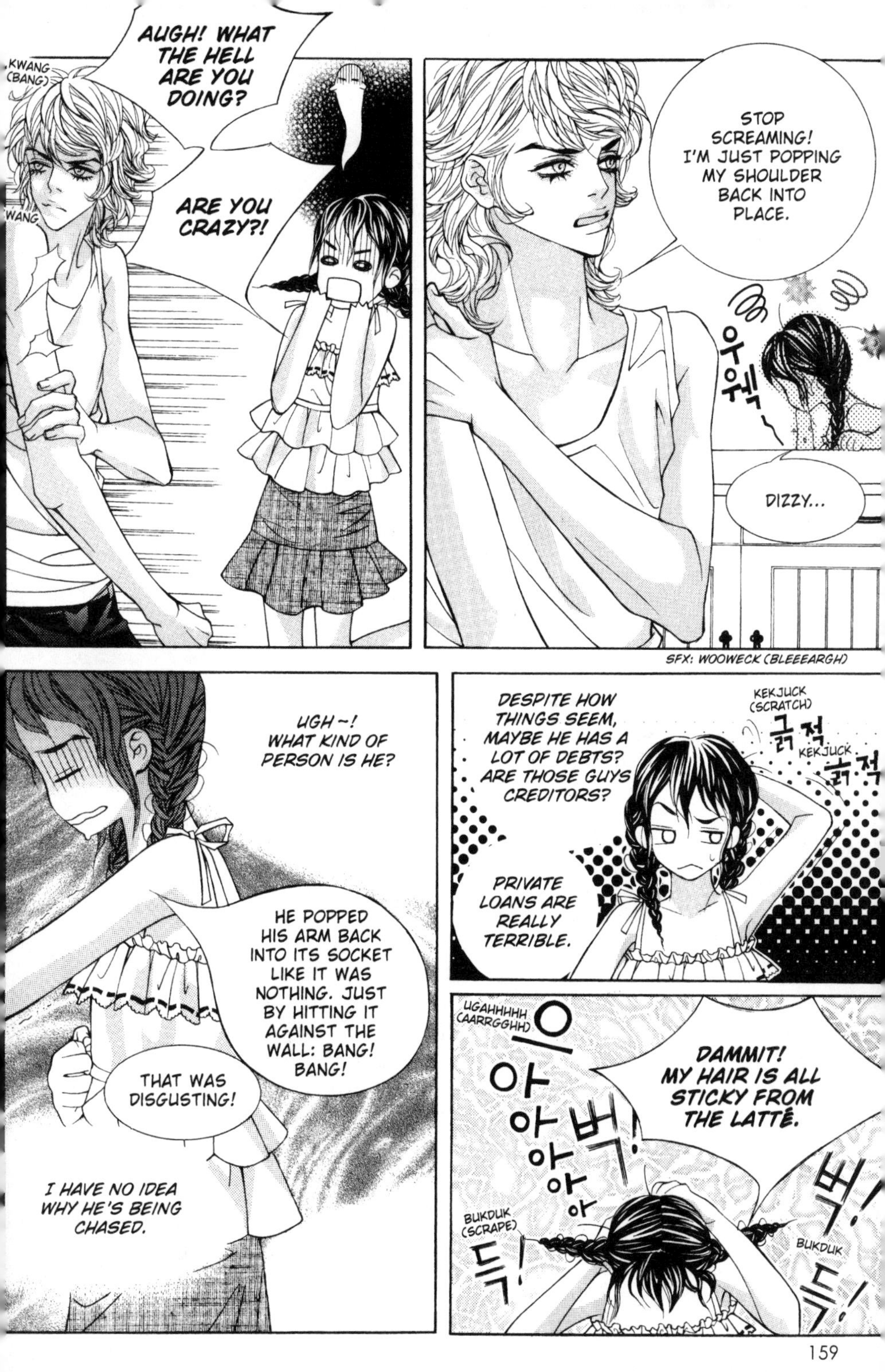
KWANG (BANG)
AUGH! WHAT THE HELL ARE YOU DOING?
WANG
ARE YOU CRAZY?!
STOP SCREAMING! I'M JUST POPPING MY SHOULDER BACK INTO PLACE.
우웩~
DIZZY...
SFX: WOOWECK (BLEEEARGH)
UGH~! WHAT KIND OF PERSON IS HE?
HE POPPED HIS ARM BACK INTO ITS SOCKET LIKE IT WAS NOTHING. JUST BY HITTING IT AGAINST THE WALL: BANG! BANG!
THAT WAS DISGUSTING!
I HAVE NO IDEA WHY HE'S BEING CHASED.
DESPITE HOW THINGS SEEM, MAYBE HE HAS A LOT OF DEBTS? ARE THOSE GUYS CREDITORS?
KEKJUCK (SCRATCH)
긁적
KEKJUCK
긁적
PRIVATE LOANS ARE REALLY TERRIBLE.
UGAHHHHH (CAARRGGHH)
으아아아아아
DAMMIT! MY HAIR IS ALL STICKY FROM THE LATTÉ.
벅!
BUKDUK (SCRAPE)
득!
벅!
BUKDUK
득!

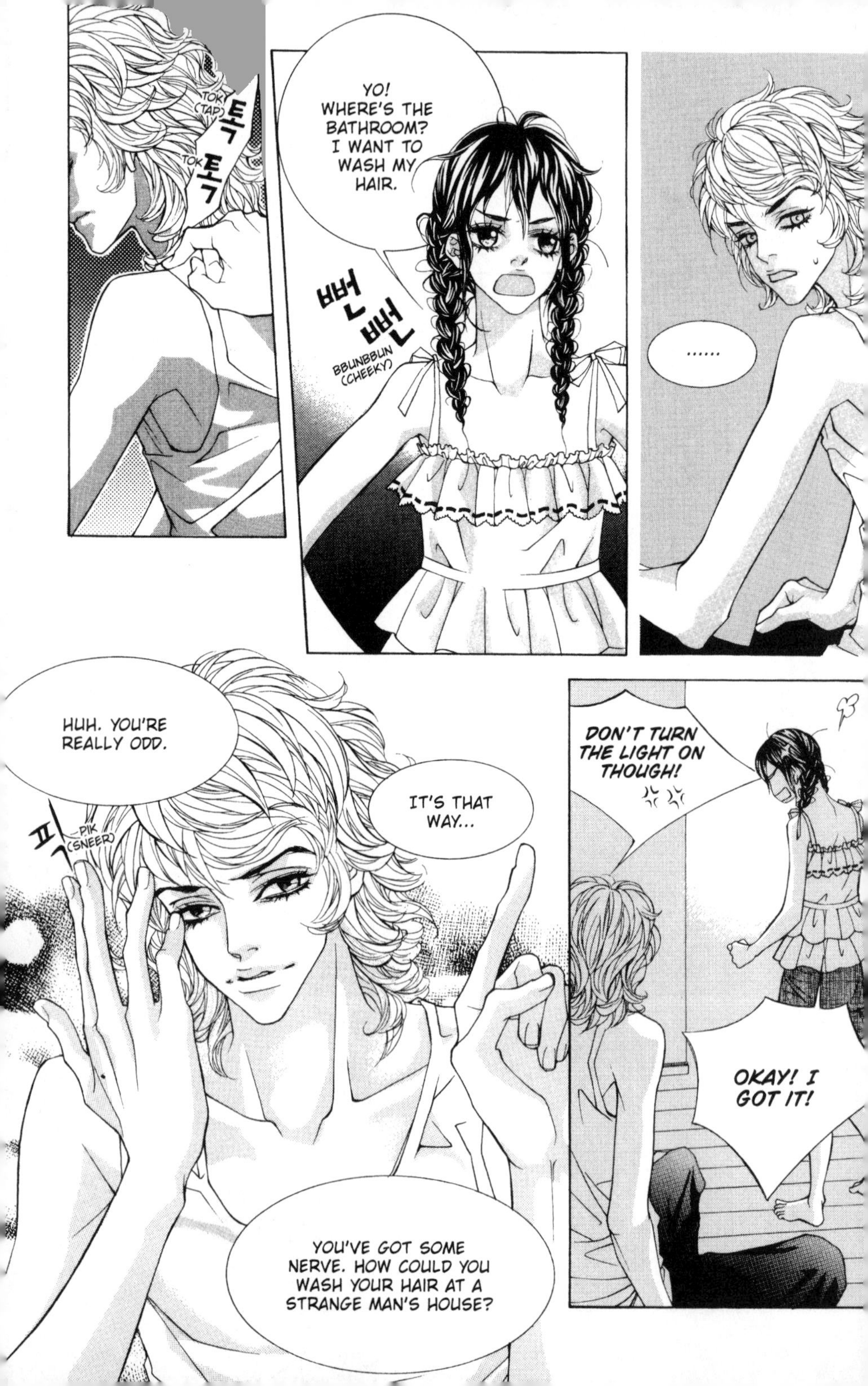
톡 TOK (TAP)
톡 TOK
YO! WHERE'S THE BATHROOM? I WANT TO WASH MY HAIR.
뻔뻔 BBUNBBUN (CHEEKY)
......
HUH. YOU'RE REALLY ODD.
피 PIK (SNEER)
IT'S THAT WAY...
YOU'VE GOT SOME NERVE. HOW COULD YOU WASH YOUR HAIR AT A STRANGE MAN'S HOUSE?
DON'T TURN THE LIGHT ON THOUGH!
OKAY! I GOT IT!

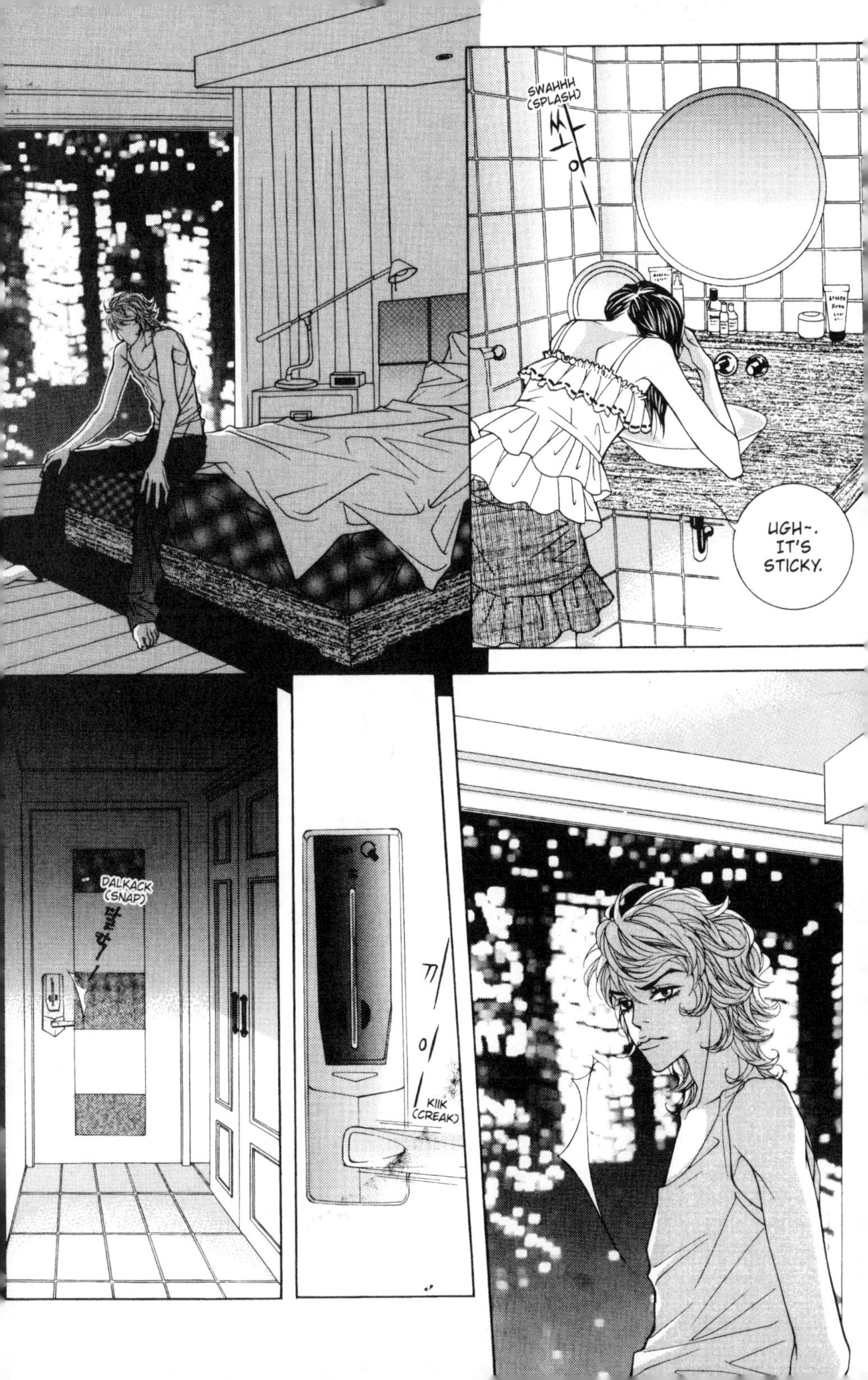
SWAHHH (SPLASH)
쏴아
UGH~. IT'S STICKY.
DALKACK (SNAP)
끼이
KIIK (CREAK)

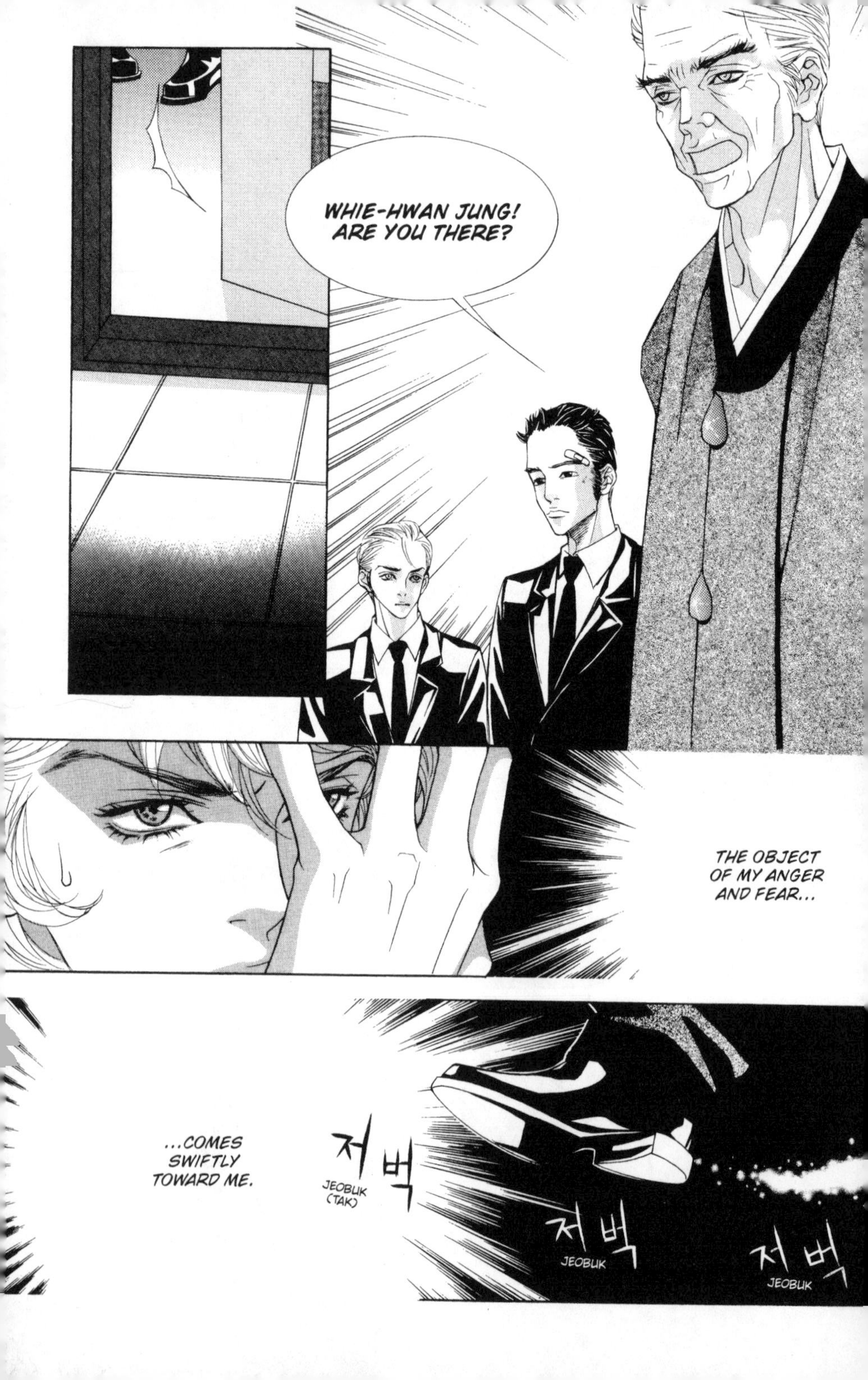
WHIE-HWAN JUNG! ARE YOU THERE?
THE OBJECT OF MY ANGER AND FEAR...
...COMES SWIFTLY TOWARD ME.
저벅
JEOBUK (TAK)
저벅
JEOBUK
저벅
JEOBUK

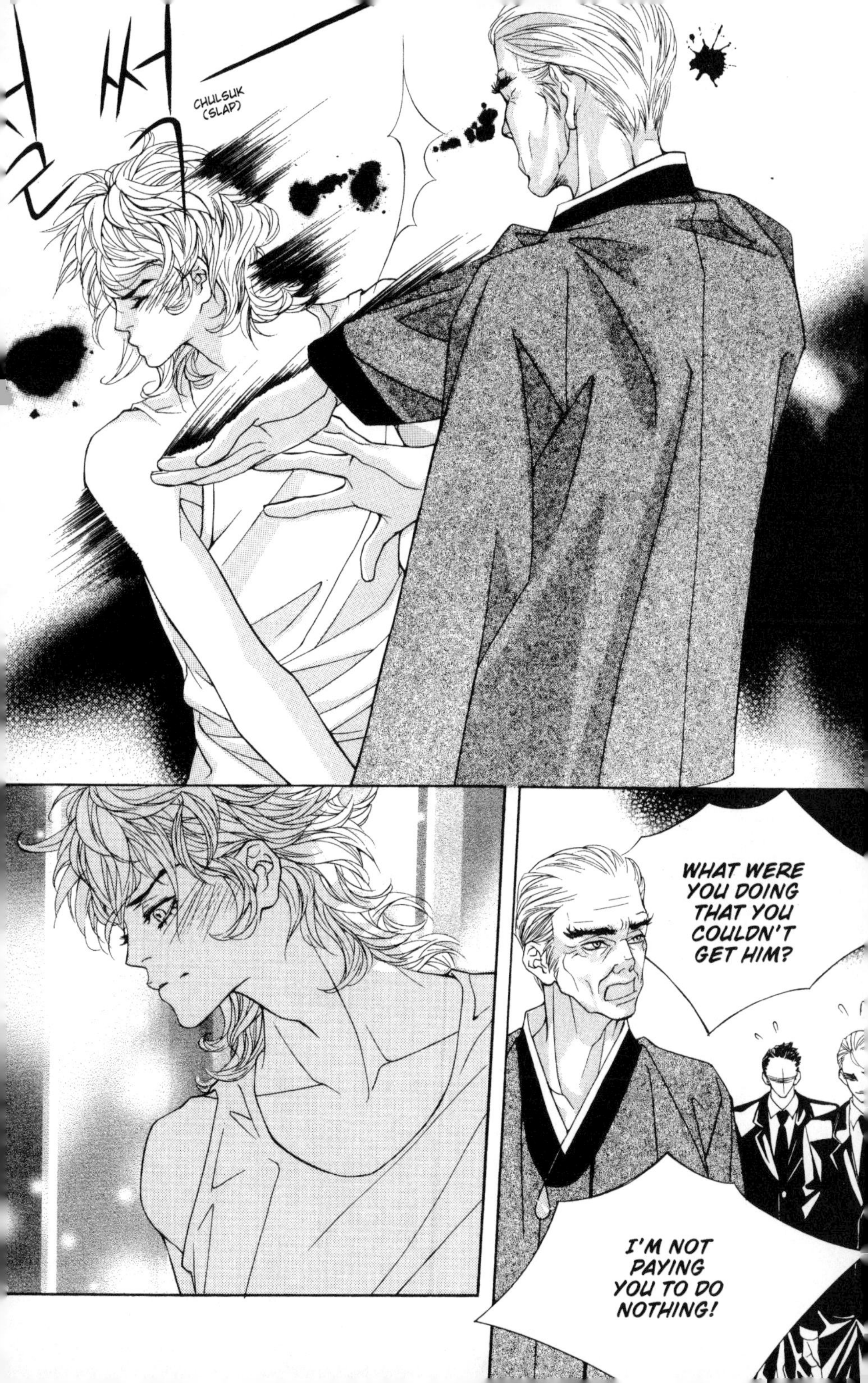
CHULSUK (SLAP)
WHAT WERE YOU DOING THAT YOU COULDN'T GET HIM?
I'M NOT PAYING YOU TO DO NOTHING!

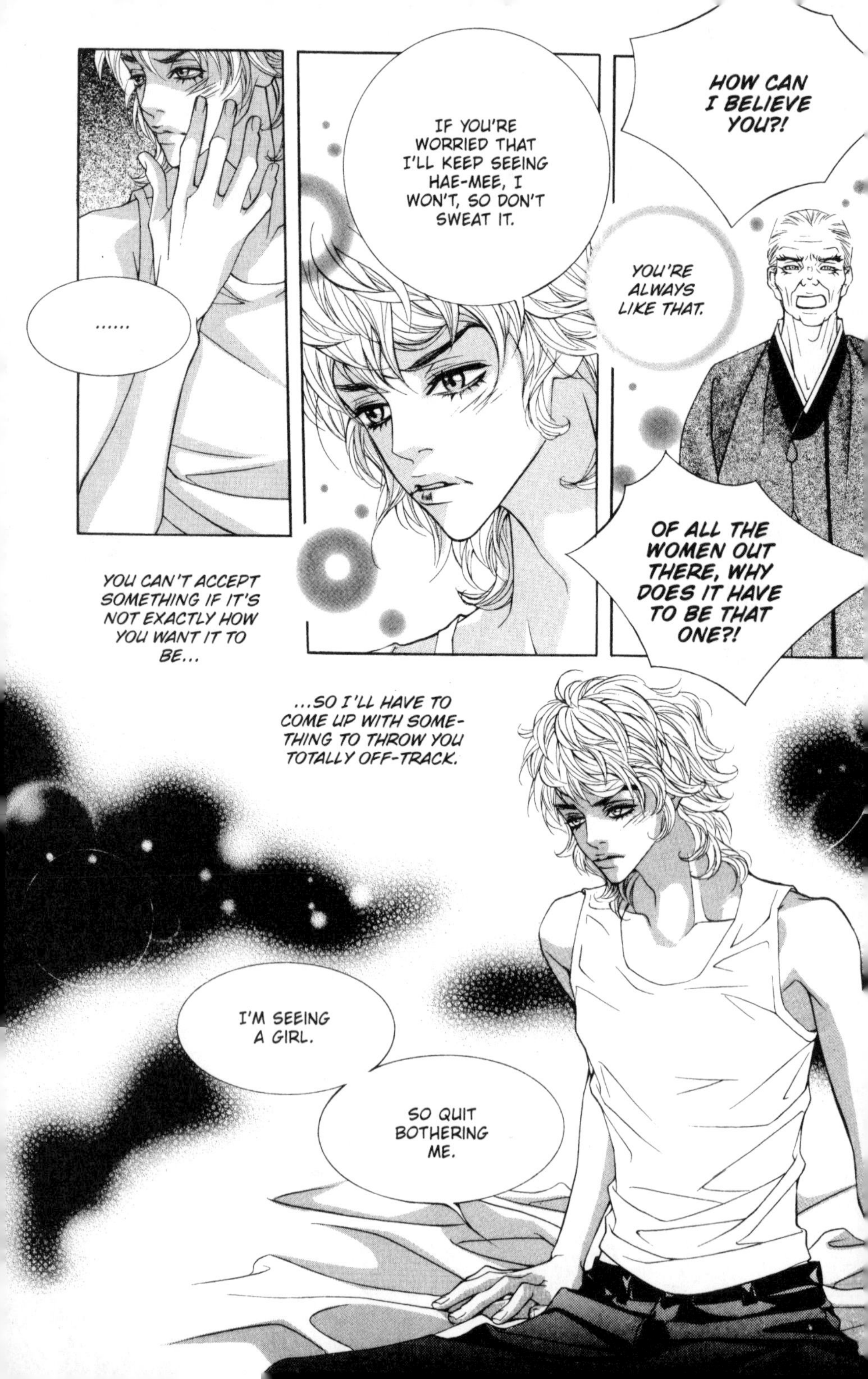
......
IF YOU'RE WORRIED THAT I'LL KEEP SEEING HAE-MEE, I WON'T, SO DON'T SWEAT IT.
HOW CAN I BELIEVE YOU?!
YOU'RE ALWAYS LIKE THAT.
OF ALL THE WOMEN OUT THERE, WHY DOES IT HAVE TO BE THAT ONE?!
YOU CAN'T ACCEPT SOMETHING IF IT'S NOT EXACTLY HOW YOU WANT IT TO BE...
...SO I'LL HAVE TO COME UP WITH SOMETHING TO THROW YOU TOTALLY OFF-TRACK.
I'M SEEING A GIRL.
SO QUIT BOTHERING ME.

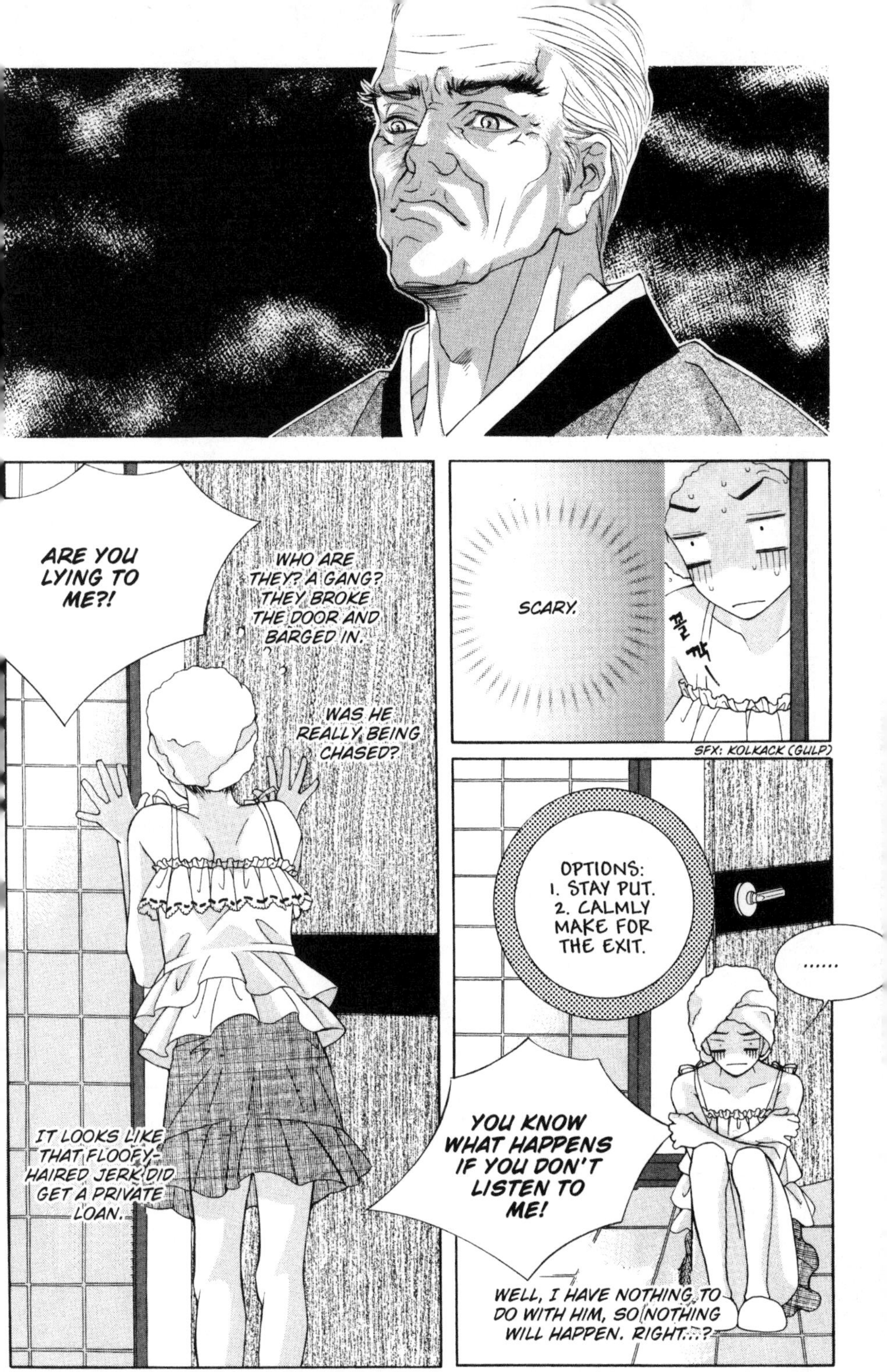
ARE YOU LYING TO ME?!
WHO ARE THEY? A GANG? THEY BROKE THE DOOR AND BARGED IN.
WAS HE REALLY BEING CHASED?
IT LOOKS LIKE THAT FLOOFY-HAIRED JERK DID GET A PRIVATE LOAN.
SCARY.
SFX: KOLKACK (GULP)
OPTIONS:
1. STAY PUT.
2. CALMLY MAKE FOR THE EXIT.
......
YOU KNOW WHAT HAPPENS IF YOU DON'T LISTEN TO ME!
WELL, I HAVE NOTHING TO DO WITH HIM, SO NOTHING WILL HAPPEN. RIGHT...?

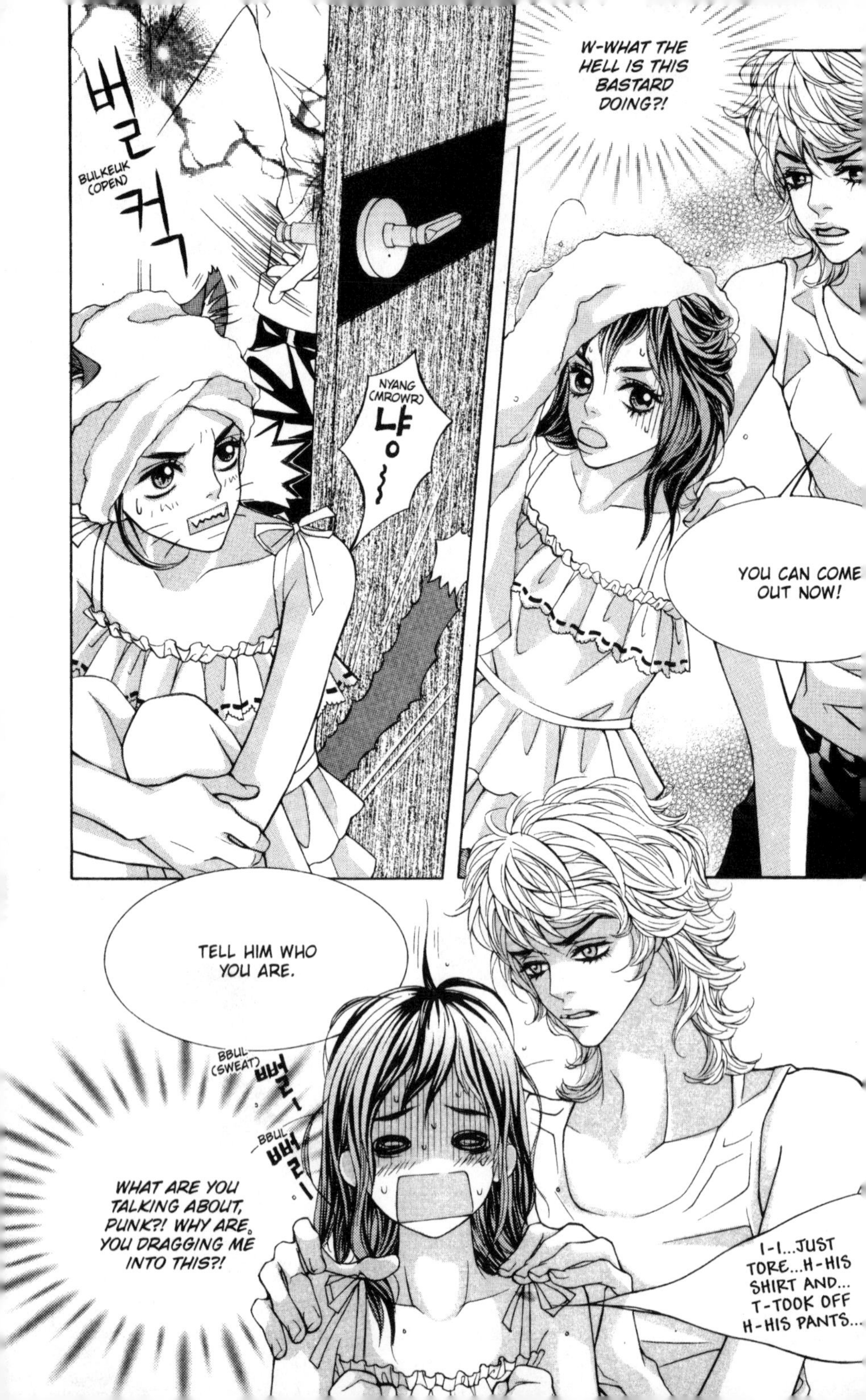
버럭
BULKEUK (OPEN)
NYANG (MROWR)
냐ㅇ~
W-WHAT THE HELL IS THIS BASTARD DOING?!
YOU CAN COME OUT NOW!
TELL HIM WHO YOU ARE.
BBUL (SWEAT)
삐질
BBUL
삐질
WHAT ARE YOU TALKING ABOUT, PUNK?! WHY ARE YOU DRAGGING ME INTO THIS?!
I-I...JUST TORE...H-HIS SHIRT AND... T-TOOK OFF H-HIS PANTS...

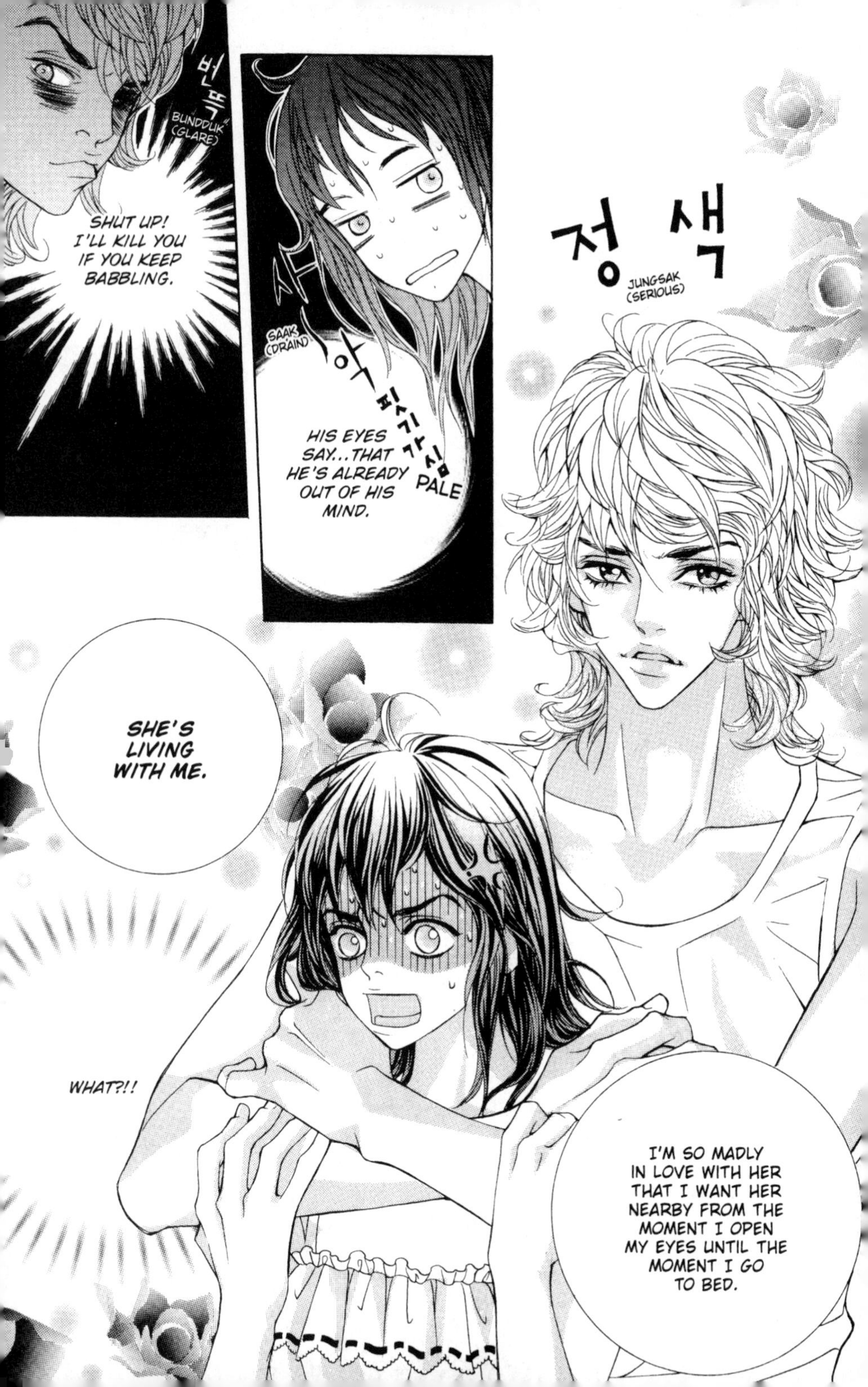
번뜩
BUNDDUK (GLARE)
SHUT UP! I'LL KILL YOU IF YOU KEEP BABBLING.
사악
SAAK (DRAIN)
HIS EYES SAY...THAT HE'S ALREADY OUT OF HIS MIND.
핏기가싱
PALE
정색
JUNGSAK (SERIOUS)
SHE'S LIVING WITH ME.
WHAT?!!
I'M SO MADLY IN LOVE WITH HER THAT I WANT HER NEARBY FROM THE MOMENT I OPEN MY EYES UNTIL THE MOMENT I GO TO BED.

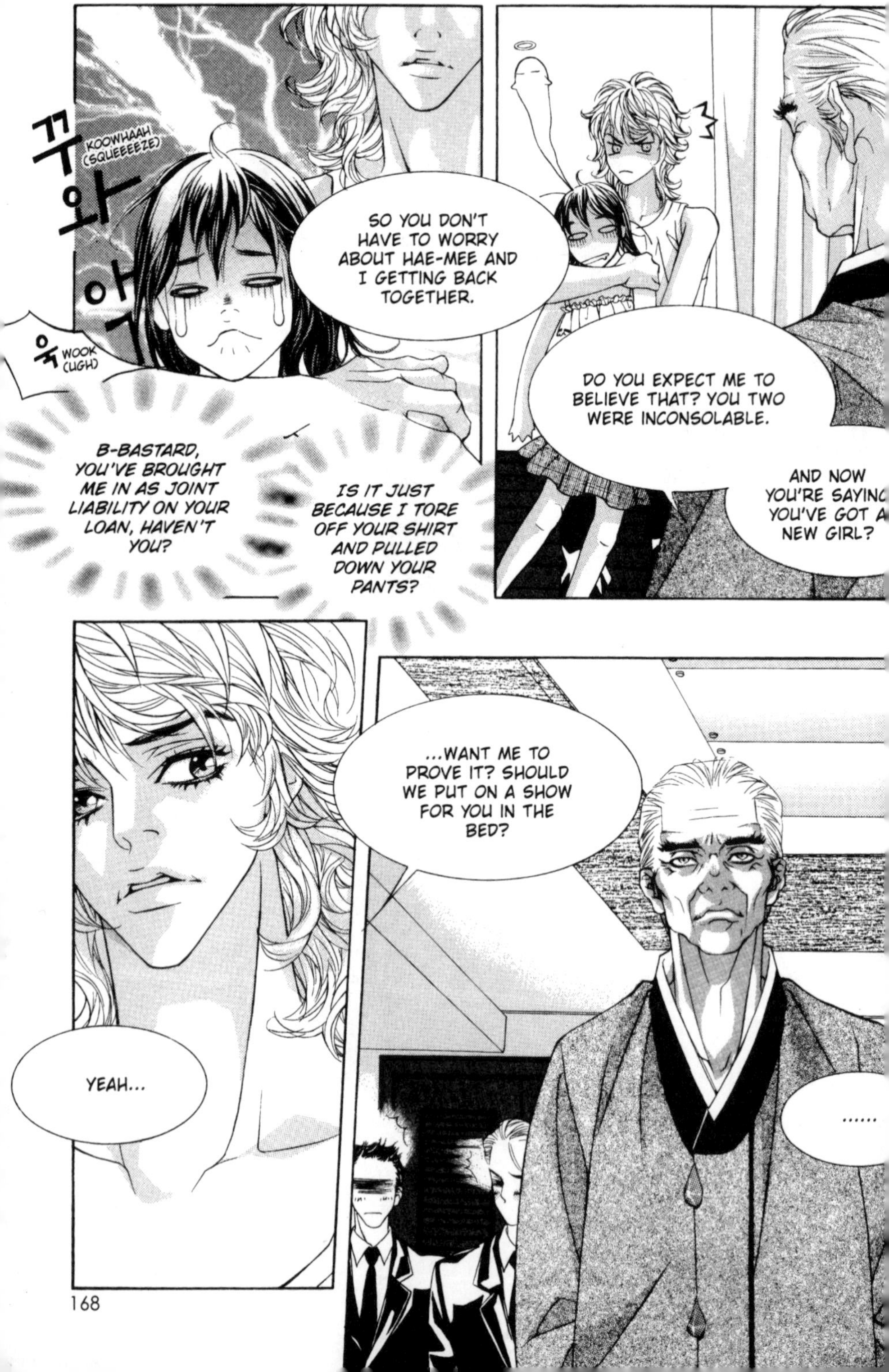

꾸와악
KOOWHAAH (SQUEEEEZE)
SO YOU DON'T HAVE TO WORRY ABOUT HAE-MEE AND I GETTING BACK TOGETHER.
욱
WOOK (UGH)
B-BASTARD, YOU'VE BROUGHT ME IN AS JOINT LIABILITY ON YOUR LOAN, HAVEN'T YOU?
IS IT JUST BECAUSE I TORE OFF YOUR SHIRT AND PULLED DOWN YOUR PANTS?
DO YOU EXPECT ME TO BELIEVE THAT? YOU TWO WERE INCONSOLABLE.
AND NOW YOU'RE SAYING YOU'VE GOT A NEW GIRL?
...WANT ME TO PROVE IT? SHOULD WE PUT ON A SHOW FOR YOU IN THE BED?
YEAH...
......

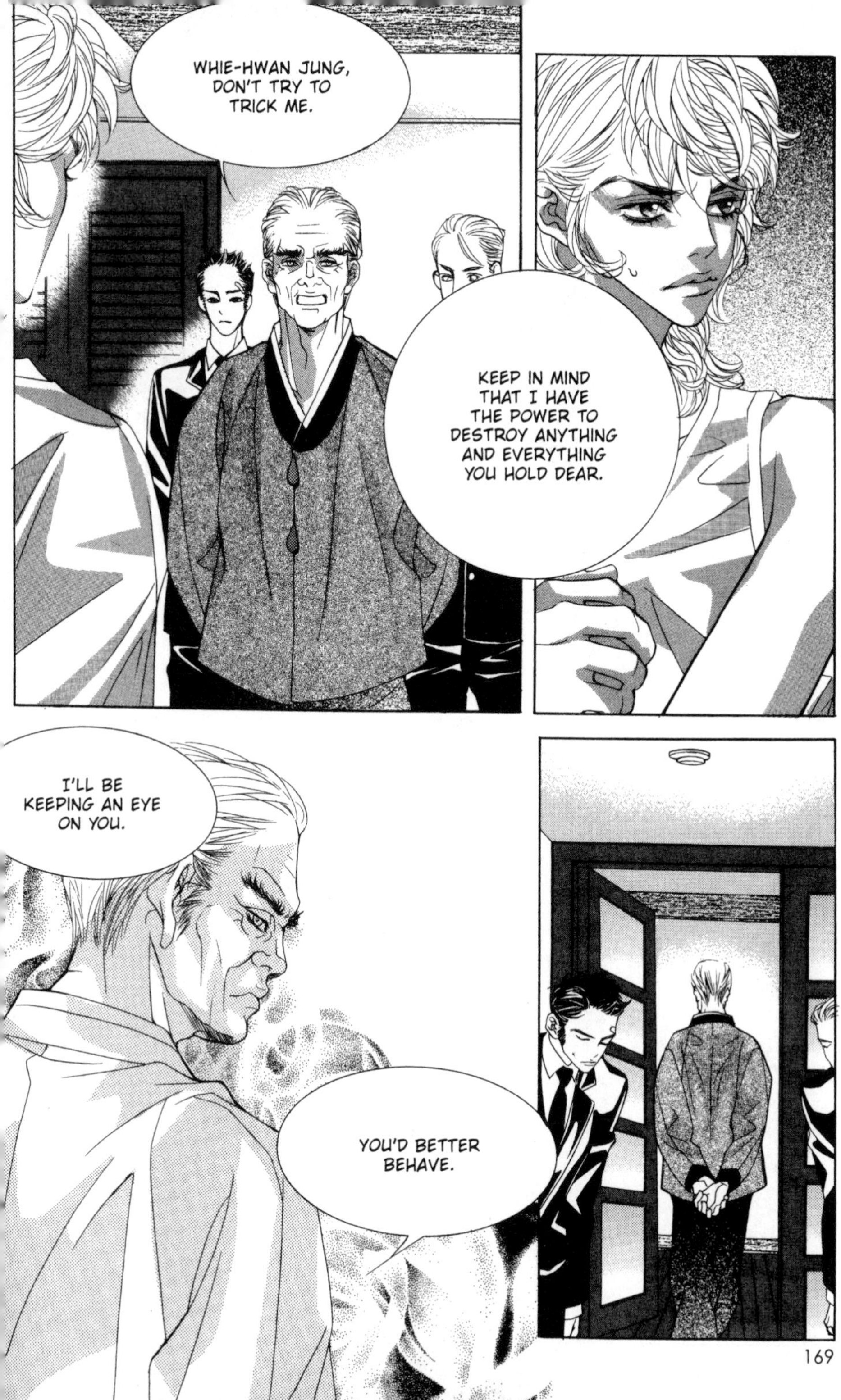
WHIE-HWAN JUNG, DON'T TRY TO TRICK ME.
KEEP IN MIND THAT I HAVE THE POWER TO DESTROY ANYTHING AND EVERYTHING YOU HOLD DEAR.
I'LL BE KEEPING AN EYE ON YOU.
YOU'D BETTER BEHAVE.

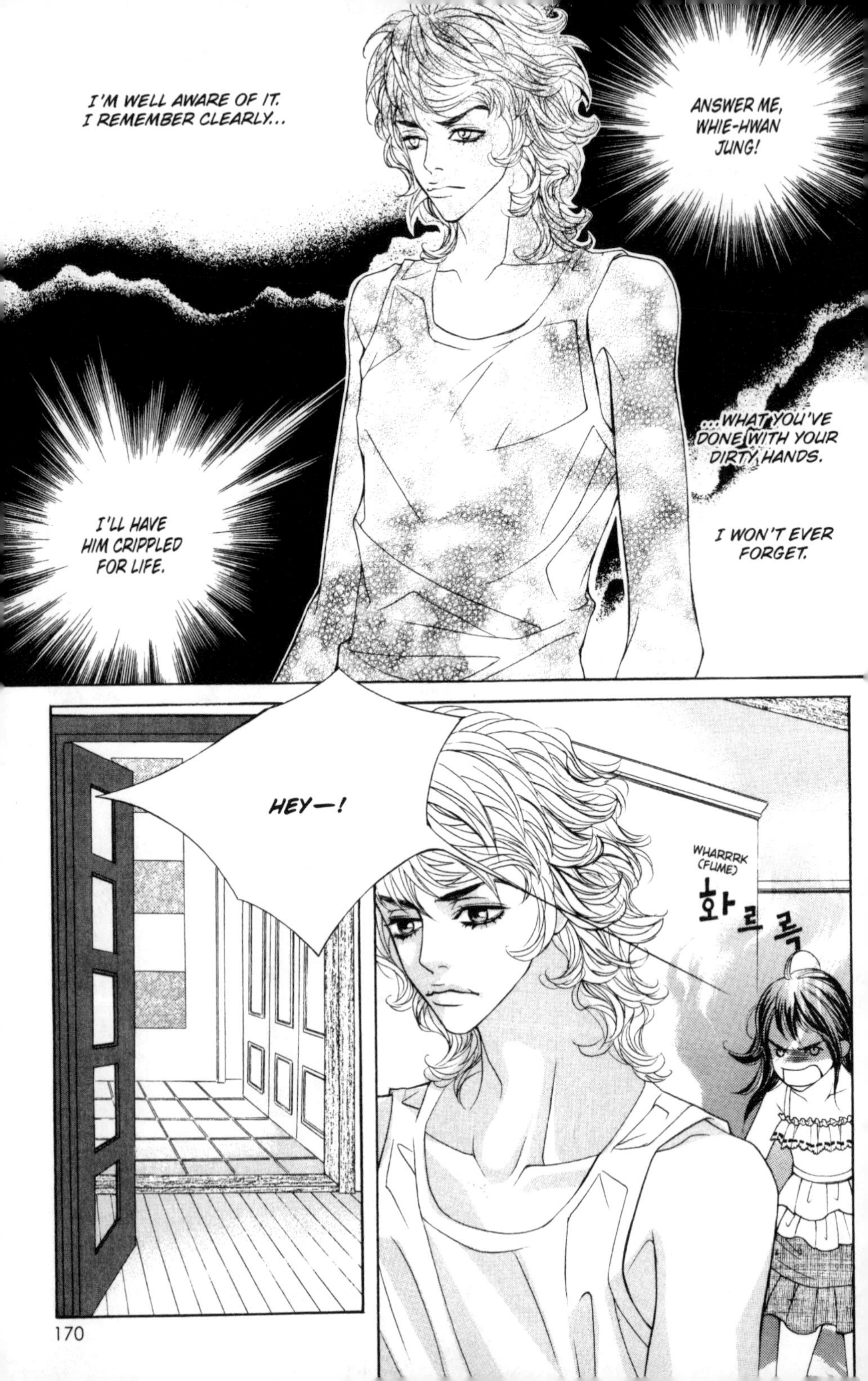
I'M WELL AWARE OF IT. I REMEMBER CLEARLY...
ANSWER ME, WHIE-HWAN JUNG!
I'LL HAVE HIM CRIPPLED FOR LIFE.
...WHAT YOU'VE DONE WITH YOUR DIRTY HANDS.
I WON'T EVER FORGET.
HEY—!
WHARRRK (FUME)
화르륵

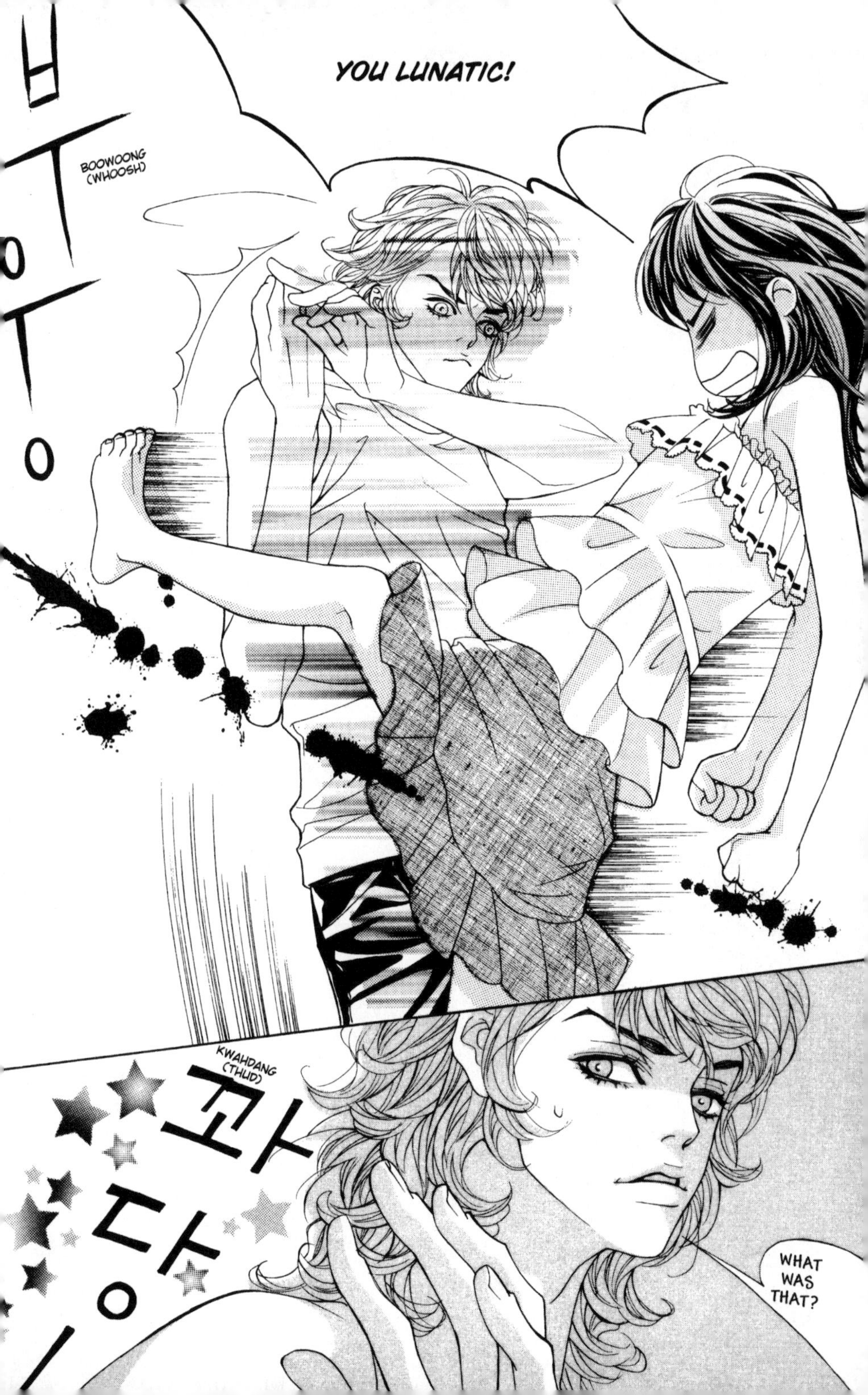
부웅
YOU LUNATIC!
BOOWOONG
(WHOOSH)
KWAHDANG
(THUD)
콰당
WHAT WAS THAT?

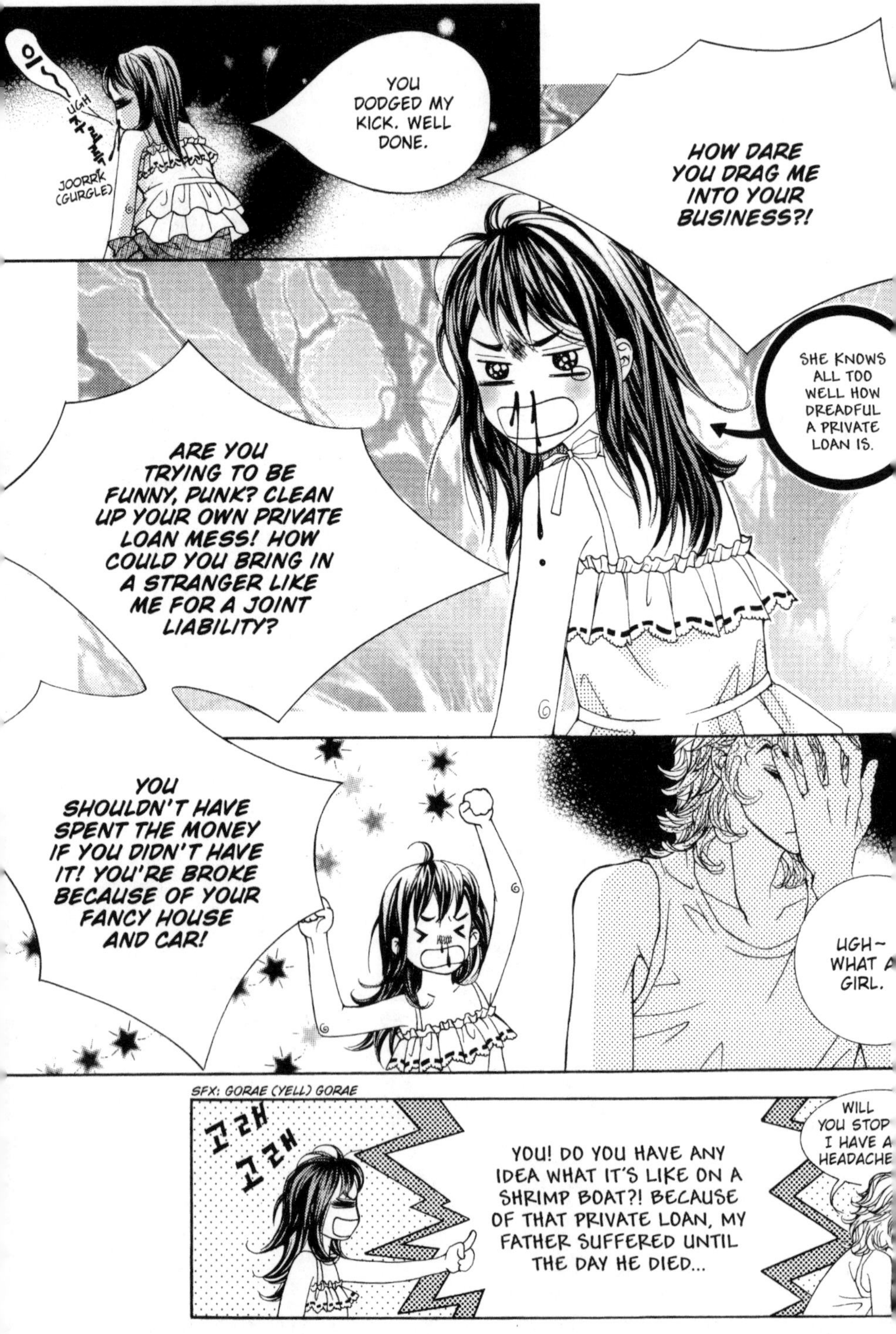

이~
UGH
주르륵
JOORRK (GURGLE)
YOU DODGED MY KICK. WELL DONE.
HOW DARE YOU DRAG ME INTO YOUR BUSINESS?!
ARE YOU TRYING TO BE FUNNY, PUNK? CLEAN UP YOUR OWN PRIVATE LOAN MESS! HOW COULD YOU BRING IN A STRANGER LIKE ME FOR A JOINT LIABILITY?
SHE KNOWS ALL TOO WELL HOW DREADFUL A PRIVATE LOAN IS.
YOU SHOULDN'T HAVE SPENT THE MONEY IF YOU DIDN'T HAVE IT! YOU'RE BROKE BECAUSE OF YOUR FANCY HOUSE AND CAR!
UGH~ WHAT A GIRL.
SFX: GORAE (YELL) GORAE
고래 고래
YOU! DO YOU HAVE ANY IDEA WHAT IT'S LIKE ON A SHRIMP BOAT?! BECAUSE OF THAT PRIVATE LOAN, MY FATHER SUFFERED UNTIL THE DAY HE DIED...
WILL YOU STOP I HAVE A HEADACHE

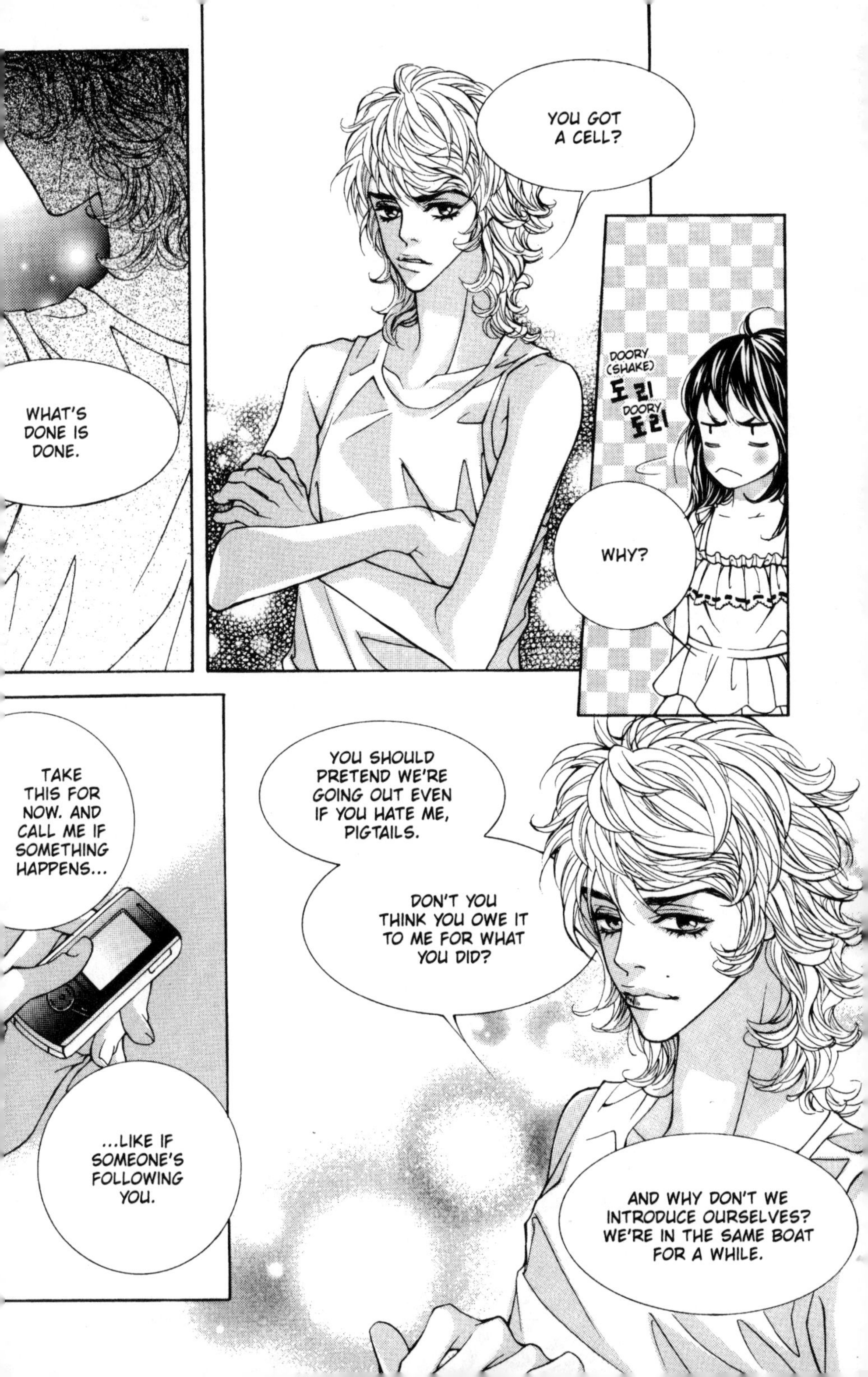
WHAT'S DONE IS DONE.
YOU GOT A CELL?
DOORY (SHAKE)
도리
DOORY
도리
WHY?
TAKE THIS FOR NOW. AND CALL ME IF SOMETHING HAPPENS...
...LIKE IF SOMEONE'S FOLLOWING YOU.
YOU SHOULD PRETEND WE'RE GOING OUT EVEN IF YOU HATE ME, PIGTAILS.
DON'T YOU THINK YOU OWE IT TO ME FOR WHAT YOU DID?
AND WHY DON'T WE INTRODUCE OURSELVES? WE'RE IN THE SAME BOAT FOR A WHILE.

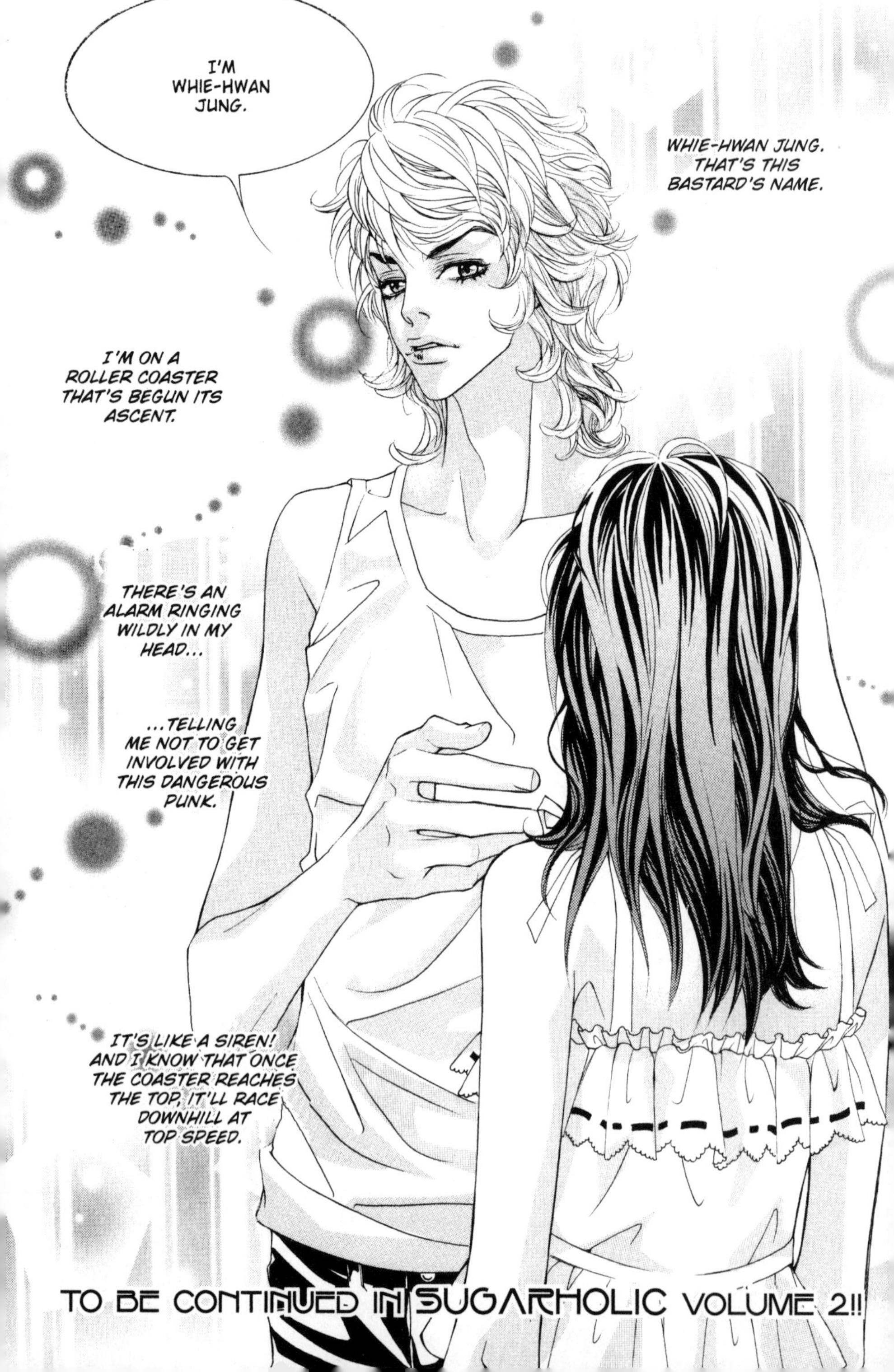
I'M WHIE-HWAN JUNG.
WHIE-HWAN JUNG. THAT'S THIS BASTARD'S NAME.
I'M ON A ROLLER COASTER THAT'S BEGUN ITS ASCENT.
THERE'S AN ALARM RINGING WILDLY IN MY HEAD...
...TELLING ME NOT TO GET INVOLVED WITH THIS DANGEROUS PUNK.
IT'S LIKE A SIREN! AND I KNOW THAT ONCE THE COASTER REACHES THE TOP, IT'LL RACE DOWNHILL AT TOP SPEED.
TO BE CONTINUED IN SUGARHOLIC VOLUME 2!!

TRANSLATION NOTES

Page 32
The "background music" here is from the Korean cartoon *Run Hany*.

Page 140
Mongkon is the headband worn by Muay Thai athletes.
Praciat were bands worn around one or both of the boxer's biceps. Traditionally, both the *mongkon* and *praciat* were infused with magical powers believed to protect and strengthen the boxer.

Muay Thai, literally "Thai Boxing," is a form of martial art that originated in southeast Asia. Matches are fought in a ring similar to Western boxing, but combatants are allowed to strike with not only their fists, but also with their elbows, shins, and knees.

Page 145
Bae-Dal Choi, also known as Masutatsu or Mas Oyama, was the founder of Kyokushin karate in Japan, one of the first styles of full-contact karate.

Page 147
The **Ram Muay**, or "Boxing Dance," is a dance-like ritual performed by Muay Thai fighters before a competition as a show of respect for their trainers and supporters.

Page 170
In Korea, people may sign up to work on a shrimp boat to earn extra money, but the work is terribly grueling.

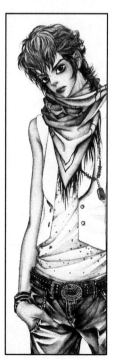

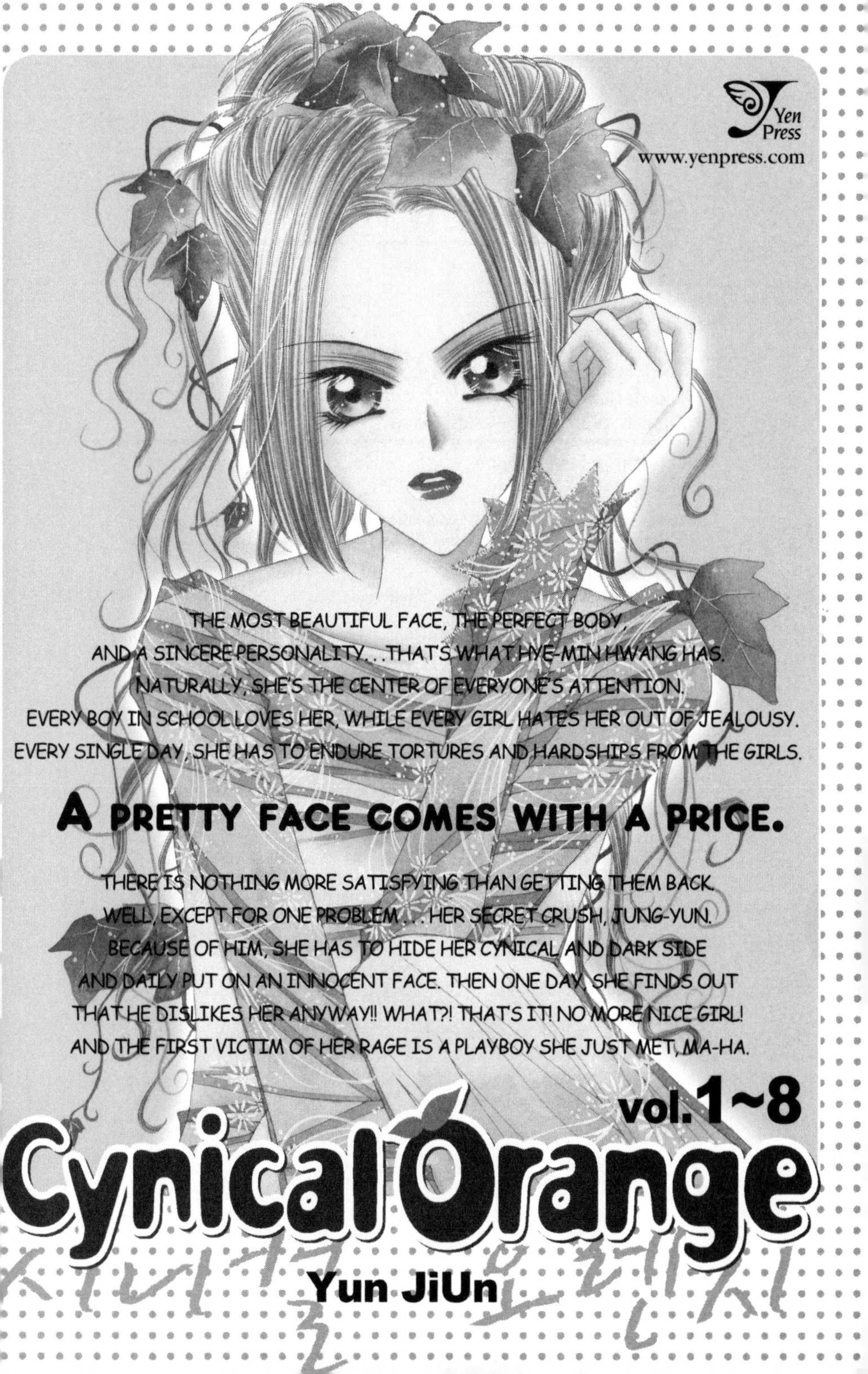
Yen Press
www.yenpress.com
THE MOST BEAUTIFUL FACE, THE PERFECT BODY,
AND A SINCERE PERSONALITY. . .THAT'S WHAT HYE-MIN HWANG HAS.
NATURALLY, SHE'S THE CENTER OF EVERYONE'S ATTENTION.
EVERY BOY IN SCHOOL LOVES HER, WHILE EVERY GIRL HATES HER OUT OF JEALOUSY.
EVERY SINGLE DAY, SHE HAS TO ENDURE TORTURES AND HARDSHIPS FROM THE GIRLS.
A PRETTY FACE COMES WITH A PRICE.
THERE IS NOTHING MORE SATISFYING THAN GETTING THEM BACK.
WELL, EXCEPT FOR ONE PROBLEM . . . HER SECRET CRUSH, JUNG-YUN.
BECAUSE OF HIM, SHE HAS TO HIDE HER CYNICAL AND DARK SIDE
AND DAILY PUT ON AN INNOCENT FACE. THEN ONE DAY, SHE FINDS OUT
THAT HE DISLIKES HER ANYWAY!! WHAT?! THAT'S IT! NO MORE NICE GIRL!
AND THE FIRST VICTIM OF HER RAGE IS A PLAYBOY SHE JUST MET, MA-HA.
vol.1~8
Cynical Orange
Yun JiUn

SUGARHOLIC ①

GONG GOOGOO

Translation: JiEun Park
English Adaptation: Natalie Baan

Lettering: Terri Delgado

SUGARHOLIC, Vol. 1 © 2005 GONG GOOGOO. All rights reserved. First published in Korea in 2005 by Seoul Cultural Publishers, Inc. English translation rights arranged by Seoul Cultural Publishers, Inc.

English translation © 2009 Hachette Book Group, Inc.

Yen Press
Hachette Book Group
237 Park Avenue, New York, NY 10017

Visit our Web sites at www.HachetteBookGroup.com and www.YenPress.com.

Yen Press is an imprint of Hachette Book Group, Inc. The Yen Press name and logo are trademarks of Hachette Book Group, Inc.

First Yen Press Edition: August 2009

ISBN: 978-0-7595-3074-4

10 9 8 7 6 5 4 3 2 1

BVG

Printed in the United States of America